Radegundis Stolze

The Translator's Approach – Introduction to Translational Hermeneutics

Hartwig Kalverkämper/Larisa Schippel (Hg.)
TRANSÜD.
Arbeiten zur Theorie und Praxis des Übersetzens und Dolmetschens
Band 41

Radegundis Stolze

# The Translator's Approach – Introduction to Translational Hermeneutics

## Theory and Examples from Practice

Verlag für wissenschaftliche Literatur

Umschlagabbildung: © Klaus Stolze, aufgenommen im August 2010
Das Foto stellt die Durchfahrt unter der Tjeldsund-Brücke in der Provinz Nordland in Norwegen dar. Diese Brücke, 1967 erbaut, verbindet als E10 das Festland mit den Vesteralen-Inseln nahe dem Ort Harstad, nördlich des Polarkreises.
In dem Bild zeigt sich eine Beweglichkeit der Fahrt, wie sie für das Übersetzen typisch ist.

ISBN 978-3-86596-373-4
ISSN 1438-2636

© Frank & Timme GmbH  Verlag für wissenschaftliche Literatur
Berlin 2011. Alle Rechte vorbehalten.

Das Werk einschließlich aller Teile ist urheberrechtlich geschützt.
Jede Verwertung außerhalb der engen Grenzen des Urheberrechtsgesetzes ist ohne Zustimmung des Verlags unzulässig und strafbar.
Das gilt insbesondere für Vervielfältigungen, Übersetzungen, Mikroverfilmungen und die Einspeicherung und Verarbeitung in elektronischen Systemen.

Herstellung durch das atelier eilenberger, Taucha bei Leipzig.
Printed in Germany.
Gedruckt auf säurefreiem, alterungsbeständigem Papier.

www.frank-timme.de

# Table of contents

**Introduction** ........................................................................................................... 9

**1 In search of a new paradigm in Translation Studies** ................................. 13
  1.1 Practice, theory, research and knowledge ................................................ 13
  1.2 The goal of faithful translation .................................................................. 15
  1.3 The first paradigm of interlingual transfer for equivalence ..................... 19
  1.4 Descriptive and prescriptive rules in translation ...................................... 25
  1.5 Translation as a dynamic task ................................................................... 30
  1.6 The translators' subjectivity as an integral element ................................. 33
  1.7 Misunderstanding in the academic discourse ........................................... 36
  1.8 Words for concepts .................................................................................... 41

**2 The paradigm of translational hermeneutics** ............................................. 45
  2.1 Foundations of hermeneutics with Schleiermacher .................................. 45
  2.2 Historicity in language .............................................................................. 47
  2.3 Oral and written communication ............................................................... 50
  2.4 The medial act of reading .......................................................................... 52
  2.5 Game playing and habitus ......................................................................... 56
  2.6 The phenomenological problem ................................................................ 58
  2.7 The hermeneutical circle and our memory ............................................... 60
  2.8 Complementary research interest in Cognitive Science ........................... 64

**3 A translator's relationship to texts** ............................................................. 68
  3.1 Grounded understanding of content .......................................................... 68
  3.2 The link between translation and original ................................................ 73
  3.3 Responsible reading and expertise ............................................................ 75
  3.4 Translation between rules and play .......................................................... 78
  3.5 The bifocal view on texts .......................................................................... 81

**4 The limits of subjectivity** ............................................................................ 85
  4.1 How much text analysis is needed? .......................................................... 85
  4.2 What is interpretation? .............................................................................. 89
  4.3 Textual growth in multiple in re-translations? ......................................... 94
  4.4 Is meaning captured? ................................................................................. 98
  4.5 Manipulating translations? ...................................................................... 101

**5 Hermeneutical orientation in the world of texts** .................................... 105
  5.1 The situative background ........................................................................ 105
  5.2 Features of ecological and material culture ........................................... 107
    5.2.1 Features of social and religious culture ........................................ 108
    5.2.2 Communication for specific purposes .......................................... 110
    5.2.3 Problems of legal texts .................................................................. 111
  5.3 The discourse field .................................................................................. 113
    5.3.1 The place of ideology .................................................................... 113
    5.3.2 Domain-specific communication .................................................. 114
  5.4 The meaning dimension .......................................................................... 116
    5.4.1 Key words ...................................................................................... 117
    5.4.2 Terminology ................................................................................... 121
    5.4.3 Vagueness of legal terms ............................................................... 122

| | | | |
|---|---|---|---|
| | 5.5 | The predicative mode | 125 |
| | | 5.5.1 Style and mood of text | 125 |
| | | 5.5.2 LSP phraseology | 126 |
| **6** | **Writing as an autopoietic process** | | **128** |
| | 6.1 | Experiences from self-translation | 128 |
| | 6.2 | Authentic formulation in empathy and embodiment | 130 |
| | 6.3 | Tentative writing for optimization | 135 |
| **7** | **Rhetorical text production in translation** | | **138** |
| | 7.1 | Creativity in formulation | 138 |
| | 7.2 | The evolutionary character of a version | 141 |
| | 7.3 | Strategies of problem-solving | 144 |
| | 7.4 | Translational hierarchy as a coordination problem | 149 |
| **8** | **Fields of attention in translational writing** | | **153** |
| | 8.1 | Genre | 153 |
| | | 8.1.1 Appearance of the text | 153 |
| | | 8.1.2 Formatting problems | 154 |
| | 8.2 | Coherence | 156 |
| | | 8.2.1 Dealing with lexical lacunae | 156 |
| | | 8.2.2 Isotopy as a semantic web | 157 |
| | | 8.2.3 Technical terminology | 160 |
| | 8.3 | Stylistics | 161 |
| | | 8.3.1 Sociolects, word play and other features | 161 |
| | | 8.3.2 Condensing phrases | 164 |
| | | 8.3.3 Functional style in LSP | 166 |
| | | 8.3.4 Expert-lay communication | 168 |
| | | 8.3.5 No decision-making as to syntax | 169 |
| | 8.4 | Function | 171 |
| | | 8.4.1 Visualizing a literary scene | 172 |
| | | 8.4.2 Specialist communication across language barrier | 172 |
| **9** | **Elements of translation competence** | | **177** |
| | 9.1 | Dynamic interaction of memory and language proficiency | 177 |
| | 9.2 | Discerning priorities in the texts | 181 |
| | 9.3 | The tool of lexicography | 184 |
| | 9.4 | The translator's growth | 187 |
| | 9.5 | A systemic model of translation | 188 |
| | 9.6 | Perspectives on the quality of translations | 195 |
| | | 9.6.1 The translator's dynamic interest for an adequate formulation | 195 |
| | | 9.6.2 The client's prospective interest for useful texts | 196 |
| | | 9.6.3 Translation criticism with a static analysis of shifts | 198 |
| **10** | **Practice: Discussion of translation examples** | | **200** |
| | 10.1 | Translating in communication for specific purposes | 200 |
| | | 10.1.1 A technical text | 200 |
| | | 10.1.2 A science text | 203 |
| | | 10.1.3 A legal text | 210 |
| | | 10.1.4 A publicity ad | 214 |
| | | 10.1.5 An economic text | 217 |
| | | 10.1.6 A pragmatic text | 220 |
| | | 10.1.7 A multimedia text | 222 |

|  |  |  |
|---|---|---|
| 10.2 | Translating literature | 228 |
|  | 10.2.1 Extract from a novel | 228 |
|  | 10.2.2 A short story | 237 |
|  | 10.2.3 Bible quotations in literature | 257 |
|  | 10.2.4 Text from an arts catalogue | 260 |
|  | 10.2.5 A poem | 263 |
| **11** | **References** | **269** |
| **12** | **Index** | **289** |
| 12.1 | Subject index | 289 |
| 12.2 | Author index | 295 |

# Introduction

This book is an introduction to the theory of translational hermeneutics and will explain the hermeneutical foundations of translation as a human activity. Translating is understood, here, as the human task of faithfully presenting a text's message in another language for readers in a different culture. What is needed for the translating person is to know how to cope with any new text to be translated, independently from its domain. A strict methodology for this strategic process has not yet been found in Translation Studies, and maybe it isn't even possible in human translation. If so, machine translation systems could easily take over.

In a normal professional situation, for instance in the language industry, translators are constantly faced with different types of texts. In today's market, highest flexibility, quick adjustment to new tasks, and a very broad knowledge of elements in the globalized world is required. Often, translators are the only non-specialists in the whole communication process to be enabled by translation, while authors and even target readers may be members of a similar group sharing the same interests. The task of creating a presence for the message in a translation means to authentically continue the communication initiated by the original text and intended between author and readers across the language barrier. The core problem is: how can one understand that message, how can one enter in that strange world of discourse? And how will one find the right words for it?

The paradigm for personalized translation activity is based on the modern language philosophy of hermeneutics, and the book aims to explain the hermeneutical outlook to the task of translating, which starts from the viewpoint of a translator as a socially embodied individual. Translation is conceived of as an assignment yet to be completed, and all translational decisions are to the full discretion of the translator. He or she is alone responsible, and this responsibility calls for critical reflection.

There are two ways of tackling with the practical problem of translation, either a methodology-based one, or a decision-based one. The problem with methodology is that it tends to be 'objective' and neglects the subjective parts in a translator. Descriptive approaches only tell us what has already been done elsewhere, while prescriptive approaches offer answers before any questions have been raised. This book has originated out of the author's unsatisfactory experience of traditional translation teaching where a great amount of examples from ready-made translations were presented and discussed, but this very often did not help to solve the problems at hand in a new translation assignment.

The cognitive aspect of translation has been taken for granted so far. In present-day Translation Studies (TS), we find a lot of descriptive studies focusing on so-called translation universals observed *post festum*, such as 'clarification', 'expansion', 'ennoblement of style' etc. that are based on the comparison of language structures in the target text (TT) and the source text (ST), without questioning any possible reasons for the observed data. There is also a great variety of studies discussing the cultural pressures supposedly governing translation, and the sociological effects of translations as products of a power struggle. Strangely enough, there is no questioning whether the translators did their job well and managed or at least tried to understand their texts, or whether this is at all possible.

Whilst various translation methods have already been developed in the academic literature, the decision-making process for translating was not yet explained sufficiently. The translator's strategy varies constantly, depending on the given knowledge base and its growth. A person's situated cognition is flexible and thus strangles all rules. That means, in every single case one would have to design one's strategy anew, and the translator may rely more on the own competence than on the application of any given method. For this purpose we need some reference points for orientation.

The book therefore discusses the medial character of translational reading in order to understand a text, and combines it with the text-processing activity debated in cognitive science and rhetoric. The question of how to transcend the familiar world of one's given knowledge and to enter the strange world seen in the translation texts is discussed here in its phenomenological significance. But translation does not stop there. The core issue of how to find the right words for a message once understood, and how to revise one's solutions according to rhetorical goals in view of the target text's purpose is then taken up, presenting the relevant fields of attention in the translator's approach. Saying that translation is "quasi the same ideas expressed in other words" (Eco 2006) is not enough. The issue is to describe that process of searching linguistically in order to find criteria for backing-up one's translational decisions, both in technical communication and in literature. Whereas understanding a text is a holistic, global, schematic act of cognitive processing, the production of a translation text in a target language will concentrate on language details including readers' expectations.

The lines of orientation in translational reading, such as the situative background, the discourse field, the meaning dimension, and the predicative mode as visible in the source text are discussed and confronted with fields of attention in translational writing, such as genre, coherence, stylistics, and function. Translation is described, here, as a co-authored text production in the sense of a social service for the purpose of intercultural communication, rather than an interlinguistic transfer. Finally, the results concerning prioritizing of translation problems, quality assessment, the necessary life-long learning, and the intellectual growth of the competent translator is mentioned.

The translator's approach to texts of various kinds, as outlined here, will be explained at the end with examples from both literature and specialist translation in the language pair of English and German. But this translator-centered approach is not language-specific, as it discusses elements of a translation competence in general. Comparable ideas are today, often with a different terminology, discussed in cognitive science, game theory, relevance theory, complexity theory, creativity research and process research. We will refer to relevant studies, where appropriate.

Even if producing practical advice is not the interest of theory, it is true that theory will give the adequate framework for practice, and various theories of translation may render different practical behavior. Therefore it is worth occupying oneself with theory in order to empower the translators for their practical work. Underlying this book is the notion that knowledge of theory can affect the way we translate. Professionalism is characterized by expertise in one's work and the ability to critically reflect on it.

Darmstadt, April 2011

# 1 In search of a new paradigm in Translation Studies

## 1.1 Practice, theory, research and knowledge

As the intended presentation will focus on both aspects of theory and of practice, it is necessary to first of all clarify some terms. Often their interrelationship is not clear.

*Practice* is the field of concrete activity in the profession. In the field of language this includes translators, interpreters, technical authors; among linguists it includes language teachers, journalists, media reporters, university professors in language studies, advertisement texters etc. The concrete problems comprise the tools to use, such as special dictionaries, computers, translation memories, automatic translation systems, literature, libraries, but also the personal role in project management and the working team, the proper time management, the behavior with clients and colleagues, payment, accounting modalities, tax issues and salary. The goal is professionalism in the activity.

*Professionalism* is a quality that characterizes workers who not only do their job well, but who can also reflect on it with self-criticism. They dispose of adequate specialist knowledge, use the adequate tools and are ready for investment and constant further training. They can generalize problems and work methodically. They can back-up their decisions with self-confidence in a scholarly manner, but they also developed a time-saving routine. This attitude requires expert knowledge, which is not yet given in students.

*Knowledge* is an economic good and is the basis of working in theory and practice (Budin 2002). Expert knowledge may be described in detail:

**Ability** for something is the condition for knowledge, it's the born-in talent to learn something and to perform it.

**Proficiency** is an implicit, subjective knowledge about certain activities, we may also call it skill.

**Competence** means the totality of all object-related and methodical forms of knowledge on a certain process which we are performing in our professional activities consciously and which a certain target (experts, specialists).

**Social and intercultural action knowledge** means that you have to know your own culture and also the foreign one in order to become aware of communication barriers, to react adequately in the encounter with foreigners, to well deal with clients and to lead negotiations.

**Knowledge on language and communication** is a nearly perfect knowledge about the languages involved in translation. This includes grammar, functional stylistics, lexicon, text type conventions, rules of comprehensibility, special signs (semiotic knowledge) and other extra-lingual communication means (illustration, text arrangement, etc.). Simply studying a foreign language is not sufficient for proper translation.

**Terminology** knowledge refers to specialist terms in domains of science and humanities. Terminology is the collection of special words, i.e. terms with specific concepts as their word meaning.

**Domain-specific knowledge:** as specialization is growing in all scientific disciplines, in the fields of economy, law, social sciences and all engineering fields, we are forced to acquire domain-specific knowledge on the on the hand, and to specialize in certain areas on the other hand.

*Experts* are different from lay persons because they are not only intuitively able to do something well, they have expressly studied and learnt it. The concept of expertise is relative, because everybody can become an expert in a field, the competence is developing constantly through life-long learning (Kalverkämper 1998:24).

*Theory* stems from gr. θεωρία, the vision, contemplation. Theory is the complex of ideas regarding a scientific field, the modeling. The theoretician is a scholar who deals principally with an issue. Regarding translation the issue is about "what translation is", how this functions, and not about any concrete working instructions or the development of practical tools. The goal of theory is to find definitions, and for this purpose hypotheses are created which then are being examined. This is the place of basic research. Theory cannot give prescriptive propositions for practical action. It isn't even sure whether theoretical insights have any effect for practice. The occupation with theory, however, is legitimate because the human interest in things simply wants to know, what is behind the phenomena and observable procedures. And a new theory as a novel view of the object may eventually also generate different practice. Theory is based on research.

*Research* is the basis for developing theories. It includes such methods and means that are applied in order to develop theoretical models, to describe objects and to verify hypotheses. Research is either *descriptive* when objects are analyzed and compared in case studies, or *empirical* when questionnaires, protocols or corpora are evaluated, or *experimental* when laboratory designs are made to test reactions or when machines monitor processes of action. A triangulation of various methods is considered as fruitful, because qualitative data from interviews can be strengthened by quantitative data collected empirically (Hansen 2006:23).

## 1.2 The goal of faithful translation

Translation has been used ever since humans communicated with one another. And translation was also the subject where thinking about the act of translating has initiated.[1] Translation is not communication in itself, rather it is a social service of mediating in order to enable communication. Texts are being made accessible to readers in another language because those cannot understand the original, either for reasons of historical distance or for linguistic barriers. This view includes the concept that a translation substitutes the original and that a translator becomes a co-author of the text's message, and is burdened with the responsibility to translate faithfully. Readers assume that a translation transports the original text's content. Otherwise it would not make sense to read a translation.

We are discussing here the issue of how a translator can cope with this task of faithful translation, which is a very important task in society and should not be subdued. We doubt whether W. Wilss is right in his statement: "Both, TS and translators in their professional work, have to accept the fact that the essence of translation is relativization and compromise […], and this awareness sometimes dampens our translation motivation" (Wilss 1996:38).[2] Not at all, we would say,

---

[1] See Translators through History. Edited and directed by Jean Delisle and Judith Woodsworth (1995).

[2] He holds a pessimistic assumption: "Metaphorically speaking, translators are a kind of 'displaced persons' who plug their own communication system into the translation network, hoping that in the course of their activity they can gradually filter out the uncer-

translators are workers with their own professional competence and ability of judgment.

As this is difficult, though, practitioners repeatedly urge translation theorists to equip them efficiently with practical hints on how to translate. But this is not possible, since theory is the legitimate attempt to just view, analyze and describe a problem – for instance the "act of translating" or "what translation is" or "the factors of the translation process" – in order to create novel insights that perhaps would some day generate new approaches for the task of teaching translation.

We distinguish between *translating* as the act of rendering written input from one language by means of another language in written form (and thus revisable) with the product of a *translation*, and *interpreting* as the act of oral rendering a message heard in another language. *Interpretation,* on the contrary, is the explanatory exegesis of a foreign text from a certain viewpoint, mostly in religious or ideological environments. In general language, "interpretation" is a synonym for "understanding".

Translation Studies have seen considerable changes during the past fifty years as they gradually developed into a discipline. The scholarly interest shifted from a description of language differences to the social role of translation in the literary context, and to an analysis of the translation process. Over the years, various translation theories have appeared.[3] It is a difference whether you conceive translation as a linguistic transfer procedure, rather than an intercultural mediation, or as a power struggle for meanings. The translator's approach to the given task will be a different one in each case, because he or she will direct attention to varying aspects.

The early translators reflected on their activity and sought for some explanation for their decisions regarding the goal of faithful translation. Following St. Jerome, who translated the Greek Bible into Latin, medieval translators developed tools for very precise and literal translations in order to be faithful to the original text, what later even influenced the translation of secular texts (Brenner 1998:6).

---

tainty which makes itself unpleasantly felt in many translation processes" (Wilss 1996:142f).

[3] See *Übersetzungstheorien. Eine Einführung.* 5th edition (Stolze 2008).

In the 16th century, important impulses for translation came from Martin Luther with his German translation of the Bible. In his reflection on translation[4] he motivated his choice of a non literal target-oriented translation even for the holy text to confer the message in a powerful way. He created the term *verdeutschen*, that means to speak German so that people may understand. Such a translation is of course 'free', it may transform the original at a certain point. On the other hand, the so-called 'faithful translations' were seen philologically as sticking to the original's word structure, and this is then *verfremdend* (alienating), it makes the text 'strange' for the target reader.

That old tension between the two methods of "free translation" and "faithful translation" has brought along the demand for clear rules of translation, not least for the purpose of educating translators. For centuries, the struggle between these two methods characterized the theoretical debate, where theory was deducted from practice as its foundation and motivation. The commentaries on translations give evidence of the translators' difficulties, but this did not grow soon into a real translation theory. In language courses in school until today, students are being taught to translate "as literally as possible and as freely as necessary". But this is a circle, since "possible" and "necessary" are interrelated plausibilities, no definitions.

In the 18th century, A. Tytler gained some importance. He put up the following valid requirements for a good translation: knowledge of both languages, insight of the subject discussed, good style, and an understanding of the author's intention. He described the relationship between translation and original (Tytler 1797:16):

> I. That the translation should give a complete transcript of the ideas of the original work.
>
> II. That the style and manner of writing should be of the same character with that of the original.
>
> III. That the translation should have all the ease of the original composition.

This statement clearly is a description of the individual goal a translator as the author of a target text would set himself, just as all the self-reflecting translators

---

[4] Cf. "Sendbrief vom Dolmetschen" (1530), in: Störig (1973:1-13). – See a comment on that in Lefevere (1977:7-9).

did. Still recently it was proposed that translation competence, understood in its totality, would cover individual sub-competences, for example: (1) language competence, (2) textual competence, (3) subject competence, (4) cultural competence, (5) transfer competence (Neubert 2000:10). In its generalization, this is not very different from what Tytler had established.

Until the 19th century, translation was considered an art, and the assignment was always to make audible "the author's voice", that is to follow the ideal of a philologically faithful translation. The German Romanticism had formulated a certain understanding of the "genius of a language" as the medium of expressing a people's character, presenting examples of untranslatable words (Humboldt 1836/1971). As a part of the culture, all languages are different from each other, and translation, in the end, would remain a vain effort. Language and culture constitute a closed world for the intellect, and the language even affects the way of thinking. A classical text, a piece of art, was conceived of as the external appearance of a nation's spirit, because writing is identical with the language. When we see it this way, then indeed translation will become rather impossible.

It was only in the 20th century, with the development of modern linguistics, that the focus has shifted. Language is seen now as a semiotic system and the objective is to design a general methodology of translation, with a view to automation.[5] Nonetheless, the human translator is still needed, as the amount of texts to be translated worldwide is growing tremendously in size and variation.

Thoughts about translation originated – as we have said – in the self-reflection by individual translators who had set their own goals. It is a misunderstanding when A. Chesterman collects various similar observations – such as "the translation should resemble the original" or "the translation should show a good style and avoid unusual words and expressions" – and suggests: "Hidden beneath these prescriptive statements about the universal characteristics of good translations there actually lie predictive hypotheses" (2004:4) (see also Chesterman 1993). No, this is not necessarily so, even if many might have understood it in

---

[5] The "science of translation" was initially used as an auxiliary discipline for the target of formalizing language in a way as to make texts translatable by computers. Though the target of Fully Automatic High Quality Translation (FAHQT) has not yet been reached even today, many useful applications have been determined for huge technical texts of a similar structure.

that sense. These statements just constitute individual goals set by translators for themselves and used as a justification for their work.

## 1.3 The first paradigm of interlingual transfer for equivalence

The modern scientific analysis of languages gave a new perspective. Language as a means of communication was no longer seen merely as a mirror of individuality, but as a medium of expressing one's thoughts in a rational way. Language appears as a system of signs to be analyzed, and research now focuses on language structures rather than peoples' ideology. On the surface, translation appears as an exchange of source language material by target language material (Catford 1965; Kade 1968).

On a purely linguistic basis Catford (1965) dealt with "translation shifts" defining them as "departures from formal correspondence in the process of going from the SL to the TL" (1965:73).[6] And this view is still valid thirty years later: „Translation is a process by which the chain of signifiers that constitutes the source-language text is replaced by a chain of signifiers in the target language which the translator provides on the strength of an interpretation" (Venuti 1995:17). Thus translation was defined as an "interlingual transfer" of information, requiring a "code-switching process" in the channel of communication in order to preserve the information unaltered (Wilss 1996:5). This created the paradigm of translation as an uni-directional "transfer" of information from one language to the other:

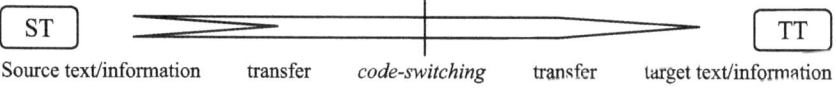

Source text/information     transfer     *code-switching*     transfer     target text/information

The resulting "problem of translation" was defined as the task of obtaining "translation equivalence" between two languages with different signs and structures, and there were extracted four kinds of "potential equivalents", such as the *one-to-one (total equivalent), one-to-many (facultative equivalent), one-to-part*

---

[6] Snell-Hornby (1988:19) has criticised that Catford's definition of textual equivalence were "circular", his theory's reliance on bilingual informants "hopelessly inadequate", and his example sentences "isolated and even absurdly simplistic". She asserts that the translation process cannot simply be reduced to a linguistic exercise.

*(approximate equivalent), one-to-zero (non-equivalence) or gap* (Koller 1992:229). This definition regards individual lexemes, and later on it found wide application in contrastive linguistics and lexicography.

The discipline of Contrastive Linguistics, originally designed for explaining difficulties in learning a foreign language, also influenced Translation Science as it offered the instruments for translation criticism and error analysis (Spillner 1990), and this was mainly based on comparative stylistics first developed in Quebec. The problem of an information transfer over a code-switching led to the discipline of *Stylistique comparée* describing the transfer in a particular language pair. There are studies for English-French (Vinay & Darbelnet 1958) and German-French (Malblanc 1968) translation, inferring some "transfer procedures".

> Comparing existing translations with their source texts, they described seven procedures supposedly applied by the translators, namely *emprunt, calque, traduction littérale, transposition, modulation, équivalence, adaptation*. The first three are a substitution of single words, *transposition* and *modulation* are a non-literal paraphrasing of units for stylistic reasons, *adaptation* is a shift for extratextual reasons, *equivalence* a substitution of idiomatic phrases. These procedures are seen as reactions to the ST structure on the syntagmatic level.

Translation Science thus could be defined as the task "to develop operating procedures which will make it possible to factor the transfer from a SLT [sc. source language text] to a TLT against the background of the intended meaning in the SL, to organize the individual factors in a plausible frame of reference and extract from them a logical model of description and explanation..." (Wilss 1982:63). This equivalence-based concept is still maintained in Wilss (1996) where we read:

> Translation is a specific kind of linguistic information processing based on the principle of code-switching. It is basically characterized by the interaction of three communicating partners, the ST author, the translator, and the TT reader (1996:5). – Except for instances where it has become a routine, translation is a form of linguistic performance requiring subtle skills of ST/TT synchronization on all translationally relevant levels. In accomplishing a translation, translators are aware that they face the ST as a "silent object". They must first penetrate it receptively (semasiologically) and then reproduce it in the TL (onomasiologically) (ibid. 9). – As a "higher-level" discipline, building upon the insights of contrastive linguistics and sharing with it the notion of "tertium comparationis", TS [sc. Transla-

tion Studies] seeks optimally inclusive rules of ST/TT coordination (10). – A specific feature of translator activities is that they are in principle norm-determined (42). – In order to help the translator, TS must develop procedural standards on an empirical basis. The primary aim of TS is to work out efficient strategies and norms of behavior... (44f). – The main property of translation is coordination between the ST and the unfolding TT at the semantic, stylistic, and pragmatic levels. Unless a translator can proceed in a predominantly or all-out routinized manner, this coordination is a demanding task, although (or because?) translation is essentially a reproductive activity (45). – Translators do not produce a primary text; they produce a secondary text. Translators do not really have a decisive say in performing their task; they are bound by the situational demands to which they are exposed (46f). – We all agree that translation is a goal-directed activity which basically consists of a decoding and an encoding, or more precisely, "recoding phase" (recoding, because the ST has already been encoded in the SL) (78). – What characterizes translation activity is the fact that it is immersed in a basic framework of mental activity - the perception, the reorganization (restructuring), and the evaluation of strings of linguistic symbols (126). – ...translation is a mental activity, in which occur internalized, "elementary" translation procedures, such as literal translation, and more intricate transfer procedures, such as obligatory or optional non-literal transfer procedures (137). – Certainly, the recognition of the centrality of the lexicon in translator performance and the (near-)automatic reproduction of textual configurations are top targets for translation efficiency (137). – Translation is a situationally optimal synchronization of the ST and the TT (175).

The idea seems to be that TS has to "analyze data" (ibid. 57) by comparing target texts with source texts in order to detect hidden rules of translational behavior that might then be operationalized and taught in translation pedagogics. Translation is defined „as the quoting, in sequential chunks, of the wording of a written, oral or signed text, with an imitative purpose" (Mossop 1998:231). The theoretical basis for this collecting data is to be found in G. Toury (1995) who called for descriptive analyses in order to better define the discipline of Translation Studies, and to state principles of translating in the sense of "translational norms" (ibid., 58). But the idea was there earlier.

Rooted in general linguistics, E. Nida (1964) has developed a guideline for translators based on the syntagmatic analysis of ambiguous structures for transfer and restructuring. His principle of a "dynamic equivalence" (Nida/Taber 1974:13) derives from a thorough analysis of semantic and syntagmatic structures, and it is situated within the paradigm of interlingual transfer in translation. He even expressly talks of "transfer" when he suggests to find the "closest natural equivalent" (ibid. 13) by translating the deep structure of "kernel sentences" and then rearranging them on the surface level in the other language (ibid. 33). The problem with Nida's program is the fact that he only focuses on syntagmas, without taking any larger sentence structures or even a paragraph into consideration.[7] We have to admit, though, that Nida's concept was directed towards translating for mission at exotic places with less developed languages, and this is still applied today in respective bible translation projects.[8]

Translation is seen didactically as a series of technical procedures to be applied, and this has decisively determined the orientation of translation pedagogics in the 1960s and onwards. Many translation handbooks even today still follow this language-pair model, because it is also a useful instrument for translation evaluation in the class room. J. House (1997) has developed a model of translation quality assessment aiming at a "scientific translation critique". Its purpose is to measure whether a translation has an (optimal) equivalence relationship to the original on all linguistic levels, regarding words and sentences in terms of their deviation from a literal translation. She argues that ST and TT should match one another in function: "Translation is constituted by a 'double-binding' relationship both to its source and to the communicative conditions of the receiving lingua-culture, and it is the concept of equivalence which catches this relationship" (House 1997:29).

House suggests that it is possible to characterize the function of a text by determining "situational dimensions" in the ST. The translation should employ equivalent situational-dimensional means to achieve the function wanted (ibid., 49). The idea is to find instruments for comparing texts and translations in every

---

[7] There are various examples of ambiguous biblical phrases that follow Greek language structure, and which, according to Nida, should be disambiguated in a translation:
| | |
|---|---|
| the will of God | God wills |
| the God of peace | God causes/produces peace |
| the Holy Spirit of promise | God promised the Holy Spirit |
| the word of truth | the word is true |
| the riches of his grace | he shows grace richly/abundantly |
| the day of the preparation | the day when (people) prepare (for the Sabbath). |

[8] Meanwhile Nida has left the strict, biased syntactical view, when he notes (1985:119): "We are no longer limited to the idea that meaning is centred in words or even in grammatical distinctions. Everything in language, from sound symbolism to complex rhetorical structures carries meaning."

linguistic detail so to determine the degree of equivalence between both. This later on could perhaps serve to operationalize "translation rules" in the sense of a descriptive presentation of the adequate translation reaction to source text structures, based on a systematic linguistic-pragmatic analysis of the language function in the situational context.[9]

Whereas Nida's concern had been the issue of a faithful representation of the message, though in a different form, in order to gain equal response to it amongst the target language audience, the focus shifted totally towards the addressees in other functional approaches. The so-called Skopos Theory sees translation as part of Action Theory and gives highest rank to its purpose, over and above any coherence relationship of the target to the source text (Reiß & Vermeer 1984:119). The general guideline of translation should be its purpose, the question for whom and to which end we are translating (Vermeer 1996a). Even if this is a strong argument for shifts, the reference point of argumentation, still, is the source text structure. In explaining "functionalist approaches", C. Nord (1991:17/21) discusses for instance the adaptation of lexical or syntactic structures – now called "functional units" – to the system of the target language by means of translation procedures such as "modulation" and "transposition" known already from Stylistique comparée.

In stressing the need for "creativity" in the translator regarding his or her linguistic decisions for purposeful translation, Kußmaul (1995) designed a model of training the translator. Based on a cognitive foundation of translation teaching, his interest is "to explore various aspects of the methodology of translation" (1995:2).[10] A didactic learning effect is seen in the critical discussion of the re-

---

[9] In order to compare TT and ST, a "textual profile" has to be established. For example: "The absence of elliptical clauses or comment parentheses" is a sign of written language, "e.g. in an information letter" (House 1997:49f). Or: "The presence of strong textual cohesion due to the employment of several mechanisms of theme-dynamics and clausal linkage" is a textual means of indicating the province as the situational embedding.

[10] Kußmaul (1995) discusses the following topics:
What goes on in the translator's mind?
Creativity in translation
Pragmatic analysis
The analysis of meaning
Text analysis and the use of dictionaries
Evaluation and errors
A summary of strategies.

sults, however without any categories of evaluation. The interest is in analyzing the origination of formulations that are structurally different from the source text as the point of reference. Any non-literal translation, thus, is defined by him as "creative", just because it implies a modification of the form, compared with the original: "As soon as we have to realize such changes in virtue of linguistic constraints, we are creative to a certain extent" (Kußmaul 2000:22, *my translation*). And he again recalls the procedures of "transposition" and "paraphrase" invented by Stylistique comparée, even defining a scale of "more or less creativity" (ibid. 29).

In the French tradition, there has been designed the alternative of "sourciers" (source-text related types of translators) and the "ciblistes" (those focusing on the target text). The former tend more to stick to the ST structure in a literal translation preserving form and sense, while the latter create deviant new formulations to present the meaning. Unfortunately, J.-R. Ladmiral himself, the author of those terms, does not give a concise definition of what he thinks "translation is". In an article dealing with "a pluralistic concept" of translation (1995) he argues on a pragmatic level,[11] but he fails to give a definition of "translation", only an account of its instances. Ladmiral himself, though, seems to be a cibliste. In view of the source text-oriented translators (*sourciers*) he speaks of an utopian attempt to "repeat the original text" (1995:417; 1993:297), but his account does not explain how to make it better and still leaves us without a definition of the term *translation*. And this deceptive state is neither resolved five years later in his article on the "aporetic concept of translation" (2002), where he even defines translation as "equivalence", just to say that this is a tautology (2002:126; 1995:417). He also mentions the problem of literalness for a "truthful translation" (2002:123) as had been requested by the poet Walter Benjamin.[12] Obvious-

---

[11] Ladmiral differentiates among spontaneous translation L2-L1 by pupils in foreign language acquisition (surcodage mental, 1995:410), the pedagogic translation exercises in schools (version, thème), the professional translation of literary and technical texts in the sense of presenting a "real text". Literary translation is subdivided into the translation of the works of literary art, philosophical texts, and holy scripture (ibid., 423).

[12] In fact, Benjamin had stated in 1923: "Rather the meaning of fidelity, which is assured by literalness, is that the great longing for the complementarity of languages should make itself felt in the work. Real translation is transparent, it does not hide the original..." (Lefevere 1977:102).

ly, this approach too is neither able to give a convincing definition of what translation is nor to oppose the circular statement put up by Ladmiral: « Tous les arguments contre la traduction se résument en un seul: elle n'est pas l'original ».[13] Even if the translation "is" not the original, it functions "as it". Ladmiral's repeated attempts to find a semantic definition of the concept of translation are fruitless.

The relationship between languages has now been analyzed to every respect, on the theoretical level (*langue*) as well as on the practical level (*parole*), when translations are being compared with their originals. The framework of an "interlingual transfer" is never transgressed. And this is even understandable since, at surface level, the target and the source text actually do show some similarities in their wording and structure. An equivalence-based textual criticism will always show some "shifts", but such resulting formal deviations cannot be taken as a theory of translation.

## 1.4 Descriptive and prescriptive rules in translation

Wilss (1996:10) describes the task of TS to operationalize "rules of ST/TT coordination". A "rule" has various meanings:

> 1. governing power, 2. an authoritative direction, 3. a customary course of action, 4. a statement that describes what is true in most or all cases, 5. a standard procedure, and others (*The American Heritage Dictionary*).

The search for supposedly basic principles of translation in a language pair was not always systematic. P. Newmark, in his numerous books on translation, renders uncountable examples of translation cases called "rules" (Newmark 1973; 1979), obviously thinking that this collection would lead to a general insight in how to address the task. His micro-stylistic approach is clear when he writes (1980:127):

---

[13] *Translation:* "All arguments against translation are resumed in one only: it is not the original." See Ladmiral (1995:418; 2002:127) citing here both times Georges Mounin (1955:7).

You can no more teach someone to become a good translator than to become a good linguist. All you can do is to give some hints, give some practice and if you're lucky, show more or less how the job can be done.[14]

Newmark's "rules" appear subjective and proto-academic. Most of them are circular comments presented by the teacher in a prescriptive way, but they cannot serve as a general guideline. As every text is different, and as the "case studies" always just refer to one specific case, this is not very illuminating. But how can individual goals and achievements become general rules of translation? The reason lies in the structural focus of argumentation.

The idea is to link translational effects to text structures as their cause (Chesterman 1998), because in the interlingual transfer paradigm translations seem to be just a reaction to source text structures. Texts are being personalized, and researchers analyze text types as "a general translational behavior of texts" (Reiß/Vermeer 1984:204)[15], in order to describe the "factor model of translation" (ibid. 148). In reality it is the translators who show a certain behavior.

Descriptive Translation Studies set out to analyze the behavior pattern of translators by analyzing their results. "Real science", according to Toury (1995:1), is only empirical science. He requests to "do more empirical research" (Toury 2004:23), obviously meant for later on constructing some "rules" found, that could be taught in the classroom for translators. He accepts the forming of a theory if the empirical studies lead "toward the establishment of a full-fledged, multi-facet theory of translation of a high explanatory power" (Toury 1995:240).

---

[14] Newmark obviously thought that there are as many types of translations as there are texts. The title of one of his articles reads: "Twenty-three Restricted Rules of Translation" (1973). Maybe those didn't seem sufficient, so he wrote another article: "Sixty Further Propositions on Translation" (1979). One "rule" thereof reads: "42. Translation balancing-act – On the one hand, the translator should not use a synonym where a translation will do, in particular, where the translation is a 'transparently' faithful cognate or the standard dictionary equivalent and has no special connotations. On the other hand, he should not translate one-to-one where one-to-two or -three would do better, nor, reproduce a SL syntactic structure where he can recast the sentence more neatly."

[15] *Read*: "Es ist für die Translatologie, deren Gegenstände u.a. die Erforschung der Bedingungen und Möglichkeiten der Übersetzung ist, eine der Textsortenklassifikation vorgeschaltete, gröbere und abstraktere Differenzierung von Texten im Blick auf ein *generelles translatorisches Verhalten* von Texten von Interesse, die Klassifikation nach Texttypen."

However, all this appears as a naïve inductionism, since any interpretation of data implies subjective aspects as well. The way we perceive some things, or whether we perceive them at all, is determined by our own experience, our own perspective as a researcher. The pure, 'objective' collection of data does not make sense, unless they were purposefully collected on the basis of a specific research hypothesis. D. Gile (1991:154) calls for "real research" by the extensive collection of data, even without much hypothesis beforehand: "Systematic observation of reality is a valuable scientific act *per se*" (ibid. 166). And even he sticks to the old idea of textual transfer when he defines translation as "a process P acting on an input I and producing an output O, where both input and output are entirely contained in written documents" (ibid. 155).

The bulk of corpus studies works according to this empirical paradigm, when for instance the recurrence of certain collocations is analyzed in translations (Sinclair 1991). Corpus-based methods of enquiry have given impetus to the quest for the so-called translation universals, i.e., "features that typically occur in translated text rather than original utterances and which are not the result of interference from specific linguistic systems" (Baker 1993:243). Explicitation, simplification, normalization, the "law of interference" and "the unique items hypothesis" have been investigated with monolingual comparable and bilingual parallel corpora.[16] E. Steiner (2004:17) makes it clear that corpus analyses are being used for translation criticism – showing patterns of translational behavior (Teich 2003), but no instruction for translating itself as a task. The systematical description of given translational solutions focuses on facts on the surface level, what for some researchers even intuitively turns into prescriptive statements. The idea of "predictive hypotheses" (Chesterman) includes the assumption that "it must be so", all the more that the mainstream results shown in such corpuses confirm that. The problem in such corpuses, though – be they large or small – is that it is "dead language material" or a "silent object" (Wilss 1996:9).

On the contrary, utterances by speakers are always marked by the individuality of the respective situation and the speaker's evolving linguistic proficiency, as well as the knowledge of the individual. Any recorded speech only fixes a past situation. The utterance could well have been pronounced in a totally different

---

[16] For an overview of corpus studies on universals see Klaudy (2009); Laviosa (2009).

form, as the way people speak is highly unpredictable. What is predictable is only grammar, the correct idiomatic usage of certain syntagmas, what very often not comes to the conscience of the user. A corpus thus fixes momentary "language games" (Wittgenstein 1953:§7) what makes it an arbitrary construct with no strong relevance for any future linguistic behavior. Corpora age quickly, and this reduces their relevance as data-sources for linguistic analysis, and of course as examples for future linguistic activity in particular, in communication just as in translation.

The analysis does not lead to a convincing motivation of such solutions seen, nor to any improvement of them. How should we draw a pattern for future translating activites therefrom? Wittgenstein had pointed out that language is "language in use", when he called a language-game "the whole, consisting of language and the actions into which it is woven" (ibid.). Despite repeated calls for a "collection of rules" for translating, such works have not yet been put on the table. Perhaps, it is not even possible because there are too many exceptions.

We have to distinguish between "prescriptive rules" of methodology and "descriptive rules" of behavior patterns, i.e. between rule description and rule observation. Prescriptive rules are those presented by Newmark, though without any synthesizing order and without answering any questions. Descriptive rules, on the contrary, are a result of empirical analysis, they stem from the experience, that things happen to be the same in various cases (but not in all). They need not become prescriptive rules for the sake of majority. The empirical scientific concept as an analysis of facts or a verification of simulated models of action implies the idea that the problem of how an individual translator approaches his or her work, and which quality standards he or she will apply, were already solved. But this is not at all the case. Translational behavior is not predictable.

The way of dealing with texts to be translated is no direct consequence from the discussion of given examples and methods, as didactics often presupposes. The traditional description of "translation processes" has no other reference points than language structures. However, it is not yet clear whether translational activity in practice really works with such linguistic structures as grammar and syntax. That concept of comparing language structures for the purpose of defining a model of translation fails its subject. Rightly, Stecconi (2007:15) supports semiotics, because "it redefines the traditional image of translating as transfer".

The human translator really thinks differently. S/he asks *why* something has been done and whether it could be done better, rather than simply observing *what* and *how* it has been done. Many researchers state that translations are "in principle norm-determined" (Wilss 1996:42; Koller 1992:209). Toury (1995:55) speaks of "norms in translation" which are "acquired by the individual". He is thinking of social norms and conditions of the translation activity (to be descriptively analyzed in TS) while Wilss thinks of linguistic rules of ST-TT transfer. But translators do not apply such "rules".

The idea of translation as a rule-governed activity – both descriptively and prescriptively – much influenced by machine translation, appears to us as a completely wrong concept of human translation. Wilss' book on the "Knowledge and Skills in Translator Behavior" (1996) does not even describe such "behavior", he only compiles numerous quotations from the literature about the scientific analysis of "knowledge structures" and necessary skills such as translation techniques on the sentence level.

Translation is a process, based on the individual strategy within a social setting, rather than a translator's quasi automatic behavior as a "response to the ST" (Wilss 1996:99) in view of "operational prediction" (ibid. 31). And "strategy" is a plan for action, rather than rule application. Ladmiral (1988) called descriptive approaches a "translation science of yesterday" (*traductologie d'hier*), because it comes too late for the act of translating, but he does not exploit his own idea when he simply stresses the need for translators to decide here: « Condamné à être libre, le traducteur est un décideur […] dans une alternative stratégique de décision traductive » (1993:291f).[17] Hönig (1993) had already stressed the necessary self-assurance of the translator who may decide by himself and defend his or her solutions.

---

[17] *Translation*: Condemned to freedom, the translator has to decide, in a strategic alternative of translational decision.

## 1.5 Translation as a dynamic task

Nowhere is the translator mentioned as a historically and culturally rooted person using the languages. Levý (1969:25) regrets that nearly all "theories of literary translation are neglecting the translator's part in the process of translating" (*my translation*). Translation, as seen by the translating person herself, is a dynamic assignment, since the target language text is yet to be produced. In the moment of translating there is no target text to be correlated, and any examples from descriptive translation criticism are only of limited relevance to the given assignment, because they refer to past translations in a different context. The issue of "equivalence" is a static concept from translation criticism, as "I cannot translate equivalently" (Stolze 2003:17). Findings from Stylistique comparée explain the differences in a language pair, but are no "transfer procedures" (Wilss 1977:10). Debates about the relationship between source and target texts on the theoretical level always come too late or too early. The translator rather needs orientation for his translation strategy.

Standard translation theories – either in the transfer paradigm or in the comparative cultural paradigm – always see a direct move from the ST to the TT. However, this is not the way the translator's approach is working. Any translation is ultimately guided by an implicit or explicit understanding of the source text. Translation is no „navigating on a sea of words between languages and cultures" (Bassnett 2000:106) but, rather, the task to represent a message, understood from a text, in another language. We then have to strictly distinguish between the mere comprehension of that text, and the strategic move of writing a translation.

The translator will only translate what he or she has understood beforehand and what is now cognitively present in his or her mind as the message. Any features of the text ignored by the translator will be lost (but may reappear in a later translation). There is only one message cognitively present, which will flow from one language into another language's frames. So it is wrong what Jakobson (1959:233) said: "Translation involves two equivalent messages in two different codes". Unfortunately, this idea has governed generations of scholars regarding their translation theories.

Wittgenstein has underlined the differences between reasons and causes (cf. Richter 2004:43): reasons justify while causes merely explain; and what we need is justification. We know our reasons for acting in a certain way, whereas we might not (be able to) know the causes of our actions; and any chain of reasons ever comes to an end in the person, which needs not be true for chains of cause and effect. An infinite regress of theory by inference, therefore, is not helpful in social action. Teaching translation means teaching an activity, rather than a linguistic relationship or a pattern. And human activity is never totally governed by "recurrent patterns" (Collini 1992:7).

Any translation – in the act of writing and subsequent revision – is an open task, a design of formulation (*Entwurf*) which in that moment is entirely subjective. Reflection, testing against objective knowledge, and dialectic response to criticism will then result in another draft, and finally back-up the end-result of the translation work. This is the inner perspective of translators, that so far has not yet been sufficiently discussed in Translation Studies.

If translation were an operation fully directed by rules to be operationalized in factors, then it should not be possible that one text receives several different translations, as it is the case whenever translated by humans and not by a machine translation system. As long as still persons and teams are doing the job and future translators are being trained in schools, their approach to dealing with texts – from their own inner perspective – should be made the subject of scholarly consideration.

Experience shows that thought and volition, even if referring to each other in the acting person, are also ineluctably separate. The wish does not lead in a logically compelling and fully guaranteed way to the respective action, neither does command. You want to do the good, but emotion hinders you. Factual knowledge is not automatically and necessarily a knowledge of sense in human life, and regulations are not always direct orientations for the individual, as Bubner (1976:136) has stated, and laws do not become immediately customs (even if rulers hope so). Ever and ever again, dissenting opinion and diverging activity is possible, and ethical responsibility exactly originates from that necessity to socially motivate one's acts.

If we ask: "How should I as a translator approach my texts, whereto should I put my attention", the scholarly interest will be shifted from the description of structures, data, facts and external processes towards the individual perspective and motivation of the acting person within the framework of his or her given cultural situation. One might call this the "hermeneutical paradigm", while a so-called liberal arts paradigm of translation research comprises case studies in both comparative literature and translation criticism. Due to the interdependence between understanding and translation, there is an intrinsic link between hermeneutics and translation as a dynamic task.

The personalized approach will also change the system of co-ordinates in Translation Studies. The issue is no longer the question whether TS should rather be "more descriptive or more prescriptive" (Chesterman & Arrojo 2000), it will instead become more reflective. We will have to focus on the person who questions and reflects about the decisions to be made by him- or herself.

A dynamic approach to translation can go a long way in the effort to overcome the extreme binaries that often play a role in TS. Such binary structures include: source text/target text, translatability/untranslatability, written/oral, literal/free, specialist languages/literature, form/content, foreign/familiar, static/dynamic, translation unit/whole of text, explicitation /implicitation, overemphasis/ simplification, subconscious decision/ mechanical application of methodology, etc. These binaries are supposed objectivations of human activity or thought which, however, is very different in every individual. With hermeneutics, there is no longer the mutual exclusion of extremes but, rather, different positions that complement each other (Hu 2004).

Such a view of language and translation also leads to different questions in research. For instance, the question is no longer whether a text unit is translatable or not, but *how* one can find an adequate translation. There is no longer the search for a definite equivalence-relationship between target and source text but rather the question of *how* the source-cultural message, now cognitively present the translator's mind, can assume another linguistic form. We do not look for a unified methodological paradigm to finally delineate a translatological discipline. The question is rather *how* a certain translational behavior can be motivated. The discipline is a field of various activities (Holmes 1988). There is a move from quantitative to qualitative research.

## 1.6 The translators' subjectivity as an integral element

The primary problem is how to understand the text to be translated and to connect it with successful target language text production, and this is not solved by designing models for the "interlingual coordination of semiotic structures" (Wilss 1996) or "intercultural transfer". The translator as a person finds no help in patterns or other examples, since translation is not merely an application of rules.[18] We will have to revolve our perspective to hermeneutics.

Hermeneutics distinguishes – from a personalized world view – between objects/facts with their analysis/cognition and human activity with its inner motivation, i.e., between objectivity and subjectivity, analysis and evidence, method and decision, rationale and intuition, inference and evidence, proof and argumentation.

Language comprises aspects of both objective features in grammar & lexicon uniting all members of a speakers' community, and subjective features of individuality, because language is also created and evolves by situated utterances in a culture. Both aspects shall never be kept separate from each other, they can only be seen alternately, in a more or less clear emergence, depending on the individual case. Any contrastive grammar or stylistics or text analysis will only grasp one half of a language reality, and, on the other hand, individual assurance of having understood rightly may be prone to the relativity of a naïve subjectivity. So this calls for critical reflection.

"Translation is an activity that varies as we pass from one translator to the next, from one ST to the next", admits Wilss (1996:42). However, this is not a "defect" but a fundamental characteristic of translation. F. Paepcke (1986:161)

---

[18] "The aversion of propagators of this [hermeneutical] approach against any kind of objectivization, systematization and rule-hypothesizing in translation procedures leads to a distorted view of translation, and a reduction of translation research to examining each individual translation act as an individual creative endeavour" (House 1997:3-4). – As it were.

makes it clear that "the translator is *acteur*, not *voyeur*; he is an actor, an active participant, not a wise observer of translation" (*my translation*).

The fear of subjectivity has probably been introduced into Translation Studies by Nida (1964), who has a short chapter on "The Role of the Translator" where the last part has the telling title "Dangers of Subjectivity in Translation" and where he commits the translator to full "fidelity" to the source text, understood in linguistic features, warning:

> No translator can avoid a certain degree of personal involvement in his work. In his interpretation of the source-language message, his selection of corresponding words and grammatical forms, and his choice of stylistic equivalents, he will inevitably be influenced by his overall empathy with author and message, or his lack of it. (Nida 1964:154)

We will have to extensively discuss later on whether this is a correct understanding of "subjectivity" and what "interpretation" really means, or how to prevent "intuitive personal speculation" (Gile 1991:166). We see a difference between a normal speaker/reader and a responsible translator who, of course, cannot only stick to "personal predilection" (Wilss).[19] The translator's responsibility to faithfulness in his work does not come from an order, but from the readers' confidence, who normally believe that a translation gives them a correct idea of the original text.

Subjectivity in human activity is an ontological given, and it should therefore be reflected upon and integrated into the model. This creates responsibility. And individual variance of texts and situations is an offspring of it, equally not to be eliminated in the studies. In our view, the translator's approach is not a "behavior" but an attitude and outlook towards texts leading to a strategical action. The question is: How can a translator adequately deal with a given text to be translated? And this dealing with texts and coping with their difficulties as an approach is in fact seen here as "one coherent translation theory" which is so vehemently rejected by Wilss (1996:45). In the following, the practical effect of this concept and its theoretical foundation will be discussed.

---

[19] Wilss makes the sweeping statement: "Since individuals tend to engage selectively in different aspects of their textual environment according to their personal interests, predilections, and capabilities, no quick answers to our questions are available or expectable" (1996:79).

Some feel that, because of the subjectivity in every individual, understanding among each other were quite impossible. Our conviction, to the contrary, is that a translator basically is able to take part in a foreign world of thought, s/he can accept the opinion of another person as manifested in a text. There is no proof against this idea, but it is expressly opposed for instance by H. Vermeer (1996b:5/23). He refers to the above-mentioned relativist language theory of Humboldt supporting a world view determined by individual languages of different nations, and he points to the theory of monads by Leibniz concerning those units of spiritual substances living side by side "without windows". He writes:

> "[...] trotz aller ausgesandten Signale also sitzt jeder einzelne letzten Endes wie Leibnizens Monade in der Formel *seiner* Wahrheit befangen und in *seine* Welt eingesponnen da" (cf. Vermeer 1996b:35, 121, 182, 261). (*My translation*: despite all signals sent out, every individual in the end sits there like Leibniz' monad, locked in his truth and cocooned in his world). – Thus Vermeer considers true understanding to be impossible: "Meiner Ansicht nach handelt es sich um eine Annäherung, die allemal noch eine Differenz bestehen lässt" (1996b:59) (= I think it's a narrowing that ever leaves a difference). – Vermeer neglects here an important aspect in Leibniz' philosophy: he had stressed that these monads are living in "harmony with one another", each one at his predetermined place. Even here there is a higher level of unification.

But already 19th-century philosophers have pointed out the aporetics of sole subjectivism and extensively described the constitution of intersubjectivity as "Vergemeinschaftung der Monaden" (a collectivisation of the monads) (Husserl 1950:199). We may cite some 20th-century cognitivist researchers as well:

> When people who are talking don't share the same culture, knowledge, values, and assumptions, mutual understanding can be especially difficult. Such understanding is possible through the negotiation of meaning. To negotiate meaning with someone [...] you need a talent for finding the right metaphor to communicate the relevant parts of unshared experiences or to highlight the shared experiences while de-emphasizing the others. (Lakoff/Johnson 1980:231) – The authors also criticize what they call "the myth of objectivism in western philosophy and linguistics" (ibid., 195).

Accepting subjectivity in the translator, and also in research, may not correspond to modern ideas of scientific discourse. Nonetheless, it is ever possible, but it includes reflection and responsibility.

## 1.7 Misunderstanding in the academic discourse

The problem of understanding among researchers in TS who apparently come from different worlds of discourse is virulent. The difference between these two worlds is marked by the terms of the Liberal Arts Paradigm (LAP) and the Empirical Science Paradigm (ESP) – two paradigmatic approaches to doing research in TS (Stolze 2009).

The widely discussed interdisciplinarity of Translation Studies (Kaindl 1999) has provoked some doubts about its methodological clarity, as is shown by the title of a recent book *Doubts and Directions in Translation Studies* (Gambier et al. 2007). The discipline itself lacks a clear definition and an established name: it is alternately referred to as "science of translation" "translatology" or "translation studies". As a result, the need to enhance the precision of terminology is keenly felt in the field (cf. Gambier & van Doorslaer 2007).

Weaknesses regularly observed and reported in studies conducted by TS researchers seem to reflect lacunae in basic rather than advanced skills and methods (Gile & Hansen 2004). This concerns not only the research methodology, but also the nature of academic writing. The doubts seem to be partly caused by a problem of mutual misunderstanding. Outsiders or newcomers to a given academic discipline with a given type of discourse do not always have a clear perception of the conventions adhered to and the academic skills relied on in the given world of discourse. Therefore, in order to promote peaceful coexistence and fruitful cooperation in TS, it seems necessary to make the representatives of different worlds of discourse more aware of the implicit norms of other worlds of discourse.

The progress of scientific knowledge is based on constant communication among researchers. Science can be defined as "scientific communication", since the objects as such, e.g. the words and objects like 'car', 'apple', 'gene' or 'translation' have no inherent scientific quality. It is always a question of the researcher's perspective, what he or she "sees" on them and talks about (Kalverkämper 1998:31). Moreover, the norms of academic writing also differ considerably in various linguistic communities (Ventola & Mauranen 1996), even if these differences are becoming increasingly blurred as English is consolidating its role as the *lingua franca* of international research and academic publication.

But this only aggravates the situation, as authors tend to unconsciously apply their own cultural or institutionally trained attitude to text construction, even when writing in English, and that, again, may cause some serious problems of understanding.

Science has the goal of objectivity which is to be reached by a very precise analysis of the objects. This requires the so-called "scientific method" of doing research, as is explained in many textbooks, see a.o. Strauss and Corbin (1998). Empirical research first established itself in the natural sciences, but has now become common in the humanities, too: psychology, neurophysiology and economics are prime examples. Translation Studies can also be seen as a science with an empirical research dimension (Toury 1995:1).

The norms of writing a report on empirical studies are strict. Scientific publication, here, requires that a dissertation or thesis begins with the clear presentation of aims and objectives of the research, followed by a detailed description of tools and methods that were used. Next follow the results and a critical discussion of them, completed by a summary. A review of the literature is also necessary, plus references to all relevant previous studies, surveys and/or experiments.[20] Nothing should be left implicit, as the publication will serve as a model for methodological replication and evidence regarding the results. As the results are most important they are also summarized in the abstract, which may be read in order to know whether the article will be interesting. Anthologies of abstracts give an overview of research completed.[21] Readers in ESP are trained to check every statement by looking at the data and quotation reference given. In this way the content of a paper reveals itself "point by point" in a linear arrangement.

The researcher, here, has a special perspective on the objects and determines the data to be analyzed in view of the research project. Different researchers may be interested in different data, and this does not necessarily mean that they "misin-

---

[20] This may explain why scientific prominence is being measured with a citation index. The ISI Web of Knowledge, now owned by Thomson Reuters, is a searchable database of scientific research. One of its products is the Journal Citation Reports (JCR), which ranks journals on the basis of the times articles are cited. TS journals are largely overlooked and rated poorly.

[21] See for instance the online *Translation Studies Bibliography* of John Benjamins.

terpret reality" (Gile).[22] Doubts about the social relevance of working in TS mirror some uncertainty about the relationship between concepts such as *theory*, *research* or *science*. Gile asks: "Do research projects need to be socially useful?"[23] Whereas some exotic analysis may well be done in ESP, the social relevance is always the point of departure in the humanities (Beiner 2009:118). Strauss and Corbin (1998: 22) define theory in this way:

> For us, theory denotes a set of well-developed categories (e.g. themes, concepts) that are systematically interrelated through statements of relationship to form a theoretical framework that explains some relevant social, psychological, educational, nursing, or other phenomenon.

These categories are themselves theoretical constructs because they depend on the researcher's perspective or problem-awareness. Theory creates concepts, definitions, and models. Hypotheses are then tested and refined by research methodology, and this is dependent on the subject matter to be investigated. Empirical science includes the narrowing of one's perspective to focus on one specific phenomenon that will be analyzed extensively and deeply with an appropriate methodology. That means looking at data and analyzing them, ideally with a rigorous logic, systematically, objectively, cautiously, drawing on the collective work of the scientific community.

All research is guided by an inherent theory, and this is the field of LAP. In TS there is a continuing debate about the question of how translation is being conceived of as such, what "it is". There are various theories regarding translation, e.g. translation as interlingual transfer, as a linguistic response to language input, as intercultural mediation, as purposeful text production, as target language formulation of a message understood, as a localization product, and so on. There are so many ideas about translation that new textbooks on the "theories of translation" are continuously being written and compiled, see for instance Gentzler (1993), Stolze ($^5$2008), the book series *Translation Theories Explored* by St.

---

[22] D. Gile says: "When scientists start investigating a phenomenon, they often have a theory which they seek to prove. This may (*inter alia*) make them sensitive to some parts of reality and less so to others. Thus, they may misinterpret reality and "see" facts where other scientists with different theories would 'see' other facts". See Daniel Gile on "Scientific facts", website www.est-translationstudies.org/research issues, posted January 2005.

[23] See website: www.est-translationstudies.org/research issues, posted August 2007.

Jerome Publishing, the *Handbook of Translation Studies* of Benjamins, the *Routledge Encyclopedia of Translation Studies,* etc.

The first impulse for developing a theory, creating new hypotheses, opening new ways of reasoning, or testing new scientific methods is always an intuitive idea, an unexpected observation arousing interest, astonishment over an unfamiliar phenomenon, a problem seen that needs solving, a dissatisfaction with results so far obtained. This effect is bound to the subjectivity of the researcher. The evolution of theories will then emanate from research as scientific activity, and new theories may lead to new research activity. If somebody presents a more convincing theory, the former might be given up or, at least, the latter will find more followers.

Discourse in the Liberal Arts Paradigm is about ideas, and theoretical argumentation is different from reporting on research completed. Most so-called theory-oriented papers and studies belong into this tradition. The researcher, who is a scholar rather than a scientist, works on theories and models of relationships or activities, on processes or developments, on motivation of social action. He or she asks "why" things are as they are according to empirical description, and sometimes even makes suggestions on how things "should be". This is the prevailing approach in the humanities as a field of research (Beiner 2009), and TS belongs to the humanities, too. Our hermeneutical approach is also located in this paradigm.

In academic discourse we will start with an inter-subjective plausibility of the terms we are using and hope that the audience will understand us. Opinions and arguments are based on personal conviction and implicit values. Otherwise there would be no point in entering into a debate. Scholars must first agree on what it is that may be called a "fact" before they can talk about it. This kind of debate in LAP is closely linked with the respective scholar as a person, and therefore subjectivity is always present and determines the procedures of doing research and communicating it.

Such contributions pose a question, problematize a concept, or suggest a practical application, e.g. for pedagogic purposes. The intention in all cases is to modify the status quo with respect to a theoretical view. A large part of scholarly work in LAP is based on critical analysis of other scholars' publications and is, in this way, done in the library. Referees from the ESP paradigm have sometimes difficulties to understand this kind of discourse and argumentation (cf. Stolze 2009:8).

The question arises whether this has something to do with hermeneutics. This branch of modern language philosophy is studying the conditions of understanding by a human being in his or her cultural setting and attitude towards the world (Stanley 2005). Hermeneutics does not explain or guide understanding, but asks whether and how understanding is at all possible. Hermeneutics is ever confronted with the problem of non- or misunderstanding.

> Its problem consists in the fact that it is able to take its course only insofar as a kind of non-understanding is essentially involved in it. As understanding has been defined as the way of coming to terms with the foreign and unfamiliar, or as subsuming the singular under the already established rule, non-understanding should be considered as the disruptive intrusion of the unfamiliar into the field of knowledge, or the subjective response to what Friedrich Schlegel called incomprehensibility (Markowski 2008).[24]

This is also relevant in academic discourse, because in LAP there are "schools of thought" in the framework of which researchers develop their theories. Readers will need some specific knowledge in order to understand the text. Hermeneutics calls for critical self-awareness regarding this problem: one must always ask oneself whether sufficient knowledge is given for understanding, translating, and entering into a debate, or whether some learning strategies are still needed. Finally, orientation in the world does not only mean understanding, but also acting, for instance as a translator or a translation teacher, and researcher.

But there is a difficulty: Practical activity is geared towards the future. It is not certain that the description of past events (corpuses, behavior, rules) will have any impact on a present action. The individual must always decide according to the case at hand, there are no general rules (Risku 1998:11). In theoretical articles on translation, for instance, one will think about strategies and try to integrate as many aspects as possible. That is why respective texts not rarely "sound prescriptive", a critique often heard from referees.

---

[24] See Michał Paweł Markowski, Keynote paper at the International Conference on "Hermeneutics and the Humanities", 27-28 March 2008, Jagiellonian University, Kraków.

As theory-oriented papers *per se* are not focused on so-called objective facts but on ideas, the related "facts" cannot be presented and regarded as evident. Theoretical conclusions in LAP follow from a scholar's line of reasoning, which s/he will present repeatedly, using various expressions. This may explain why LAP articles tend to appear circular or unclear at first sight to ESP-trained readers. A LAP scholar will first express his or her idea and then try to back it up with examples or arguments, whereas ESP scholars will derive conclusions from careful analysis of the data. Logical inference in ESP, supposedly leading to results valid for everybody, is in sharp contrast with apparently circular argumentation in LAP, which gives the impression as if the author had difficulty in expressing him/herself, and was searching for words in order to convince readers.

The need for dialectics is easily acceptable if we imagine a group of persons sitting in a room. After some conversation they all will agree on a topic, this is their truth now. Then suddenly somebody else comes in, and, being briefed, he answers: "But this is not at all how I see it." And the entire process of dialectic exchange and sharing of opinions will start again.

## 1.8 Words for concepts

LAP contributions aim to make a case for some claim, and the inherent subjectivity creates a serious problem regarding the use of terminology. As the concepts created are placed within a specific "school of thought", readers will need some specific knowledge in order to understand the terms found in a text. Theories are not technical fixations like in a scientific terminological system. N. Pokorn speaks up "In defense of fuzziness" and states in her abstract:

> In Translation Studies the definitions of the concepts *native speaker* and *mother tongue* have been uncritically adopted from linguistics and are regarded as defined and clarified as far as their meaning is concerned, despite the fact that neither linguistics nor translation theory can offer an objective and water-tight definition of the terms. A similar desire for univocal terms can also be detected in the claims for the need of one, universally accepted term for the same phenomenon where various competing terms already exist and are in use. [...] The article questions the desire for the univocal and argues that it is high time we all learn to live with more fuzzy definitions. (Pokorn 2007:327)

The words used in LAP are not created artificially, as in many cases of terminology in the natural sciences where we have a "terminus technicus" with a fixed meaning. This problem is also relevant in the process of specialized translation, particularly in the humanities. M. Thelen asks, ignoring the answer:

> What makes up the distinction between term and word? In the process of specialized translation, terms can in some cases clearly and without any problem be distinguished from words, whereas in others this is not so obvious, especially in cases where terms turn out to behave like words as in such disciplines like psychology, sociology, art & art criticism, leisure & tourism, etc. (Thelen 2005).[25]

The words as signifiers for theoretical concepts in LAP are taken from the general language existing in a community. Their meaning is anchored within a specific school of thought or a cultural background, and relevant knowledge is hermeneutically essential to understand that meaning. At the same time, these given and formally identical words are legitimately being used by other scholars in another context as well, often with a slightly different meaning. This fact accounts for some of the fuzziness of terminology in the humanities. Terms such as *subjectivity, intuition, creativity, experience, decision, responsibility,* etc., which according to many scholars are unclear terms, should not be eliminated from TS but, rather, their effect in the concrete decision-making process of translation should be discussed. Wilss calls for a *caveat* in this respect:

> There is a universal human tendency to give rather uncritical credence to terms we have become attached to, because we hope they can help us to understand better what we do when we translate. Such terms are cognition, complexity, simplicity, intelligence, experience, efficiency, relevance, behavior, and above all, knowledge. (Wilss 1996:39)

However, the fact that there is "a universal human tendency" should have told him that it is not possible to speak of such terms other than giving them "initial credence" (Paepcke 1986:248). These terms designate invisible contents of thought, cognitive representations, and any discussion about such content ever starts by giving credence to those terms in a primary evidence, later on describing them in one's scholarly paper as precisely as possible.

Discourse in LAP is based on the assumption of plausibility regarding the terms that are founded in the general language. The terms and concepts are self-evident in the sense of a collective understanding of their form, but the semantic

---

[25] Marcel Thelen 30 July 2005, m.m.g.j.thelen@hszuyd.nl – see also website www.est-translationstudies.org/research issues, posted 30 July 2005.

content of terms such as "translation", "creativity", "culture", "interpretation", "meaning", "literary effect", "learning", "understanding", and so on, is interpreted slightly differently by every individual researcher. The whole cultural background is there and influences the interpretation of lexis.

Thus, for example, the terms used within a given field of research may easily "wander around", allowing their meaning to develop in various directions. Terms like "cognitive environment", "relevance" (Relevance Theory) or "embodiment" (Cognitive Science), "binding" (Deconstruction), "grounded theory" (Psychology) or "self-reflection" (Expertise Studies) or "loyalty" (Skopos Theory) are explicitly discussed and defined in these fields of scholarly work. However, they are not confined to these domains, and no individual author has a patent over them. We will find them in other fields, too, such as psychology, phenomenology, hermeneutics and creativity theory. They are general language words, in each case with a specific, often even subjective scholarly meaning. Authors presuppose their plausibility for readers in the same language. Readers, on the other hand, may not be absolutely sure and ask themselves critically whether they dispose of the relevant knowledge base or whether some research is still needed. The exactitude of scientific terms is missing.

When someone from a different theoretical field uses terms from an adjacent field, s/he need not refer to their original interpretation as long as one defines the own understanding precisely. Trying to corroborate personal claims exhaustively by references to any other usage or by quotation from other authors would only mean the boring repetition of already known content which in a given case is considered irrelevant.

Content in LAP is not created by inference based on other contributions but, rather, by authorial reasoning. Authors see their texts as a contribution to discussion (and this explains why libraries are so full of books). Readers may themselves find out about interrelationships with other articles. It is especially this interrelationship, established over the bridge of general language, wherein the terms are rooted, what enables new thinking, based on reading. There is much more common ground shared between the various theoretical approaches in TS than their representatives normally would like to see (Chesterman & Arrojo 2000).

In order to overcome the basic problem of understanding, an explicit definition of the concepts used is needed in every single contribution, whilst in ESP given terms are being used as a matter of fact. At the same time, the use of terms with similar signifiers in other disciplines can also not be forbidden.[26] If a referee criticizes the rash "borrowing" of concepts or the "appropriation" of ideas (by using some words), one might even reply that these other fields obviously did not see the potential of their own terminology, because they used it in a rather narrow context. In this way, it is a vain attempt to try to fence in the words used in LAP. Consequently, the discussion process is continuing constantly, and only when the meaning of a term changes too much will a new term be created.

Papers in LAP will put more emphasis on internal argumentation within the scholarly thinking, owing to the lack of self-evident objective facts. They try to convince the reader by themselves, without reference to other studies. Their argumentation would only be hindered by repeated reference to similar studies. Of course, all thinking builds on what one has read beforehand, but creative thinking cannot be exhaustively backed up by reference to other publications, it evolves "by association" (Risku 1998:155). On the other hand, argumentation is an invitation to further debate. Authors expect a holistic response from their audience, which is called upon to think critically themselves. They will not check every statement by looking at the data or the references, but by examining the plausibility of the argumentation itself.

In LAP, even the structure of articles is not strictly regulated. There is a certain freedom regarding reasoning, style and concluding statements. Because intuition is a cognitive factor, many things may remain implicit, unlike as in ESP, where science presents itself as an explicit logical chain. The two approaches to academic writing are complementary to each other. This should be borne in mind in reading the present book which expressly follows the LAP model.

---

[26] There may only arise a translation problem, e.g. with words like *cultural translaton* or *interpretation*. We will discuss this extensively later on.

## 2 The paradigm of translational hermeneutics

### 2.1 Foundations of hermeneutics with Schleiermacher

Centering the translator as a competent person, we situate ourselves within the paradigm of hermeneutics, which reflects on the conditions of comprehension as a human outlook towards the world. Understanding has something to do with one's orientation in the world, and with dominating that world. It becomes a problem when interpretation and experience of that environment tend to fall apart, and this, for instance, is the case in translation, where the tension between the foreign and the familiar is constantly sensible. The Tower of Babel designates the hermeneutical situation of origin, when nobody understands the other, and the experience of Pentecost is the hermeneutical utopia of all people understanding one another.

Hermeneutics is exploring the possibility of understanding otherness. It was only in the 20th century that hermeneutics advanced to the place of the leading paradigm of language philosophy.[27] Philosophical knowledge is always based on earlier insight, even if older opinions gradually might be outdated by new findings. Grondin (1994:XI) terms hermeneutics as the *koiné* of present-day philosophy, and its claim of universality has not been disproved so far.

In recent years, hermeneutics has moved in the English-speaking world from being regarded as a subsidiary aspect of European philosophy to being one of the most widely debated topics in contemporary philosophy. It has to do with "an empathic projection of the interpreter's desire to understand into the activity s/he is attempting to understand" (Robinson 1998:97). Tribute is paid to the founding role played by the German Protestant theologian and philosopher F. D. E. Schleiermacher (1768-1834). He had offered new insight as he reflected on

---

[27] For a good overview of the historical development see Peter J. Brenner (1998): *Das Problem der Interpretation. Eine Einführung in die Grundlagen der Literaturwissenschaft.* Tübingen: Niemeyer. – For an explanation of its relevance in Translation Studies see R. Stolze (2003): *Hermeneutik und Translation.* Tübingen: Gunter Narr Verlag, 41-83.

the understanding of texts, with a view to Bible translation.[28] He argued that neither the logical reasoning, nor the individualistic evidence of Idealism in their absolutism can be a proof for the certainty of truth in talking about language.

Schleiermacher in fact never saw interpretation in empathetic terms, seeing it rather in terms that now sound surprisingly relevant to contemporary philosophical accounts of language and epistemology. In the introduction to his translation, A. Bowie[29] develops about concepts such as *spontaneity* and *receptivity* (p. ix), or *feeling* and *intuition* (p. xi), *dialectic* and *hermeneutics* (p. xix) as were used by Schleiermacher. He sees parallel ideas in modern cognitive thinking to those also central to Schleiermacher's philosophy.

> Modern philosophy sees it, he says, that "in our cognitive relations to the world the deliverances of receptivity already draw on capacities that belong to spontaneity',[30] so that 'We must not suppose that receptivity makes an even notionally separable contribution to its co-operation with spontaneity' (ibid.). Related locutions are common in Schleiermacher: 'the original being posited of reason in human nature [in the sense of that part of nature which is human] is its incorporation into the receptivity of this nature as understanding and into the spontaneity of this nature as will'.[31] 'Spontaneity', the activity of the mind which renders the world intelligible by linking together different phenomena, and 'receptivity', the way the world is given to the subject, therefore cannot be finally separated. In consequence, the link between the subject and the world cannot be conceived of in terms of a dualism which gives rise to all the problems of how the two relate to each other in an intelligible manner (…)" (Bowie 1998:ix).

The modern concept of the role of language is different from the ancient tradition. Originally, the words were seen as an imprint of signs with a direct relationship to the objects covered, and truth could be obtained by an assimilation to the ideas and an analysis of the signs hiding these objects (Stanley 2005). Modern language philosophy, on the contrary, sees language itself as a medium of creating truth. And any interpretation is an achievement by the individual sub-

---

[28] The most important textual basis to understand the hermeneutical theory of translation according to Schleiermacher is his article "On the different methods of translating" (*Über die verschiedenen Methoden des Übersetzens"*, 1813. – English translation 1977).

[29] Andrew Bowie: "Introduction". In: Schleiermacher (1838/1998): *Hermeneutics and Criticism*. 1998, p. vii-xxxi.

[30] John McDowell, *Mind and World*, London 1994, p 41.

[31] F.D.E. Schleiermacher, *Ethik* (1812-13), Hamburg 1990, p. 14.

ject, not a mere imprint of given ideas where a logical reasoning would suffice to convince people. The main objects of hermeneutics are written texts, as their message requires a back transformation into language in order to be intelligible. Comprehension plays a central role.[32] This is relevant for translation.

F. Paepcke, who was strongly influenced by Schleiermacher, then Heidegger and above all by Gadamer, was one of the first scholars to advocate the hermeneutical approach in TS (Paepcke 1986). After his efforts in the 1970s, this approach was further developed by other German speaking scholars (Stolze 1992; 2003; Kupsch-Losereit 2008; Bălăcescu & Stefanink 2006). These scholars attempted for the first time to approach the act of translating systematically from an hermeneutical perspective and to present the results in complex theories (Stolze 2003). Hermeneutics is more than the "art of interpretation" (*Kunst der Auslegung,* Kußmaul 2007:12).

Interpretation of an author's individual language usage can be reached, according to Schleiermacher, in a double perspective: partly by way of a psychological interpretation or divination, and yet it must also be placed on a solid fundament by reference to the general language system in the grammatical interpretation and in the procedure of comparison with other texts of the genre. This combination of two aspects forms a constant controlling instance and a possible corrective element for subjectivity. By this double methodology Schleiermacher prevents arbitrary interpretation, and, at the same time, he foresees the hard-core issue of a necessary permanent linguistic motivation of hermeneutical hypotheses (Cercel 2010) and so also of translation solutions.

## 2.2 Historicity in language

Schleiermacher sees the original text as a subjective expression of its author. Therefore, the task of the understanding reader (and of a translator) is not only

---

[32] This idea, which plays a role in all modern hermeneutical theories of translation, was first formulated clearly by Schleiermacher: "Whoever has mastered this art of understanding through the most diligent cultivation of a language, through precise knowledge of the whole historical life of a nation and through the lively representation of single works and their authors, he and he alone may wish to lay open the same understanding of the masterpieces of art and scholarship to his contemporaries and compatriots" (Schleiermacher 1977:72).

to grasp the meaning of certain text passages, but also to understand the text's genesis, i.e. the intention and motivation of the author within the context of his or her life and epoch.[33] Schleiermacher also draws attention to the existence of an individual moment in all language usage.

> It is a central issue in Schleiermacher's hermeneutics that language utterances should be considered as a complex of both the core meaning to be derived from the general system of language and the creative individuality given into a message by any speaker: "On the one hand every man is in the power of the language he speaks" and "the shape of his concepts, the nature and the limits of the way in which they can be connected, is prescribed for him by the language in which he is born and educated", but on the other hand "it is the living power of the individual which creates new forms by means of the plastic material of language" (Schleiermacher 1977:71). Since authors "constitute a new element in the life of a language itself" (ibid., 71), their texts being expressions of "a peculiar way of thinking and feeling" (ibid., 72), and as the translator should also implement "his powers of observation" (ibid., 80) based on factual knowledge for an adequate comprehension, it is true that he can act himself creatively in the language but his task will "always be of relative and subjective value only" (ibid., 81).

The truth of a text grasped in understanding is historically determined. The language, the individual, and understanding are defined by Schleiermacher as "historical phenomena". The disregard for history, which characterized reflections on translation from the Romans until the nineteenth century, was definitely ended by Schleiermacher. The growing historical awareness, and in particular the historicism of the Romantic movement led to Schleiermacher "historicizing" the objects of understanding: "language is an historical fact" (Schleiermacher 1977:76), a fact constantly changing and evolving by the innovative insertions of its speakers in the course of time. Based on historical awareness, it should be acknowledged that no aprioristic knowledge of things in themselves exists independently from an interpretation by individuals. Individuals (authors, translators, readers of texts) cannot be severed from their historical world; language and in-

---

[33] This is best visible in a famous passage of Schleiermacher's article on translation: "Either the translator leaves the author in peace as much as possible, and moves the reader towards him: or he leaves the reader in peace, as much as possible, and moves the author towards him" (ibid, 74).

dividuals determine each other within their respective historical situation. This is seen anew today by current philosophy (cf. Beiner 2009).[34]

F. Apel developed the poignant idea that translations are determined by time and history, and he even "radicalized" it by discovering an entire pyramid of historicizing levels in literary texts (Apel 1982:26). The original itself is a historical document of its time, any translation represents a different historical reception of the text first given, any analysis of a translation is subject to the historical background of the translation critic, and finally even any translation theory that builds on knowledge from translation practice and translation critique is anchored within the variability of history.

At the same time language has a uniting function for the members of a language community. Wittgenstein in his later work emphasizes the importance of agreement in language.

> *Philosophical Investigations* §242 implies that agreement in judgment is a precondition for language to be a means of communication. In §241 he puts it that agreement in language is agreement in form of life. Both agreement in judgment and agreement in form of life here seem to be presented as being internally related to agreement in language (that is, to what it means to have the same language). (21). In §355 he says that all language is founded on convention. (54) (see Richter 2004:21/54).

But any meaning of words, any culture-specific understanding of an object, any scientific method is never absolute, as it also will change in history.

> The phenomenologist Schütz claims that "every word and every sentence is [...] surrounded by 'fringes' connecting them with past and future elements of the universe of discourse to which they pertain and [...] with a halo of emotional values and irrational implications which themselves remain ineffable" (Schütz 1970:97).

---

[34] In the 20th century translational hermeneutics received a dramatic development by its expansion into three different disciplines. In philosophy, the topics of translation have a special standing in the works of Martin Heidegger, Hans-Georg Gadamer und Paul Ricœur. This is now documented in the growing amount of secondary literature on that subject. The interest for translation stands in close connection with the primary linguistic nature of philosophical debates at the time. With his *Tractatus logico-philosophicus*, Ludwig Wittgenstein initiated a "linguistic turn" in Anglo-Saxon philosophy, and parallel to this the hermeneutical tradition of continental philosophy was strongly influenced by an intensive occupation with the phenomenon of language.

Historicity is decisive, as the language of a people is evolving constantly, persons are no static objects, but they change permanently in their living together within their culture. The objects of research in humanities are objects having developed in time (Beiner 2009:31). Paul Ricœur's observation of a permanent "translation" within a language community – in the form of commentaries in other words to previous discourse – refers for him to the work of the language "on itself". (It's the people who are working it.) An "identical sense" cannot be found, simply because of the fact that one may express the same message with different words just as well, an idea that you can also find in Eco (2006). Any speech fixes only a moment, and at other times it will/may have a different form.

There is no quasi objective, ever unchanged truth in society. In our quest for the "truth of a text" we will therefore have to seek dialogue with others as a critical reference. Truth is only found dialectically, in a discussion process within a group, and in one historical period of time. Any understanding experienced as a learning process even influences and enriches the reader's mind, what then will open new horizons for further understanding.

## 2.3 Oral and written communication

The hermeneutical issue concerns processes of understanding, both written and oral. But the question should be raised whether there isn't a difference in the ways of dealing with the texts. This question is important, as there is actually a significant difference between interpreting as an oral reproduction of speech heard, and translating as a reproduction of written texts in intercultural communication. In speech acts, with a shared presence of speaker and audience, speakers may well negotiate their comprehension of texts with others.

According to Sperber and Wilson's (1986) Relevance Theory, communication depends on the "principle of relevance", in that hearers adapt their interpretation of an utterance through an optimization of means and resources. Speakers are supposed to say adequately what they mean (Grice 1975:42). Relevance theory applies to "ostensive-inferential communication making manifest to an audience one's informative intention" (Sperber & Wilson 1986:54). The underlying cognitive strategy of all humans is to select the most plausible assumption from the momentary cognitive environment.

It is based on the general principle of spending as little cognitive processing effort as possible on supplying contextual information. The crucial mental faculty which enables humans to communicate with one another is the ability do draw inferences from people's *behaviour*. Gaining new information requires "that the outcome of an act of communication has to modify some previously held assumptions in order to be found rewarding". (Gutt 2000:28)

This functions only in direct oral communication, when the speaker and the audience are both present and share the same context of the utterance. Temporary misunderstandings are gradually eliminated within the prevailing situation or by debate.

A written text, on the contrary, is a means of communication carrying a message fixed in a language to other times, places and cultures and to unknown readers. Written texts are severed from their original situation, and there is no overt behavior given as a context. Non-professional readers and translators run the risk of inferring inappropriate text meanings, because there is no "cognitive environment that is *mutually shared* between communicator and audience" (Gutt 2000:27) apt to invoke the principle of relevance.[35] We may cite Gadamer who writes:

> Thus, precisely because it entirely detaches the sense of what is said from the person saying it, the written word makes the understanding reader the arbiter of its claim to truth. The reader experiences what is addressed to him and what he understands in all its validity. What he understands is always more than an unfamiliar opinion: it is always possible truth. This is what emerges from detaching what is spoken from the speaker and from the permanence that writing bestows. (Gadamer 1990:394)

Hence, the understanding of written texts requires a mental reconstruction of the situation of origin. Even if texts materially do "transfer" information from an author to a reader, this information is only "revived" in the relationship between the translator as a reader and the text, as it induces a cognitive representation. Texts allow us to look beyond the text structures and to view a distant, external world. This occurs when the textual input creates a cognitive scene in the reader's mind (Fillmore 1976:63). The identification of a specific topic in a visual scene is one of the most important comprehension tasks at written texts. Those

---

[35] This, for instance, is the case in the lay translation of a text for specific purposes. Practitioners know all too well that this case is not so rare.

texts have lost the direct stimulus character of utterances; they are now open to various interpretations.

While oral interpreting actually is bound to a momentary linear sequence of textual input, the written text and translation remains present for a while, and is ready for repeated rereading. This enables a more global approach for the translator, as he or she might even comprehend the beginning of a text only in the light of its end, an effect that in the interpreting situation is not possible.

There is rarely an author to be contacted personally for a written text, so his intention can only be derived from understanding his text in a more or less adequate manner. (Of course it is helpful to contact an author and ask him questions about his text, but sometimes authors don't remember what they have written some time ago.) There is no partner to negotiate the sense, no matter how available the text remains for repeated reading. Translations are no "interactions" between author and readers. Readers, and in particular responsible translators, therefore, have to reflect on their textual understanding, as comprehension can never be taken for granted. Many tend to exclude subjectivity, but this is a vain effort. Initial inference of supposedly relevant "objective" information may later prove inadequate and thus be transformed during the whole reading process.

## 2.4 The medial act of reading

How can we and what do we understand? In the 20th century, it was Martin Heidegger who gave new impetus to an ontological and existentialist conception of hermeneutics. Heidegger raised the question about the "significance of existence", and he presented understanding as the proper of human existence. It becomes *Auslegung* (*SuZ*, 161, "interpretive understanding") – not so much of the object to be understood – than of the understanding subject itself, who always raises the question about the "sense of being as such" (*Sein des Seienden, SuZ*, 37)[36]. The "dasein" of mankind has its existential foundation in language, as

---

[36] For reasons of space we use the abbreviation "SuZ" for *Sein und Zeit*, and "BaT" for the English Translation *Being and Time* of 1962.

language is "the house of being".[37] The world appears to the subject as a "totality of meaningfulness", and understanding, then, is an act of "making sense out of it": Meaning is not a quality of an object to be discovered by analysis, meaning is what is articulated by interpretive understanding of the world, and this happens in language: The sense of human existence is expressed and understood through language.[38] In the hermeneutical view, the subject/object dichotomy and the focus on things are faded. Understanding is not a process based on any scientific meta-concept.

The event of interpretive understanding underscores the location of the subject who wants to understand. This seems important for our purpose here, since translators are carrying out their job in various times and situations. We may cite Gadamer[39]:

> Thus written texts present the real hermeneutical task. Writing is self-alienation. Overcoming it, reading the text, is thus the highest task of understanding. Even the pure signs of an inscription can be seen properly and articulated correctly only if the text can be transformed back into language. As we have said, however, this transformation always establishes a relationship to what is meant, to the subject matter being discussed (*TaM*, 390f).

That idea of Gadamer's hermeneutics has been exemplified by P. Eberhard (2004) with the "middle voice" (as derived from Greek grammar). Eberhard makes explicit the mediality of the event of understanding in reading which is implicitly evoked in the many middle-voiced expressions that punctuate Gada-

---

[37] I.e. "Haus des Seins" see Heidegger in his letter on humanism, *Wegmarken*, GA vol. 9, 1976, p. 313; later, in *Unterwegs zur Sprache*, Pfullingen: Neski, 1959, p. 90, he sees this in a self-critical way.

[38] A characteristic feature of the philosophical dealing with the problem of translation is that, here, translation is primarily understood in an ontological sense and that the concrete work of translating is considered derivatively, as secondary to this primary concept. In particular Martin Heidegger does not so much envisage concrete communication or the work of translating. Rather, he sees language and translation as belonging to the existential structure of humankind: the world wherein we are living is constituted by language and is being "translated" by language. One interprets this world by speaking about it. The interlingual process of translation, in philosophical hermeneutics, represents a more secondary form of the ontological translation as a transfer of thought into words.

[39] Hans-Georg Gadamer: *Truth and Method.* Second revised edition. Translated by W. Glen-Doepel and revised by J. Weinsheimer and D. G. Marshall. New York: Crossroad, 1990, 256f. – In our quotations we will use the abbreviations "WuM" for *Wahrheit und Methode,* and "TaM" for *Truth and Method.*

mer's texts.[40] And Gadamer himself calls the structure *"sich lassen* + infinitive" medial: understanding a text is a medial event. There are also expressions in Gadamer like "history does not so much belong to us as we belong to it", "in conversation we are more led than leading", or "language speaks us rather than we speak it", "we belong to tradition and it belongs to us."[41] All these examples have, according to Eberhard, a middle-voiced ring: they all situate the subject within the event that befalls that subject, without though subjugating him or her.

The central claim of Gadamer is his famous phrase *"Sein, das verstanden werden kann, ist Sprache (WuM,* 450) [Being that can be understood is language, *TaM,* 474]. The quote taken from Schleiermacher reads: *"Alles Vorauszusetzende in der Hermeneutik ist Sprache" (WuM,* 387). Now Eberhard (2004:96) points out to the medial aspect therein: "Language is no object. It is an event-like medium that encompasses the speaker".

> Gadamer uses the example of the "dialogue", he mentions the *Vollzugsform des Gesprächs* (*WuM,* 392). In the revised English translation of "Truth and Method" a periphrastic expression is necessary to render this one word *Vollzug*: "what takes place in" (*TaM,* 388). In fact, *Vollzug* seems particularly difficult to translate. To give only a few examples: in the same revised translation "Vollzug" is also translated with "act" [ix], "occurrence" [103] "process" [307] and "to be practiced" [473]. Interestingly, the meanings of "event" and "performance" are equally present. "This one word means happening and doing at once. It is middle-voiced" (Eberhard 2004:64).

Reading texts reveals the practice of hermeneutics in its full mediality, as it applies to everything we understand. And Gadamer also explains this medial character of being influenced and simultaneously being active in reading, with the example of the game: it is presented in front of us, and we are torn into its activity, more and more taking part ourselves. Gadamer's notion of game helps bringing to the fore the inadequacy of the dichotomy between subject and object.

The necessary basis for this to happen is "openness" or receptivity (Schleiermacher), not blocking ourselves against the input of the new experience. Then

---

[40] Eberhard states: "As it is the case with the middle voice, these expressions often go unnoticed. By far the most frequent expression suggesting the middle voice is the refrain like *sich etwas sagen lassen* or *sich etwas gesagt sein lassen* (to let something be told to oneself)" (2004:62).

[41] For references see Eberhard, op.cit. 63.

the author I am reading will "tell me something". The examples stress the event-like character of understanding, its happening, its *Vollzug*, its *Ereignis* and the subject's location within it. Gadamer intends to describe the hermeneutical act like a game "as it happens to the subject", rather than to set up guidelines for a subject in charge of his or her action. In understanding, truth reveals itself to the subject, it is not detected through analysis by the latter. The question is: what happens to us when we understand, and this is also relevant for translators.

Paul Ricœur, in the hermeneutical tradition, sees an œuvre, a text as a unity of sense detached from its original conditions, able to challenge the the recipient's world view, even capable to modify it. What we have understood is addressing us, it enlarges our horizon. Ricœur localizes the aesthetic effect of a text also in view of the concrete linguistic structure and its explanation during reception. Thus he has demystified Gadamer's approach and strengthened Schleiermacher's ideas (Jeanrond 2009:92).

We might state for the translator that openness is required, and it also needs some time. Who wants to understand has to look behind the words at the intentions and messages of authors. Then understanding will happen and arouse affirmative reaction in the reader. This idea is supported by cognitive research:

> Understanding does not consist merely of after-the-fact reflections on prior experiences, it is, more fundamentally, the way (or means by which) we have those experiences in the first place. It is the way our world presents itself to us. And this is a result of the massive complex of our culture, language, history and bodily mechanism that blend to make our world what it is. *Image schemata and their metaphorical projections are primarily patterns of this 'blending'*. Our subsequent prepositional reflections on our experience are made possible by this more basic mode of understanding. (Johnson 1987:104)

Understanding implies being receptive and active at the same time. We might even mention the term of „Achtsamkeit" (*attentiveness*) underlined by Heidegger, which includes a far-reaching attention to the environment, in the sense of receptivity. And precisely this has been found to be an important basis for creative action in contemporary creativity research (Brodbeck 1995): We open ourselves for new content, and at the same time our interest is critically focused on the concrete details of the input creating that interest.

The example of the game gives evidence of the fact that the experience of art is no subjective and instant impression only, that would lack any cognitive significance. In viewing a picture, for instance, there is the interplay between being emotionally impressed, and trying to analyze the specific techniques used to provoke that impression. Though not conversational in the same way as a dialogue, the experience of art nevertheless takes time; it is not a matter of immediate insight, but it plays itself out between the onlooker and his or her world (Dostal 1994, n.32). The double effect of impression and scrutiny is decisive. This attempt of explaining the critical reading by a translator goes one step further than Gadamer, who just underlines the being drawn into a game.

## 2.5 Game playing and habitus

Hermeneutics is always interested in social and ethical relationship. The motivation of our action and the understanding of others, and what they want to tell us, is important, not the analysis of given objects. There is the "consciousness of being affected by history" (Gadamer, *TaM*, 301 – *historisches Bewusstsein*). The experience of history as a critical appropriation of a nation's tradition is also the basis of cultural identity. There is no free autonomous existence, we all live in traditions that are present and handed down in our language, and in our minds they will determine our understanding of everything. "These all are modes of experience in which a truth is communicated that cannot be verified by the methodological means proper to science" (Gadamer, *TaM*, xxii).

Comprehension is not impossible, as language is a medium of communication, but any encounter with alterity is also subject to a limited personal pre-knowledge. Gadamer's (1990:490) concept of "games" as the infrastructure to his hermeneutics links the referential totality of any individual to the larger culturally and historically determined "lived world" as shared by speakers in a language community. Thus, even though translational hermeneutics takes as its point of departure any given individual translator's perspective and endeavors to take his or her subjectivity into account, the notion of game playing offers a conceptual tool that helps move research beyond the merely subjective to include historical, cultural and pragmatic elements within the structure of human understanding.

This conceptual tool provides us with an excellent model to understand human behavior, in as much as its dynamic structure arises through and, yet, simultaneously governs (human) interaction. All games rest upon rule-like structures, but these structures are modified constantly due to interactions with "reality", with other games and players: the similarities to the role played by cultures in societies are apparent. The dynamic structures of games allow us to link purposeful action (pragmatics) directly to speaking about those actions; likewise, the actions can serve as a frame of reference when moving beyond the limits imposed by a specific language. When there is not much in common in the actions – the game playing –, the malleability of the rules governing the language games is similar to the permeable structures and value systems inherent in culture, and here we find a model that helps explicate the interaction between cultures.

The basis for this to get a chance is seen in an education handing down the common sense of a culture (*Bildung*). What we can recognize is something we have in common with others, and it is changing in the course of history. Consequently, it is true that no exact description of rules will lead with a compelling logic to a singular expression of human behavior. Different convictions and deviating actions are always possible (even if not desired in the game).

Translation as an activity is socially embedded and, here, some "power relationships" are at work. There are "power-driven processes of the representation and production of knowledge, and the construction of identities and cultures" (Prunč 2007:309) (*my translation*). For modeling the effective cultural conventions governing social activity, such as translating a. o., one might refer to the French sociologist Pierre Bourdieu (1984).

Starting from the role of economic capital for social positioning, Bourdieu pioneered investigative frameworks and terminologies such as cultural, social, and symbolic capital, and the concepts of habitus, field or location, as well as symbolic violence, to reveal the dynamics of power relations in social life. His work emphasized the role of practice and embodiment or forms in social dynamics and worldview construction, often in dialogue and opposition to universalized Western philosophical traditions. The actors in a social field do follow preferences acquired by learning and socialization, and this inner tradition shows in their "habitus" and is prolonged by it. So the habitus determines the behavior of individuals and social groups who have internalized the rules of the game.

Regarding translators, one may interpret their habitus in a way that they simply have adopted the dominant norms, e.g. of faithful translation. But there are also examples of how certain translating personalities have themselves contributed to forming translational norms and created a relatively autonomous field of literary communication by translating (Gouanvic 2002). By their translations they had accumulated sufficient symbolic capital to be brought into the discourse (Gouanvic 2005).

However, the translators' habitus is not only dependent on their individual socialization, but also on the status given in a culture to cultural contacts and to the importation of foreign cultural goods. The higher this status, the more symbolical capital can be drawn from it for translators and gives them more freedom. This has consequences for their work in the modern, global market for literature. In a marginalized position, translators really are subject to power relationships between politics, editors and the image of languages. The translator will have to reflect on this fact critically at any single assignment, because this touches his or her responsibility.

## 2.6 The phenomenological problem

We are convinced that a translator can only translate what and how he or she has understood. However, the surface appearance of objects, e.g. a text, is not the ontological reality of the object itself, a text may be misunderstood. Rather that reality has to be construed cognitively by a human being, in transcending one's own world view (Husserl 1950:282). The strange reality is always seen from a specific individual perspective, a "seeing-as" (Stanley 2005:357). And, of course, all individual perspectives are different and some are inadequate to the foreign culture. Truth is never found "as such", neither objectively by methodology and logical reasoning, nor subjectively by evidence and conviction, but only dialectically in a relation to history, in sharing with others by learning, and in reflecting on one's habitus. Phenomenology states that an individual vision of things cannot reach objectivity, because it is bound to the personal world view.

The phenomenologist E. Husserl (1950:254) extensively discusses that problem as neglected in the scientific world view (ibid. 229) and calls for an "intentional conscience" (ibid. 206) to be activated, in order to constantly try to transcend superficial/subjective/provisional understandings, and to critically reflect on one's own understanding, until an integrated cognitive representation will be created in the reader's (translator's) mind. There is ever an "intentionality" of our conscience tending to transcend mere phenomenological evidence, by creating "real objects" in the mind, within our living situation. Cognitive research confirms this idea: "Every time we see something as a *kind* of thing, for example a tree, we are categorizing" (Lakoff 1987:5). (Meanwhile, neuro-physiological studies have defined engrams in the brain as structures that transport repetitive and similar information. Frequency of input strengthens their function.)

Of course, ontologically, the things have a quasi objective identity on a higher level, but this is not experienced directly – that would be a naïve subjectivity – but only by an intentional work of transcendence, going from the single to the general. The structures of perception are the same in all people (like the rules of a game), but their perspectives are different. Things appear to us in an individual appearance, everyone sees something different in the "same thing". And every time when we change our perspective, we also are able to detect some new visions of the thing. It is important to be aware of the fact that things (ideas and objects) are not "as they appear to us", as we can see them. But occasional evidences as phenomena in a familiar world may motivate the conscience to transcend them and to constitute ontological identities. And this happens in reflection. The translator's conscience is able to transcend the primary impression towards a more comprehensive and more scholarly understanding of texts. It only needs the disposition and goodwill for it.

We need to cognitively transcend our own worldview, be open for other visions. For the purpose of translation, this means that a self-critical attitude of the translator has to be exercised, by changing one's perspective and repeatedly trying to understand better. Understanding should never be taken for granted, said Schleiermacher. Often we read statements like the following: "A translator as a reader of the source text is socially and historically positioned, and how he or she translates the source text will be deeply shaped by this fact" (Sunil Sawant).[42] This is tue and not true at the same time. We will have to reflect on our own position and not let us be induced into subconscious cultural adaptation. On the other hand, when analyzing old translations from colonial times, one might come to that conclusion (because the translators did not critically question their work).

Gadamer underlined that we inevitably stand within a tradition dominating us. He called this "the verbal constitution of the world" (1990:444). Language is being inherited. Jacques Derrida similarly once said:

> « Je me sens héritier, le dépositaire d'un secret très grave auquel je n'ai pas moi-même accès. La parole ou l'écriture que je promène dans le monde transporte un secret qui me reste inaccessible mais laisse voir ses traces dans tous mes textes, dans ce que je fais et je vis. » (*Magazine Littéraire*, avril 2004: 29).[43]

The subjectivity of personal translation strategies is not an individualistic power position (Steiner 1975:298), but rather a cultural imprint that we cannot put away. We rather have to critically reflect on it. Hence, the cultural position and habitus of a translator and his strategies based on experience have to be integrated into empirical research (Inghilleri 2003). G. Hansen calls this the "translators' profiles" and defines it as the "individual preconditions, experiences, feelings, qualities, attitudes, behavior and abilities which are having an influence on the activity during the translation process and so also on the product" (Hansen 2006:23) (*my translation*). By her empirical analysis, she tries to raise awareness of these facts.

## 2.7 The hermeneutical circle and our memory

Interpretive understanding (*Auslegung*) does not work phenomenologically cleared of any pre-judgment, because human existence in its perception of the world is ever bound in itself.

---

[42] Sunil Sawant (India) in his paper proposal on the study of the "interface between parallel literary polysystems" for the Conference on *Research Models in Translation Studies II*, Manchester, 1 May 2011.

[43] Read: "I feel myself an heir, a depository of a serious secret to which I have no access. The word or writing that I carry through the world transports a secret inaccessible for me, but it leaves its traces in all my texts, in my deeds and my life" (*my translation*).

> When something is understood but is still veiled, it becomes unveiled by an act of appropriation and this is always done under the guidance of a *point of view*, which fixes that with regard to which what is understood is to be interpreted. In every case, interpretation is grounded in *something we see in advance* – in a *fore-sight*. This fore-sight 'takes the first cut' out of what has been taken into our fore-having, and it does so with a view to a definite way in which this can be interpreted. (Heidegger, *BaT*, 191)

In understanding something, one starts from one's own familiar world knowledge, and any phenomenon appears subjectively against the backdrop of this given individual fore-knowledge, as explained. This is the so-called "hermeneutical circle" saying that, for to understand, I already need to dispose of some related pre-understanding. Outside that circle of knowledge there is no understanding, but this circle does not fence us in. The core problem is, rather than escaping from it, how to get into that circle by learning processes.

> Heidegger writes: "It [the hermeneutical circle] is not to be reduced to the level of a vicious circle, or even of a circle which is merely tolerated. In the circle is hidden a positive possibility of the most primordial kind of knowing. To be sure, we genuinely take hold of this possibility only when, in our interpretation, we have understood that our first, last, and constant task is never to allow our fore-having, fore-sight, and fore-conception to be presented to us by fancies and popular conceptions, but rather to make the scientific theme secure by working out these fore-structures in terms of the things themselves" (*BaT*, 195).

> Gadamer explains it more clearly: "What Heidegger is working out here is not primarily a prescription for the practice of understanding, but a description of the way interpretive understanding is achieved. The point of Heidegger's hermeneutical reflection is not so much to prove that there is a circle as to show that this circle possesses an ontologically positive significance. The description as such will be obvious to every interpreter who knows what he is about. All correct interpretation must be on guard against arbitrary fancies and the limitations imposed by imperceptible habits of thought, and it must direct its gaze 'on the things themselves' (which, in the case of the literary critic, are meaningful texts, which themselves are again concerned with objects)." (*TaM*, 266)

Language determines the possibility of understanding one's existence. Language signs refer beyond themselves, the sense is never totally enclosed in them and in their syntactics. Therefore, linguistic analysis will not render the truth of a text. Ricœur focuses on overcoming the naïve misinterpretation (1969:22) and the search for a "hidden sense behind the obvious sense":

> J'appelle ici herméneutique toute discipline qui procède par interprétation, et je donne au mot interprétation son sens fort: le discernement d'un sens caché dans un sens apparent. (Ricœur 1969: 260)

Interpretation as searching for the sense will then allow to find a potential plurality of senses in time. We will depart from the text in its entirety and then "construct one or several senses in reading, coming from the formal elements" (Wilhelm 2009:93f) (*my translation*). Ricœur now pleads for a phenomenological attitude, different from the objectivicizing attitude of linguistics as a semiotic science viewing a closed system of signs to be analyzed, and he sees language as a "milieu" in which and by which a person is presenting herself in and to the world. Ricœur notes that a system of signs as an autonomous entity of internal dependencies does not know either a subject nor an outside (*ni sujet ni dehors*) (1969:85 and 246-250) and, hence, is only one half of the whole thing. For the author, who wants to say something, language is not only a means but also a medium.

In reading a text, a learning process will take place – starting at what is already familiar to us and then integrating the new –, and finally this should lead to the famous "fusion of horizons" (See: *TaM*, 306 – *Horizontverschmelzung, WuM*, 289) between the understanding individual within his/her horizon, and the text mirroring the foreign author's voice. Author and reader are held together, according to Gadamer, in the "common sense" given by tradition, i.e. the cultural identity of a group, a nation or the whole humanity (Gadamer, *WuM*, 26). The cultural common sense is a source of truth, since it constitutes the general characteristic within a certain group of speakers. Truth always claims general validity, and this happens in a culture (and only there).

It stands to reason that knowledge is connected to our memory, as we are historical persons. So it is broadly accepted that "translation involves memory", this being even an "integral part of the very concept of translation" (Toury 2004:19), and the predicate represents a cognitive variable. Now Kintsch (1998:18) states: "Knowledge is primarily stored in the world, not in the individual brain." This is true if we look at objects as the result of human activity, and at texts as carriers of relevant information. However, when the memory of the human brain does not contain any element of encyclopedic knowledge to be linked with new input, there will be no fruitful understanding, neither of texts, nor of any foreign objects. Knowledge, therefore, is also stored in memory, combined with the talent for constant extension by learning.

Our memory is the container of linguistic and world knowledge. A holistic representation of the world in memory, that results from the individuals' metalinguistic ability to interact with their environment (Piaget 1947), finds its metaphorical comparison in the virtual model of a connectionist memory network like the Internet (Hintzman 1986). Cognitive research has shown that any contextualization by the individual is closely linked to personal life experiences which are gathered in one's memory (Lakoff 1987:312f).

Language serves as a basis of understanding among people, if we accept that cognitive concepts are prototypical entities with flexible borders, rather than clear-cut categories. Persons have, for instance, made the experience that the meaning of words, though used in a variety of situations, is always more or less the same. Understanding, then, is a process of inference, initiated by the visual input of written texts, that interacts with given relevant knowledge. Where there is no experience-based conceptual level, it will be created in analogous projection by the "metaphorically (idealized) cognitive model" (Lakoff 1987:303). Understanding implies intuition: „Verstehen ist die allmähliche Hinordnung des Bewusstseins auf einen Sachverhalt und zugleich die intuitive Erfassung seiner Eigentümlichkeiten" (Paepcke 1986:160).[44]

We might also question the so-called "difficulty of texts". R. Barthes (1970:10) has defined an "hermeneutical code" amongst five "semic codes" to be used as analytical tools for reading the "open text". Barthes treats the text as an object, and the "hermeneutical code" is defined by him as anything "unconventional in a text, whether in its texture, denotative image, or connotative sense". However, the problem with that definition is obvious: what appears to be "unconventional" or hard to understand depends on the reader's competence, and is not an objective text characteristic.[45] The difficulty of a text is not a feature of it. What I un-

---

[44] Read: Understanding means the gradual adjustment of awareness towards a statement of facts, and at the same time an intuitive grasping of its peculiarities. (*My translation*).

[45] What perhaps is difficult for me to understand might be totally clear for another reader who had already travelled the country and seen certain things, or who knows the author, or, being a scientist, has access to the relevant domain of science.

derstand depends from what I know already;[46] reading will never leave the hermeneutical circle.

## 2.8 Complementary research interest in Cognitive Science

Cognitive science has produced much insight that can be taken as a proof for the traditional assumptions in the hermeneutical language philosophy. Cognitive linguistics is based on the assumption that meaning is embodied and it attempts to explain language in terms of properties of the human mind and body.

> A cognitive language approach to language is in line with modern strands of education-oriented applied linguistics and useful to second language pedagogy, especially because of its focus on the motivated, meaningful connections between forms that are often ignored by other theories of language" (Verspoor et al. 2008:21).

However, its research interest is different. Whereas hermeneutics reflects philosophically on the medial event of understanding and its conditions, when truth is felt revealing itself in reading, cognitive science does research into analyzing just this cognitive process of thinking, of intellectual reasoning, seen as an active comprehending strategy while reading.

Hermeneutics implies a receptive attitude of openness so that truth may show itself intuitively. By contrast, cognitive science analyses the activity of the brain trying actively to grasp information needed for a special purpose. As information retrieval, this is a selection process, different from the holistic approach of comprehension in hermeneutics. The relationship between intellectual situations, information processing, mental processes, and conscience is the object of research here. This external perspective is different from the internal hermeneutical perspective, which is more interested in the content of thought than in its processing lines.

In an interdisciplinary view, cognitive science integrates results and methods from various disciplines, like psychology, neuroscience, computer science, artificial intelligence, linguistics and psycholinguistics. The analysis of cognitive

---

[46] Heidegger says: "(Die Auslegung) bewegt sich als Verständniszueignung im verstehenden Sein zu einer schon verstandenen Bewandtnisganzheit" (*SuZ*, 159) – The appropriation of understanding, the interpretation operates in Being towards a totality of involvments which is already understood - a Being which understands (*BaT*, 191).

processes appears primarily of interest for questions of didactics, where it is important to teach fast reading for the purpose of an extraction of meaning from texts.

Methods of "text processing", strategies of understanding and intellectual processes stand in the focus (Grzesik 1990). This implies an active behavior in the reader: cognitive text processing is conceived of as a strategy directed towards creating mental representations by adapting information input (Rickheit 1995:15). The concept of the term "understanding" is different in cognitivism and in hermeneutics. The human brain is compared with a computer and called an "information processing system" (Rickheit & Strohner 1993:84). Understanding, then, is the search for the acquisition of knowledge via relevant information, and this of course excludes intuition. Hermeneutics, on the contrary, focuses on the whole of a message from another person addressing the receptive reader who experiences this address and may be influenced by it.

And there is another difference: while information retrieval is geared towards single units of valid information, hermeneutical receptivity is open for a whole message, be it useful or not. In the learning environment one may rightly state: "Reading is a much more self-directed activity than hearing" (Rickheit (1995:17). Text processing for information retrieval is a selective "construction of sense" in a determined learning situation, while hermeneutical understanding is, rather, an "experience of sense" in a medial act. The interest is to grasp the "whole of a text" and its entire message, and not only to extract selected information that will be relevant for a certain purpose. And this hermeneutical approach seems particularly adequate for translation conceived of as a faithhul rendering of a source text (to be processed later by the recipients).

In the constructivist region of cognitive science, the structuring of knowledge as stored in memory is the object of research. The research is done by means of tests and questionnaires with the aim of simulating processes in systems of knowledge management, e. g. over key words, and knowledge representation is the input for the mind (or machine) as an information processing system.

It has been proved that knowledge and personal experience are stored in our long-term memory in a certain order, neither in an incoherent list nor simply en bloc. There are Thematic Organization Points (TOPs) (Schank 1982), associatively related among each other. This experience may even be verified by introspection (Hansen 2002:9). Memory as the means of a critical adaptation of tradition is all but a mere assimilation of available pieces of information appearing to us, it structures them flexibly. Cognitive science is interested in that structure of conceptual meaning, and *language* is used "as a window to the mind" (Baldauf 2003:48), whereas hermeneutics sees *texts* as a "window to the world", through which we receive messages.

A central idea in cognitive research is the "concept" as an image schema, and studies led to "the granularity of conceptual knowledge and its categorization influence" (Lewandowska-Tomaszczyk 2004:135). Concepts are the units of thinking, a kind of "mini theory", that structure and constitute knowledge.

> Concepts are cognitive structures, independent from actual acts and perception (Deppert 2001:25). Understanding, here, is seen as a closed circle of interdependent processes of "assimilation" and "accommodation": *Assimilation* is the application of a given structure onto one's experience, whereas in the second process of *accommodation* the concepts may even be modified themselves." (Deppert 2001:28). "Understanding remains (...) a dynamic process in which the content to be understood shall build upon that which is already given, but where it also goes beyond it" (ibid. 31). [*My translation*]

"Understanding as a dynamic process" (Deppert) describes just what hermeneutics has always been saying: The "hermeneutical circle" is an open helical process of an ever growing horizon of knowledge, but we cannot get out of it in the sense of an access to "objective" knowledge. It may be stated: "Cognitive semantics considers image schemata as universal *dispositions*" (Zelinsky-Wibbelt 2003:4), quite in the sense of the hermeneutical *receptivity*. Hermeneutics is not interested in the kind of structuring that knowledge, but only in the fact that it is given or not.

Various results of research tend to give evidence of older hermeneutical assumptions. The difference is in the depth of analysis. While cognitive research focuses on the description of individual aspects, for example words, hermeneutics is interested in the human understanding of his/her environment as a whole, in order to motivate social activity. The exact form of knowledge storage is not of interest in hermeneutics, where it is only stated that some encyclopedical knowledge should be given and be critically reflected.

Recently a new area of interest came up within the framework of "situated cognition" (Clark 1997). The brain is now studied as a system with a capacity to interact with environment, artefacts and fellows. This corresponds more to the hermeneutical vision, than a brain as a simple storage place for knowledge. Just as hermeneutics stressed the importance of the "historical consciousness", cognitive science now acknowledges that the momentary situation of a person, together with the individual history of cultural development, is an integral part of the processes of thinking and behavior. We see: both approaches complement each other.

Culture is handed down by tradition and education and is thus a common background for understanding, a source of common perspectives, as the effect of history filters out the particular determinations and leaves only the general ones. This includes a receptivity in embodiment applying personal experience for categorizing phenomena. In understanding a text with its message, I will not understand the individual (silent) reasoning by an author, but I will gain an insight into his or her cultural background and get in touch with the questions dealt with by the text.

Recent experimental research on translation processes focuses on the cognitive activity by analyzing its results (Göpferich et al. 2009). A combination of retrospective interviews, key-logging records and eye-tracking will lead to a description of the translating work as a physical process, as it is visible from the outside. It will say nothing about the inner motivation of translational strategies.

# 3 A translator's relationship to texts

## 3.1 Grounded understanding of content

We say that a translator needs to understand his/her text well. But the difference of concepts is important. *Auslegung* (interpretive understanding) is what the translator first will do intuitively just as everybody and develop a subjective understanding of the text, based hermeneutically on his or her given pre-knowledge in the hermeneutical circle. But then one should become aware of one's own historical background, in situated cognition, as the medial act of understanding always includes the question "Where am I?" Only with this self-reflection will it be possible to eventually see the limits of one's perception too – in the sense of unquestioned interpretation – and become aware of the necessity for relevant further research, to go beyond idiosyncrasy, when a text "does not make sense" or could appear too biased, when we are honest.

As long as there are still lacunae of understanding in a text as a whole, there is the requirement for further research so that truth can reveal itself. Bălăcescu and Stefanink (2006:63) mention the reader's "dissatisfaction" (*Unzufriedenheit*) as a sign of problem awareness in the translator. We have to enter the necessary hermeneutical circle of the cognitive environment. The objects' evidence has a "subject-relevant being" in their occasional appearance as a phenomenon, but this is to be transcended towards their "ontological being" (Husserl 1950:282). Husserl rightly criticized the fact that we are often taking the subjective seeing-as for the objective being of things. Eventually, when I have learnt something, the object will have gained a new subject-relevant being for me on another level: it is better understood now.

This touches the central issue of translation work in practice. Quite often, authors and target readers are members of the same group of communication, only the translator is not, he or she is an outsider. The question, now, is whether I responsibly understand what the other person is telling (in the written text), or whether I (want to) understand only what is of interest for myself. The attitude of receptivity as an outlook is basically the same for both the literary and the technical translator, as both worlds are alien to him or her. The expert translator in every field of communication has to reflect on the own knowledge, perspective and depth of understanding.

Responsible translation implies the transition from a subjective interpretive understanding (*Auslegung*) to an – as we will call it – "grounded understanding" (*informierte Auslegung*) of the text. The translator will consciously have to place him or herself within the relevant cognitive environment of knowledge. This relevant world knowledge, be it in a scientific domain or within an unfamiliar foreign culture, must be acquired beforehand. The hermeneutical circle should be widened. That problem is also explained by Gutt, out of a cognitive approach:

> Thus, very often the translator cannot simply use his own cognitive environment when trying to understand the original; rather he has to metarepresent to himself the mutual cognitive environment shared between the original communicator and original audience. Otherwise, a secondary communication situation will result, prone to lead to misinterpretation. [...] If the translator's efforts are to succeed, he needs to be aware of their [sc. the receptors'] cognitive environment, too, that is, he needs to metarepresent it. (Gutt 2004:81)

"Metarepresentation" of a foreign cognitive environment means to approach an object, e.g. a text, right from the beginning as being embedded in that foreign context. A specialist text shall not be tackled with from a layman's opinion, and a foreign culture in a literary text has to be accepted as different from the own familiar one. Such "grounded understanding" as the basis for an adequate translation will lead to a correct positioning of the source text within its relevant background and enable adequate comprehension and later on responsible translation. That background normally is given in the source of the text.

In a knowledge-based approach, technical texts will then be situated by the translator within their professional domains, and literary texts are conceived of as an aesthetic life description against the backdrop of a specific cultural world. Already Schleiermacher (1838/1998:203) had called for a systematic analysis of the context in which an original text had been written.[47] This of course has decisive implications for the adequate disambiguation of cultural key words or of specialist terms found in those texts.

---

[47] Schleiermacher's initiation gave rise to the so-called historical-critical research for Bible studies.

According to hermeneutics, real understanding is always possible, manipulations are not a rule. Gadamer (*TaM*, 394) mentions "possible truth" as emerging from texts. It is possible, but it requires the reader's good will (Gadamer 1984:59).[48] The textual truth will disclose itself to receptive readers prepared for a grounded understanding. Gadamer "says that to understand is always to reach an understanding with each other about a *Sache*. Understanding is underway no matter what" (Eberhard 2004:79).

What is needed is adequate knowledge and openness for the message. Both source and target cultures as knowledge systems get into contact within the translator's mind, in a fusion of horizons, and the translator's mind is reaching out into different cultures and various fields of scientific knowledge and gets a share in both. This is meant with "grounded understanding". It is enabled by targeted learning.

"Interpretation", on the other hand, is a derivative way of explaining a text's meaning in the light of a specific ideology or science. In the context of Christian Bible text exegesis, interpretation is normally offered in a sermon. We find for instance a feminist, a fundamentalist, a liturgical, a liberation-theological or a historic-critical interpretation of the texts from the Gospel. Very often, and particularly in specialist communication, *Interpretation* and *Auslegung* may actually fall together, into one adequate grounded understanding, i. e. when the respective insider cognitive environment is already given in the communication and must not be transcended. Heidegger has pointed out that we unconsciously tend to blur that difference.[49] The reason for this is the functional versatility of language and we will discuss this more in detail below.

---

[48] Gadamer says: "Goodwill is what Platon calls 'eumeneis elenchoi'. That means: we do not try to keep right, we rather try to strengthen the other side as far as possible so that his/her assertion becomes somewhat convincing. Such an attitude seems to me essential for any interpretive understanding" (*my translation*).

[49] Heidegger (*SuZ*, 152): „Alle Auslegung, die Verständnis beistellen soll, muß schon das Auszulegende verstanden haben. Man hat diese Tatsache immer schon bemerkt, wenn auch nur im Gebiet der abgeleiteten Weisen von Verstehen und Auslegung, in der philologischen Interpretation. Diese gehört in den Umkreis wissenschaftlichen Erkennens. Dergleichen Erkenntnis verlangt die Strenge der gründenden Ausweisung. Wissenschaftlicher Beweis darf nicht schon voraussetzen was zu begründen seine Aufgabe ist. Wenn aber Auslegung sich je schon im Verstandenen bewegen und aus ihm her sich nähren muss, wie soll sie dann wissenschaftliche Resultate zeitigen, ohne sich in einem Zirkel zu

Gutt (2000) also mentions information about the background as a decisive point for understanding a text. He defines translation as an "interlingual interpretive use" of language: "a translation would be a receptor language text that interpretively resembled the original" (Gutt 2000:105). Texts must be relevant for the audience, otherwise they are not intelligible:

> The central claim of relevance theory is that human communication crucially creates an expectation of *optimal relevance*, that is an expectation on the part of the hearer that his attempts at interpretation will yield *adequate contextual effects* at *minimal processing cost*. (Gutt 2000:31f)

The resemblance between a translation and an original, according to Gutt, concerns mainly the aspects of relevance for the addressees, just as Skopos theory has stated. If aspects in the ST should not be inferable from the cognitive environment in the target culture, the translator is allowed to add explanations,[50] without violating the principle of faithfulness, and we can subscribe to this idea:

> These conditions seem to provide exactly the guidance that translator and translation theorists have been looking for: they determine in what respects the translation should resemble the original – only in those respects that can be expressed to make it adequately relevant to the receptor language audience. They determine also that the translation should be clear and natural in expression in the sense that it should not be unnecessarily difficult to understand. (Gutt 2000:107)

Gutt's general statement that translations should resemble the original and should be relevant for the audience is certainly right, but it says nothing about the concrete process of translating and how to access that text as a translator in

---

bewegen, zumal wenn das vorausgesetzte Verständnis überdies noch in der gemeinen Menschen- und Weltkenntnis sich bewegt." – *Translated:* Any interpretation which is to contribute understanding, must already have understood what is to be interpreted. This is a fact that has always been remarked, even if only in the area of derivative ways of understanding and interpretation, such as philological Interpretation. The latter belongs within the range of scientific knowledge. Such knowledge demands the rigour of a demonstration to provide grounds for it. In a scientific proof, we may not presuppose what it is our task to provide grounds for. But if interpretation must in any case already operate in that which is understood, and if it must draw its nurture from this, how is it to bring any scientific results to maturity without moving in a circle, especially if, moreover, the understanding which is presupposed still operates within our common information about man and the world?" (*TaB*, 194).

[50] This reminds us of the distinction between "overt translation" and "covert translation" (House 1997:29).

order to finally produce relevant target texts.[51] (His definition of an "interpretive use" ignores the problem of the subjectivity in understanding.) Alves and Gonçalves (2007:50) tested translators and proved that the novices, called "narrow-band translators", "worked mostly on the basis of insufficiently contextualized cues". A lack of specialized knowledge is the main barrier against grounded understanding to infer "the relevant cognitive environment".

Translators need a profound idea, in the sense of grounded understanding, of the topic presented in the text, whilst "interpretation" goes one step further. Here, the reader subjectively applies the new information to the own life or explains it for others, viewing it from a certain scientific or ideological point of view. There is a difference between "What does the text actually say", and "What does that mean (for the addressees)"? The social role of translating as a service – in order to help people to themselves understand and react interpretatively to a text across the language barrier – asks for rendering the text's saying (Eco 2006:17). This will only be possible if this text is presented to them authentically, and not in an ill-considered subjective or ideologically pre-formed or culturally distorted interpretation by the translator.

The ideological interpretation of a text's content blocks our receptivity to the full message presented in that source text which, however, should be represented in the translation. We may cite Johann Wolfgang v. Goethe[52]: "Man verändert fremde Reden beim Wiederholen wohl nur darum so sehr, weil man sie nicht verstanden hat" [= We are probably changing foreign speech so much in citing, because we didn't really understand it]. But only after we have grasped that full message – be it an information conveyed in scientific communication, or a calling in a political speech, or a legal text embedded in the foreign legal system, or a novel from a foreign culture, or a letter from a culture in the distant past like in Bible translation – we will be able to responsibly judge which parts of that mes-

---

[51] Of course, Gutt (2000) offers extensive discussion of examples for "translation units" on sentence level and primarily from oral communication and interpreting. For some cases Gutt (2000:198) even recommends not to translate at all and instead use another form of text production – a queer statement in a general translation theory. There is an unclear distinction between the theoretical definition of translation and individual practical decision-making by a translator.

[52] Goethe, Johann W. 1962. *Gedenkausgabe der Werke, Briefe und Gespräche* (ed. by E. Beutler). Zürich/Stuttgart: Artemis, p. 499.

sage need special explanation or even should be dropped or adapted in view of a target intellectual environment. We are implying full receptivity by a translator based on grounded understanding – even if this, in the end, might be an utopian ideal. Translation will only reach an optimal solution.

## 3.2 The link between translation and original

Often, translation is defined as „bridging cultures".[53] This has been the intention of translators since centuries. They want to prepare a way for messages to pass from one cultural setting to another in an intelligible way. It's worth questioning whether this translational work done by human beings goes without any transformation – be it of the message, of the target culture or of the translator him/herself. But is there any bridge?

By translating an authored and thus culture-bound text from one language to another one we enable the growth of texts by offering them a different audience (Steiner 1975:319). The message of those texts will be enlarged, if not transformed by a divergent interpretation in the target area. The bridge, here, is somehow 'ungraded and rough'.

The target culture is also being enriched through the influx of novel ideas in the translations. This may even have an impact on the literary polysystem there. The assumed bridge between the cultures is actually a 'waterfall', because translation as a process is always mono-directional.

Looking finally at the translating persons, what is their contribution to building bridges? They are domesticating foreignness, otherness, because they present it as they have understood it. Translators are cognitively living in two cultures – the foreign and their own one -, rather than building bridges over or between them. They themselves ‚are the bridge' and not a solid one.

In translating, the translator is constantly transformed himself in various ways. As Steiner (1975) explained, the experience of translating may disturb the translator and even silence his own voice. But it may also enlarge his horizon, as any translation confers a new knowledge input. There will be a growth of the translator.

---

[53] See for instance the title of the F.I.T. Congress in San Francisco in August 2011.

Translators are rooted in one culture, and, by having access to the other, they cognitively reach out into both. Translators do not stand in "between cultures" (Bassnett 2000:113) transferring any information from here to there. The two systems rather establish contact among each other within the translator's mind. The adequate grounded understanding that comes near to the author's intention is best gained when one tries to enter the author's situational context, his or her world of thought in history. This argument is not, in the first instance, meant as a prescriptive rule, it is rather a goal set from the professional translator's perspective.

This concept also has to do with the relationship between translation and original. There are not two texts in equivalence (Jakobson), but there is only one message (in the translator's mind) appearing in two different language forms.

The translators will never translate other than what they have understood beforehand, what is now cognitively present in their mind. This is a dynamic task and one needs reference points for orientation. Important aspects are understanding, precision and responsibility. We will have to reflect on the mental activity performed in gathering information about a source text, finding criteria for a strategic decision, setting translation principles, doing stylistic text work and target-oriented editing.

The modern professional working post is characterized by a great variety of clients to be served and of texts to be translated. Thus, the translator requires professional expert competence, and we will have to discuss its elements. As a model of relationship this shows the translating person vertically in his or her outlook towards various texts to be understood and translated (Stolze 2003:134):

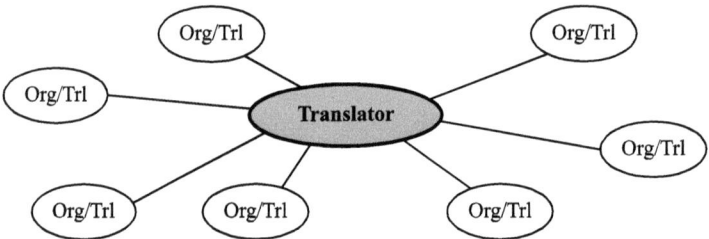

Translators are challenged to find orientation in the worlds of languages, cultures and sciences. Mossop presents the following description:

As readers of the source-text, translators are outsiders, translating texts not addressed to them. But as writers of the translation, they are insiders, acting as ghostwriters for source-text authors. [...] Such considerations lead naturally to reflection on the power and duties of the translator, as well as on the nature of authorship. (Mossop 1994:405)

Comprehending a written text creates a mental representation which then will be represented in the translation. Any translation is linked to the original – not by structural equivalence – but by its mental representation in the translator's mind. The relationship between translation and original is mediated cognitively by the translating person.

In reading a text, we listen to the author's voice speaking to us. This means that texts are viewed as an integrated entity carrying a message. However, since comprehension of written texts is not a matter of fact but has to be worked out (Schleiermacher), it is the great flaw of traditional translation studies, which focus on linguistic structures only, to silently imply that understanding the text were no problem, or that any problems were already solved.

## 3.3 Responsible reading and expertise

Phenomenology has argued that objects appear to humans as a phenomenon only at their surface, they have a "subject-relevant being".[54] In order to approach the virtual "objectivity" of the thing seen, we cannot insist on our own perspective, we have to move, or employ factual knowledge.[55] In the same way, the text appears on its surface as language signs, and still we know that it "means" something. The message or information conferred hereby is not exhaustively contained in these words and sentences, our memory will add relevant information. The text, as it were, is ontologically a holistic phenomenon activating multiple perspectives in readers. This is why different readers may interpret a text in many different ways. Texts in communication offer a "multiperspectivity"

---

[54] Remember the famous Leibniz' example in which wanderers from the four directions of the compass head towards a town and each wanderer sees the same town but (only) from an individual perspective. All are right when they say the town looks this or that way as they see it. But it is only their individual perspective of the town that is seen, not the town as a whole.

[55] The human subject, seeing for example the façade of a house, is well capable, based on experience, to know that in reality what s/he sees is more than this surface.

(Paepcke 1986:103) as they contain inter-subjective elements of grammar integrated with individual aspects of intention. Meaning can never simply be extracted by linguistic analysis of the text structure.

Readers of a translation assume that their text represents the message first given by the original author. This reader-expectation charges the translator with the responsibility for a faithful rendering of the original text's content. Precision is the goal for translation on all linguistic levels (Stolze 2003:181). And this, of course, raises the question of "responsible reading" as a feature of translation competence. Translators are asked to observe loyalty – not only to the author but also to the expectations of truth in their readers (Nord 1991a:91). There is the commission and the responsibility to grasp the sense of a text and to faithfully render it – not only to follow a subjective interpretation. C. Nord even sees here, with reference to Chesterman (2001:145ff) an "ethics of conflict-management, of confidence-building, of professionalism and honesty" (*my translation*) (Nord 2004:237). And Levý (1969:74) rightly stresses: "In translating, probably more than elsewhere, a homogeneous concept is needed, i.e. a clear idea of the œuvre and a consistent outlook towards it."[56]

Cultural and professional knowledge and experience determine the adequate interpretation of phenomena, as we have stated for the hermeneutical circle. Any naïve reading which exclusively would concentrate on the text structures is inadequate for a translational approach to texts. The crucial translation problem, then, is not the text structure, but the translator's background knowledge stored in memory. Gadamer rightly could stress "Bildung" or education as the indispensable condition for social life.

The fixation onto one aspect or problem only is phenomenologically questionable, since every phenomenon itself has to be seen within its environment and against its background, rather than isolated. It appears to be very fruitful for translators to include in their interest as many dimensions of life as possible, at the price of losing the depth of analysis. This lack of scientific profundity is

---

[56] *My translation.* Read: "Beim Übersetzen ist wohl mehr als anderswo eine einheitliche Konzeption vonnöten, d.i. eine feste Anschauung von dem Werk und eine einheitliche Grundeinstellung ihm gegenüber."

counterbalanced by a cognitive overview helping to create awareness of those points where further relevant research is still needed.

It appears that the translator's competence is a very complex system, as so many different aspects are constantly to be interlinked and viewed together. This is the primary difficulty in translation pedagogics, where often only one single aspect is being taught as a scientific object, while in reality it gets its translational significance only in combination with other aspects. "Situated cognition" (Risku 2000) might be seen as a scholarly designation of an effect which is present in everyday life as well. When we see an object and would like to understand it, the hermeneute will not say: 'What's this object like? Let's analyze it!', but rather: 'Where am I standing when I see it?' 'Should I walk over there?' This would imply the medial act of reading.[57]

When I consciously locate myself in relation to an object, I will also need some reference points of orientation to determine this location. At first, one will look at a larger area around oneself and gradually come down to the own situation. Such a situated cognition, which of course runs intuitively in the person's mind, also includes the realization whether I am in the position at all to understand that strange object or whether I have to ask questions. And this is also true for understanding texts. The reader will start with a top-down movement, departing from the own historical embedding. Translational criteria of orientation will be discussed in detail below. It is part of the translator's responsible reading and expert knowledge to critically reflect on his or her own capability.

We have to distinguish between merely experienced professionals and experts. Expert knowledge in general (Presas 2004) has been found to be *abstract* since experts are able to reduce the superficial characteristics of a problem to its functional principles and thus approach it holistically. Expert knowledge is also *strategical* in terms of an application of any methods which it uses prospectively in

---

[57] Such an attitude might help in viewing a palace and distinguish the front from its sides, or in analyzing a sick tree by taking into consideration the wood and environmental pollution around it. It might help in reading a map correctly, as this is dependent of one's own placement, either on the right or on the left hand side of it. The natural tendency to locate oneself in relation to others is also visible in the practice of mobile phoning, when we hear people say: Where are you? I am travelling on this and that route right now, etc. This helps people to orientate themselves in the world.

view of the overall goal. Expert knowledge is *proceduralized* as the experts apply their strategic knowledge automatically in commanding problem analysis. And last but not least, it is *self-reflective* as experts concisely reflect upon their problem-solving behavior and thus are able to direct it. Expertise, in its overall strategic approach, is intuitive and strategic at the same time. Both attitudes cannot be kept separate from each other. This applies for translation as well.

## 3.4 Translation between rules and play

Having said that grounded understanding of a text in responsible reading is the condition for adequate translation, we might ask: Is translation an art? Gadamer has introduced the metaphor of game. More adequately, Paepcke (1986:121) has defined translation as an activity "in between rules and play".

> Using the example of sportsmen, he stressed that the athlete has already prepared a strategy before beginning the contest; he knows the fixed rules, and still the moment of their application remains spontaneous, and the result is not guaranteed (Paepcke 1986:123). Any sport has certainly some rules as a methodology, they are strategic plans. And, at the same time, achievements are being made by intuition which is the driving force behind human action. Rules concern all repetitive aspects, but "the application of rules ignores a rule" (ibid., 124). That is the difference to the law as an absolute chain of cause and effect. In the translators' approach to texts, their intuition in full embodiment will constantly produce creative solutions, combined with "precise imagination in the uniformity of the rule" [*exakte Phantasie in der Einförmigkeit der Regel*] (ibid. 125).

Both attitudes, intuitive outlook in receptivity and methodical procedure, are effective in dealing with texts. Schleiermacher in his book *Hermeneutics and Criticism* has given some hints on how to get firm ground for this. He said (1838/1998:283): "The rules of analysis have no recipe for their application. It remains an art." But he also designed four factors of an hermeneutical process: grasping a subject (e.g. a text passage), its conditions of origination, its situational background, and its placement within a larger text type entity (Vermeer 1994:174). This is conformant with phenomenological awareness, and it produces a dynamization of that object.

In order to overcome mere subjectivism, Schleiermacher (1838/1998) called for a combination of both a "grammatical analysis" with genre comparison, and a "divinatory understanding" as a psychological explication of the passage. We read (ibid., 92): "For the whole procedure there are, from the beginning, two methods, the divinatory and the comparative, which together, because they refer back to each other, also may not be separated from each other" (§6, Part II). The vision of a text in its historical embedding and the comparison with similar text genres for more precision should be linked, in an interplay between rule and intuition. There will be phases which are more driven by methodology, and others where intuition is the leading strength.

> Schleiermacher (1838/1998) writes (p. 52): "In the application (of grammatical analysis) to the N.T. the philological perspective, which isolates every text of every writer, and the dogmatic perspective, which regards the N.T. as One work of One writer are opposed. Both become closer if one ponders the fact that with regard to the religious content the identity of the school, and with regard to the subsidiary thoughts the identity of the language area, become relevant" (§23+24, Part I).

The basis for this to happen is grounded understanding, as we said, and according to Schleiermacher a knowledge of the topics treated and of the language necessary for understanding and also mastered by the author (who shall not be severed from his or her individual text production) is decisive (cf. Vermeer 1994:174). In order to back-up one's understanding of a text and to expound its meaning, Schleiermacher established several alternating antinomies of analysis as a method. We paraphrase what we read in Schleiermacher:[58]

- There is a circle of understanding between the whole of the text and the single element in it. Both determine each other and are not well understood separately. The whole is more than the sum of its parts, of which it is made up.
- There is a circle between constitution and effect of the text. The author might have had other intentions than are now visible from the written text at first view from a reader's perspective.
- There is a circle between primary and secondary text features. What has been focused by the author, for instance with subtitles? The translator should pay attention to that.
- There is a circle between the individual text form and the analysis compared with other similar text genres. Good understanding will do the comparisons.

---

[58] See also the elaboration in Rübberdt/Salevsky (1997:305).

For translators, this might be a hint whereto direct their interest, combining intuitive outlook in receptivity and methodical procedure. Conscious of the own standpoint, the translator will first take a global view on the text. Cognitively speaking: top-down-processes come before bottom-up-processes. Schleiermacher said (1838/1998:27, §23): "Even within a single text the particular can only be understood from out of the whole, and a cursory reading to get an overview of the whole must therefore precede the more precise explication." Only when I know where I am standing can I see probable ways for advancement.

The hermeneutical approach to translation presented here includes the idea that the translational dealing with texts is basically the same for all text genres – only the required knowledge base and language proficiency is different. This concept stands in contradiction to a broadly defended conviction that translation of creative literature were an act totally different from technical translation. For instance, Wilss (1996:153) sees a special nature of literary translators with "inborn capabilities".[59] But this is an unnecessary mystification, derived from his automate concept of translation as an inter-linguistic transfer procedure. Others see a clash between different worlds of translation.

> The report on a conference on "Interlingual crossings. Translation worlds in comparison" (Udine, May 2006) shows this supposed clash. Bruno Osimo writes: "The structure itself of the meeting tended to emphasize the differences between the two approaches: on one side the impressionistic approach to translation, in which all the questions are considered in terms of the translator's mood, in a Romantic-like view in which, since translation is inspiration, also translation criticism and translation theorizing are based on experiences, reflections, or even – in one paper – dance; in this view, *terms* (*versus* *words*) are considered inelegant, too technical; on the other side the scientific approach to translation, in which efforts are made to use terms with clear-cut definitions (…). It is not an accident that, in the latter group, there were many papers from the area of semiotics.[60]

---

[59] He writes: "Literary translators are something more than biological beings with inborn (nativist) capabilities; they are creative, highly skilful agents, uniquely patterned and deserving a special effort to explore and interpret their nature. – This shows that there is a distinction between literary and technical translation. Literary translators are less inclined than technical translators to react to textual stimuli in more or less fixed ways which are standard operational. They determine their strategy in harmony with the total semantic and stylistic impact of the ST and activate their skills accordingly" (Wilss 1996:153).

[60] EST-Newsletter, No. 29 (November 2006, p. 7). www.est-translationstudies.org.

The hermeneutical approach precisely overcomes the "impressionistic approach in terms of the translator's mood" by ever stressing the role of the hermeneutical circle. Language is a means for many different purposes, and the words themselves are neutral; they only get their real meaning when seen against the relevant background, the different cognitive environments. For this reason the meaning of words and sentences is not accessible only by linguistic analysis on system level.

Literary styles or cultural aspects are as strange as functional styles of communication and technical terms for the translator. The relevant knowledge for both areas has to be acquired beforehand in a self-critical awareness. The idea of translation being merely a subjective mood and impression is not part of the hermeneutical theory of translation, which also includes precision and methodology. The translator's mind is reaching out into all worlds, to different cultures and to various fields of scientific knowledge. Both regions of activity (literature and science) are a field for translation competence in dealing with texts.

The text as an individual message consists not only of semiotic structures apt to analysis; it also contains some singular aspects that may be perceived intuitively. Language is always an intrinsic combination of both linguistic rule application and intuitive creation of meaning by human beings. This cannot be severed, with the consequence that neither syntactic analysis alone nor impressionistic feelings will come up to truth.

## 3.5 The bifocal view on texts

Schleiermacher has pointed out to some circles in the move of understanding a text. Textual elements have their meaning only in relation to the whole of the text, but it's those elements that carry meaning. For Schleiermacher, the analysis of a text, made in order to gain a reliable understanding of it, is always a variation between grammar and the individual sense of the utterance, between the text in its appearance and similar known text types, between the single word and the overall text meaning. The meaning of a text is more than a simple addition of the words and sentences. Holistic pre-understanding guides the textual analysis.

Language is an indissoluble complex of grammatical *and* individual elements. So translators have a double perspective on texts: *both* viewing the cultural and/or technical constellations out there in the situation, *and* "analyzing the text structure to find confirmation for their initial understanding" (Coseriu 1980:116). Once you have understood a message holistically you may go back to the text level in order to find certain words or sentences which had induced it. Any understanding has to be backed up by linguistic confirmation, but it cannot be derived from the ST structure. It is a holistic affair, not one of construction out of particles.

Cultural awareness has ever been stressed in TS looking beyond mere linguistic analysis. The main difference of the hermeneutical approach is that it does not try to deduct sense from the language structures, and it includes an outlook in grounded understanding – viewing a whole text with insider eyes already, rather than starting with "problem awareness" (Henschelmann 1999; Nord 1991) on the text level. The latter would make understanding much more difficult, because it focuses on single aspects instead of the holistic reference. Focusing on individual problems as they occur on the text level requires an activation of the background knowledge at every single point anew, whereas hermeneutical positioning excludes the apparition of such "problems". And on the other hand, it enables detecting certain points in a text where "problem awareness" is actually required. Looking at those points neutrally (without given pre-knowledge) I might even miss them. Where should the problem awareness come from? It is an effect of the hermeneutical metacognition. Therefore, an hermeneutical approach to texts in translation will be holistic and not reduced on an analysis of syntax.

We need an approach of integratively dealing with texts. Paepcke (1986) has given some hints on how to treat the translation text as a reader/translator, explaining his ideas at an example (1986:158-175).

> Paepcke, following Schleiermacher, points out to the need for first looking at the cultural and historical background of the text (1986:163); then translators should consider their own embedding and the purpose of the translation work (ibid. 165); one should look at the overall structure of the texts with the main ideas presented therein, so that we find an orientation in that landscape of a text (ibid. 163); the next step is to select the central concepts and terms in the text in order to analyze "the text's semantic program" (ibid. 169); in

focusing on the word fields and aspects of polysemy and synonymy, one should also remember the history of meaning (ibid. 170) and consider the effect. This effect in communication is varying, as languages constitute different cultural systems; the thematic structure is also relevant (ibid. 169). (*My translation*)

As Paepcke's ideas are not very systematic and only presented with the help of examples, there is the need to offer a more stringent model for bifocal translational reading. According to Iser (1978), the reader's acts of comprehension are guided by textual construction.

> The interpreter's [i.e. the reader's] task should be to elucidate the potential meanings of a text, and not to restrict himself to just one. Obviously, the total potential can never be fulfilled in the reading process, but it is this very fact that makes it so essential that one should conceive of meaning as something that happens, for only then can one become aware of those factors that precondition the composition of the meaning. (Iser 1978:22)

These factors do guide the readers' attention into certain directions. All the potential "textual strategies of a text" cannot be actualized in one reading only. This is because "fictional texts constitute their own objects and do not copy something already in existence. For this reason they cannot have the total determinacy of real objects" (Iser 1978:24).

Texts convey messages in human communication. One characteristic of texts, therefore, is individuality too. Even if a text may belong to a specific genre, it always carries an aspect that reaches out beyond that field, as Schleiermacher has taught. Texts constitute a holistic entity where every part is dependent on the whole, and the whole is more than the sum of its parts. This relationship between the whole and its parts is called by Schleiermacher the "interpretive circle" (*Zirkel des Verstehens*) (1998: §23), not to be mistaken for the "hermeneutical circle" (*hermeneutischer Zirkel*) dealing with the relevant knowledge base in the reader. Following hermeneutics, we might argue that any text analysis should ever be preceded by a holistic interpretive approach. This idea is adopted in cognitive science as well: holistic text processing in understanding is seen as both

> "bottom-up, that is data-driven, from the lexical level up to the text level, and top-down, theory-driven, from the text level down to the lexical level, such that the text meaning feeds back to and may revise the interpretation of its components" (Zelinsky-Wibbelt 2003:203).

And Beeby (1996:92; 95) states, in a more generalizing manner, that professional translators' communicative competence "consists of the specific grammatical, socio-linguistic, discourse, and transfer [sub]competences", all interdependent – she adds – in "a continuous bottom-up/top-down interaction." – We would rather say it is a "top-down/bottom-up helical movement".

In line with the language philosophy of hermeneutics, we have been deliberating on the "conditions of comprehension" such as language proficiency, relevant subject knowledge, and openness. The understanding will happen intuitively in a "fusion of horizons". If this statement sounds like a mere repetition of what professionals are doing anyway, they might take it as a theoretical confirmation of their work.

In Translation Studies, much literature has been developed to describe and teach translational work. A great deal of this endeavor aims at overcoming the translators' subjectivity. Before proceeding with a concrete explanation of the hermeneutical orientation in the world of texts for translation, we will therefore have to discuss the limits of subjectivity in translating.

# 4 The limits of subjectivity

## 4.1 How much text analysis is needed?

In this respect, traditional TS is lop-sided. By and large in Translation Studies, a "translation-relevant text analysis" is posited as the prerequisite of adequate translating, see for instance Nord (1991:17). Text analysis is meant to guarantee comprehension, overcome subjectivity and secure the concept of a translation as an inter-linguistic transfer and multi-level equivalence of a ST and a TT to be measured in a "translation profile" (cf. House 1997:52). However, the reduction of the language problem onto locally analyzable text structures is an illicit restriction of the holistic concept of language in communication which includes both objective and subjective aspects.[61] Maybe one should also better give up the traditional terms of "source" and "target" texts, because it is only "one message" we are dealing with.

Schleiermacher (1977:74f) commented on his two translation methods: "The two separated parties must either meet at a certain point in the middle, and that will always be the translator, or one must completely join up with the other, and of these two possibilities only the first belongs to the field of translation." The usual linguistic approach has always been the analysis of

<u>morphemes – semes – lexemes – in texts –</u>

<u>as a genre – in a situation – in a culture.</u>

This should be reversed. The translator does not analyze linguistic objects, he or she is confronted with

---

[61] Traditional translation studies tend to follow the "interlingual paradigm" and to extensively discuss such grammar structures for equivalence, see Kußmaul (2000:81) who discusses how an English participial construction could be translated as a temporal sentence in German. – See also Wilss (1992:91) on "translating procedural paradigms" concerning the threefold translation of a pre-modifying English participial construction. – See also Wilss (1996:155): "Turning now to translation method (translation methodology) it is advisable to define translation as a two-phase operation, with a ST-analytic and a TT-synthetic phase. [...] In my view, the two-phase model (with the additional dimension of feedback between the two phases) is more in line with translation reality...".

<u>cultures – in a discourse field – as texts –</u>

<u>with words – carrying sense.</u>

Translators as the actors of translation are individual human beings integrated in their own culture and having gathered knowledge of the relevant cognitive environment (through language acquisition, social sciences, practical experience, specialist studies, travels, learning of facts) about the other culture or scientific domain. Both cultures as a system of knowledge get into contact within his or her mind, in a "fusion of horizons".

It seems a platitude to say that every text should be viewed within its context, however this affects the understanding of that text. The same linguistic signs against a different cultural or scientific background may have a completely different meaning, and that, by the way, is the reason for polysemy. Language serves as a means of communication among all speakers. Linguistic signs are referring to a meaning beyond themselves (on system level), as there are no special signs for all and every situation (on usage level).[62] The translator needs sensitivity for the differences in sign usage:

> In order to recognize the relevant relationships the mental representations of source and target language speakers have to be considerably more explicit than those which speakers represent in monolingual communication. (Zelinsky-Wibbelt 2003:206)

Gadamer had called this fact "highlighting". He writes (1990:386): "Translation, like all interpretation, is a highlighting. A translator must understand that highlighting is part of his task. Obviously he must not leave open whatever is not clear to him." This might be an explanation for the pattern of *explicitation* found in corpus analyses as a "universal of translations" (Klaudy 2009). When translators are not conscious of their situation as a translator scrutinizing the text, they will forget about going back to normal style in writing their translation, and instead explicitate too much.

---

[62] *Examples*: The clause "Just get me that spoon, could you?" is a question in the grammatical form, but it is often interpreted as a polite demand. – The clause "It is rather cold in here" is a grammatical proposition, however in some cultural contexts it means "please close the door" (Hall 1976: 98). – The term flow, for instance has a different meaning in painting, engineering, physics, linguistics, journalism, etc.

Skopos theory argues that the first step in a translational text analysis should be the analysis of the target readers' expectation. Skopos is a "basic rule dominating the translational decisions" (Reiß & Vermeer 1984:95) while the original of the text "is de-throned" (Vermeer 1986:42). Translation is defined as "a purposeful activity" (Nord 1997) linked with the suggestion that first a "translation commission" should be defined, by analyzing the addressees' comprehending ability and their interest and expectations for use, before translation for functional adequacy could take place. Text analysis is dependent, here, on the addressees' world, rather than on any difficulties found in the original (as traditional translation theories saw it).

> This should help to decide which parts of the source text material may be preserved, and which ones should be changed for cultural or purpose reasons, and the target text will be a function of this skopos fixed. Nord discusses the "adaptation" of source text material identifying and isolating those ST elements which have to be preserved or adapted in translation (Nord 1991:17/21).

Nord discusses the adaptation of conventions regarding text genre to target norms by "paraphrases", or even the adaptation of verbalized and non-verbalized information to the knowledge of the target audience by expansion or reduction (Nord 1991a:96). All this is done with reference to the respective structures in the source text.

Nord (1991) discusses several "translation problems", caused by ST structures, pragmatics, cultural divergence and language pair differences. In this connection she develops a scale of texts ranging from easy to difficult, with a view to translation teaching and to structuring the lessons. The problem is that not all students have the same level of knowledge, for some of them the texts might be too easy. And again, this does not lead us beyond the comparison of translations and source texts within the equivalence-based transfer model.

Nord (1991:9) advocates a description of the instructions for translating, as they "should contain as much information as possible about the situational factors of the prospective TT reception, such as the addressee(s) or possible recipients, time and place of reception, intended medium, etc.". The basic statement is: "Being culture-bound linguistic signs, both the source text and the target text are determined by the communicative situation in which they serve to convey a message" (ibid., 7).

But the target text is not there while the translator is dealing with the source text, and the "possible recipients, time and place of reception" are unknown even after the translation as a written text has been completed. It is clear that Nord's approach is oriented towards translation criticism with "evaluation standards", rather than aiding the preparation of a translation. This is seen differently by Nord herself who fears individuality and gives prescriptive instructions:

> If reception is absolutely dependent on the individual conditions, there will be no chance whatsoever of finding evaluation standards which will take into account every single reception process. The only way to overcome this problem is, in my opinion, first to control ST reception by a strict model of analysis which covers all the relevant text features or elements, and, second, to control TT production by stringent "translating instructions" which clearly define the (prospective) function of the target text. (Nord 1991:17)

In the light of our hermeneutical approach it is simply not possible to „control ST reception by a strict model of analysis", since understanding is a medial event (it happens or not) and it is more than text analysis. Moreover, the reference to "text elements" as fixed points of decision does not overcome the old paradigm of interlingual transfer by reusing or exchanging text portions in translation, and it is no real "objectification" either, since the decision about which elements "have to be preserved or adapted" is again dependent on the translator's understanding. A "text analysis" of this kind is of no use for the hermeneutical translator, who asks for reference points of orientation, to be competently applied in "every single reception process".

The analysis of facts remains on the surface. The more detailed one aspect is being analyzed, the more all the other multifarious aspects in the text are being excluded.[63] The hermeneutical translator would not, for instance, note grammatical forms or particles because they are unimportant. Any idea can just as well be formulated in another way, different from the model translations and different from structures in any corpus. Hermeneutics deals with social action among people.

---

[63] This is a feature often lamented in the discussion of students' behavior in Think Aloud Protocols. They tend to focus on one point only and forget about the rest, see e.g. Bălăcesku & Stefanink (2006) or also Kußmaul (2000).

"In retrospective interviews during process studies, professionals accounted for their decisions [holistically] in terms of skopos, intratextual coherence and stylistic considerations. Kussmaul's analyses of translation processes show the importance of cognitive strategies, such as scene activation, chains of associations, ... for decision making in translation" (Schäffner).[64]

"Scene activation" is only possible within the relevant "cognitive environment" (Gutt) of the domain concerned. This is also an argument for the statement that a holistic approach is being used by professionals, rather than syntactic text analysis.

## 4.2 What is interpretation?

In science there is much suspect against subjectivity, because it relativizes the general validity of knowledge. This is an important objection, and it has to be discussed here. When we talk of understanding as a prerequisite of translation, the concept of "interpretation" is closely connected. It is a common opinion in TS that any translation were already an "interpretation", and thus ever subjective.[65] Vermeer sees this as inevitable and concludes that

> es eine nicht abgeschlossene Zahl von Translationen gibt (geben sollte), aus denen sich jeder Rezipient die ihm am meisten zusagende aussuchen könnte" (2003:256) [There is (should be) a never ending number of translations so that recipients could select the one they prefer].

After all, "interpretation" is not the same as "understanding". Text understanding, as it were, is a kind of dialogue about the content of texts based on foreknowledge, and Gadamer asks the reader to make clear what he has understood or not: "Obviously he must not leave open whatever is unclear to him. He must show his colors" (*TaM*, 386). In a chapter on "Verstehen und Auslegung" (*SuZ*, 148ff) Heidegger defines *Auslegung* (interpretive understanding) as the understanding from one's own perspective, i.e. a subjective interpretive understand-

---

[64] See Chr. Schäffner in her abstract on the paper "Metaphor in Translation: Reflections on Translation Process Research" for the Conference on *Research Models in Translation Studies II*, Manchester 1 May 2011.

[65] In the English translation of Gadamer we find that "any translation constitutes already an interpretation" (*TaM*, 384) (= Jede Übersetzung ist daher schon Auslegung, *WuM*, 362). Eco (2006:273) repeats this idea, stating that "Auslegung" is "Interpretation". We will discuss this below.

ing. He distinguishes it from *Interpretation* as "an area of derivative ways of understanding" (*BaT*, 194) ["eine der abgeleiteten Weisen von Verstehen" (*SuZ*, 152)]: "The latter belongs within the range of scientific knowledge. Such knowledge demands the rigor of a demonstration to provide grounds for it" (*BaT*, 194). The German term "Interpretation" always appears in a collocation with an attribute, such as *philological, historiological* (*BaT*, 194), *ontological* (150), *existential* (241), *Descartes'* (130), *Hegel's* (484) *Interpretation*. It is the explanation and functional understanding within an ideology or science.

In talking about the issue of understanding, there is a problem of translating those terms from the German into the English language, and this may cause major confusion.

> See *Being and Time,* translated by John Macquarrie & Edward Robinson. (London: SCM Press Ltd, 1952). The translators note (p.1): "Heidegger uses two words which might well be translated as 'interpretation': 'Auslegung' and 'Interpretation'. Though in many cases these may be regarded as synonyms, their connotations are not quite the same. 'Auslegung' seems to be used in a broad sense to cover any activity in which we interpret something 'as' something, whereas 'Interpretation' seems to apply to interpretations which are more theoretical or systematic, as in the exegesis of a text. We shall preserve this distinction by writing 'interpretation' for 'Auslegung', but 'Interpretation' for Heidegger's 'Interpretation', following similar conventions for the verbs 'auslegen' and 'interpretieren'.

Let us present some examples giving various renderings of German philosophical works in the English translation. Gadamer and Heidegger use the term "Auslegung" when they refer to the process of interpretive understanding of the world by an individual, of one's existence, of the "Sache" (content) present in the language:

> (1) Gadamer speaks of: "**Auslegung**, die der Übersetzer dem ihm vorgegebenen Wort hat angedeihen lassen." (*WuM* 362) *This has been translated:* „The **interpretation** that the translator has made of the words given him." (*TaM*, 384).

> (2) Gadamer cites from Heidegger about the hermeneutical circle: „In ihm verbirgt sich eine positive Möglichkeit ursprünglichsten Erkennens, die freilich in echter Weise nur dann ergriffen ist, wenn die **Auslegung** verstanden hat, dass ihre erste (...). Was Heidegger hier sagt, ist zunächst nicht eine Forderung an die Praxis des Verstehens, sondern beschreibt die Vollzugsform des verstehenden **Auslegens** selbst. (...) Alle rechte **Auslegung** muss sich gegen die Willkür von Einfällen abschirmen." (*WuM*, 251)

*This has been translated:* "In the circle is hidden a positive possibility of the most primordial kind of knowing, and we genuinely grasp this possibility only when we have understood that our first, last, and constant task in **interpreting** is never to allow our... What Heidegger is working out here is not primarily a prescription for the practice of understanding, but a description of the way **interpretive understanding** is achieved. (…) All correct **interpretation** must be on guard against arbitrary fancies. (*TaM*, 266f)

(3) Gadamer writes: „Das ist aber genau das Verhalten, das wir als Auslegen kennen. Übersetzung ist wie jede **Auslegung** eine Überhellung. Wer übersetzt, muß solche Überhellung auf sich nehmen. Er darf offenbar nichts offen lassen was ihm selber unklar ist." (*WuM*, 363)

*This has been translated:* "But this is precisely the activity that we call **interpretation**. Translation, like all **interpretation**, is a highlighting. A translator must understand that highlighting is part of his task. Obviously he must not leave open whatever is not clear to him." (*TaM*, 386)

(4) Heidegger defines: "Das Entwerfen des **Verstehens** hat die eigene Möglichkeit, sich auszubilden. Die Ausbildung des Verstehens nennen wir **Auslegung**. In ihr eignet sich das Verstehen sein Verstandenes verstehend zu. In der **Auslegung** wird das Verstehen nicht etwas anderes, sondern es selbst. **Auslegung** gründet existenzial im Verstehen, und nicht entsteht dieses durch jene." (*SuZ*, 148). „**Auslegung** ist nie ein voraussetzungsloses Erfassen eines Vorgegebenen. Wenn sich die besondere Konkretion der **Auslegung** im Sinne der exakten **Textinterpretation** gern auf das beruft, was "dasteht", so ist das, was zunächst „dasteht", nichs anderes als die selbstverständliche, undiskutierte Vormeinung des Auslegers, die notwendig in jedem **Auslegungsansatz** liegt als das, was mit Auslegung überhaut schon „gesetzt", d.h. in Vorhabe, Vorsicht, Vorgriff vorgegeben ist. (*SuZ*, 150)

*This was translated:* "The projecting of the **understanding** has its own possibility – that of developing itself. This development of the understanding we call "**interpretation**". In it the understanding appropriates understandingly that which is understood by it. In **interpretation**, understanding does not become something different. It becomes itself. Such **interpretation** is grounded existentially in understanding; the latter does not arise from the former." (*TaM*, 188). An **interpretation** is never a presuppositionless apprehending of something presented to us. If, when one is engaged in a particular concrete kind of **interpretation**, in the sense of exact textual **Interpretation**, one likes to appeal to what 'stands there', then one finds that what 'stands there' in the first instance is nothing other than the obvious undiscussed assumption of the person who does the **interpreting**. In an **interpretative approach** there lies such an assumption, as that which has been 'taken for granted' with the **interpretation** as such – that is to say, as that which has been presented in our fore-having, our fore-sight, and our fore-conception." (*BaT*, p. 192)

The problem of rendering both concepts (*Auslegung* and *Interpretation*) with "interpretation" in English causes misunderstandings by blending with the German word "Interpretation". And in fact, this happens whenever there is back translation from English to German, if the translator isn't aware of that point, and this easily leads to the misconception that any understanding automatically were "Interpretation" to a certain extent.

> One striking example is found in Risku (1998a:121): In referring to cognitive science, she writes that connectionist networks „bei bloßen ‚Andeutungen' umfassende Muster aktivieren und je nach situativem, textuellem und internem Kontext unterschiedliche ‚Interpretationen' anstellen". This is not only an awkward statement but clearly a mistranslation of 'varying interpretations' with the meaning of 'understandings' (Deutungen).

The idea that "translation is interpretation" in English may even go back to Roman Jakobson in his famous article of 1959 "On Linguistic Aspects of Translation". He argues that the meaning of a word is classified within the lexical system of a language, so that it may be replaced by other words that seem equivalent, and he calls this "interpretation of a linguistic code-unit". The German translation also speaks each time of *"Interpretation sprachlicher Zeichen"*, a clear blending with the English term as a false friend (Jakobson 1981:191).

> He distinguishes three kinds of "interpretation of a language sign": (1) intralingual translation or *rewording* as "an interpretation of linguistic signs by means of other signs of the same language", (2) interlingual translation or *translation proper* as "an interpretation of signs by means of another language", and (3) intersemiotic translation or *transmutation* as "an interpretation of linguistic signs with signs of a non-linguistic semiotic system" (Jakobson 1981:190).

It is important to note that we do not subscribe to this concept of "interpretation" as rewording which, according to Eco (2006:269) was obviously influenced by the diction of Charles S. Peirce. Interpretation, on the contrary, is a cognitive act, closely linked to the way of understanding, but from a specific point of view. As a matter of fact, "interpretive understanding" (*Auslegung*) as a natural, subjective understanding, and "interpretation" (*Interpretation*) as a scientific or ideological understanding are not the same, as both imply different cognitive environments and intentions of the comprehending individual.

In ordinary language usage, this fine distinction is not made. "To interpret s.th." and "interpretation" mean "to explain, to expound, to set forth the meaning of s.th." (For this sense see Jakobson as mentioned). And interestingly enough, the language dictionaries also present this unspecified meaning of the word:

In the *Oxford English Dictionary* (1989) we read: ***To interpret*** - to explain, expound, translate, understand, also in pass. sense to be explained, mean. But also "To make out the meaning of, explain to oneself". And: ***Interpretation***: "The action of interpreting or explaining; explanation, exposition". And on ***interpretative***: "having the character, quality or function of interpreting; serving to set forth the meaning (of something); explanatory, expository."

In the *American Heritage Dictionary of the English Language* (2000) we read for ***to interpret***:
**1.** To explain the meaning of (interpreted the ambassador's remarks. Synonyms at explain.) **2.** To conceive the significance of; construe (interpreted his smile to be an agreement; open door as an invitation.) **3.** To present or conceptualize the meaning of by means of art or criticism. **4.** To translate orally.

Intr. **1.** To offer an explanation. **2.** To serve as an interpreter for speakers of different languages (-> adj. Interpretable, interpretableness, interpretability)." On ***interpretation*** - **1.** The act of process of interpreting. **2.** A result of interpreting. **3a.** An explanation or conceptualization by a critic of a work of literature, painting, music, or other art from; an exegesis. **b.** A performer's distinctive personal vision of a song, dance, piece of music, or role; a rendering (-> adj. interpretational)."

And in German lexicons we see the same assertions: *Wahrig*: **interpretieren** etw. (sprachlich, sachlich, künstlerisch) erklären, auslegen, deuten. Einen Text, eine Aussage, ein Musikstück interpretieren. **Auslegung** – Erklärung, Deutung des Sinnes (Bibel, Recht.). Bodenbelag. **Ich deute**: - erkläre, suche den Sinn herauszuholen 2. zeige darauf, 3. lässt daraus erkennen, 4. lege aus – suche zu enträtseln.

*Brockhaus. Handbuch des Wissens* (1923): **Interpretation:** Erklärung und Auslegung von Schriften, Gesetzen, Verträgen sc., wobei man grammat. und sachl. I. unterscheidet. **Auslegung** von Schriften im allgemeinen, s. Hermeneutik, Exegese und Interpretation

**Exegese** – Erklärung, Auslegung, bes. Bibelerklärung. **Hermeneutik** –. „Lehre von der Kunst der Auslegung einer Rede oder Schrift", die es v. a. mit der richtigen Anwendung der exegt. Hilfswissenschaften zu tun hat (unter „Auslegung).

In the German dictionaries, there is no differenciation between *Erklärung, Deutung, Auslegung, Interpretation*. All mean a sort of "explaining", "expounding the sense". But it is exactly against this concept that Heidegger had put his view of "Auslegung":

Die Auslegung wirft nicht gleichsam über das nackte Vorhandene eine "Bedeutung" und beklebt es nicht mit einem Wort, sondern mit dem innerweltlichen Begegnenden als solchen hat es je schon eine im Weltverstehen erschlossene Bewandtnis, die durch die Auslegung herausgelegt wird. (*SuZ*, 150). – "In interpreting, we do not, so to speak, throw a 'signification' over some naked thing which is present-at-hand, we do not stick a value on it; but when something within-the-world is encountered as such, the thing in question already has an involvement which is disclosed in our understanding of the world, and this involvement is one which gets laid out by the interpretation" (*TaM*, 190f).

For Heidegger, "Auslegung" is not "explaining" but "understanding". Therefore we may translate this with "interpretive understanding", a solution also found in Gadamer's English translation. A translation will not "explain" a text but "present" it in an intelligible manner.

In literary studies *Interpretation* means the process of searching for a precise meaning to understand. When I have not yet gained a satisfactory understanding of the text in my intuitive reading, then I will interpret, "when I am not satisfied with a normal grade of understanding, but try to find out how in the friend the passage from one thought to the other was made" (Schleiermacher 1838/1998:320).

In Translation Studies the difference between understanding and interpretation, based on a process of searching for meaning, seems to be unclear. Reiß and Vermeer (1984:19) state:

> Der Translator geht von einem vorgegebenen, von ihm verstandenen und interpretierten Text aus. Ein Text ist sozusagen ein Informationsangebot an einen Rezipienten seitens eines Produzenten. (*My translation*: The translator starts with a given text, understood and interpreted by him. A text is an information offer given to a recipient by a producer).

## 4.3 Textual growth in multiple in re-translations?

Nord (1991a) also sees a double binding of the translator – to the ST author and to the TT recipients –, just as Wilss who states: "Translation is ... the interaction of three communicating partners, the ST author, the translator, and the TT reader" (1996:5). However, the translator has only the text at hand, and the target audience data are not yet given in an objective form, they can only be postulated by the translator. Translators cannot look into the minds of people – neither those of authors nor of readers – they can only try to imagine questions of a cultural situation or a scientific domain to be answered in a text.[66]

The result of Skopos theory is that different addressees require a different strategy of translation, a fact which is not requested for original texts.[67] We encounter this idea in the constant call for new Bible translations, see e.g. Berger and Nord (2000:216). Quite similarly, Ricœur spoke of unending retranslations of the great works because there is no absolute translation (*retraduction incessante des grandes oeuvres*, 2004:15). In order to approach the truth of a text one would need various translations, they say.[68] We doubt whether a collection of several translations – which constitute an accumulation of different subjective understandings – could lead to any "objective" translational meaning and be satisfactory for a reader. How long will we have to go on with this procedure? The asymptotic narrowing of textual meanings is open-ended and thus not adequate for a proof.

What needs to be reflected, here, is the viewpoint from which the academic discourse takes place. Talking about a textual "growth" in endless reinterpretations, even including an "inflationary hermeneutic process" (Steiner 1975:319) or a multiperspectivity of works that "grow" with every new reading, envisages the œuvre as an object (Iser 1978). In view of its pragmatics, a text appears as an ontologically multiperspective object, including the potential of arousing various reactions in readers. The perspective, here, is reversed from the

---

[66] Nord (1991:16) in her textbook *asks the impossible* of a translator: "He is a 'critical recipient' who is aiming at least to achieve an objective, conscientious, and verifiable comprehension of the source text. He receives the text on various levels: (a) on the level of a SC-competent recipient (in his own TRL situation), (b) on that of an analyst who puts himself in the situation of both the intended ST recipient and a possible real ST recipient, and (c) from the standpoint of a TC-competent recipient, who reads the ST 'through the eyes' of the intended TT recipient and tries to put himself in his shoes as well."

[67] Nord (1991:33) defines: „The first step ... in the translation process is the analysis of the TT skopos, i.e. of those factors that are relevant for the realization of a certain purpose by the TT in a given situation." That means that for different purposes there have to be produced different translations. – We think that the same translation might well be used for any purpose, just like any original text.

[68] The authors argue that addressees of their new Bible translation are "all those, whether theological laymen or experts, being interested in the relationship between ... several translations of the same original, and expecting that by an unprejudiced comparing vision of various translations they would get to know more about the source text" (*my translation*) (Berger & Nord 2000:216).

translator to the text and its so-called behavior. Any object once grasped includes the potential of growth: a text is not limited to the author's intention, but can be understood anew in many new readings (*Zuwachs an Sein*, Stanley 2005:359). But this addition is only virtual.

Regarding individual understanding (what is the goal of any translator), it remains a speculation, since the idea of any meaning being clarified by multi-translation, or a "growth of meaning", cannot be verified consistently. It remains open. Not many readers will actually read several translations of the same text in order to get "more truth". In such a quest, they would rather try to read the original – and then again get only their own truth. The comparison of different translations creates a deep uncertainty in the reader as to what that text is "really saying".

We are arguing here from the hermeneutical viewpoint of the single translator faced with a text and trying to make sense of it as integratively as possible. Virtual "objectivity" of a thing is not obtained by many different contributions, but by flexible thinking of one observer who phenomenologically tends to be as broad as possible.

The idea that many different translations would render more "truth" sounds strange, since source texts always appear in only one form and still are being read (and perhaps even understood) by various readers.[69] And scientific or ideological readers' interpretations may even vary to a large extent – though based on one and the same text or (faithful) translation – when the readers have a different opinion with which they approach that text. But this is the readers' task and freedom, one cannot force one specific interpretation onto them.

The source text is being "interpreted" here in the construed interest of the supposed target text recipients – and not in the perspective of an informed translator taking into consideration the source text's background. This kind of target text orientation – to our opinion – is an inadequate form of *Interpretation* focusing ideologically on a so-called purpose, instead of the message to be translated. It implies two problems: (i) The question of first understanding the source text re-

---

[69] Advocates of "functional translation" themselves assume that the translations of their own books and articles are faithful, so that the intended addressees might get the message (without reading various translations).

mains out of focus, thus opening all ways for a subjective misunderstanding of that text and excusing this with any target readers' needs. (ii) The target readers are an unclassified quantity, they are not known beforehand. The purpose-driven translation even includes a second subjective interpretation, since the "needs of the target audience" are a mere postulation by the translator himself. When, for instance, fluent readability becomes the utmost purpose of a translation, any cultural specificity will readily be eliminated from that translation. And when intelligibility for certain target readers is the main purpose, the translator runs the risk of either skipping scientific aspects in an LSP text or of over-simplifying it (because he himself does not really understand it).[70] The production of a translation as an act is mistaken here as the fulfillment of a social purpose which, however, will be carried out by the readers themselves. Translators make themselves the lords of the source text, even reducing its meaning:[71]

> After reading the text himself, he [sc. the translator] is going to convey to them, by means of his translation, <u>a certain piece of information from or about the source text</u>. The translator's reception (i.e. the way he receives the text) is determined by the communicative needs of the initiator or the TT recipient (Nord 1991:10). (*my underlining*).

Such a form of reductionist "functional translation", which in reality is an ideological interpretation of the source text, seems not adequate for the theoretical concept of faithful translation as a re-presentation of messages – that later on

---

[70] Examples of this stance are discussed in Stolze (2003:285, note 570).

[71] Nord (1991:33) presents for this the example of an eye-witness report, and it is not understandable which text elements he may use for his own purpose: "A report by an eyewitness of the 'soft revolution' in the former GDR on November 9$^{th}$, 1989, has been recorded on tape and subsequently transcribed. An American journalist asks for a translation of the transcript because he wants to use the information for a book on the political changes in Eastern Europe in 1989. In view of this intended TT function, the translator will pay special attention to any information explicitly or implicitly contained in the report, neglecting, however, the features of spontaneous, informal speech and the rhetoric clichés used by the eyewitness to impress the interviewer, as these are of secondary importance for the journalist's purpose. However, if the transcript is to be translated for publication in an American newspaper as an 'eyewitness report', the features of spontaneous and emotional speech are of particular interest because they will signal the text type "eyewitness report" to the readers" (Nord 1991:33). – Our comment: Such a translational behavior is unacceptable. The American journalist asked for a "transcription" of that report, and he can himself neglect spontaneous features, if those aren't of special interest to him for his book. The TT recipient could just as well read the full translation himself and decide himself what to do with it within the own communicative needs (if he didn't expressly ask for a short conclusion).

will have to be interpreted by the readers themselves for their own purposes. If we already present a pre-interpretation, a "fore-having" (Heidegger) to them, there will not be left much to be interpreted by the readers later on. (Of course we are aware of the fact that some interesting transformations in history go back to manipulating translations, but it happened unintentionally.)

Skopos theory finds its strongest argument in the need of correcting any objective defects, such as unclear statements a. o. found in a translation text. This of course is done by any responsible translator who will not stick to inter-lingual transfer. Nord states (1991:35): "In professional translation, source texts are very often defective, and yet they have a communicative function, which they normally fulfill, and, what is more, they have to be translated." That sweeping statement about many defective texts in its generality is rather absurd, considering the high specificity in technical texts given in real professional translation situations (Schmitt 2004). Some so-called "defects" detected in a text might even derive from misunderstandings by the naïve translator.[72]

## 4.4  Is meaning captured?

The question was also raised whether translators shouldn't make clear their own ideology in order to become more visible, since for centuries translators have only been the minor servants of their authors (Albrecht 1998:69). This question again focuses more on the purpose of a translation than on its content. When translation is conceived as a mediating service being rendered by a responsible translator with professional expertise, then the translator's voice is never subdued. It finds its expression in an adequate understanding and a good formulation of the text message, just like a co-author. It is not the task of translators to make clear, for instance, their critical opposition to a text message.[73] They rather

---

[72] In a practical situation, a direct enquiry with the commissioner might help to better understand the text they presented for translation. The clarifying questions are not only: "For which purpose do you need the translation?", but also: "Where does that text come from?"

[73] Risku (1998:85) writes that a translator for instance could "translate a socio-critical novel who's intention is not understandable for the target society, or which would not be ethically acceptable for the translation, as a kind of neutral report about a strange society". We think that this is pure ideology and not helpful. If such a text in reality would actually be translated, a corresponding note in the foreword would do it as well.

should translate it as faithfully as possible (or not at all), in order to enable target readers to criticize it too, themselves. One might eventually write one's personal opinion in a foreword or, better, a postscript, but the translation as such is not an instance of just changing that text into a more acceptable form.[74]

This observation stands in clear contrast to opinions within feminist translation studies, where it has been argued that women should take the right to change texts into a more acceptable form.[75] This is a political and ideological stance, but it cannot be part of a theory of translation.

That broadly accepted conviction finds theoretical backing in Steiner's (1975) mimetic language theory. Steiner is interested – not so much in preserving meaning in a translation but – in creatively unveiling that meaning at certain points in a dynamic concept of evolution. He describes understanding in a subjectivist manner with rather violent terms:[76]

> His [sc. the translator's] "hermeneutic motion" on a first level starts with an "initiative trust that will ordinarily be instantaneous" and open for the "the 'other' as yet untried, unmapped alterity of statement" (ibid. 269).- For Robinson (1998:97) "the translator who stops at this stage produces painfully literal renditions: the SL words in their original sequencing are too wonderful to force into TL habitats".- Second: In confronting the text the "manœuvre of comprehension [becomes] explicitly invasive and exhaustive, leaving the shell smashed and the vital layers stripped" (ibid. 298). "The translator invades, extracts, and brings home" (ibid). The third level is "incorporative, in the strong sense of the word embodiment. [...We] come to incarnate alternative energies and resources of feeling" (ibid. 299) by a "complete domestication, an at-homeness" of the translation (ibid. 298).- For Robinson (1998:98) "The translator who stops at this stage (since it is difficult to stop at the second, without bringing anything back), produces assimilative translations so thoroughly conformed to TL norms as to bear no trace of their origins in the SL".- The forth level leads to a balancing: "The aprioristic movement of trust puts us off balance. We 'lean towards' the confronting text [...] The system is now off-tilt. The hermeneutic act must

---

[74] In the case of translating, for instance, an historical text which perhaps once had a dangerous ideological impact, the translation will have to be very precise in order to show these effects.

[75] For references see Wolf 2005, Prunč 2007, Arrojo 1994.

[76] As a representative of the hermeneutical approach to translation, Paepcke uses similar terms: Der Originaltext wird „aufgesprengt, umgestellt und in fortgesetzt neue Konstellationen gebracht" (Paepcke 1986:108) (= The original text is being forced open, rearranged and put into permanently new constellations).

compensate. If it is to be authentic, it must mediate into exchange and restored parity" (ibid. 300). - Steiner sees a permanent "inflationary hermeneutic process" (ibid. 319), based on the human "compulsion to otherness" (ibid. 236). He sees every translation as adding and extending the meaning, thus constituting an interpretation. Literary translation, for Steiner, is an artistic act wherein the literary tradition generates new ideas and groups of readers.

Steiner's concept opposes our idea of translation as an attempt to faithfully represent a message understood from a text. His stance is also unclear, as he first speaks about the act of comprehension, but soon switches to the description of the effects of translations, "generating new ideas". His "inflationary hermeneutic process" reminds us of the multiple retranslations already discussed. Mixing up prospective and descriptive aspects of translation is theoretically weak. But his work gave rise to much research on creativity in translation.

Steiner sees himself as a representative of the hermeneutical translation. But his aggressive impression of the "invasive manoeuvre of comprehension" has nothing to do with hermeneutical understanding, because a text is not scattered and destroyed when somebody receives meaning from it. It remains there for further understanding by other persons. Robinson (1998:98) states in view of Steiner: "The translator has invaded the SL and stolen some of its property; now s/he makes restitution by rendering the SL text into a TL that is balanced between the divergent pulls of the SL and TL cultural contexts". But texts are no "silent object" (Wilss 1996:9) or dead material for the translator to extract the message they carry. Nonetheless, Steiner's imagery had an aftermath in the later discussion of translations as a "power struggle for meaning".

> Carbonell (2002:238) calls "to relate to the culture into which the translated text will be integrated, the culture that finally has given space for the publication of a foreign text expressed by the language and experience of a translator." (...) "The meaning is captured and abducted into unknown terrain" (ibid. 235).

In an approach of this kind, the polysystem of a culture is mistaken for the individual text approach by a translator who never, though, is merely the representative of "a culture" and its (colonial) strive for power, and understanding texts is not the same as the subjugation of peoples (cf. Brenner 1998:161). We should distinguish whether we are talking of acting persons such as translators, or of the reaction of a literary polysystem in the target culture.[77]

The good translator is the "faithful" one, not the one with the politically correct conviction, or the one presenting a subjective interpretation. What readers today expect is an authentic translation in the sense of reconstructing the author's ideas, but abstaining from mixing one's own preferences with the reading of the text. Accepting and faithfully presenting foreign ideas is more difficult than just to tell one's own opinions.

## 4.5 Manipulating translations?

Another idea of subjectivity and its supposedly inevitable obstacle for true understanding and translation is advocated by the supporters of the "manipulation school" within Descriptive Translation Studies. There is the opinion that any translation is manipulation, deviation, betrayal per se (*traduttore traditore; les belles infidèles*). The subject of research, here, are manifestations and possible extralingual ideological reasons for observable textual shifts (in the interlingual transfer paradigm). In Hermans (1985:11) we read: "All translation implies a degree of manipulation of the source text for a certain purpose", and Lefevere (1992:13) says: "Rewriters have to be traitors, but most of the time they do not know it, and nearly all of the time they have no other choice." This view – gained from the descriptive analysis of old translations – is epistemologically problematic if no other opinion is admitted anymore.

Venuti (1995:93) states that translations are characterized by "asymmetrical relations" and that, being "fundamentally ethnocentric", there could never be a communication among equals. Correcting this by an express foreignizing strategy is seen as the "ethical" act by translators in some post-modern approaches.[78] Such an observation might be true when looking back at some naïve translations from colonial times, but it is an effect of the translators' inability to do their job.

---

[77] See also Goethe: „Die Gewalt einer Sprache ist nicht, daß sie das Fremde abweist, sondern daß sie es verschlingt" (*Maximen und Reflexionen*, 979; cited from Paepcke 1981:121). The talk is of the polysystem of a language, not of a person trying to assume the strange.

[78] See for instance Arrojo (1997), Shing-yue (2002), Bassnett & Trivedi (1998), Tymoczko (2006), a. o.

The apodictic argument of manipulation obscures the fact that translators, with goodwill of course, can be able to grasp and represent the sense of a foreign original. That has ever been their goal, that is the social motivation of translating, and it is not proven that it were impossible. It requires competence, self-criticism and openness. Therefore, actual "manipulations" empirically observed in comparison at any structural level cannot simply be turned, in a logical reversal, into a theory of translation. Structural observation does not detect "general rules" of translating but only some mistakes by individual translators. An old misconception of taking the text structure already for its content is outed here:

> Translation is a process by which the chain of signifiers that constitutes the source-language text is replaced by a chain of signifiers in the target language, which the translator provides on the strength of an interpretation. (Venuti 1995:17).

It is of course true that the linguistic form of the text is transformed in translation, but this may also be done in the service of a better and more authentic presentation of the message, an idea that E. Nida already advocated with his "dynamic equivalence" (Nida 1964:159).

It's not illegitimate for a translator to try to "understand" the strange in a foreign culture and to convey it. We are not "translating cultures", and there is no cultural transfer.[79] The point is, rather, to get oneself acquainted with divergent world views and to cope with alterity. And then it should be possible to talk about this self-experienced knowledge, but in one's own target language words. We need not "promoting activist translation practices" (Tymoczko 2006) in a way over-alienating what is already alien to us. What is true for strange cultural systems is also true for records from the past (Eco 2006:191). Translation is a service to enable communication.

The point is to become aware that something is strange, to accept and sustain otherness, to see the own differences and to prepare for learning. Tymoczko's approach is the application of Venuti's far-echoed claim:

---

[79] The talk about „constructing cultures" by translation (see Bassnett & Lefevere 1998) comes from a descriptive view: The image of cultures is easily shaped by the way their texts have been translated. However, this is an effect which cannot be controlled by the working translator himself. In the creation of stereotypes there are many other factors active as well. It is always tempting but inadequate to raise any descriptive observation into a theory of translation.

> I want to suggest that insofar as foreignizing translation seeks to restrain the ethnocentric violence of translation it is highly desirable today, a strategic cultural intervention in the current state of world affairs, pitched against the hegemonic English-language nations and the unequal cultural exchanges in which they engage their global others. Foreignizing translation in English can be a form of distance against ethnocentrism and racism, cultural narcissism and imperialism, in the interest of democratic geopolitical relations. (Venuti 1994:20)

This meanwhile popular distinction between "domesticating" or "foreignizing" translations goes back to a misinterpretation of Schleiermacher who in 1813 had stated two "methods of translating" (Schleiermacher 1977). There is an English translation of his article (Lefevere 1977:66-89), where the decisive passage reads as follows:

> But what of the genuine translator, who wants to bring these two completely separated persons, his author and his reader truly together, and who would like to bring the latter to an understanding and enjoyment of the former as correct and complete as possible without inviting him to leave the sphere of his mother tongue – what roads are open to him? In my opinion <u>there are only two. Either the translator leaves the author in peace, as much as possible, and moves the reader towards him; or leaves the reader in peace, as much as possible, and moves the author towards him.</u> The two roads are so completely separate from each other that one or the other must be followed as closely as possible, and that a highly unreliable result would proceed from any mixture [...] <u>The translator tries to communicate to the readers the same image, the same impression he himself has gained</u> – through his knowledge of the original language – of the work as it stands, and in doing so he tries to move the readers towards his point of view, which is essentially foreign to them.
>
> But if the translation wants to let its Roman author, for instance, speak the way he would have spoken to Germans if he had been German, it does not merely move the author to where the translator stands, because to him he does not speak German, but Latin, rather it <u>drags him directly into the world of the German readers and transforms him into their equal</u> – and that, precisely, is the other case. (Schleiermacher 1977:74, *my underlining*).

Venuti only cites four lines from that text and over-interprets them in an aggressive way:

> Admitting (with qualifications like „as much as possible") that translation can never be completely adequate to the foreign text, Schleiermacher allowed the translator to choose between a <u>domesticating</u> method, an <u>ethnocentric reduction</u> of the foreign text to target language cultural values, bringing the author back home, and a <u>foreignizing</u> method, a <u>ethnodeviant pressure</u> on those values to register the linguistic and cultural difference of the foreign text, sending the reader abroad. (Venuti 1995:20)

M. Snell-Hornby (2004:337) has clearly explained that terms like "ethnocentric reduction" and "ethnodeviant pressure" are not recognizable semantically in Schleiermacher's text, being a feature of the language of a 20th-century American scholar. She also points out that Lefevere's translation with its formulation "rather it *drags* him directly into the world of Germans and transforms him into their equal" instead of "places him within the world of the readers and transforms him into one of his own kind" (what would be more precise) could have been an impulse to this kind of violation of the original text in a translation by Venuti. Whereas Schleiermacher spoke of dealing with content, Venuti thinks of target cultural norms.

It is striking, after all, to see how little there is mentioning, in so many contributions to Translation Studies, of content, of semantics, of a message to be conveyed. And precisely this is the central point of interest in hermeneutical translation.

A theory of human translation work would have to define its subject as a motivated, dynamic process that is performed in languages where the translator has a share in both and, here, an interlinking between theory and practice is indispensable. We should not forget that "ideas without a concrete content are sterile, but practical opinions without a concept are blind" (Kant).[80] Theory should envisage practice, and practice should be aware of theory. Then the latter might appear as a reflected practice in terms of motivating it, and as a systematic setting and foundation of such practice. One will ask how a translation is developed, against the backdrop of the translator's familiar experience and the foreign world of languages, cultures and scientific disciplines, and how a translation competence could evolve. This is now described in detail in the following chapters.

---

[80] I. Kant: „Gedanken ohne konkreten Inhalt sind leer, Anschauungen ohne Begriffe aber blind." – This much cited phrase is also read as: „Praxis ohne Theorie ist Leerlauf, Theorie ohne Praxis blind." (Practice without theory is ineffective, theory without practice is blind.)

# 5 Hermeneutical orientation in the world of texts

## 5.1 The situative background

The hermeneutical approach is an outlook for "what the text is saying", it is content-oriented with semantic and stylistic questions being more important than syntax, grammar or pragmatics. The responsible translator will activate a kind of "reflected subjectivity" in grounded understanding, in the sense of an individual approach following general lines of orientation. These will be described below as "categories of attention" in translational reading.

The translator will pose questions to the text and they will get an answer, just like in a dialogue with others. These questions regarding the text are not sufficiently answered by means of the famous Lasswell-formula: "Who says what with which means when and how?" Often in TS this was presented as a relevant text analysis (Nord 1991:42), but it would only render what I can know if I read the text in an early interpretive understanding. And accordingly, the Lasswell-formula[81] was an instruction for reporters and journalists on how to present messages in newspapers to be grasped easily. It does not focus on the translational relevant points.

We see a vertical model of human action in embodiment, using reference lines for orientation. Relevant results from empirical research, if so found, may fruitfully be employed (Hansen 2006).[82] The translator needs a "cognitive landscape" in order to see where to go.

---

[81] Originally, this formula containing five w-questions (*who, what, when, where, why*) has been created by the American political scientist Harold D. Lasswell in 1948 within the surge of mass communication. It applies to the lead principle of journalist articles: the most important part of the news shall appear first, so that texts can be abbreviated from their end.

[82] Often it is thought that bilinguals were better translators. This is not true, they are worse. The problem is that they have lost their subjective standpoint within one mother tongue, from where one would see the world and acquire any foreign language. Studies have shown that bilinguals, even if speaking and writing independently with excellence in both languages, were rather bad in translating. Suddenly, they mixed up rules or became uncertain fearing mistakes (Hansen 2006:163).

Hönig and Kußmaul (1982) in their textbook *Strategie der Übersetzung* (The strategy of translation) state rightly: „The embedding situation potentially influences the text's language on all levels" (1982:70) (*my translation*). But instead of explaining how this fact is dealt with in translations, they just enumerate the so-called "factors", such as social relationship, familiarity among speakers, geographical origin and social class, sex and number of speakers, kind of medium and field of usage". This factorial description is of no use if not really tackled with by a translator in his or her hermeneutical outlook. As usual the perspective of translation scholars views the external factors, and not the translator as a person with her questions.

The initial step will be an expert "positioning" of the text within its situation, and this may then activate the translator's knowledge base regarding any cultural characteristics and features of specialist communication that may show up on the text level. In this sense the famous Lasswell-formula has been adequately extended by Wilss (1996:125) to point the translational reader's interest to the background of the text.[83] However, this background is not emerging from the text's surface level (even if I ask for it), it has to be either known beforehand, or it will emerge from extra-textual integrative information.[84] One might justly ask the question of how far history, the major frame in which a human life is spent and by which it is shaped, is responsible for the expressive choices, and even for the topics about which literary writers poured their creative production. And

---

[83] This formula was first introduced by Hönig (1986), Nord (1991:42) and others as a starting point for the "translational text analysis". It answers questions also answered by simply reading the text. The formula, as was proposed by Wilss (1996:125) in more detail, reads:
"Who says something?
What is the sender talking about?
Who is the addressee of what the sender says?
What is the sender's communicative purpose?
What is the spatio-temporal setting of the communication?
Which are the linguistic means that the sender employs to get the indeed meaning across?
Katharina Reiss has expanded the formula by adding another question: What does the sender not say in view of implicitly shared knowledge between himself and the addressee?"

[84] Advocates of literary translation often say that a translator should have read all the books the author read himself. As this ideal, of course, is not possible, one will observe the cultural background of the epoch.

what is the scientific domain wherein specialist communication is taking place when we translate.

The translator might start with considering the SITUATIVE BACKGROUND of the given text assignment, that means first doing research into to the text's embedding context, even before looking at the linguistic structure of it. Where does that text come from? What do I know about that culture or domain? There must be extra-textual information on the culture of origin, the time of origination of that text, the author, the place of publication, etc. The respective findings will decisively guide any further translational decisions, as the translator now – in a grounded pre-understanding – will focus on the adequate meaning of signs right from the beginning. The hermeneutical circle is a different one, whether we have to translate a children's book or an instruction manual, a report for the radio or a legal document, or a classic novel (the professional translator is often confronted with so many different tasks). This is apt to enlighten the text's beginning, which at first sight appeared vague. Redundancy in texts towards their end is a well-known feature from text linguistics.

This SITUATIVE BACKGROUND must be known before beginning the translation work. The translator will have to orient him or herself in order to become aware of what is part of his/her own familiar world and what is foreign, either in terms of a strange culture or of a scientific domain of specialist knowledge where he or she is not specializing in. Cultural elements are mirrored on the text level. Nida (1945:68ff) has proposed a valuable classification of "types of cultural problems in determining semantic equivalence":

## 5.2 Features of ecological and material culture

Ecological diversity may be extreme among territories, and it is often not anticipated. This is a special difficulty in Bible translation, but also in literature in general.

> For example, in Yucatan, Mexico, practically no correspondence can be found to the four seasons we know in the temperate zones. It is often difficult in tropical countries to render the word *desert* as a place which has sparse vegetation (Nida 1945:69). It is inconceivable to a Maya Indian that any place would not have vegetation, unless it had been cleared for a maize field, and a cleared field is not the cultural equivalent of the desert in Palestine. Ac-

cordingly, one must translate *desert* as an 'abandoned place', for culturally the two places are similar in that they both lack human population. – The Australian *bush* or the Japanese *love hotel* or features of *Swiss snow* are difficult to translate without explanation. But explanation is easy when one has seen it.

Sometimes translators try to preserve the foreign word and integrate it as a borrowed lexeme into the target language, but this is not always well understood. Almost the reverse type of tendency, but equally unguided, is found in the insistence of some translators upon 'preserving' the target local language 'clean' and looking at all borrowed words as some type of contamination.

> In one of the Indian languages in Latin America, a translator went so far as to translate *ass* as a 'small long-eared animal', even though the people of the particular tribe were well acquainted with the burros and used the Spanish name *burro*. (Nida 1945:69)

Features of material culture often are even more complex than the ecological ones. On the other hand, there are many items of close equivalence, for instance between the Palestinian culture of Bible times and the cultures of many of the so-called 'undeveloped' peoples today. The *ox goad,* the *millstone,* and the *stone water jar* have equivalents for translation there.

> But there are also various differences, for instance processes and plants of agriculture. In those parts of the world where the *dibble stick* is used for planting, e.g. rice, the biblical illustration of the sower who scattered seeds on various types of ground seems incredible. It needs much explanation to convince the Indian that the sower in the famous parable was not out of his mind. (Nida 1945:70)

> Also, the villages of most aboriginal people are quite different from the walled cities of ancient times, and they have no *gates.* So what to do with a respective text passage? The phrase 'give us our daily bread' is incomprehensible for Eskimos who only know fish for their nutrition. And there are thousands of other similar examples. (ibid. 70)

### 5.2.1 Features of social and religious culture

The social organization is often different. This is also relevant for novel translations.

> For example, in the Maya language there is no term for *brother* and *sister* as such, but one must designate whether the person is an older or younger brother or sister. Often in the biblical account there is no specific indication as to the age relationship. The only clue we have in Hebrew or Greek is that the elder's brother or sister's name normally occurs before the younger one's. (Nida 1945:71)

The social implications of actions described in the Bible are a subject of interest.

> When the Totonac people read about *a man carrying a jar of water* (Mark 14.13; Luke 22.10), they are tremendously amused. It seems very silly to the women to think of a man doing women's work, and the men are astonished at the men's ignorance of propriety. (ibid. 72)

> If there happens to be a society that considered the Jewish custom of circumcision at a male infant as a cruel act to a baby, the story in Luke 1:59 might cause objection. In such a case the translator might perhaps write something like "the time came for presenting the child in public" or the like.

It is decisive for an adequate understanding by the reader to dispose of certain contents of memory regarding the foreign sociology.

> Example: *"We are living at the left side of the highway."* This sentence heard in Germany might be a neutral indication of the residence. In South Africa, however, it could also be a reference to the social class when uttered e.g. by a colored person. Until the end of apartheid, the different races had been forced by law to live in separate housing areas. A translator who has never heard of the Group Areas Act might have difficulties to understand.

> Eco (2006:198) has the example of words in a different cultural background, saying that "coffee" is not translatable since it means different things in Italy and in the U.S.A.: "Consider these two sentences, one from an Italian novel, the other from an American one: 'Ordinai un caffè, lo buttai giù in un secondo ed uscii dal bar' (literally, 'I ordered a coffee, swilled it down in a second and went out of the bar'); and 'He spent half an hour with the cup in his hands, sipping his coffee and thinking of Mary'." However, this sentence in a whole text of which we know the situation is easily translatable. The Italian *caffè* is in German „ein Espresso" and the American *coffee* is „eine Kaffeetasse" or „ein Becher Kaffee".

We have to leave the word level of false friends and get to the scenes. This shows the explanatory potential of Fillmore's Scenes-and-frames-theory (1976), and the hermeneutical theory says we have to look through language into the world. Translation concerns possible worlds, not language contrasts.

In matters of religious culture, the problems of translation are often the most perplexing ones. The names for "deity" are a continued difficulty.

> The indigenous term may have a connotative significance which makes it awkward to use. On the other hand, a foreign word often implies an alien God. And even more difficult are the words for *sanctity* and *holiness* (Nida 1945:72). One translator in Africa attempted to construct an expression for holy Spirit. He rather naïvely asked for indigenous expressions

for 'holy' and then for 'spirit' and combined the two words into the title for deity. The first word had the basic meaning of 'taboo', and this was usually produced by contact with an evil spirit. And most spirits were negative, so people could not understand how a good god could have such a spirit (ibid.:73) These are only a few of various examples encountered in translation practice, mainly in the past times.

Nida states righty: "Languages are basically a part of culture, and words cannot be understood correctly apart from the local cultural phenomena for which they are symbols. This being the case, the most fruitful approach to the semantic problems is the ethnological one. This involves investigating the significance of various cultural items and the words which are used to designate them. A combination of analytical social anthropology and descriptive linguistics provides the key to the study of semantics" (Nida 1945:78). Knowledge about cultural features is stored in the reader's memory, and it is fruitful to recommend that translators travel a lot to get to know foreign countries and cultures, as the influence of places and the climate as well as history are decisive for the creation of cultural concepts (Born 1996:14).

Often the role of the necessary pre-knowledge for the hermeneutical circle is not seen. Fleischmann (1997:409) points out to the „problems of the interpretation and representation of sacral objects and names in the history of art" (*my translation*), the ignorance of which affects the understanding of the text. Vermeer (1978:102) for instance speaks of „Jakobsstraße" meaning a Medieval pilgrim way towards Santiago de Compostela in Spain, which however to German Christians of all denominations is known as the *Jakobsweg*. Such problems appear not only in religious texts to be translated, but in many literary texts.

### 5.2.2 Communication for specific purposes

The SITUATIVE BACKGROUND of a text is equally relevant for specialist translation where it concerns the respective domain of science. The sciences as specialized communication systems reach out beyond cultures and are identical all over the globalized world, but seen from the outside, they are as strange for the translator as any alien cultural system. Disciplines are created by such specialist communication. There are no "scientific features" in objects, but it is the scientist/scholar talking about that object from his/her perspective who creates the science (Kalverkämper 1998:32).[85]

The establishment of the relevant cognitive environment in the domain will mentally exclude all other possible linguistic meanings, and eventually lead to an adequate understanding of the terms in the text, avoiding naivety. If the translator finds that he or she does not dispose of sufficient specialist knowledge, e.g. in medicine for translating a medical text and be it only a simple "medical certificate" in everyday document translation, then first research has to be done, before the translation work can proceed any further (Hönig 1995:88). Mere linguistic text analysis will not be helpful.

Extra-textual information about the author and the time and medium of publication also is necessary to determine whether we are confronted with state-of-the-art technology, or rather with some historic findings. Multimedia texts mostly belong to specialist communication as well, as their contents mainly refer to a professional environment, like in science and technology, politics, economy, sports or others.

### 5.2.3 Problems of legal texts

The SITUATIVE BACKGROUND of a legal text is decisive. Legal concepts as regulators of the living-together of a people have been developed out of the regional tradition. The main problem in legal translation is the underlying difference between the case law in Anglo-American societies, and the Civil Law based on the Roman constitution in European continental societies (Šarčević 1988:38), as well as other local law traditions. It is of no use to keep the foreign term untranslated within the target text.

In a hermeneutical positioning of the text to be translated within its jurisprudential domain, one will at first determine the number of legal systems involved, and we may distinguish three main cases of legal translation (Kjaer 1999:65):

---

[85] *Example:* What is an "apple" in the eyes of a farmer, a hungry school child, a biochemist, a trade official, a cargo driver, a baker, a theologian? – What is the difference of an antenna mast for users of mobile phones, radio listeners, researchers wanting to minimize costs, or for neighbours fearing maximum radiation exposure?

Translation within the framework of one national bilingual or multilingual law system, e.g. Switzerland, South Tyrol, Finland, Belgium, Luxemburg, and Canada;

Translation of texts from an international or supranational law, e.g. international conventions or European directives;

Translation of texts based within one national law system into another language for purposes of legal transaction, e.g. an American divorce decree or a licence agreement into the German language for practical use. All these cases of translation pose different problems.

The law is always rooted in the cultural background, and this becomes most virulent in confronting legal systems (Pommer 2006). As the basic approach to jurisdiction – either following the precedents or observing the legal codes – is completely different, respective texts may be considered as "untranslatable" to some extent.

> A German *Eheschließung* and a British *marriage* and an Italian *matrimonio* are linked by their common sociological meaning of "marrying", but these concepts are not the same as there are different legal provisions regarding this civil contract, according to the local legislation.[86] The names of national institutions constitute a similar difficulty, as a translational transfer of such an entity into a target system is inadmissible, because this would delude the reader into thinking of a false equivalence. Only a literal translation of such designations is adequate, in order to indicate the difference.

Nonetheless, such texts have to be translated when somebody wants to establish a right in another country, or when international bilateral or multilateral agreements are reached. Translators should be able to consciously evaluate their translation practice as a routine, subconscious mental activity. The necessary strategic meta-knowledge is stored in their memory.

We claim that translators are indeed capable of performing this evaluation by changing from automatic routine to conscious problem-solving. They do so by mentally locating themselves on a higher level, in a kind of reflected subjectivity, where they have meta-knowledge at their disposal as the necessary problem awareness for evaluating their translation behavior. Weak translations typically result from a translation practice consisting only in practical skills and which

---

[86] See for instance the celebration by an officiating civil registrar, and/or church pastor, or any other official; there are differences regarding spouse's maintenance, years of separation required for divorce, etc. (Eco 2006:40)

therefore lacks any super-ordinate distance to itself (Zelinsky-Wibbelt 2003:202).

## 5.3 The discourse field

Translation has been defined as an "intercultural transfer" (Vermeer 1986:30), but what is "a culture"? The cultures are no homogeneous entities, they are composed of various sociolects within various fields of social discourse, they are a dia-cultural system. Every field of communication has its specific concepts and these recur in the texts.

There are various dia-cultures within one cultural system. There are special groups of scientists, housewives, church people, political parties, translation teachers, staff in the European and international institutions, medical doctors, business men, engineers, soccer players, journalists, etc., all rooted in their own "native" culture, and at the same time producing texts in communication for specific purposes. People can adopt several roles, thus having cognitive access to various dia-cultures in their system. They are active in various DISCOURSE FIELDS.

### 5.3.1 The place of ideology

An idio-culture is the culture of one specific person, the habitus, always placed within a dia-culture as well, even if unconsciously. Individual differentiations within the common dia-culture are possible, as everybody also wants to keep something for himself in interacting with others. The dia-cultural way of speaking is mirrored in the texts. Special social groups, e.g. feminists, or left-wing activists, or business people, will use a specific selection from the potential of their language, based on their ideology.

Hence, biographical data on the author are important, in order to know who this author is. In their DISCOURSE FIELDS, speakers sometimes are closer to foreigners than to their own fellow nationals. A message circulating among people has its motivational background, it answers certain social or technical questions, and that is what translators try to discover. Translators' special expert competence is their access to a variety of specializations as dia-cultures, not only to the one an author has in his own field of work. For translating specialist texts, the differences in the domains of sciences or humanities are decisive (see the earlier described difference between research methods in an empirical science or a liberal arts paradigm). Without a respective pre-knowledge in addressing such texts, an adequate translation will be impossible.

The ideological or the professional background of the text determine the relevant DISCOURSE FIELD where the author is at home. The focus, now, is on the author's social setting and the field of communication, on the questions of the époque or scientific research (old or new), which are being answered in the text. This again will give us hints about the author's ideology, possibly reflecting in his text to be translated.[87] Grounded understanding will help that certain problems of misinterpretation might not even arise in translational reading.

### 5.3.2 Domain-specific communication

In LSP translation, the special discipline as a DISCOURSE FIELD within a general domain requires specific knowledge. The level of communication (expert/lay) in a particular discipline will reflect in various text structures. Internal specialist communication among scientists on the same level in a domain is different from communication between scientists or scholars and lay people in that domain, or in other fields.

Recognizing a respective DISCOURSE FIELD in the source text will help to establish a corresponding DISCOURSE FIELD for the translation, and to observe the required functional style, provided that the translation commission does not request other. The translator's attention is not directed towards grammar structures (such as relative sentence orders or attributive constructions or particles, etc.), but more generally on the style in the linguistic formulation of a text type. Style is dependent on the formulation requirements in the respective DISCOURSE FIELD. At this point the translator can make use of knowledge produced by linguistic analysis of LSP: We distinguish a. o. between scientific, laboratory and sales communication in a domain (Stolze 1999:24f), and differences in the information presentation according to the social relationship (equal standing or teacher

---

[87] Understanding will be favoured if the translator knows, for example, that the author of a novel is rooted in feminist thinking, or that the author of a political text is a representative of a socialist party, or that the text given is a legal sentence and not a contract, and so on.

to student) in communication have been analyzed (Baumann 1992:34f). However, there is one difficulty: Results of linguistic research in LSP mostly are not found with a view to translation, but from a general linguistic perspective. It is the task of translation teaching to gather and sort out the numerous individual results from the scholarly literature, and to adopt them for the purposes of translation.

Focusing on the DISCOURSE FIELD of legal texts, for instance, there is the field of the domain, e.g. criminal, civil, works, international, trade law and others, and the problem of the confrontation of two different legal systems in translation, as mentioned. Not seldom it is rather difficult for the translator to establish the relevant DISCOURSE FIELD in advance as a subfield of the situative background. But there is another hermeneutical effect: As Iser (1978:22) has stated, the reader's acts of comprehension are guided by textual construction. These insights from the aesthetic reception theory are not only valid for literary texts, but for technical texts as well.

Those texts refer to a special scientific or legal system of thought that constitutes their background. Kalverkämper (1983:155) points out that technical terms can never be analyzed independently from their extra-textual context as a DISCOURSE FIELD. Many aspects remain implicit, and the text as such contains gaps of meaning. These gaps have to be filled cognitively by the reader, and this is often easily possible with a view to the whole text within its discipline, concerning the DISCOURSE FIELD. It is a well-known observation, that texts have more redundancy towards their end. That means, if we read the entire text to be translated (even if it takes time), many questions raised at the beginning will have been answered on the way, by the text itself. There is no need for a laborious analysis of some "difficult" terms in it when their explanation is given three passages later.[88] And this effect is even valid beyond the text border.

---

[88] Kußmaul (2000:23f) discusses the translation shifts in the English/German language pair, stating: "Gradually stronger modifications will result if words are replaced by such words that at first sight have a different meaning" (*my translation*). He discusses the translation of the syntagma *new products and processes* in an economic text in the field of microelectronic industry, stressing that it might be difficult for the readers to know what kind of "processes" are meant here. However, from the observation that this is an economic text it will become clear which processes are being discussed implicitly.

*Example*: A professional translator might have to translate a short certificate saying that the person frequented a course in "fashion and cut". At first view one might infer the scene of model designing. Then there is a second certificate with the subjects taught and marks obtained in the examination, and there we read something about "hair dressing". Now it is clear what the respective discourse field is, and we can responsibly translate the text, even if the words as such might not be changed. The translator does not need to transfer his own lack of specialist knowledge at the possible readers by trying to explicate this in the respective text or by footnotes.

## 5.4   The meaning dimension

Every discourse field has its particular MEANING DIMENSION and this, according to cognitive linguistics (Verspoor et al. 2008:21) recurs in the texts, reflecting in cultural associations, specific metaphors, key words, image schemas, and terminology to be found in a text. That is why semantics is more important than syntactics for translation. The title or opening of a text is a clue for understanding, it sets the general theme. In translational reading, one will now focus on the text structure itself – after having checked the situative background and discourse field and read the whole –, taking into consideration particularly the semantic aspects. Regarding language learning, it has been stated:

> One of the potentially most serious problems for translators involves differences in the structure of conceptual categories and differences between SL and TL prototypical category members. Prototypes of even most frequent concepts can be different in different languages. [...] Connected with the problem of language-specific prototypes are non-equivalent ranges of inferences that are acceptable in texts written in these languages and possible conceptual/inferential mismatches between SL and TL texts. (Lewandowska-Tomaszczyk 2004:140)

The translator needs metalinguistic awareness of this problem of varying concepts. Only in conscious deviation from the familiar reader's perspective, will there also appear different phenomena to be processed cognitively, so that "non-equivalent ranges of inferences" become salient.[89] And this is exactly what

---

[89]   Based on traditional contrastive linguistics, Lewandowska-Tomaszczyk (2004:141f) describes some "cross-linguistic problem areas", such as "displacement of senses, multisemy, phrasal grammar and discontinuous syntax, derivational patterns, collocations". These problems are more prevalent in language acquisition than in translation, since the translator with a holistic approach may solve these problems on a higher level of discourse field, beyond the linguistic equivalence. Lewandowska-Tomaszczyk (ibid., 143)

translators do when they have to translate texts reaching out beyond their own personal worlds.

The MEANING DIMENSION with its key words is indicated by the title and subtitles as well as the very beginning of the text, as Schleiermacher already has pointed out. It is astonishing to see that in many reading tests (carried out by myself) the readers simply ignored the title and then had difficulties to get the semantic focus of the theme.

### 5.4.1 Key words

Key words within the MEANING DIMENSION of the discourse field in a culture may be recognized holistically on the overall text level, by means of searching for a certain isotopic semantic network of significant appearance, where concepts appear surrounded by neighboring synonyms and in repetition of the same words. Cultural meanings and metaphors representing stereotypes are relevant here, as particular sociological groups tend to use a particular selection of words from the lexicon, and this reflects the author's ideology in correspondence with his/her group. The linguistic meaning of a word may be specifically shaped by the relevant DISCOURSE FIELD, and even by the particular idio-culture if discernable.

What we understand in reading has its ground in the text structure. "Every text has a theme or topic. Regarding the text semantics, this means that the lexemes therein do not come from just any region of the vocabulary, but that they already belong to certain groupings. One might call this word nets, and they constitute the text's conceptual meaning" (*my translation*) (Weinrich 1976:14). The word groupings (*Wortfelder*) comprise words sharing a common conceptual feature what constitutes an isotopy, a semantic web. Semantics assumes that the meaning of lexemes, the concept, is built up of various semes as sense carrying particles. Recurrent semes are the basis for synonyms and paradigmatic relationships between words. Prototype semantics (Kleiber 1993; Wierzbicka 1996) has

---

calls for the "development of pattern matching", we would rather subscribe that "the translator has to invest some effort to liberate himself from the SL system and in fact, defeat the routinized lexical, phrasal, syntactic, discursive SL-TL equivalents not to let himself in a false-friend trap" (ibid., 145). This may be achieved by viewing the text as a holistic semantic entity.

stated, that most words, except for exact scientific terms, have a core meaning and fuzzy edges, so that they are flexible to a certain extent in their usage.

Isotopic chains are being created by the recurrence of a key word or thematic lexeme in its complements. It is plausible that meaning in texts is mainly constituted by semes found in several lexemes of the semantic web all over the text. As titles have the function of informing about the subsequent information in a text, they also will evoke associations which then are being realized by a corresponding semantic network in that text.

> There is a very impressive example for this effect found in Snell-Hornby (1988:71). She presents a text from Somerset Maugham written in 1921. The theme of the European in alien surroundings and his emotional disintegration in the heady world of the tropics is a familiar one in Maugham's works. Snell-Hornby writes: "In the 1920s, when the British Empire was still flourishing, such far-off tropical zones had a meaning for the educated English reader even outside his personal experience. Hence the title is not merely a geographical name, but is used to evoke associations in the reader's mind" (ibid. 70).

### THE PACIFIC

> The Pacific[1] is inconstant[2] and uncertain,[2] like the soul of man[2]. Sometimes it is grey like the English Channel[3] off Beachy Head,[3] with a heavy swell,[1] and sometimes it is rough,[1] capped with white crests, and boisterous.[2] It is not so often that it is calm[1] and blue. Then, indeed, the blue is arrogant.[2] The sun shines fiercely[2] from an unclouded sky. The trade wind gets into your blood and you are filled with an impatience for the unknown. The billows, magnificently rolling,[1] stretch widely on all sides of you, and you forget your vanished youth,[2] with its memories,[2] cruel and sweet, in a restless, intolerable desire for life.[2] On such a sea as this[1] Ulysses sailed when he sought the Happy Isles. // But there are days also when the Pacific[1] is like a lake[1]. The sea[1] is flat and shining. (…) You sail through an unimaginable silence[2] upon a magic sea.[1] Now and then a few gulls[3] suggest that land is not far off, a forgotten island[3] hidden in a wilderness of waters;[1] but the gulls,[3] the melancholy[2] gulls, are the only sign you have of it. You see never a tramp,[3] with its friendly[2] smoke,[3] no stately[2] bark[3] or trim[2] schooner,[3] not a fishing boat[3] even: it is an empty desert,[1] and presently the emptiness[1] fills you with a vague foreboding.[2]

> Snell-Hornby (1988:74) analyzes that text adequately: "The title 'The Pacific' is immediately taken up as the theme of the first sentence, which itself acts as a *Leitmotiv* for the entire text: the characterization of the Pacific as 'inconstant,' motivating the comparison with 'the soul of man.' This triggers off a clear-cut *duality* in the text-structure, marked by adjectives (*inconstant, arrogant*) which normally indicate human characteristics, but are used here to refer to the Pacific Ocean. A further important perspective is added by the *in-*

*clusion of the reader* in the text, who is repeatedly addressed as *you* and is himself implicitly *characterized* as regards age (*vanished youth*), origin (one familiar with Beachy Head) and cultural background (reference to Ulysses). Thus a second duality is created in a kind of *counterpoint technique*, whereby the Pacific is linked personally to the reader." – We see three main impressionistic sketches creating scenes in the reader by means of three lexical fields, the progress of which we can trace in the text:

| sea[1] | soul of man[2] | cultural background[3] |
|---|---|---|
| Pacific | inconstant | |
| | uncertain | |
| | soul | (English Channel) |
| heavy swell | | (Beachy Head) |
| rough | | |
| capped/crests | | |
| calm | boisterous | |
| | arrogant | |
| | fiercely | |
| | impatience | |
| billows | | |
| rolling | | |
| | vanished youth | |
| | memories | |
| | restless | |
| | intolerable desire for life | |
| such a sea as this | | Happy Isles |
| Pacific | | |
| lake, sea | unimaginable silence | |
| magic sea | | few gulls |
| wilderness of waters | | |
| | | forgotten island |
| | | gulls |
| | melancholy | trump |
| | | friendly smoke |
| | | stately bark |
| | | trim schooner |
| empty desert | | fishing boat |
| emptiness | foreboding | |

The three columns on the diagram represent the lexical fields mentioned above as forming the semantic framework of the text. Noting such isotopic networks has consequences for the selection of corresponding lexemes in the target language.

The existence of a semantic web or isotopy on the text level represents the primary semantic content of that text in its MEANING DIMENSION, and thus it is a key to understanding. Isotopic structures may arouse whole scenarios (Bălăcescu & Stefanink 2006:59), a scenario being a mental representation of the overall text message that is composed of various scenes.

It is useful, therefore, to first search, when reading a text, for significant key words, distributed over the entire text. Understanding is a process of lexical inference, initiated by the visual input of written texts interacting with memorized knowledge, what leads to a "fusion of horizons". And where there is no experience-based conceptual level, it will be created in analogous projection by the "metaphorically (idealized) cognitive model" (Lakoff 1987:303).

Sometimes there are also thematic strings, i.e. a longitudinal repetition of signs or textual interrelationship over larger parts within the text as macro-contextual structures of stylistic visibility (Frank 1988:486). This is not visible at sentence-wise analysis, but may be important for text understanding.

In such a way, texts become quasi "self-explanatory" as to their content, and selective problems will disappear with a view to the whole. In order to process new thinking, as is seen necessary for grounded understanding, the translator has to lift up from the respective language structure and contemplate independently about the scene. This is often neglected by students, as numerous tests have shown.[90] Of course, the sentence-oriented versions are 'not wrong' in terms of semantics, in word equivalence, but a different form would enhance the overall text coherence.[91]

While the notion of a language game (Gadamer) can be used as a theoretical construct to understand linguistic communication, Wittgenstein's notion of family resemblances serves as a helpful conceptual tool to address the issue of the relative ease or difficulty of translating across cultural and linguistic bounda-

---

[90] See e.g. Kußmaul (2000:43) and also the corpuses discussed in Bălăcescu/Stefanink (2006).

[91] The German translation of Erich Fromm's *The Art of Loving* is very inconsequent in the use of terms, as Hesseling (1982) has shown in her translation critique. The problem is that the translator obviously translated sentence by sentence and did not focus on key words which in this case come from the conceptual world of psychology. Thus the psychological background of the whole work remains unclear and the use of "central concepts" is incoherent in the translation (Hesseling 1982:85). A different approach consciously focusing on these terms in their conceptual framework of the scholarly discourse field would have enabled more coherence in the translation.

ries (cf. Stanley 2011). When working in cross-cultural communication, we are often faced with linguistic material that is difficult to translate simply because there are no exact parallels in the culture of the target language (cf. Nida 1945). The method of looking for similar practices in the target culture – i.e., practices that are comparable due to either common historical developments or related pragmatic concerns – is given a sound theoretical foundation within the framework of language game theory. These axioms render a paradigm that is dynamic in character and underlines not only the importance of linguistic elements in the translation process, but also provides us with a theoretical matrix that can account for the relevance of pragmatic and cultural elements in the same. Humanity is a fundamental ground for mutual understanding.[92]

### 5.4.2 Terminology

In specialist texts, with their MEANING DIMENSION defined by their terminology, there is a difference in the terminological conceptualization between exact definitions with a systematic deduction in the sciences, and academic convention and interpretation of concepts in the humanities (Stolze 2003:201). This distinction between sciences and humanities is important as it has consequences in the construction of terminology. Recognition of the relevant terminology and its distinction from general language words is relevant in order to prevent naïve understanding of a specialist text.

The terminology in natural sciences serves to recognize and describe objects and facts. It contains exact terms within the framework of a terminological system, and their amount is constantly growing in the course of scientific progress. This makes terminological standardization necessary. A definition in the exact sciences is the determination, by the researcher, of the relevant characteristics of *quality, function* and *relation* of the object to be defined (Stolze 1999:33). Then the researcher looks for a new word to design this definition, and this is the scientific *term*. Terms are registered in terminological glossaries and databases, and the translator should be acquainted with the methods of terminography and term extraction. One will mainly focus on the equivalence of terminology by a

---

[92] Berger and Nord (2000:221) are doubtful about the "existence of anthropological constants through time and space" that would not be verifiable empirically.

comparison of the conceptual systems in two languages and a discussion of translation problems like polysemy or lacunae (Arntz/Picht/Mayer 2002). Instead of defining a semantic web, the translator might establish the hyperonymic terminological structure of that text including conceptual lines and oppositions.

The terminology in the humanities, social sciences and philosophy, on the contrary, is open for interpretation. It serves for the description of development processes and the interpretation of the history of life (Beiner 2009). The terminological definitions as the content of such concepts are not inferred systematically nor fixed as a terminology, they are rather agreed upon by convention among the scholars in their academic discourse. Often the concepts remain contentious. A scholar therefore will usually define his or her terms explicitly, before proceeding in the statement. Any concept and scholarly statement is only understood adequately against the backdrop of the relevant philosophy or ideological school. The debate on the "real meaning" of words or the correct use of terms never ends, and fills libraries.

> In a hierarchical model of knowledge structures (Schank 1982), high abstractness implies high flexibility of use, while specificity is bound with rigidity, but at the same time it allows numerous combinations. Recent research indicates that speakers utilize stored, specific knowledge, beside schemata, to orient themselves in domain-specific situations (Markman 1999). This is especially true for the humanities, where terminology often is not easily recognized from its mere linguistic form.

### 5.4.3 Vagueness of legal terms

Looking at the MEANING DIMENSION of a legal text, we may find that the law is part of the humanities with all terminological consequences different from those in the sciences. Law or jurisprudence as a specialist declarative knowledge would easily function with only an exclusive and fixed technical terminology, a kind of "sanitized language". Expert communication among lawyers and judges does not require general intelligibility, and for the sake of precision the law has to create its own definitions. However, legal texts – such as codes, sentences, certificates, decrees, agreements – do rule the living-together of persons in their respective country. So these texts must also appeal to general language, in order to be understood by the people.

Legal language as a specialist language has two kinds of addressees, the lawyer and the lay person. Central terms have a double coding – a specialist concept and a general meaning, but they use the same linguistic frame, as legal terms stem from general language. And on the other hand, there is also a very exact terminology in the jurisprudential theory, collected in special dictionaries. This can cause misunderstanding. Hence, it is a well-known topic that legal language is "vague" to a certain extent (Endicott 2000).[93] Uncertainty of meaning may appear on all linguistic levels, such as the word, the phrase and the text. We distinguish between *ambiguity* (double sense), *vagueness* (sense not discernable) and *contradiction* (sense inconsistent), a problem with specific relevance in legal texts. Texts do not only include scientific jurisprudential concepts, but cultural aspects as well.

In the law we are faced with the phenomenon of a representation of expert concepts on various levels of abstraction carried in lexemes from standard language (Stolze 2003a:363). In one and the same linguistic frame at surface level, schemata of lay and expert meanings may associate. The specific problem of translating is to recognize such expert concepts in a text which, at first glance, may seem to present itself to "normal" understanding.

> A number of studies have aimed at describing the lexicon and knowledge of laymen vs. experts. Putnam (1975) argues that the meaning of a word emerges from a linguistic division of labour among experts and lay users of a language, and the word's meaning could be divided into a stereotypical intentional part and an extensional scientific part. Full extension might not be part of the linguistic knowledge of persons with everyday competence.
>
> A contrary view is expressed in the vertical semantics of Wichter (1994:71) who talks about similar word forms connected with different meanings. Wichter takes the word form as a point of departure and investigates the different meanings connected to it by different

---

[93] In many legal systems there is a legal doctrine derived from the principle of fairness underlying the law. This requires, for example, that an individual may not be held criminally liable for conduct which he or she could not reasonably understand to be proscribed. What is statutorily prohibited must be defined with appropriate definiteness and denounced with sufficient legislative precision. There must be ascertainable standards of guilt, otherwise a statute is 'void for vagueness'. Vagueness, though, is an indispensable element in the regulation of human conduct through legal rules (Christie 1964:885). There is an 'air of paradox' in the contrast between the fact of vagueness in laws, and the opposed determinacy demand intrinsic to the requirement that laws be framed explicitly in a way that makes them capable of being obeyed.

user groups. – We doubt whether the two approaches mentioned are adequate for legal terms.

As legal language must address both experts and lay persons, there must also be a semantic connection between the stereotypical and the expert concepts. Law departs from everyday life and its conflicts within a specific culture. The expert concept originating in social life is not, in our opinion, a kind of "extension" of a stereotypical meaning, it is rather the opposite. The natural meaning is being "narrowed" by legal definition (Fuchs-Khakar 1987:39). The expert concept constitutes a specification of the stereotypical lay concept into a specialist one, still standing beside the former.

Legal language is characterized by its system-boundedness. Due to legal pluralism, the differences in legal conceptions from within different legal cultures may provoke conflicts between opposite meanings, in particular with regard to basic vague legal notions like *property, contract, agreement*, etc. Such notions are often debated at court.

> A "father", for example, is not only a person who procreated a child, but he is also legally responsible for its maintenance (according to varying national rulings on the transfer of support payments), and in this meaning he is treated in all legal writings. Or: A "dog" is not only a beloved animal, a pet, but an object with a certain material value to be determined in a case of damage. Such terms are much less evident than laymen would believe.

The coexistence of specialist terms with ordinary language words constitutes a problem for understanding and translation in any text, if the correspondent cognitive environment is not inferred at once. Even if an equivalence of terms, therefore, cannot absolutely be expected, in most cases there is a kind of partial relationship between the SL and the corresponding TL concept, and the translator will apply the principle of "transparent translation" (Stolze 2005) enabling – in rather literal translation – an outlook to the foreign conditions. This is the case with all terminology in the humanities, and therefore translators have to consider the relevant academic "school" that determines the precise meaning of such words.

## 5.5 The predicative mode

After having checked the text's meaning dimension as a whole, the professional translator's interest will focus on the PREDICATIVE MODE, the concrete way of expression and stylistic structure found in the text to be translated.

### 5.5.1 Style and mood of text

This shows in the particular mood of the textual message characterizing its author. The translator considers it important to note whether the text is speaking in the first voice, e.g. in a literary text expressing a figure's world view, or whether there are other voices. It may also speak in the third voice or passive voice thus indicating a neutral role, often seen as a characteristic of specialist texts.

Ways of focusing show what was important to the author, and who speaks, an aspect already underlined by Schleiermacher. Verbal reference indicates the author's perspective, e. g. in irony, past tense indicates literary story telling. At this point, literary computing may gainfully be applied for detecting possible repetitive stylistic structures, which would remain invisible in a sentence-based text analysis. The PREDICATIVE MODE will of course be determined by the meaning dimension and the discourse field, as mentioned. This shows that the categories of attention in translational reading are closely interlinked.

Focusing on the form of the text as the PREDICATIVE MODE, the translator will identify specific styles or usage norms as features of an author's idio-culture or a text type. The textual elements that evoke idio-cultural systems include phraseological, syntactical, lexical and supra-segmental aspects on the text level. Hermeneutical understanding, advancing top-down from the situational background over the discourse field and the meaning dimension until the concrete predicative mode, leads to an expansion of the text by added information, which is complementary to the bare linguistic information found on the text's surface structure.

Emotion is often expressed in sentence rhythm, sometimes there is alliteration and rhyme. Searching for such features helps to better grasp the text's meaning. There might be various voices in the text with different idioms. This not seldom poses severe problems in translation as to register or regional dialect. The aspect of intertextuality will show in quotations, but also in implicit reference to other texts or well-known concepts. Footnotes refer to scientific communication. It is useful, for the translator, to have an eye on such features, as they are less visible in a sentence-oriented text analysis. But once detected, they will find their adequate translation.

Discourse markers may be found structuring the message, like intermediate titles, enumeration, signals of paragraph beginnings, etc. That helps to deepen our understanding and it will later clarify the formulating of the translation, particularly in specialist translations.

### 5.5.2 LSP phraseology

Regarding the PREDICATIVE MODE in specialist texts that often belong to a certain text type, we observe verbal speech acts and passive voice indicating administrative rules or directives, as well as third person voice for scientific neutral reporting. Standard text blocks are a characteristic of certain text types. For reasons of the required precision in specialist, e.g. legal or technical texts, the difference between speech acts in the form of performative verbs, and the designation of such speech acts themselves has to be observed.[94]

Specialist texts are "informative, anonymous, and concise" (Gläser 1998:206). Quotations may indicate intertextual relationships, the use of footnotes refers to a scholarly publication. The role of expliciteness in a talk depends on the audience with its comprehending ability. In specialized instruction of the public and in teaching, where often outsiders have to be instructed, talk must be very explicit.

In our discussion of the translational category of PREDICATIVE MODE it might have become clear that we mainly focused, in a kind of vertical outlook, on holistic aspects, such as: who is speaking, what sort of argumentation do we have, how is the text structured as a whole? This is sufficient for adequate translational understanding as a first step. The task to be fulfilled in translation, then, is not a horizontal coordination of a ST and a TT on all linguistic levels (Wilss

---

[94] Example: *The parties herewith stipulate that ... / The contractual stipulations shall be effective as of ...*
S. Göpferich (1995:322ff) has analyzed speech acts in directives, Trosborg (1994) has analyzed speech acts in legal texts, particularly in contracts.

1996:5/41) or the attaining of total "equivalence" between two texts (House 1997) in their functional form.[95]

When we finally have acquired a global idea of the source text message, supported by the growing redundancy towards the text's ending, translation work will begin. The translation task does not end in text understanding. The task is rather to create a "presence" in the translation for that message understood, so that it may appear like an original text about one's own opinion. That is what readers expect.

As a conclusion, we present here a table of the **categories of attention for translational reading**, as discussed above:

| Translator's reading | | Literature | Specialist communication |
|---|---|---|---|
| Understanding | SITUATIVE BACKGROUND | Country, epoch, editor, author, cultural community, realia, geographical names | Area of sciences or humanities with state of development, time, author, medium of publication |
| | DISCOURSE FIELD | Social setting in culture, author's ideology, world view in text, genre, kind of text presentation | Domain with special discipline, text type, level of communication (expert/lay), text function |
| | MEANING DIMENSION | Titles, key words, isotopy, cultural associations, metaphors, thematic strings | Terminological conceptualization (definition/ deduction vs. convention/ interpretation) |
| | PREDICATIVE MODE | Speaker's perspective, idiolect, sentence subjects, deixis, focusing, verbal tense, irony, quotations, intertextuality, register | Speech acts, phrase construction, passive form, standard text blocks, anonymous voice, directives, cohesion markers, formulae, footnotes |

---

[95] The corresponding extensive analysis is linguistically correct, but would be inadequate for the approach by a translator, because it distracts his or her attention from the hermeneutically important aspects in the text.

# 6 Writing as an autopoietic process

## 6.1 Experiences from self-translation

Readers accept a translation as a substitute for the original. The real problem in translation, then, is not reception, but production. The translator will try to produce a translated text as if it were an original, s/he acts like a co-author – in grounded understanding and loyal to the author's intention, conscious of the adressees' requirements.

Our concept of the translational relationship of a hermeneute to texts finds a reference in the experiences connected with self-translation. Shuttleworth and Cowie (1997:13) write in their *Dictionary of Translation Studies*: "Little work has been done on autotranslation; however, it is possible that closer study could yield some interesting insights into the nature of bilinguals and the relationship between language, thought and personality." So far, self-translation has been considered as a borderline case in Translation Studies. Such translations mostly are made by the authors themselves – in both literature and science – into a foreign language different from the original author's mother tongue. This, for the established scholars, has been conceived of as a non-systematic phenomenon.

Santoyo (2004:227f) has brought together various citations from self-translators, not only stating why and how they made it, but also relating about their experiences.

> In view of their competence as translators Santoyo notes that most self-translators show very adequate competence in the languages concerned, in cultural competence, and of course as regards competence in the subject dealt with, which is their own. Authors who translate themselves not only know well about the ... source language, but also are best familiar with their subject. And this is also true for textual competence in the systematic of discourse.
>
> Santoyo goes on: "However competent self-translators may be in both languages, in textual domains, in subject and cultures, still [...] their translator behavior, de facto, is a long way away from many of the theoretical assumptions and presumptions of the discipline we know as Translation Studies: adequacy, faithfulness, equivalence, correspondence or acceptability, for instance, are terms with definitions which may not fit closely into this sort

of translations. For the simple reason that self-translations may *and may not* be translations, if translation is understood in a 'traditional' way" (Santoyo 2004:228f).

When the writer is himself the translator, he can allow himself some bold shifts from the source text which in other cases would not pass as an adequate translation. The reason for this is explained by an autotranslator, very similarly to many relations by other self-translating authors:

> There is no doubt that the process of self-translation often results in a loss, in a betrayal and weakening of the original work. But then, on the other hand, there is always the possibility, the chance of a gain. Yes, the possibility that certain words or expressions in the other language may have the advantage of metaphorical richness not present in the first language. So that even though the self-translator always confronts this possibility of loss, he also hopes for a chance of gain.. [...] Yes, we rarely forgive such liberties, and consequently expect the bilingual writer who translates himself to remain faithful to his own texts. On the contrary, one should allow the writer-as-self-translator some *freedom*, some room for play within his own work, if only for the sake of enriching that work. And of course, I allow myself such playfulness. (Federman 1993:81, *cited after Santoyo 2004:231*)

Consequently, Santoyo (2004:229) notes that "two distinctive factors are brought into play, i.e. *freedom* and what I would call *complementariness*". Authors who translate themselves, independently from the language direction, are working with their own texts, their own messages and ideas. A new version gives the opportunity to find better expressions. "Words develop in order to reach meanings" (Heidegger: *"Den Bedeutungen wachsen Worte zu";* 1927:82). This gradual, autopoietic process of „finding words" for ideas which are already there stands in clear opposition to the traditional concept of linguistics to „find the meaning of words" via text analysis.

> Schleiermacher had mentioned the fact that „we will understand the author better than he did himself, since much of this kind (sc. regarding the language field, specificity of formulation) is unconscious to him what has to become conscious to us (as interpreters), partly in general at the first reading, partly in detail when there are difficulties".[96]

Translation, here, is a formulation of a message and the permanent strive to „even better express what one had wanted to say". Gadamer underlines:

---

[96] My translation from Schleiermacher: *Hermeneutik und Kritik* (ed. by M. Frank), Frankfurt: Suhrkamp 1977, p. 104.

> That is why a hermeneutically trained consciousness must be, from the start, sensitive to the text's alterity. But this kind of sensitivity involves neither "neutrality" with respect to content nor the extinction of one's self, but the foregrounding and appropriation of one's own fore-meanings and prejudices. The important thing is to be aware of one's own bias, so that the text can present itself in all its otherness and thus assert its own truth against one's own fore-meanings. (*TaM*, 269)

The translator of any text as the co-author is free to find dynamic expressions for what he or she "really" wants to say. Then, translation is a re-creation or re-writing. Both texts, the original and a later version as a translation, are complementary to each other. They refer to the "same message", the second however in a more developed linguistic form.

## 6.2 Authentic formulation in empathy and embodiment

This concept of autotranslation backs up our understanding of the task of a translator: to present a message understood in empathy with it "as if it were his/her own opinion" (Stolze 2003:179), that means to really identify oneself with that message and to try to express it in an appropriate manner. An author – and a translator – who are fully aware of the original and now want to write a translation, they both have learnt something in the meanwhile. A hermeneutical learning process, a widening of horizons has taken place which is irreversible in time. And this may eventually lead to some changes in the translational formulation, visible in comparison with the original's text structure, but not so much visible in view of the same overall message (in the translator's mind).

> Original and translation become interchangeable, twin-texts mutually complementary to each other; both modulate and complete each other. The translated text – which chronologically comes later – is no longer seen as a replica of the original, but as a sort of textual rebirth in another language, a follow-up of the previous text, independent and alive by itself. (Santoyo 2004:230)

Instead of textual "equivalence" achieved by "transferring information" we have here a status of "interwoven textuality". This, of course, also shows that the point of reference cannot be the translator's critical opinion or any target readers' expectations or preferences for fluent reading, but the "Sache" (the content) of the message itself to be presented with precision in the translation. And it requires an open, interdisciplinary attitude. Snell-Hornby (1988:31) has rightly stated that translation theory actually is a production theory wanting an "integrated approach".

One may think of the concept of "simpatico", introduced and almost immediately undermined by Venuti (1995) in his sixth chapter. An analysis of Venuti's use of the concept (Strowe 2011) shows that his dismissal of it is largely based on the assumption that it must be defined through sameness and identity (in form). His definition of the term can be examined to show that this is impossible. But when we widen that concept by redefining it in terms of similarity rather than sameness, we will reach an hermeneutical view. This broadening allows not only a subjective flexibility to enter into the description of translator-author relationships but also a historicization, that in Venuti had to be specifically prohibited in the name of identity.

Responsible hermeneutical translation is discredited a bit by George Steiner who sees a continuous "inflationary hermeneutic process" (1975:319) which he traces back to a „compulsion of otherness" (ibid. 236). He thinks that humans ever tend to stretch rules of meaning and to resist to "contemporary requests of uniformity", affirming that "a study of translation is a study of language" (ibid. 49). The hermeneutical outlook of a reader, saying "there is something there to be understood" and "there is more than meets the eye" (ibid. 312), is reversed by Steiner into a human tendency for expansion, diversity, expression of personality. (He is being cited as an advocator of creative writing.) And indeed, he is not much interested in translation competence.[97] Contrary to that, we would focus on the text's content rather than on different forms found in every translation. The reason for a reformulation is not a "compulsion of otherness" but, rather, the opposite: a compulsion of assimilation.

There will be "empathy with the message in translation" (Stolze 2002). Such an empathy with the text may not always surge at first glance, but grow slowly in the course of repeated readings, and it includes responsibility. With "empathy" we understand a kind of deep comprehension of the text message that may lead

---

[97] G. Steiner (1975:126) says: "One finds few answers to these questions in the literature. Indeed, they are not often asked."

to more authenticity in translation regarding the original text message, and this leads to a more natural formulation in the target text.[98]

Having called for an empathy with the message, we may also turn back to the medial act of understanding. A shared interest in the message is a basic requirement for faithful translation. In hermeneutical receptivity and openness, the message – as the "Sache" of that text – will disclose itself to the mind of the translator who may then be able to re-write it creatively.[99] When messages are being presented convincingly, the translator becomes a multiplier, he or she will open up new worlds for the text. Steiner (1975:423) quotes a reference to Dryden: "A translator is to be *like* his author." And an author writes in a way s/he thinks might be intelligible for intended readers (whether this has been achieved can only be verified later). Vermeer describes this fact according to communication theory:

> If the sender wants to communicate, he attunes himself to the recipient's personality, or, to be more precise, he adapts himself to the role which he expects the recipient to expect of him. This includes the judgment which the sender has of the recipient (*cited after* Nord 1991:15).

This "attuning" is done intuitively as the author/translator concentrates on the message to be expressed. Gadamer says:[100] "When I wrote the sentence: 'Being that can be understood, is language' [*TaM*, 474], then this meant that the existing can never be understood totally. Everything that carries a language ever refers beyond what is being expressed. That is the hermeneutical dimension in which the being 'reveals itself'." In translation we see how Being that reveals itself linguistically may become language again.

---

[98] Contrary to that, Wilss understands with empathy a sort of affection that is "disquieting" for his concept of TS: "This means that, in assessing the quality of a literary translation, TS [sc. Translation Studies] is in the uncomfortable, disquieting, and often frustrating position of having to take account of the translator's full range of knowledge and skills, translation experiences, literary (stylistic) value system, and, last but not least, "empathy" with the work which he or she translates" (Wilss 1996:153). – And Koller (1992:210) sees a moral category in our identifying empathy.

[99] We cannot simply "report about a text", a text is more than an "Informationsangebot" (offer of information) (cf. Vermeer 1982). See also Wilss (1996:37): "information-processing procedures" for translation. We do not see only a "transfer movement within the communication channel" (Kade 1968).

[100] See Gadamer (1984:28), *my translation* from German.

The idea that a translation could never be really "faithful", for reasons of different language structures, has been claimed for centuries. Ricœur sees the reason in the fact that there is missing, regrettably, a benchmark for evaluating the fidelity of the translation:

> Such a criterion would be found in a tertium comparationis allowing to compare the source text and the target text with a third text which would be the carrier of the identical sense that should go from the first to the second one. (*my translation*)[101]

Walter Benjamin had called for a "pure language" to be "reached only by the plenitude of their complementary intentions" (Lefevere 1977:102), but this nostalgic concept did not materialize. Even Steiner (1975:301) maintains that "the true interlinear is the final, unrealizable goal of the hermeneutic act." Paul Ricœur does not see the potential of his own view when he states that a "third text" in between the source and the target versions was needed as a *tertium comparationis*. Exactly this text is there: it is the cognitive representation of the message understood which is now present in the translator's mind and attracts new frames. Original and translation "are the same text", since all what a translator can translate is what he or she has understood beforehand. Ricœur advises the translator to do grief work in the Freudian sense and to renounce to the ideal of perfect translation: "A good translation may only tend to a presumed equivalence, not founded in a demonstrable identity of sense; and the only way to criticize a translation is to propose a new one, presumed, pretended, better or different" (*my translation*).[102]

Any criticism by proposing a new translation, that's precisely the revision of initial drafts prepared tentatively by the translator himself in the revision process. Seen in this way, translation is forever a hermeneutical design (*hermeneutischer Entwurf*, Paepcke 1986:86), as long as the informed and self-critical translator is searching for the right words deemed adequate to express the message understood and intended to convey.

---

[101] *Read:* Un tel critère serait donné par un tertium comparationis, permettant de « comparer le texte de départ et le texte d'arrivée à un troisième texte qui serait porteur du sens identique supposé circuler du premier au second ». (Ricœur 2004:39)

[102] *He says:* « Une bonne traduction ne peut viser qu'à une équivalence présumée, non fondée dans une identité de sens démontrable; et la seule façon de critiquer une traduction, c'est d'en proposer une autre présumée, prétendue, meilleure ou différente » (Ricœur 2004:40).

The idea in one's mind tends towards expression. The real problem in translation is to find "the right words" apt to precisely express what one has understood and wants to say in a translation.

> Heidegger had pointed out that "Finally assertion has been accepted from ancient times as the primary and authentic 'locus' of truth. The phenomenon of truth is so thoroughly coupled with the problem on Being that our investigation, as it proceeds further, will necessarily come up against the problem of truth." (*TaB*, 196) [Schließlich gilt die Aussage von alters her als der primäre und eigentliche 'Ort' der Wahrheit. Dieses Phänomen ist mit dem Seinsproblem so eng verkoppelt, daß die vorliegende Untersuchung in ihrem weiteren Gang notwendig auf das Wahrheitsproblem stößt (*SuZ*, 154)]. – " 'Assertion' means '*communication*', speaking forth." (*TaB*, 197). [*Aussage bedeutet Mitteilung, Heraussage* (*SuZ*, 155)].

Eberhard (2004:96) notes with reference to Gadamer: „The emphasis on language means something like 'linguisticability' because the ability to put something into words is the way to understanding it." The entire complex process of transferring a thought into words – from the initial vague idea up until the orderly utterance – has already been described in Medieval times by Thomas Aquinas with his threefold scheme of the "word of heart" over the "picture of the inner word" until the "external word".[103] Speaking or writing, then, is a kind of translating, according to Gadamer:

> Thus the inner word is certainly not related to a particular language, nor does it have the character of vaguely imagined words that proceed from the memory; (…). Since a process of thinking through to the end is involved, we have to acknowledge a processual element in it (*TaM*, 422).

We admit that Gadamer's usage of the term *translation* is too general, when we think of translation as an intercultural communication. Grondin (1993:151) points out a trend of universalizing translation for hermeneutics: any "translation" in language philosophy is "understanding". Human existence means "to translate the world", says Gadamer: "A person who is trying to understand a text is always projecting. (…) Working out this fore-projection, which is constantly

---

[103] In *Quaestiones Disputatae de Veritate I*, qu. IV 'de verbo' art. 1 c; ed. Raymund Spiazzi O.P. Torino/Rome 1949. See also the representation in Blank (1977:87) and in Stanley (2005:61). See also Stolze (2003:97), Gadamer (1960:397). The origin of ideas by Sinnesreiz has also been discussed in Fillmore's (1977) Scenes-and-frames theory.

revised in terms of what emerges as he penetrates into the meaning, is understanding what is there" (*TaM*, 257).

But this opinion is shared by others as well. Chesterman (1997) argues that one of the most recurrent ideas in translation (his "supermemes") is "all writing is translation". Interestingly, in cognitive science we also find such a concept, following the studies of Hayes and Flower (1980) who had verified the process of professional text production, defining the phases of *planning*, e.g. tentatively translating one's ideas into text structures, and *reviewing* the solutions according to global communicative goals:

> The function of the TRANSLATING process is to take material from memory under the guidance of the writing plan and to transform it into acceptable written English sentences. (Hayes & Flower 1980:15)

Translation, when carried out by humans, involves all aspects of human activity including intuition. The "philosophy of embodiment" explores the philosophical ideas behind the fact that we are acting here in dynamic and emergent processes of embodied interaction with our socio-physical environment. The embodied self (*Leibhaftigkeit,* Paepcke 1986:125) is the whole human being, neither a body with solely a mind, nor only a mind in a body; it is the whole interactive, co-inhered self. Studies of human activity should therefore include, among others, linguistics, phenomenology, cognitive psychology, ideological thinking, and social studies. Robinson (1991) rightly explains that translation is also affected by attitudes, feelings, and experiences of the translating person.

## 6.3 Tentative writing for optimization

The impulse to formulate in the target language is an intuitive cognitive movement, and finding adequate words for its content is based on linguistic creativity in the translator. Translation is, like communication, never a conscious application of linguistic rules, but an utterance. The attempt will, at last, remain unfulfilled, since any new consideration or "better idea" for a formulation will again lead to a new draft translation replacing the first one as a revision. Rewording is ever a tentative act, and the goal can only be reached optimally.

Such a cognitive event is an "autopoietic process" of semiosis (Stolze 2003:207). "Poiesis" means transformation of something, i.e. the cognitive scenery gained. The basis for the formulation is given in the original text, it is not a creation out of nothing: *nihil ex nihilo* (Stefanink 1997:169). And autopoiesis is a characteristic feature of living systems, such as human beings when they act as translators. The message changes its external linguistic form in the process of attracting target language words. And why should this be impossible? When I know what to say, I will also find the right words for it in communication. Thus, intuition proves to be a core aspect of translation.

The relationship is between the translator and the message, and not between two texts in different cultures. The act of presenting a perceived message from another language in a translation is rather similar to acting on stage in full embodiment, where an idea – one's own one or a received one from the drama author – is "made present" for the audience. What I translate is the same as what I have in my mind, what I have understood – be it right or wrong. This problem has not been solved by traditional translation theory with its assumption of two separate texts: a source text and a target text.

Practise is: you want to say something, and the word lies on your tongue, but you don't manage to get it out. On the other hand, thoughts and formulations rise intuitively into our mind, we have creative ideas and don't know where they come from. Speaking is located in a very special way on the border between consciousness and the unconscious (Stolze 2003:210).

A comparison of various drafts does not give "more truth", it only reflects the translator's evolving cognition. "A good translation is nothing else but the verbalization of one's comprehension processes. This seems to be true at least for the cases where the world knowledge and the cultural expectations of source-text readers and target-text readers are fairly similar" (Kußmaul 1997:243). Given the constant flow of development, this kind of rewording a message remains a tentative act in an "intuitive formulation impulse" (Stolze 2004:48). And again, memory containing formulation proposals, is decisive here.

Attempts for an ever better target text formulation do not change the meaning and are no manipulation, or subjective distortion, or ideologically dominant abduction but, rather, the effect of the "historical consciousness" (Gadamer 1990:231). As the translator is constantly learning himself, the readiness for a revision of initial drafts at a certain point is part of the translation competence.

The autopoietic formulating impulse is connected with a cognitive process of knowledge activation (Anderson 1983). Three routes of activation have been determined: *perception of signs, spreading activation of brain,* and *focusing* as a conscious concentration on one point so far not sufficiently activated. This corresponds to research activities when the translator feels a lack of sense in his text passage, hindering the immediate apparition of a translational draft.

> What the translation does not reveal of the original is not a loss but something that you can never gain. The original may still reveal its secrets, but only to the *next* translation. Most crucially, the resistance of the original is precisely what makes translation possible. In fact, what people call 'loss' results from one of the conditions of translation semiosis – namely difference. (Stecconi 2007:22)

As Gadamer stresses, a text forever includes a "surplus of sense", which makes it possible for an old text – fixed in words on a paper – to become meaningful once again. The fact that a translation will never grasp the "complete potential" of a text in one given instance, what many critics call a 'loss', is in fact an inherent characteristic. Any creative association of ideas may later even lead to new thoughts (Boden 2001:99), but this is the effect of a translation, not the act itself. According to Paepcke (1986:162) we should "consider the target text not as something static once and for all, but as dynamic in accordance with the flux of present-day modes of expression" (*my translation*).

Translating as a cognitive act presents itself for an analysis of the differences in understanding and in writing. Both aspects of human orientation in the world – comprehension and expression – are by no means symmetrical, as some have thought. Text production was long seen as a kind of "reverse reception" of texts, including comparable restrictions (Antos 1989:6), and translation theory is often seen as a question of how "to 'synchronize' ST reception and TT production" (Nord 1991:11). Rickheit and Strohner (1993:23) speak of cognitive language processing as "a situated and communicative production *and* reception of linguistic texts by cognitive systems" (*my translation*), a relatively awkward statement. When we examine this more closely, some differences will appear.

# 7 Rhetorical text production in translation

## 7.1 Creativity in formulation

A reader's comprehending competence is organized globally, as it does not focus on grammar structures but creates a cognitive scene (Fillmore 1976:63), whilst a writer's productive competence really focuses on details on the text level, regarding rhetorical formulation aspects (Antos 1982:119). Translational text production is realized in a dynamic process of text formulation and repeated optimization.

Translators do not "apply rules", they competently communicate by writing a translation. Even if language usage in communication is – in theory – an (intuitive, subconscious) application of linguistic rules, in practice it is not. It's just utterance. And the same is valid for translation. Translation is, as we have said, an activity in between valid rules and free play. An inherent characteristic of all individual action is subjectivity. Any external, quasi "objective" factors cannot fully account for the result of an individual act which also includes social motivation and personal experience. In modern society, individuality and subjectivity have been reduced in estimation, in favor of the individual seen as part of a system. This involves cooperation, flexibility and creativity (Walter Fricke). But these concepts, still, are open for individual interpretation and free solutions, even within the system.

That is why creativity[104] is a great issue today. Being no longer confined to cultural expressions only, it is rather an expression of modern life and work as such.

> Research in the field of psychology usually defines creativity as "the ability to produce work that is both novel (i.e. original, unexpected) and appropriate (i.e. useful, adaptive concerning task constraints), and that also requires to be accepted as creative by society" (Sternberg 1999:3), see also Preiser (1976:1-7).

---

[104] For an evaluation of the relationship between intelligence and creativity see Sternberg (1999:251-273).

Creativity belongs to the human being, just as intuition and subjectivity. "Creative acts can therefore be expected, no matter how feeble or how infrequent, of almost all individuals. […] The conception that creativity is bound up with intelligence has many followers among psychologists" (Guilford 1968:81f), but trying to "measure" creativity is fruitless.

> Wilss (1996:48f) speaks of the "extraordinarily complex and cumbersome issue of translation creativity" which "is still (and probably will remain to be) a 'smoke-screen' concept". Helplessly, Wilss must state: "Research on creativity has not yet reached the degree of explicitness needed to attain the criteria of objectivity, simplicity, and completeness that ideally characterize scientific endeavors" (ibid., 49f).

And this is not even necessary. We will never get through it by trying to press it into a fixed grid of research methods. Instead, we have to accept this phenomenon in an inter-subjective re-enacting of its results (*intersubjektive Nachvollziehbarkeit*; Bălăcescu & Stefanink 2006:52). "Creativity is obviously a mental 'superdatum', in which reasoning, understanding, intuition, knowledge, and textual imagination work together in an integrative way. Translation creativity, just like creativity in general, cannot be predetermined", admits Wilss (1996:52f). And also translation is commonly regarded as being a creative activity, and the result of translating is called a "creative achievement" (Kußmaul 2000a:117). Talk is even about a "creative turn in Translation Studies" (Loffredo & Perteghella 2006:1).

Being creative means playing with the way things are interrelated, and creative behavior is characterized by originality, expressiveness, inventiveness, and productivity. Creative thinking means seeing new patterns and it is usually described as expansive, innovative and unconstrained, being associated with daring, uninhibited, free-spirited, and unpredictable exploration. It is even contrasted with "critical thinking" qualified as focused, disciplined, logical, realistic, practical, dependable, conservative (Sternberg 1999:397).

However, the concept of creativity is not so self-evident here, as one might assume at first glance. What does "creativity in translation" really mean? There is the translator's (self-imposed) obligation to authentically re-present the message from a source text, in order to enable readers' future interpretation and reaction to it. Authentic translation does not mean a literal transfer as a "faithful translation" in the traditional sense. But it still includes a bond to the given original text, what might be seen as a feature restraining creativity.

> Wilss notes: "It may be argued that creativity is in contradiction to the nature of translation; its goal is to reproduce a ST in a TL. 'The translator must be willing to express his own creativity through someone else's creation' (Nida). Goethe and Schiller were creative, but their translators are not as creative as their masters. Translators are creative only within the framework of a given text. (Wilss 1996:53)

So it is often argued that translators were not committing their own ideas to paper, but were only reformulating the ideas given to them by the author of the original text. They therefore "cannot be said to plan, organize or express an authentic, but only a derived message" (Forstner 2005:100). We doubt whether this is really true. Creativity in translation focuses on the value of linguistic structures in view of their capacity to present the message envisaged (and not on new ideas regarding that message).

> Neubert (1997:19) puts it this way: "In the course of achieving something new, mediators (translators and interpreters) have to resort to novel ways of encoding an old message. They are forced to creativity because the means of the target language are not identical with those of the source language. To arrive at an adequate target language version, new resources have to be tapped. In theses efforts, creativity plays a prominent role."

We are talking here of creativity on the language level. Creativity within a system of life, here: of language, does not mean a *creatio ex nihilo,* the act of creation out of nothing (Antos 1982:100), but rather a combinational, exploratory playing with given ideas and rules, the combination of words and sentences given in the source text. Rules of language usage are acquired by learning and experience, while ideas are handed down in the history of texts through the process of understanding, as hermeneutical philosophy has explained.

> Creativity requires an established knowledge-base, and disciplined self-critical thinking. As we do not perceive anything we do not already know schematically, it is obvious that creative translations can be achieved only when translators have a high level of mastery in their working field. While knowledge of a domain does not always lead to creativity, it still appears to be a necessary condition for it. (Sternberg 1999:409f)

Forstner's definition appears to be too narrow when he requires "new ideas" for being creative. Rather, the given ideas are being newly acquired by the translator himself in empathy with them. And the initiative for creative moves is always given by dissatisfaction with the present state of affairs in the revision process, e.g. a preliminary translation draft (cf. Bălăcescu & Stefanink 2006:57), that soon may be overruled by new ideas for a better formulation, and revised.

Whereas not even the writer of the original text enjoys full artistic freedom (as he is underlying a variety of constraints imposed by the chosen medium and the broader context with its functionality), the translator is subject to both the ever present model of the source language text and to the additional limitations imposed by the medium and the target language wherein the translation has to operate. Working with, and within, constraints thus entails a shift of focus, from an absolute and free subjectivity to one "in which creativity interacts with a specific set of givens – which may again account for a notion of creativity of a series of skills" (Loffredo & Perteghella 2006:9-10). It is necessary to look at things from different perspectives, to dig below the surface, to find previously undetected patterns, to find connections among textual phenomena, and to "continue to question one's own certitudes, never immediately believe in the (seemingly) evident and obvious, and remain perceptive with regard to the superficial contradictions of the text" (*my translation*) (Fontanet 2005:438). That is the attitude of an hermeneute, and it may be explained with rhetoric.

## 7.2 The evolutionary character of a version

How does this general notion of linguistic "creativity" take concrete shape in the translation process? The mentioned innovatory, associative process of thinking is reflected in the gradually deepening hermeneutical understanding of a text, that shows in an improved translational version. When the idea concerning the content is becoming clearer, there will be freedom from the ST structures. At this point, finally, the translator's attention will focus on the target text structure to be formulated. As translators are not living in a pure, contamination-free atmosphere, this quite naturally leads to an interdisciplinarity in their approach. Translators being confronted with multifarious kinds of texts need an interest in just everything. "Multidisciplinarity allows looking to neighboring disciplines for inspiration and discover new problem approaches" (Forstner 2005:101).

Flexible understanding will then lead to creative formulations in the sense of Kußmaul (2000:29) who distinguishes among various degrees of "linguistic deviation" (more or less literal) between a source and a related target text. The extent of creativity is varying according to the translator's subjectivity. It is not measurable exactly, because the meaning of the source text is not absolutely definable in terms of the author's intention and, on the other hand, the deviation of language structures between source and target texts is dependent on both the different cultures with their idiomatic languages and the translator's proficiency.

It is true that a text in several translations by different translators, and even by the same translator at varying times, appears in different forms. This is an inherent characteristic of human translation, when the translator faithfully tries to understand that text and to find ever better words for it in the other language, in a slow evolution. Against the backdrop of the historical and cultural evolution, the language usage is constantly changing, and so the truth of a text, which in a way is understood as "the same", will come out differently on the text level. This is visible for instance in various Bible translations, where passages with undoubted content are still formulated differently, often in a "more modern, more intelligible" way. Various translations do not really change the message, are no new interpretation.

> We are faced with stylistic variations based on the translator's competence or the cultural taste. See an example from the Bible, Matthew (10:24):
>
> The disciple is not above his master, nor the servant above his lord. It is enough for the disciple that he be as his master, and the servant as his lord. (*Authorized King James Version 1960*)
>
> No pupil is greater than his teacher; no slave is greater than his master. So a pupil should be satisfied to become like his teacher, and a slave like his master. (*Good news for modern man 1966*)
>
> A student is not above his teacher, nor a servant above his master. It is enough for the student to be like his teacher, and the servant like his master. (*New International Version 1978*)
>
> A disciple is not above the teacher, nor a slave above the master; it is enough for the disciple to be like the teacher, and the slave like the master. (*New Revised Standard Version 1989*)

There seem to be endless possibilities of how to formulate this simple statement. The text's message is about superiority and inferiority and obedience. The differences between lord, master, teacher etc. are a question of target cultural understanding and recently also political correctness. No methodology will lead to one 'objective' correct translation. Rather, there is freedom of trying again and again. Nida and Taber (1974:47) called for a stylistic education of Bible translators and verified nine different versions of a sentence.

The translational writing – after a global understanding obtained – departs bottom-up from the text structures. Initial literal translation, just following the structure found on the text level, is rather normal, and only if this is no longer possible for reasons of language differences, a divergent creative formulation has to be found. In the end, the whole text has to be revised for more coherence in the overall entity, and this will eventually lead to some major shifts away from literal translation.

Nida (1945:74) has pointed out the crucial problem of different features of the languages concerned, as the special grammar characteristics of languages are a main drawback for literal equivalence in translation. Many languages, for example, express some concepts verbally, which others normally would express in nouns. As Jakobson (1981:195) has put it, "languages differ essentially in what they *must* convey and not in what they *may* convey". The differences existing between languages and the resulting adaptations needed may be treated under phonological, morphological, syntactic and lexical factors (Nida 1945:74).[105] The differences may constitute a translation problem.

All formulation is in the translator's own responsibility, but we should not forget about the fact of being bound to cultural tradition. The habitus of a translator is dependent on his or her education, life experience and the topical cultural values. All this normally is subconscious to us and, therefore, has to be reflected upon intentionally. So it could also happen that what seems creative or special to me, is in reality not much different from what others are doing as well. Particu-

---

[105] There is an example: the *phonological* systems of two languages envisaged must be compared, since it is necessary to transliterate names consistently throughout the text. The resulting words should not be homophones to some indigenous word which may be quite objectionable or confusing. For example, a transliteration of *rabbi* proved to be too closely related in sound to an obscene word in one of the Bantu languages in South Africa, and the transliteration had to be modified (Nida 1945:74). – In one of the tonal languages of Latin America, the translators found to their amazement that their translation, which they thought concerned 'sinners', was actually directed at 'fat people'.

larly regarding translation strategies on various linguistic levels of the text such findings might be analyzed and verified by corpus studies.

Corpus-based methods of enquiry have given impetus to the quest for the so-called translation universals. Some "target-oriented universals", i.e. different linguistic patterns "occurring in translational and non-translational texts produced in the target culture" (Laviosa 2009:307) could just as well cover the translator's own pattern. Translators' styles have been analyzed by corpus analysis (see Kenny 2009 for an overview). Here again, corresponding results could well contradict the translator's intuition. We have to be aware of this possibility and take it into consideration. But, nevertheless, the formulation draft in the concrete act of dynamic translating remains in the translators' responsibility. It has an evolutionary character.

Different language structures and varying cognitive representations in the cultures are the main difficulty in translation, but understanding and formulating an idea are intrinsically linked with one another. The bottom-up and the top-down movements of text processing, as analyzed in cognitive science, have been described in hermeneutics as a helical movement of approach to textual truth: the final version is not produced instantaneously but rather evolves in a gradual movement towards the optimal state. The progress of formulating even feeds back to an advance in the understanding of the original text.

A translation is a dynamic task. The uneasy nature of not yet having reached the goal must be accepted. It's like in sports: the gold winning champion has still the potential of improving his achievement next time,to do a world record. Dynamics, change, the sketchy character of writing, the readiness for revision, holistic orientation are all characteristics of the hermeneutical translation.

## 7.3   Strategies of problem-solving

Some researchers speak of problem-solving in connection with creativity in translational writing. Creative abilities such as fluency, flexibility, and originality are actually indipensable components of a realistic problem solving behavior. In fact, the relationship between creativity and problem-solving is a very close one, according to many researchers. Guilford (1968) has argued that the terms refer to essentially the same mental phenomena.

Wilss (1996:47f) has just one page on "translation as problem-solving activity" and he states that "in TS literature there is little to be found about problem-solving in the sense of a systematic descriptive method". As the shape of "translation problems" is not uniform, we propose here to distinguish between "translation difficulties" as a characteristic in the source text which constitutes a difficulty of understanding for the translator on grounds of his or her (lack of) relevant knowledge, and "translation problems" concerning the selective search for a creative TL frame for a corresponding SL frame, in formulating what has to be said.

Problem-solving is the move from a present state of formulation at a certain point into a desired state, i.e. overcoming the unpleasant situation of not yet having found the satisfactory words for the meaning to be expressed. It differs much in individuals.

> If we define a problem as a situation to which the individual has no ready, adequate response, we see that the variety of problem situations is enormously large and that problem solving is essentially as broad as behavior itself. (Guilford 1968:63)

The differences between languages have been analyzed extensively by Stylistique comparée, what we mentioned already. Given translations were compared with their originals, and seven ways of "translational reaction" on the syntactic level were found descriptively. This was then taken as a model of transfer procedures for translation teaching in the language pair, and descriptive rules turned into prescriptive ones.

However, the translator is not working in this way. Instead of focusing on a specific sentence structure, e.g. the English cleft-sentence or the resultative construction, the translator will rather ask how the message carried here might best be formulated in the target language. Translational decision-making is not a selection between several grammatical forms, but rather semantically the search for the right expression. Any translational decision can in fact lead to a "translation" (and later be criticized), but this is a descriptive result, not a translational strategy. The translator needs to liberate himself from the grammatical ST structures.[106] The so-called "translation universal" of *simplification*, for instance, might possibly derive from a lack of language creativity in the translator, and not necessarily from not having understood deeply enough. The tendency to *normalization* as also detected in corpus analyses seems to be an ill-considered attitude of rejecting the alien and rather adapting to target culture norms in text construction. Be it as it were – the mere observation of such findings does not yet improve translational solutions.

There are relevant findings of cognitivist research regarding professional expertise in problem-solving. While Husserl had called for transcending the familiar world in an "intentional thinking", cognitive science has found the concept of "lateral thinking". Langacker (1987:120) explains this effect with a "figure/ground-alignment", what means that in our cognition we always perceive a preeminent figure against a background. Viewing this background means activating one's given pre-knowledge within the hermeneutical circle. But the relationship between figure and ground is not fixed. At a change of focus, after a move, an originally ground element might come to the foreground, when we have learnt something. "Lateral thinking" as a change of perspective may provoke this effect, thus creating new insight.

This is relevant for translation, as any preliminary subjective interpretation and reformulation of the meaning is not adequate and must be deepened or extended by a conscious modification of focus. Self-critical questioning whether the understanding is integrative, may help to overcome naïveté and gain more responsibility. Langacker writes:

> Impressionistically, the guide within a scene is a substructure perceived as "standing out" from the remainder (the ground) and accorded special prominence as the pivotal entity around which the scene is organized and for which it provides a setting. Figure/ground organization is not in general automatically determined, for a given scientist is normally able to structure the scene with alternate choices of figure. However, various factors contribute to the naturalness and likelihood of a particular choice. (Langacker 1987:120)

Guilford (1975:40) sees the "problem-solving activity" of finding solutions in "divergent thinking" for problems for which the convergent or logical thinking

---

[106] Wilss, on the contrary views this in line with the automation of transfer procedures based on syntagmatic analysis (1996:223) and calls for more longitudinal studies of the translator competence. This to our opinion is not helpful here.

has not yet brought up a satisfactory suggestion. De Bono (1970:42ff) preferred the concept of "lateral thinking" compared to the "vertical thinking" of logical inference. (Both terms, though, seem to refer to the same concept.) Any item from the word to the sentence can trigger a problem-solving move. Now Wilss claims: „We cannot normally rely upon intuition; it often helps us in an emergency, but without guaranteeing success" (1996:55). We would rather say, we cannot sidestep intuition, because as a human feature, it works subconsciously and suggests translation solutions, which then may be accepted or revised. Not seldom the first solution is the best, and after intensive revision work one may even return to it.

The final step in translational text production will then be a glance beyond the language structure outward towards potential readers. They are integrated in their target culture, but this does not mean that every reader has to receive a different translation, there are social groups. If we see the various factors that influence a particular choice as the cultural factors behind language usage, the explanatory potential of the theory of scenes becomes clear. We find more support for this idea in Bălăcescu and Stefanink (2006:52) who present a review of results in cognitivist research. They present the "inter-subjective re-enacting of creative problem-solving processes" as a possibility of critically accepting solutions found by a translator for a specific word or sentence in a text.

A legitimization of creative solutions is possible with an awareness of their apparition, which came about along relevant lines of thought. Research into cognitive language processing has shown that our mental "lexicon" is not an incoherent list, but that the words are rather stored in a semantic connection, and that our language processing runs in orderly lines marked by our experience (Bălăcescu & Stefanink 2006:52, with reference to Aitchison 2003:84ff).[107] The neural network offers the lines for an associative chaining in the quest for new expressions. As these associative chains are dependent on our experiences, and as there are culturally divergent experiences for natural reasons, this may even lead to different metaphors carrying this associative chaining of frames, as La-

---

[107] There are neural links between stored experience and its representation by words or frames (Aitchison 2003:224ff). New experience tends to use given links in order to associate, thus even enforcing those present links what leads to a learning effect. Se also Schank (1982).

koff and Johnson (1980:139) have shown. This of course will only function when the respective linguistic and cultural knowledge for grounded understanding is given in the translator's memory. The phenomenon may be applied intentionally in the third phase of brain activation in "focusing", in searching for other adequate expressions as a problem-solving strategy.

In translation, "it is possible that in various cultural areas there might be a tendency to activate different associations" (Bălăcescu & Stefanink 2006:52, *my translation*). The translator has to realize both the associations activated by the ST and those possibly different associations applicable for a functional adequacy of the translation in the target culture. This, then, is the place of translational creativity on the language level, when the "same meaning" or "scene" is presented – not in literal translation – but in different linguistic frames. Phenomenology calls for the attempt of an objectification by overcoming one's own ideas or entering into a foreign domain of knowledge.

The borderline between misleading, weak translations and creative ones is floating. "We cannot define a creative product, but we know it when we see it", says the *Handbook of Creativity* (p.13). And we feel it in our own translation work, we might add. "…the objectivist philosophy fails to account for the way we understand our experience, our thoughts and our language" (Lakoff & Johnson 1980:210). On the other hand, a creative solution as a problem-solving move is not necessarily just a lucky find. It rather has been induced by the work of metaphoric "models of categorization", according to Lakoff (1987:121). These are "the intuitions behind objectivism" (ibid. 174).

Though based on a somewhat different theoretical background, Gutt (2000:136ff) has developed a collection of linguistic aspects on the surface level of comparing language structures that trigger translational decisions.[108] He sees a system of rules and states:

> It is entirely reasonable for the translator to use these observations when facing choices and decisions at the translation desk. It would be a waste of time if the translator ignored this treasure of experience and started from scratch, re-inventing the wheel for every task s/he

---

[108] He discusses various "communicative clues" arising from semantic representations, from syntactic properties, from phonetic properties, from semantic constraints, from formulaic expressions, from onomatopoeia, from the stylistic value of words, from sound-based poetic properties, etc.

faces. [...] Supposing that the rule or guideline in question has in fact been stated explicitly enough, before applying it to a specific instance of translation, the translator will need to check out how well the contextual conditions of his/her target audience agree with those for which the rule was drawn up in the first place. Though the degree that these circumstances differ from those assumed by the rule maker, the rule will be inappropriate and is likely to lead to bad results [...] In the search for optimal relevance relative to a certain contextual background the translator knows how to make a decision *in all those instances for which no rules or guidelines exist.* (Gutt 2000:226f)

We think that first searching for and then testing "rules" against any textual conditions would be itself a re-inventing of the wheel, and a waste of much time. For the hermeneutical translator there are no rules of interlinguistic transfer. Ideas in understanding and formulating come intuitively. Just as in natural language usage, grammar aspects are applied by the "competent native speaker" (Chomsky) unconsciously. Also, we should not forget about the role of the hermeneutical circle, of the necessary metalinguistic knowledge. If knowledge about any "rule" is not given in the translator, he or she will not apply it, and not even find it when reflecting upon. Understanding and presenting an individual text is not "re-inventing the wheel" but "rolling the wheel".

## 7.4 Translational hierarchy as a coordination problem

In understanding a text the translator creates a global cognitive plan for the accepted assignment of presenting that message in empathy. In a helical movement, tentative creative writing and reviewing in a problem-solving strategy are repeated several times, until a final text is produced that corresponds to the initial writing goal. Translations are not derived from their "source text", but rather written down in a holistic movement, with disregard to the linguistic structures in that source text.

The process of writing is first oriented selectively to certain points of difficulty, it is a data driven bottom-up process. This has always to be followed by revision in a top-down process feeding back towards the whole of a message.[109] Writers dispose of global structures as a kind of "production scheme" for their process

---

[109] Bălăcescu & Stefanink (2006:57) discuss the example where subjects in a think-aloud protocol have overstressed the initiating textual surface elements too strongly, and did not expose them to "examination by the top-down process".

(Antos 1989:21), focusing on pragmatic features such as intelligibility and functionality of the text, with the aim of reaching a responsible presentation of that message accepted to be expressed in empathy. They have to cope with insufficient knowledge, limited proficiency in language and genres, problems of activating and focusing one's knowledge, etc. (Antos 1989:6), all aspects of rhetoric.

> This idea is formulated in a very general way by A. Pym, as quoted in Chesterman (1997:119): "Translational competence consists of two skills: 'the ability to generate a series of possible translations for a given source text or item, and [...] the ability to select from this series one version considered to be optimally appropriate'."

In practice, this proves to be a process of coordinating the writing goals on the macro and the micro level of the texts. The specific problem in translational text production, then, is the adjustment of the various rhetorical features that will all contribute to the intended meaning of the text as a whole. Such features are formed gradually in a constant reviewing and reformulating process of the first draft, and they concern concrete aspects like text organization, adequacy for addressees, effect, style, emotion, institutional background, aesthetics, thematic progression, coherence, etc. (Antos 1989:13) on the target text's macro level.

The process of writing is oriented towards the whole of the text, following general production schemes. The problems to be solved at certain points, then, are gradually changing, since any modification at one point results in some other consequent transformation at another point. As the writing goal gets clearer, in the sense of a message gradually understood more profoundly, the rhetorical problem becomes more complicated. "The important constraints do not come from the text of departure but only from the target text" (Loffredo & Perteghella 2006:179), as writing studies have shown.

> The hierarchy of decision making, which itself is constantly evolving dynamically, is something different from the "hierarchy of the textual values to be preserved in a translation" (*my translation*) determined by Koller (1992:266). In a linguistic approach, Koller sees here a "hierarchy of equivalence norms" to be based on these static observations, not realizing that any such "norm" once stated is being overruled several times by any single translational decision made.

Problem-solving acts concentrate on some unsatisfactory or pivotal points in the text. But translation does not stop there, it has to present a whole text. The translational activity, thus, is an entire series of problem-solving acts which, again, are constrained by each other. Any decision at one single point in writing might easily be overruled by a later decision on a higher level of text linguistics. „As in speech production, speakers consider many more words than they eventually select. A huge number are activated, then those that are not required are gradually suppressed" (Aitchison 2003:239). Translation presents itself as a coordination problem on the overall text level.

It might have become clear by now, that the evolutionary helical movement of text understanding and re-formulating, which traditionally has been described as an *ever narrowing* circling around the truth (*hermeneutische Spirale*), is in reality a constant movement of attention between the translator and the text, going back and forth from bottom to top and vice versa. Top-down- and bottom-up-processes are sequentially inter-linked. Brodbeck (1995:86ff) underlines the importance of attentiveness and receptivity for all creative thinking. Both concepts are opposite to rule observation, to routine and habits only moving on the familiar lines of thought.

Empathy with the text, that expands during several readings, may also contribute to the fact that the "dynamics of the translator's macro-strategy" will be changed (Risku 1998:147), possibly several times. A full understanding in the sense of an awareness of the macro-strategy of writing used by the author is growing slowly, in the course of a dialectic to and fro between the text's situative embedding and an analysis of its structure. That is why the problems become more and more difficult, with the formulation process advancing.

According to productivity research, the individual writing goals are in the beginning relatively abstract and only globally represented. By gradually assimilating given instructions, valid conventions, etc., those goals are being accommodated, what again makes the hierarchy more elaborate and differentiated. Any longer text includes an "accumulation of coercion", because the initially open possibilities of formulation are being reduced, as the "inner logic" of the produced text is growing (Dörner 1976:96). The clearer I see my translation task, the more I feel my own limited means, the more coercion pops up in the detail. This, in the end, forces one to make a hierarchy of translational decisions.

The resulting hierarchy of decision-making may be explained with some "categories of attention in writing". The translator can back-up his or her version by means of those categories, but they might also be used in pedagogics and translation criticism as a guideline. Working with these categories is not seen as a methodology, because their consideration does not follow any specific order, they are rather considered intuitively. Also, the categories are not found in linguistic structures in the text, they rather constitute a dimension on a higher level of cognitive representation and rhetoric formulation. However, the results of the decision-making process can be described with linguistic means, since translating is still an act in language. The categories will be presented in the next chapter.

# 8 Fields of attention in translational writing

## 8.1 Genre

When we have acquired a global idea of the text message and set our writing goal, translation work will begin. The issue is coherent writing, oriented towards the target readers' level of comprehension as required for any authentic text production, combined with observing an equivalence relationship with the source text as to its meaning and overall structure.

### 8.1.1 Appearance of the text

Instead of starting work right away, the translator will first reflect upon the general setting of the translation assignment. The GENRE in which the translation will be presented is a most decisive aspect determining the translator's decisions. It might be the same as for the original and thus correspond to the PREDICATIVE MODE as found in that text. But it may also be different, if a specific translation commission has been given or was chosen. As there is no automatic transfer relationship between a ST and a TT, it is the translator's responsible task to decide about the GENRE and its respective formulation requirements. Translators will find here a first motivation for their decisions which might, possibly but not necessarily, lead to a visible deviation from the source text structure.

This is relevant, as the text's shape is a determining factor in formatting the target version. Ranking high on the decision-making order for translators, it is therefore focused in the first instance when they look at the source text more closely after having understood it. Translating a novel will normally lead again to a novel. Literary text production is ruled by specific genre norms for drama, novel, poetry, children books, fantasy, essays, etc., both in the source and in the target language. If such norms happen to be different, this might entail and explain some changes in the text structure of the translation, when we accept that a translation should follow the target culture media type. On the other hand, it may also explain the strangeness of appeal of a literary translation in the target polysystem, when the translator chose to re-present that cultural and literary specialty and to introduce a new form into the target literary system (Even-Zohar 1990). GENRE also concerns the target culture as such into which the translation will be placed.[110]

Rhyme and the verse order in poems often hinder literal translation. In publicity texts, the cultural embedding of pictures might be interesting. Quite often in such translations, it is not only the text that has to be altered for medial reasons, it might even be necessary to use different pictures for to present the message truly as such. The translator will consciously think about these aspects and thus be able to motivate the translation.

### 8.1.2   Formatting problems

In specialist texts, the layout prerequisites and the internal relationship between wording and illustrations not seldom constitute a writing problem. Non-verbal signs of page design are always there, and may even be relevant for the text's effect. The way of structuring texts in lists differs considerably in various cultures, for instance in Germany, France, Britain, America, etc. (Jamieson 1993). There are differences in indicating the time and date. Technical translations may be dominated by the space available, particularly in computer screen translation but also in paper format.

Multilingual text design (e.g. for instruction manuals) tacitly implies that the texts in various languages would occupy identical space. If this is not the case, the translator may be forced to compress. Language differences, as were mentioned earlier as a cultural aspect, include different quantities of text, due to the varying length of words. Website text translation presents specific problems in view of conformity (Foltz 1996), as modules of such texts appear on various levels of depth in the computer, e.g. in a software handbook, interface texts, glossary, help text, etc. in the online documentation. Even script fonts have culturally different effects (Schopp 2005:139). Titles are often written in different fonts. Knowledge regarding design correspondences between ST and TT mainly concerns such socio-cultural effects of the text form, and medial requirements. In

---

[110] Salevsky (2000) shows how divergent two translations of one and the same original in the same target language may come out, if they were written for two different target cultures, e.g. eastern and western Germany. (It is always the translator's responsible decision.)

legal translation, certain official provisions might be applicable by law regarding the strict representation of the original, in a kind of "documentary translation" (Stolze 2005:276). The awareness of functional norms, media, text genre conventions and ways of exotic language are part of the translator's competence regarding GENRE.

The expectations and standards required in the special text type in the target language have to be observed. You need linguistic proficiency and creativity, and you need some awareness of text type norms, styles or formulae, as they are cognitive formulation schemata and represent the utilization of already solved and meanwhile socially accepted writing problems in certain recurrent situations.

Media language and journalistic texts require a special expressive language. In fact, a text's media-mix is an identifiable feature which, in certain cases, needs to be interpreted and re-enacted in the translation. This is being researched now in studies on audiovisual translation (Remael 2010). Hypertexts combining different semiotic forms (text, image, sound) (Heine 2006), and hybrid texts resulting from multilingual influences in globalization (Prunč 2007:290), pose specific problems to a translator. The medial effects are construed by convention in the community.

Nord (1991:169f) talks about „translation errors" and, introducing a functionalist view, she defines prescriptively: „A translation error is 'a deviation from the selected (or rather, prescribed model of action', from the translator's standpoint, or a 'frustration of expectations' concerning a certain action, as seen from the recipients' point of view" (ibid. 170). An error may well be described *post festum*, but as a category of attention it is of no use for the translator in the moment of writing. Of course, in the act of translating, he or she will be convinced to fully carry out all instructions (even in consciously "deviating from the model of action" for some reasons) or at least to be on the way toward the set goal. And any revision after self-criticism will again be a new draft, and we cannot say whether this is/was an "error" whatsoever.

## 8.2 Coherence

According to hermeneutics, texts enable recipients to look beyond the language structures into the surrounding world, so that an overall cognitive scenery of a textual content will be created. For a message to be presented authentically, the text produced will have to be coherent, and text COHERENCE is obtained by semantic compatibility on the level of word fields, syntax and paragraphs, as observed under the MEANING DIMENSION.

### 8.2.1 Dealing with lexical lacunae

"Certain translation procedures are adopted by translators to handle contrastive difference between two languages" (Neumann & Hansen-Schirra 2008:135). Often translators note that for a certain word referring to a cultural concept there is no adequate correspondence to be found in the target language. This is a. o. the case with academic titles, which therefore should be transferred as such, and not translated. One will do an 'emprunt'[111] in transferring the term into the translation. In other cases one might try to creatively forge a new word. A 'calque' appears when a novel concept is found in linear translation, e.g. *Wolkenkratzer* > *sky scraper, growth rate* > *Wachstumsrate*. A 'literal translation' is apt for simple sentences not posing any problem as to style. A 'transposition' can also help to solve the problem, when several ST words obviously correspond to only one TT word. Their repetition would be tedious and flat, and one could, for example, add an explanatory adjective or an attributive construction, as suggests Koller (1992:230). Metaphoric images may be mentioned in this connection.

---

[111] In the diction of *Stylistique comparée* (Vinay & Darbelnet 1958), *emprunt* is the first of four transfer procedures in a language pair that should not transform the content. The other three are *calque* (linear translation of the word), *traduction littérale* (exchanging source text syntagmas with formally corresponding target text ones), and *transposition* (change of word type, e.g. noun > adjective). *Substitution* (one sign is translated with one or several signs of another word type) and the *over-cross-translation* (chassé-croisé) and *dilution* (several signs from several word types are there for one ST sign) and *concentration* (a phrase is reduced to less signs) are to be subsumed under "transposition". On the other hand, *modulation, équivalence* and *adaptation* are transformations in the target version with an impact on content. There is a shift of perspective (modulation), the insertion of a proverb (équivalence) and the translation according to target cultural norms (adaptation). So they are no real "transfer procedures", but rather a means of translation criticism to find meaning deviations. These "translation procedures" are today analysed in corpus-studies, e.g. for text typological considerations (Neumann & Hansen-Schirra 2008).

## 8.2.2  Isotopy as a semantic web

Thematic COHERENCE in the target text may be realized linguistically by means of a semantic web. The mental connection among concepts in metaphorical fields (Lakoff 1987) reflects on the text level in the isotopic web of semantic coherence. The theoretical concepts of coherence, theme/rheme progress, and isotopy are interrelated and complementary:

> The processes of establishing coherence, theme/rheme progression and isotopies can be described from a speaker's and a listener's point of view. Isotopy has so far only been considered statically as a result, i.e. the description of isotopic meaning levels in a produced message as a result of text analysis. Its dynamic dimension still awaits investigation. [...]
>
> Functionally the three concepts serve different, but complementary purposes: Coherence depicts the (lack of) sense continuity in a message or text and is thus the most general of the three textual parameters. Theme/rheme depicts the (more or less) continuous information flow in a text or message [...]. Isotopy depicts (more or less differentiated) meaning levels in a text and thus also indicates the coherence of a message or text.
>
> We can thus summarize that coherence, theme/rheme and isotopy can be explained as overlapping concepts which share certain conceptual features and follow a homogenous methodology but serve different, albeit complementary purposes in text constitution, i.e. to account for and make transparent the sense constitution (coherence), the informational structure (theme/theme) and the meaning set-up (isotopy) of a text or message. (Gerzymisch-Arbogast et al. 2006:356f).

Key lexemes from the MEANING DIMENSION with paradigmatic additions constitute the isotopy of a text, visible on the global text level, though possibly not on sentence level. Viewing the text as a holistic and not aggregate overall unity will help to overcome misunderstandings and errors. Isotopy is a factor of redundancy. It helps to discern various textual levels and the holistic COHERENCE.

One should always check whether there are word repetitions on the overall text level. The following example shows how a paradigmatic context works to enhance a meaning, and this can be preserved in translation. The metaphorical image of a factory is used here to create a visual idea of the HIV-virus.[112]

---

[112]  The second translation tries to observe semantic compatibility in using words like *Fabrik, Maschine, Getriebe, Spiralen, Windungen, entwirren* which all belong to the word field of ENGINEERING.

*Original:* **AIDS: A Suitable Place for Treatment?**

Like any *factory*, the virus that causes Acquired Immune Deficiency Syndrome (AIDS) is *deceptively simple* when viewed from the outside. Inside, however, its genetic *machinery* is *labyrinthine*. The *twists and turns* are just beginning to reveal themselves to scientists as they look for a place to *throw a spanner in the works*. (...) [*New Scientist*, 13.03.1986].

*Student translation:* **AIDS: Der passende Ort, um den Hebel anzusetzen?**

Wenn man es von außen betrachtet, erscheint das Virus, welches das erworbene Immun-Defekt Syndrom AIDS verursacht, täuschend *einfach* | . Betrachtet man jedoch die innere *Struktur*, gleichen die genetischen *Anlagen* einem *Labyrinth*. Die *Verdrehungen* und *Verwindungen* haben gerade erst damit begonnen, sich den Wissenschaftlern zu *erschließen*, die nach einem geeigneten Ort suchen, um dem Virus Sand *ins Getriebe streuen* zu können. [Heidelberg *Project Mental Analysis*. K. Kohn].

*New translation:* **AIDS: Ein brauchbarer Behandlungsansatz?**

Das Virus, welches die Erworbene Immunschwächekrankheit (AIDS) verursacht, wirkt von außen gesehen *täuschend glatt* wie ein *Fabrikgebäude*. Im Inneren jedoch gleicht seine genetische *Maschinerie* einem *Labyrinth*. Wissenschaftler fangen auf ihrer Suche nach einer Stelle, wo man *Sand ins Getriebe streuen* könnte, gerade erst an die *Spiralen und Windungen zu entwirren*.

Even if the text structure might have been created intuitively by an author, the words were not taken freely from the lexical inventory of a language. So the translator may – as a problem-solving strategy – ask whether there are some central concepts visible that would constitute an isotopic line and semantic web in the text at hand, as Mudersbach and Gerzymisch-Arbogast (1989) have explained. Having detected word fields of cultural concepts as an isotopy in the macrostructure, the translator might then search for some compatible lexemes within a corresponding word field in the target language (detached from any sentences) and observe interrelations by repetition.

As we are always reading with a script in mind (Schank 1982), it may also happen that inferences from our world knowledge come in and create a coherence of the scene. Certain text elements are crystallizing as pro-eminent before others (figure/ground).[113] A text's COHERENCE is constituted by the integrity of a scence

---

[113] Kußmaul (2007:127) brings an example from cognitive psychology: when we see a picture in frame, may be even doted with a title, it appears more in the distance, we perceive it as a whole entity. Without any description and frame, certain features in it become prominent, come to the foreground, even if the picture is identical.

to be grasped in the reader's mind. Fillmore (1976) has pointed out that words (frames) connect to cognitive scenes made up of partial scenes. We mentioned this already for key words found in a text.

> Bălăcescu and Stefanink (2003:519) now suggest that « le traducteur qui se retrouvera devant le problème d'un vide lexical en langue cible sera créatif si, par association, il traduit par un autre élément de cette '*scene*' qui sera prototypique en culture cible et de ce fait, lexicalisée ».[114]

An adequate reaction to lexical lacunae in the target language, thus, would also be to verbalize a different aspect within the prototypical overall scenery.

> Kußmaul (1997:241) discusses, based on TAP-analysis, the inadequate translation of the term *well-stocked convenience stores* in a text. This term is a small part of the overall scenario concerning the shape of new highway restaurants in Eastern Germany after the reunification. The individual sentences are integrated into the whole and their translation should derive from the over-summative entity of the text. We feel that Kußmaul himself, who calls for an application of the *scenes-and-frames*-theory, does not go far enough in this respect. Instead of analyzing TA-protocols sentence-wise, we would prefer to train the students' integrative view of the whole, so that the translation decisions regarding individual sentences might be based on the top-down movement and may come out differently. – Kußmaul (2000:69f) suggests that we should look for so-called "sub-modalities of situations", here invoking again the sub-scenes as mentioned.

This of course implies a translation strategy that does not stick to the sentence by sentence approach. Visual imagination also will help in that process, and one may even find translation solutions that are not registered in the dictionary. Tenuous translations, due to language interference, often prevent the creation of a cognitive scene in the reader, and do not create authenticity for the message. It is also possible that one certain lexeme appears as the focus and the overall rheme of that text. Macro-strategic text elements are guiding our attention, and any selective problem-solving act is only valid within a satisfactory overall COHERENCE of meaning.

---

[114] *My translation:* The translator, faced by the problem of a lexical gap in the target language, will be creative if he or she translates associatively with another element of this "scene" which is prototypical in the target culture and therefore lexicalised.

### 8.2.3 Technical terminology

"The present cognitive perspective of Applied linguistics holds it that the communication for specific purposes is part of the cognitive system which comprises perceptions, emotions, categorizations, abstraction processes, and reasoning. All these cognitive abilities interact with various means of communication and generate an information flow" (Baumann 2008:92). This shall not be interrupted in translation.

In order to reach COHERENCE, the equivalence of terminology in LSP-texts must be checked and consistently applied throughout the text regarding COHERENCE despite possible defects in the original, as precise terms are indispensable (see on equivalence tests for terminology Artnz/Picht/Mayer 2002). The primary problem for the translator, here, is terminology management and database retrieval. Translation memory software will help to keep terminology coherent and consistent in the entire text. A special problem are synonyms created contemporaneously by different scientists.

The technical word formation in the form of compounding, syntagmatic extension, affixation etc., and typical differences between the languages may also be considered (Stolze 1999:68ff). Language-specific forms of technical word compounding shall be used, with reference to the TL usage norm, as was acquired and is stored in the linguistic memory. A technical text is more easily understood when it is written with adequate word compounding. In an ordinary language tone it would not appear as an element of LSP. Example:

Thousands of years > *Tausende von Jahren > Jahrtausende

Council of the city > *Rat der Stadt > Stadtrat

Scope of a project > *Anwendungsbereich des Vorhabens > Projektumfang

Project dates > *Zeitangaben zum Vorhaben > Projektdaten.

Specialist texts in the humanities offer a specific problem. Since the special language is – unlike the exact sciences – oriented towards the description of developments in life and the thinking of people, rather than of external objects, the words are closer to the general language. A variation of meaning does not necessarily lead to a cumulative appearance of new terms, but rather to a redefinition or a new interpretation of the concept already existing behind the word. And such concepts are not as precisely definable as in the exact sciences, because these concepts are ever linked to the scholar's way of argumentation. It's not so much that terms are "travelling around in a discipline" (Chesterman 1997), it is the scholars who use those terms in their own specific meaning. The principal translation problem, arising from that, is the need to recognize such specialist terms in a text, which, at first glance, seem general language with general meaning. On the language system level, this phenomenon is defined as word polysemy, but for the translator, the problem is to select the adequate meaning from his/her specialist knowledge, and to find corresponding words in the target language. Since humanistic texts tend to be less linear than the technical ones, they will also present more signals of cohesion which then will guide the understanding and the order of argumentation.

## 8.3 Stylistics

Style is an important factor of meaning. Therefore the translator will – in an initial data-driven bottom-up movement in writing – focus on STYLISTICS, particularly in view of the text's GENRE and corresponding rhetorical requirements. But as the translation is not to be derived from the source text in its linguistic form, there will be no specific focus on grammar structures.

The translator needs awareness of target language rhetorical variations, the linguistic forms of how to create metaphors and their images, the stylistic value of neologisms in a language, the functional norms of text types like standard formulae, nominalization, special collocations, aspects of sound and speech rhythm, and other stylistic phenomena according to the target language norms. The STYLISTICS of the whole text is as much an integrating element of sense as is the content, and cannot be detached from its form. While the full stylistic potential of a language is realized in poetic literature, "against which ordinary language represents a reduction" (Snell-Hornby 1988:70), many other usages know a functional selection from it.

### 8.3.1 Sociolects, word play and other features

The translator will respect certain sociolects in the target language, i.e. the language of special groups like development agencies, churches, political parties, the specific diction of an association, feminist circles, etc. Membership in the DISCOURSE FIELD of a speaker's group shows in the professional jargon and ideological diction. In order to assure the acceptability of a translation, it is very important to consider such target sociolinguistic preferences and norms, independently from those valid in the source language text. Of course such differences include a reflection on the differences in cultures. However, this culture only forms a background to the activity of translation and is not schematized explicitly by the translator.

> Sometimes the metaphorical names of characters pose some problems for translators. As a mark of allegorical aspects in text, Newmark (1999:25) mentions "personification, existential metaphors and expressive names of persons and places". Those in many cases may be translated literally in order to convey their meaning (*Everyman – Jedermann, Mr. Badman – Herr Bösewicht – M. Méchant*).

In literature we need a creativity in finding stylistically novel collocations and concise formulations in order to present a specific poetical idea, what also involves some courage and confidence in one's language proficiency. Findings in view of the PREDICATIVE MODE give hints for the translation. Wherever the rhythm, or the sound, or the structure, or the physical embodiment of the text on the page contributes to its meaning, in other words, wherever the text's salient features extend beyond the simple referentiality of the words and begin to incorporate their materiality, we can speak of the text as imposing formal constraint on the translator.

Translators can productively prioritize specific material features of discourse in STYLISTICS: sound, rhythm, composition on the page. Many features observed there, e.g. characteristics of oral speech in literature, in children's narrative, etc. may well be represented in the translation, and there are numerous possibilities to express an idea once grasped, beyond literal rewording. Even if this sounds a little banal, that aspect is rather often neglected and even altered in the translation, for reasons of grammatical difficulties in the language pair.[115] In the following example the speaker's perspective was modified for grammatical reasons in the translation:

---

[115] Bălăcescu & Stefanink (2006:55) discuss a sentence of which the impact is based on rhythm.

**Example**:
A literary text begins: In my time **I have been called many things**: sister, lover, priestess, wise-woman, queen. Now, in truth I have come to be wise-woman, ...

This has been translated: Zu meiner Zeit **hat man mir viele Namen gegeben**: Schwester, Geliebte, Priesterin, weise Frau und Königin. Jetzt bin ich wirklich eine weise Frau geworden.

But it would also have been possible to maintain the personal voice of the literary speaker: Damals zu meiner Zeit **hatte ich viele Namen**: Schwester, Geliebte, Priesterin, Weise Frau, Königin.

Emotion, for instance, is always expressed in the sentence rhythm. This is important to be observed in drama translation (Haag 1984). Eco (2006:81) says: "For to preserve the level of rhythm, the translator has to free himself from an exaggerated respect for the original's wording" (*my translation*). As a principle, the value of the whole message is more important for Eco than a strict interlingual transfer. Sometimes there are certain phrases in a text that create an emotional scene: of love, of anxiousness, of melancholy, etc.

**Example**: The first sentence in Eco's *Il nome della rosa* reads: "Era una bella mattina di fine novembre." This was translated into German with "Es war ein klarer spätherbstlicher Morgen gegen Ende November". Critics mentioned that "spätherbstlich" was an illicit addition, going beyond equivalence. But it was necessary in order to invoke the feeling of that scene. Sticking to literal translation would have sounded strange in the target culture, because at this time of the year the weather normally is not nice in Germany.

Cognitive research has shown that similar rhythm as well as similar phonetic features in words attract each other associatively in writing (even as an interference with the source language), and pass from the long-term memory into the working memory while active in problem-solving strategies (Bălăcescu & Stefanink 2006:56). One aid in this process might also be the practical experience of "flow" in translating with high speed, not stopping over at individual text positions (Stolze 2003:212). Guilford (1975:40) mentions the *fluency of thinking* as the ability to produce many thoughts, associations and ideas in connection with a problem in a very short time, quasi subconsciously. Psychology has analyzed this in fluency tests (Ulmann 1968:79), and the linguistic knowledge, required for translation, could be furthered in similar tests.

Word plays, metonymy, alliterations, ambiguous words and other expressive linguistic forms in the ST are a common subject of study. This is even true for the use of "creative language" in the sense of neologisms or in "feminine literature" (Simon 1996).

> Regarding certain lexemes, this shows often in alliterations (*Kind und Karriere, Mann und Maus);* the invitation for a Halloween Party at an American seminary reads: **Ghosts, Goblins, and God***!. Dress in your favorite costume and come for food, fellowship, and fun.*
>
> *Journalists are fan of this: "Food, fashion, fitness, films, fine art or fiction, there's a tidal wave of the fit-in, fall-in-line or be-left-behind culture that's engulfing the social scene these days" (Suppl. of Sunday Times of India, 27 Feb 2011).*

When we argue that memory brings up intuitively some individual interpretation, then insights from phenomenology request a critical reflection of any such inspiration. Even if the cognitive representation in the translator has to be more explicit (in order to hermeneutically highlight one's own understanding), the verbal formulation in a translation shall not.

### 8.3.2 Condensing phrases

Also, there are indefinite formulations open for interpretation in texts. Suspense is a well-known topic of literary and reception studies. Translators can try to keep this suspense in the text, rather than fix it into a very clear proposition, in order to enable interpretation for the readers as well. This refers to the so-called translation universal of *explicitation*, when translators try to clearly say what they have understood. But cognitive studies have observed one important aspect of behavior in professional translators compared with learners, that is the tolerance of uncertainty and ambiguity in texts (Tirkkonen-Condit 1997:78). Creative and ambiguous language in an author is not easy to translate. A soft touch of words, initiating exactly the scene, is more difficult than the tackling with so-called difficult authors who have a complicated style. There are techniques of condensing phrases, so that the scene becomes more visible:

> An example: „*Lo splendore avvolto nella nube"* (Angelo G. Roncalli on the picture of a saint). Gradually the translation draft is being condensed: (1) Der Glanz, der in eine Wolke gehüllt ist; (2) Der von einer Wolke umhüllte Glanz; (3) wolkenverhangenes Leuchten.
>
> Another example: „Im Licht der untergehenden Sonne" > im Abendlicht.

How to find the balance? Here an attempt from the translator's workshop: *The mark on the wall* → *Der Fleck an der Wand* (register too low) → *Das Mal an der Wand* (register too high) → *Das Zeichen* (mysterious).

Some explicitations of the implicit in the text may just as well be superfluous, because the meaning is clear from the overall text. Paraphrasing should not be used extensively. In the following example, taken from a church self-help book (a rather common translation assignment), the sentence perspective with the uniform stressing of "40 days" in the end focus (which is a prominent feature of PREDICATIVE MODE in that passage) was not sufficiently observed in the first translation (a). Under grammatical pressure the sentence structure was unnecessarily changed here. On top of that, it contains a serious shift in the verbal tense changing the message into uncertainty. Translation (b) corrects this. The last translation (c) tried to render the importance of the focus structure to make it more impressive. The translator assimilates this message and becomes herself quasi a preacher. Here, we observe a greater distance to the ST form.

**Sample text:**

The Bible is clear that God considers 40 days a spiritually significant time period. Whenever God wanted to prepare someone for his purposes, he took 40 days:

Noah's life was transformed by 40 days of rain.
Moses was transformed by 40 days on Mount Sinai.
The spies were transformed by 40 days in the Promised Land. (...)
Jesus was empowered by 40 days in the wilderness.
The disciples were transformed by 40 days with Jesus after his resurrection.
The next 40 days **will** transform your life.
This book is divided into 40 brief *chapters. (...)*
[R. Warren: The Purpose Driven Life. Zondervan: Grand Rapids, MI, 2002, p. 9-10]

**Translation a)**

Aus der Bibel geht hervor, dass 40 Tage für Gott ein Zeitabschnitt mit großer geistlicher Bedeutung sind. Immer, wenn Gott jemanden für eine Aufgabe vorbereiten wollte, nahm er sich dafür 40 Tage Zeit:

Noahs Leben wurde durch 40 Tage Regen verändert.
Mose wurde durch 40 Tage auf dem Berg Sinai verändert.
Die Kundschafter Israels veränderten sich durch 40 Tage im Verheißenen Land.
Jesus wurde durch 40 Tage in der Wüste für seinen Dienst bevollmächtigt.

Die Jünger wurden durch die 40 Tage verändert, die sie nach seiner Auferstehung mit Jesus verbrachten.
Die nächsten 40 Tage **können** Ihr Leben verändern.
Dieses Buch besteht aus 40 kurzen Kapiteln. (…)
[*Leben mit Vision*. Gerth Medien: Asslar 2003, 9-10]

**Translation b)**

Die Bibel zeigt deutlich, dass Gott einen Zeitraum von 40 Tagen als spirituell bedeutsam ansieht. Wann immer Gott jemanden für seine Zwecke vorbereiten wollte, dauerte dies 40 Tage:

Noahs Leben wandelte sich durch 40 Tage Regen.
Mose wurde ein anderer durch 40 Tage auf dem Berg Sinai.
Die Kundschafter veränderten sich durch 40 Tage im Land der Verheißung.
Jesus gewann Vollmacht durch 40 Tage in der Wüste.
Die Jünger änderten sich durch 40 Tage in Gemeinschaft mit Jesus nach seiner Auferstehung.
Die nächsten 40 Tage **werden** auch Ihr Leben verwandeln.
Dieses Buch ist in 40 kleine Kapitel unterteilt. (…) (*first re-translation.*)

**Translation c)**

Die Bibel zeigt ganz klar, dass für Gott ein Zeitraum von 40 Tagen spirituell bedeutsam ist. Wo immer Gott jemanden auf seine Zwecke vorbereiten wollte, da hat das 40 Tage gedauert:

40 Tage im Regen veränderten Noahs Leben.
40 Tage auf dem Berg Sinai machten Mose zu einem anderen Menschen.
40 Tage im Verheißenen Land veränderten die Kundschafter.
40 Tage in der Wüste verliehen Jesus Vollmacht.
40 Tage in Gemeinschaft mit Jesus nach seiner Auferstehung verwandelten die Jünger.
Die kommenden 40 Tage **werden** auch dein Leben verändern.
Dieses Buch enthält 40 kleine Kapitel. (…) (*my later re-translation.*)

### 8.3.3 Functional style in LSP

In specialist translation, the STYLISTICS of the version will have to observe the adequate functional style, standard text blocks, formulae, controlled language, phraseology, etc., as requested by the GENRE. Technical writing is meanwhile a subject of special research and creation of writing norms, see Göpferich (2002). Since specialist translation is just a continuation of the communication for specific purposes in another language, in order to overcome the language barrier, the relevant text type is decisive for functional style. This will often result in changes in the translation, because the text type – as understood according to the DISCOURSE FIELD – has to be realized in the target language. There might be deviant norms for that, which will then determine the translator's decision.

Functional stylistics and its phraseology is also decisive to create authenticity for text and translation, since scientific contents require their adequate representation in texts (Baumann 1992:37). Such texts, if written in an ordinary style, would not be accepted by their readers as authoritative texts.

It is particularly on the level of STYLISTICS where "memorized linguistic sequences" are being applied and Bolinger (1976) has claimed that most language is remembering rather than generating creatively. Technical texts are characterized by a particular amount of "ready-made language", as "texts composed in different registers and different situations are expected to show different degrees of optimization" (Heltai 2004:57). The translator therefore should know about the adequate amount of repetitive forms in order not to fall into jargon (excessive use) or translationese (inadequate use). Psycholinguistic studies have shown that translators, under time pressure, tend to use more ready-made language than with lengthy elaborate translations, especially in team work, and we already mentioned the significance of "flow" in writing.

> This leads to the hypothesis that "a slow and analytic translation process may be subject to a higher degree of source language interference, while a faster process (when the translator 'gets into the swing') induces the translator to think holistically, which may yield a more fluent translation. 'Getting into the swing' also means finding the correct register and the ready-made units belonging to that register" (Heltai 2004:63).

A very productive language characteristic in German LSP are prefixes that show a directed movement, e.g. *auf-, ab-, an-, ver-, er-, hin-, he-, ge-, durch-, aus-, ein-, ent-, weg-* and others. Reflexive verbs also belong to this (*sich abschwächen, sich behaupten, sich bessern, sich zeigen, sich halten, sich durchsetzen*). This feature can be used in German translations, in order to enhance the idiomatic appeal of one's text. Frequent postfixes are: *-lich, -bar, -ig, -los,* a. o. Concrete verbs can be made abstract by this means of word formation, see examples below. It finds application in philosophical texts, for instance to indicate the intellectual move in narrowing a cognitive concept, mainly with prefixes *be-* and *er-* (Stolze 1999:111).

**Examples**

| | |
|---|---|
| *greifen* | begreifen, angreifen, zugreifen, abgreifen, umgreifen |
| *lassen* | verlassen, vorlassen, erlassen, anlassen, auflassen |
| *wenden* | verwenden, umwenden, anwenden, bewenden (lassen) |
| *scheinen* | erscheinen, aufscheinen, bescheinen |
| *hören* | anhören, erhören, zuhören, abhören |
| *lösen* | erlösen, auflösen, einlösen, ablösen |
| *fassen* | verfassen, erfassen, befassen, anfassen, umfassen |
| *stellen* | vorstellen, verstellen, anstellen, umstellen, bestellen |
| *drücken* | unterdrücken, verdrücken, andrücken, aufdrücken, wegdrücken |
| *fahren* | erfahren, anfahren, umfahren, befahren, abfahren |
| *bauen* | erbauen, umbauen, bebauen, anbauen, zubauen, verbauen, vorbauen |
| *bilden* | einbilden, vorbilden, nachbilden, abbilden |
| *schärfen* | verschärfen, einschärfen, usw. |

### 8.3.4 Expert-lay communication

In communication between experts and lay people, e.g. in instruction manuals, but mainly in the media, a special language for intelligibility is needed. Translation must be precise to bridge the information gap between scientists and lay persons. Kalverkämper (1988:171) calls for a „specialist hermeneutics" (*Fachsprachenhermeneutik*): the author should consider the comprehending conditions of his audience and insert explanations in a kind of „implicit didactics". Intelligibility is not in style, not in the omission of specialist content, not in exchanging terms by general language words. Intelligibility is based, as a principle, on the fact that explanations are given for special facts, which the author considers ignored by the reader. Users' manuals must be very logical, any mistakes in originals made by technical authors who do not consider their addressees shall be corrected. Only the necessary information will be given to use the machine, the reference to illustrations is decisive. One will distinguish between the logic of a constructor and the logic of a user.

As to media communication, Beier (1983:96) has analyzed the linguistic means of science-external communication in English print media, and he found „five points" (1) titles and eye-catchers, (2) reference to persons, (3) informal style,

(4) evaluations, (5) explanation of specialist facts. The important aspect of explanation can be achieved, according to Beier (1983:104), in two ways:

> 1) A fact is being explained by reference to semantic features of the respective term. (...) This procedure presupposes that the reader has already some corresponding pre-knowledge or that this was imparted already in the previous text.
>
> 2) In the explanation of a fact, there is a modification of the reference: either there is reference to other scholarly terms (of the same or of other domains) and probably there are similarities between these terms (...); or the explanation is done „externally", i.e. by a comparing reference to phenomena found in the daily environment of life experience of the recipient. (*my translation form German*).

This confirms the results of cognitive science which states: "The importance of pragmatic meanings in translation – long recognized by translation theory – can be accounted for in recent neurolinguistic and neuropsychological modes of the bilingual brain" (House 20011).[116]

### 8.3.5  No decision-making as to syntax

The issue of a sociolect or a phraseology to be considered is not a question of grammar, as Wilss sees it. Wilss (1996:174ff) discusses "translation as decision-making and choice" and brings this in connection with grammar and syntax. To the contrary, the hermeneute sees texts as messages within a culture. Ideology and sociolects appear in stylistic forms, which can of course be described linguistically on the system level. Translation, however, works on the practical level.

Decision-making is defined by Wilss as "a rational behavior" at a restricted point: "Decision-making processes do not begin until the need for decision-making is sufficiently defined within the structure of a problem-solving operation that prepares the way for decision-making" (ibid. 175).[117] But Wilss has to admit that such "operations" do not work for specific translation problems, since

---

[116] Juliane House in the abstract for her paper on „Going Cognitive: Translation and Bilingual Cognition" at the conference on *Research Models in Translation Studies II* in Manchester, 1 May 2011.

[117] He concludes: "Once a translator has gained seizable experience in handling a certain problem, e.g. the translation of **English participial constructions into German**, he or she can disregard the aspect of decision-making procedure and proceed routinely, because he or she has internalized optimization rules" (Wilss 1996:186). (*my underlining*)

the translator does not translate sentence structures but content. This is mainly relevant on the micro-contextual level.

> Because many STs contain singular (episodic) phenomena, such as semantic vagueness [...], syntactic complexity, intricate text strategies (rhetorical strategies), theme/rheme distribution, central vs. peripheral information, metaphorical expressions, wordplay, ironic text elements, distorted or non-transparent formulations, morphological idiosyncrasies or innovation, adjective/noun collocations, prepositional phrases, string compounds, lexical gaps, etc. [...] the solution obtained for micro-contextual problems can be generalized only to a very limited extend (contrary to grammatical rules). The more unique a translation problem is, the less practicable are general problem-solving/decision-making procedures, because there is no way of discerning systematic coordination principles for individual text perspectives and developing general criteria for assessing a translation situation [...] *Unique translation problems are often of stylistic nature.* (Wilss 1996:176f)

This is really true, and instead of trying to define rules, one should strengthen the language proficiency of translators, their stylistic awareness, and their idiomatic confidence. Unwillingly, Wilss offers a striking example for this effect:

> Here is an example which I take from a text on the impact of international terrorism on life in Britain and to the mounting crisis of confidence between the state machine with its larger-than-life ears and the ordinary citizen whose civil liberties are under serious attack (the article was published in the „Washington Post" some years ago, but the exact source is not recoverable). One sentence in this article reads as follows:
>
> a. The rise of terrorism on an international scale, of subversion as a respectable military weapon – recognized by such classical strategists as von Clausewitz, it is a common tool of all modern governments –, and the scope of sensitive technical information, jealously guarded by the average defence ministries, have all helped *to create a state of paranoia, and a paranoia of the state.*
>
> Apart from the complex syntax with its shift of expectancy by means of a parenthesis, it is almost impossible to reproduce in German the chiasm "state of paranoia/paranoia of the state", because German lacks a word which is as handily ambiguous as the English word "state" (in German one would have to differentiate between "state" as "Zustand" and "state" as "Staat"). Nevertheless, quite perplexingly, a highly skilful translator (Eva Rittweger), obviously not engaging in translation problem-solving operations, but activating her intuitive resources, came forward on the spur of the moment with the very impressive solution:
>
> b. (All this has created an atmosphere to the extent) *"daß sich der herrschende Verfolgungswahn in einem Verfolgungswahn der Herrschenden spiegelt".* (Wilss 1996:171f; *my underlining*)

This is how a translator will work, but to the contrary, Wilss sets out to contribute some rules because "the issue of decision-making is not well covered by recent translation research" (ibid., 177). He discusses syntactic shifts in going from English to German, falling again back into comparative stylistics.[118] Such grammatical discussions are not helpful for the translator.

On the one hand, all texts are individual entities despite their belonging to a certain text type, and on the other hand, language problems present themselves differently to various translating persons, based on their individual hermeneutical background knowledge and language proficiency. What constitutes a severe difficulty for the one, is no problem at all for the other.

## 8.4 Function

Of course a text does not consist solely of words. In a quest for authenticity of the message, the translator will finally focus on the intended target DISCOURSE FIELD for the translation, on the adressees or the intended group of readers. S/he will not stop at micro-contextual problems but raise the attention up to the overall level of the text FUNCTION in communication. Looking at the function is important, as it affects the general set-up of the target text. Skopos theory (Reiß & Vermeer 1984) rightly has pointed out the great importance of the "purpose" of any translation. But in view of the cognitive representation and translational strategies, this move is at the end of the process, and not at its beginning.

---

[118] **Examples** from Wilss (1996:178f): "We are aware that the word order shift is obligatory, because the two utterances stand in a syntactic one-to-one relation (1) *he has read the book* vs. *er hat das Buch gelesen*. Of course it is possible to modify the German sentence syntactically, e.g. by saying (2) *das Buch hat er gelesen,* but this translation would require a different theme/rheme distribution in English [...]. Things look different in cases where obligatory syntactic shifts can be accomplished in stylistically different manners. Example:
(4) *Arriving at the airport, he found his plane gone*
(5) a. Als er am Flugplatz ankam, stellte er fest, daß seine Maschine (bereits) weg war
    b. Er kam am Flugplatz an und stellte fest, ...
    c. Bei seiner Ankunft am Flugplatz stellte er fest, ...
    d. Am Flugplatz angekommen, stellte er fest, ...
For the translator, the English sentence contains a 'choice point' because German syntax lacks a corresponding participial construction." – This is all correct but we need not reflect on it.

### 8.4.1 Visualizing a literary scene

Literary translation texts need to realize their intention within the respective DISCOURSE FIELD of society, for example fantasy readers, children, feminists, romanticists, adventure lovers, theatre spectators, poetry fans etc., however not without representing the structure of the original, including tense, author's voice, and style. The function of literary translation is to present an author's world view and create interest in it.

On the language level, the aspect of FUNCTION concerns idiom. In formulating a translation in view of various aspects such as STYLISTICS and COHERENCE, the focus often is on individual phrases, what sometimes is detrimental for the overall idiom of the formulation. This can be improved by an integrative view, leaving aside now the comparison with the source text.

The background of an assertion is its cultural embedding or the scientific/scholarly way of thinking, and this determines the specific scene as a meaning in a given text. Vizualizing this scene is based on idiomatic formulation. In linguistic creativity one will have to give up literal translation forms and try to verbalise the emotion and scenery. This is very difficult in structurally rather distant language pairs, e.g. German and Hindi, or Chinese and English. The consideration of the extra-lingual background leads us out of the text towards the FUNCTION within the discourse field, addressing the specific needs of the interested audience.

### 8.4.2 Specialist communication across language barrier

In translation for specific purposes, the text FUNCTION normally remains the same, since a translation serves to continue specialist communication across the language barrier. "It is obvious that domain-specific texts, technical, commercial, narrative etc., macrocontextually raise only minor problems. It is unlikely that such texts will be assigned essentially divergent perspectives by the participants of a translation event" (Wilss 1996:176). The text type schema is a specific repository of linguistic knowledge, as text types are cognitive formulation models, and it is useful to know about target parallel texts representing some models for socially accepted and already solved writing problems (Antos 1982:119). Competent translators command certain macro-structures and apply them, as this corresponds to the addressees' reading expectations. A specialist "translation must not be deviant or strange compared to what is normal in genuine target texts of the same type", says Nielsen (1994:25).

The question regarding FUNCTION is whether the translation as a whole text contains a plausible order of argumentation (in humanities) or a logical structure (in sciences). Empathy with the message leads to co-authorship, either in repeating a literary author's creative voice, or in speaking like a scientist in specialized communication. The issue of intelligibility for the addressees now becomes relevant, as knowledge transfer is dependent on adequate formulation. There is a difference whether you write for lay persons or for specialists within a domain, as intelligibility is a relative concept referring to the respective cognitive environment.

If the translator anticipates barriers of comprehension in his intended readers, he or she will apply compensatory problem-solving strategies that explicate, paraphrase, simplify or modify the original text at a certain point (Stolze 1993). Instruction manuals, for instance, have to be logic and understandable for users of a machine, observing even the maxims of work psychology in relation to the evidence of the product logic in comparison of the users' logic (Stolze 1999:154). Any defect or unclear expression in the source text may legitimately be corrected in a translation, for reasons of the text's FUNCTION. That is what functional translation theories are calling for (Nord 1997).

The use of controlled language and standard macrostructures with fixed text blocks in the target language (even if different from the source text style) will support the intelligibility of translations, which function like an original text. The use of speech acts is relevant in legal texts: a translated certificate will again serve as a document, a legal text will follow juridical functional style in order to become authoritative. This is true even if such features do not appear or only in a different manner in the source text. (The excuse that "this is written so in the original" is not valid for professional translation.) As an hermeneutical rule, the individual elements are determined by the whole entity. The last step of revision according to FUNCTION is often neglected by beginners, as various studies have shown. But we never can avoid responsibility. For example, beginners tend to closely stick to the English attributive sentence structure which in German sounds strange and blurs the speech acts:

**From a contract:**

*The employee shall withdraw from an order if conditions develop which would impair our ability to perform the order properly.*

1) Der Mitarbeiter ist verpflichtet, vom Vertrag zurückzutreten, wenn sich Umstände entwickeln, die unsere Fähigkeit, den Auftrag ordentlich auszuführen, behindern würden. (*student translation*)

2) Der Mitarbeiter hat von einem Auftrag Abstand zu nehmen, wenn Umstände auftreten, die eine ordnungsgemäße Auftragsausführung beeinträchtigen würden.

*Each employee is solely responsible for the proper reporting of all compensation earned and paid to him/her, and for any income tax liabilities that might result from the reporting of such income tax reporting and filing requirements of all jurisdictions to which he/she is subject.*

1) Jeder Mitarbeiter trägt alleine die Verantwortung dafür, sämtliches Entgeld korrekt zu melden, das er verdient und erhalten hat. Ebenso ist er alleine verantwortlich für jegliche Einkommenssteuerschuld, die entsteht, wenn er der Verpflichtung der zuständigen Gerichtsbarkeit nachkommt, die Angaben zur Einkommenssteuer zu melden und die Unterlagen aufzubewahren. (*student translation*)

2) Jeder Mitarbeiter ist selbst für die ordnungsgemäße Anmeldung aller Einkünfte sowie für die Zahlung der sich aus dieser Meldepflicht ergebenden Einkommensteuer bei allen für ihn zuständigen Rechtsbehörden verantwortlich. (*retranslation*)

Such an approach of course appeals much to the factual knowledge and linguistic proficiency in the translators. Again, there is no methodology for them to infer the correct translation. On the other hand, it happens often that later on, after some distance to the text, and when the cognitive scene has become clear, the correct formulations will arise easily from memory.

Even if – in practice – translation work actually begins with a sentence by sentence formulating draft observing the respective GENRE, the reference point is not the ST structure but aspects like COHERENCE, STYLISTICS and FUNCTION. The usually adopted horizontal relation of equivalence is now replaced by a vertical one of holistic adequacy. This is also relevant for translation didactics, because now the focus will be shifted from the analysis of grammar structures towards the realization of the pragmatic functioning of language in a social environment.

All the described **categories of attention in translation as a text production** are relevant and inter-linked. For more clarity they are put together in the table below:

| Translation writing | | General language | LSP |
|---|---|---|---|
| Formulating | GENRE | Genre, fiction/non-fiction, shape of text, pictures, verse order, printed appearance | Medium of text type, layout, space available, illustrations, script fonts, legal prescriptions, markers |
| | COHERENCE | Titles, isotopy, paradigmatic compatibility, synonyms, syn-semantic cotext, thematic strings, allusion, proper names, geographical places | Status of equivalence of terms, concepts in humanities, specific word formation, logic in text structure, names |
| | STYLISTICS | Verbal tense, mode, numerus, prosody of emotion, direct speech, condensing forms, characteristics of milieu, suspense, word play, metonymy, alliteration, rhyme | Typical text blocks, functional style, phraseology, passive voice, impersonal expression, communicative metaphors, controlled language, style guide |
| | FUNCTION | Author's intention, text structuring, intended group of readers, intertextuality, visualizing the scene | Communicative goal, macro-structure, addressees' expectation, norms of intelligibility, vision of the topic debated |

Translators could take advantage of the fact that their text input remains – unlike in interpreting – present for re-reading it several times. Instead of a translational text analysis regarding "source text material" to be re-used in the target version, we would rather call for an assessment of the text within its situation, and a study of parallel texts in order to get familiar with text types, genres and socially accepted ways of writing.

The categories of attention for text comprehension and text production as described in the foregoing may direct the translator's sensitivity for some important features of the individual text which always has to be considered in its overall complexity. The translator has to integrate various aspects into every single translation assignment. His or her competence, then, turns out to be a networking activity based on a rich memory, as the receptive outlook and productive strategies have to be combined in the translating work.

# 9 Elements of translation competence

## 9.1 Dynamic interaction of memory and language proficiency

The translator is the central element in an hermeneutical model of translation. Hence, the issue of translation competence is crucial. Our concept is geared towards an empowerment of the translator as a person. The task consists in finding adequate words for the message understood and the approach will be integrative and envision the text as a whole entity. This is the reason why hermeneutical translation draws from as many sources as available, it is really interdisciplinary. Whereas scientific research focuses on a specific phenomenon, hermeneutics is interested in the results of that research to integrate them into the strategic motivation of social action. The model of human translation has to integrate the multiperspective activity of an embodied self in the surrounding world.

In a much cited paper, Neubert (2000:7-10) has spelled out five parameters supposedly involved in translation competence:

- *language competence*: "a sine qua non", because it is a truism that "a near perfect knowledge of the niceties of the grammatical and lexical systems of the source and target languages are basic ingredients of translation competence";
- *textual competence* in the systematic of discourse;
- *subject competence*, that is, "the familiarity with what constitutes the body of knowledge of the area a translation is about";
- *cultural competence*, which is "not at all confined to literary matters";
- and "last but not least", *transfer competence*.

We think Neubert's five parameters of translation competence should not only be quoted (as is widely done) but also analyzed in their interrelated development.

M. Lewandowska-Tomasczyk (2004) criticizes those competences as insufficient, arguing from the view of language acquisition. She rightly states that "the list of competencies does not foreground the necessary *performance* aspect involving inter alia oral and/or written *fluency* ... in TL, without which, with all other competencies present, translators would not be able to act as translators" (ibid., 135f). She finds that pattern matching, internalization of the target language concepts, and the right use of rules in appropriate contexts are all features of competent bilinguals. This alone is not yet a translation competence. To our opinion, a very good language proficiency in one's mother tongue as well as in the foreign language concerned is a prerequisite for translators, a foundation for competence. Only if this is given, hermeneutical translation can begin, and then a dynamization of those features will set in.

The human memory is not only a storage system of information data, it is a living system. Such systems are in complex interaction with their environment and evolve constantly (Hendriks-Jansen 1996). The living body with its receptive organs does not only register information offered, but it also creates such information actively and processes it. Embodiment, or *"Leibhaftigkeit"* (Paepcke 1986:125)[119], encompasses factual, historical and linguistic knowledge, and a dynamic awareness of all of this in its application. Linguistic sensitivity (*Sprachgefühl*) is very important. Translating means communicative action in the social field, performed by historically rooted persons. Single aspects of the translational action have their impact on other acts within the overall procedural system.

According to our hermeneutical concept of translation, we can now define Neubert's translation competences in more detail.

> (1) "Language competence" includes the said abilities of competent bilinguals, including the awareness of differences in both linguistic patterns and in cultural concepts. (2) The "textual competence" means style awareness in view of the source text and rhetorical assurance in view of the adequate formulation in the target discourse field including text type and genre requirements. (3) The "subject competence" is what we have called factual knowledge regarding cultural specificities and scientific facts, as this defines the borders of the hermeneutical circle. (4) Neubert's "cultural competence" is already included in the first three competences mentioned. At this point we stress the need of phenomenological self-reflection, as was also stated as an aspect of expert approaches. The translator is rooted in his or her own culture and has to reflect on the implications. (5) Neubert's "transfer competence" cannot be restricted to the way of matching two languages. In reality it is a

---

[119] With reference to Gabriel Marcel who called it *"être corps"* in French, meaning an attention geared towards the environment in which the whole being is involved, not only the intellectual part of it.

mediating competence, in that the translator, in his/her performance, has to consider both the content of the translation and the addressees' cognitive environment.

Translation competence is dynamic. Integrating as many aspects as possible ensures highest versatility as a prerequisite for professional translation. The translator does not strive "to produce an adequate replica of the original" in the static sense of "converting L1 texts into L2 texts" (Neubert 2000:10), but rather to formulate authentically. In doing this he or she will apply a dynamic memory bringing up world knowledge and memorized formulations once read or heard, integrating this in a never ending learning process.

Lines of orientation in translational reading concern the text with its SITUATIVE BACKGROUND in a certain DISCOURSE FIELD, determined by a MEANING DIMENSION that shows in the PREDICATIVE MODE. This is grasped by the understanding translator and represented in the target language, in observance of the relevant fields of attention such as GENRE, COHERENCE, STYLISTICS and FUNCTION of the translation in the target situation. The idea is that contextually embedded information and meta-cognition will direct the problem-solving moves in the strategic decision-making process.

This concept is shown in the following model:

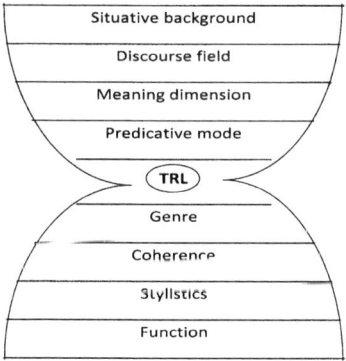

Translation means writing a text, and we have to coordinate the various aspects in our quest for creating authenticity for the message. In the revision of an initial translation draft, all the mentioned translational categories of attention will simultaneously play an important role, and they are interrelated, but never equally valid. There is a continuous helical movement between the source text structure and the translator's cognition. This idea has been taken up by cognitivist research, even though in a different terminology. Building on Anderson (1993), we see translation competence as a type of procedural knowledge, that is *knowing how*, rather than *knowing what* described as a declarative knowledge to be accumulated. Then the expert translator feels the authority to pass judgment on the own decision-making processes and also be ready to accept criticism. Relevant subject knowledge and a confidence into one's language proficiency are decisive.

In the dynamic process of translation, memory and language are interacting in an intricate manner. Target language frames associate intuitively or – as cognitivism would say – automatically with the source text ideas.

Only if there is responsibility in the professional translator will the reader accept the translation as an adequate text. Seen it this way as a responsible task, translation is no longer a servile work of slaves who would have to run after their authors and "faithfully follow the author on all ways" (Cutts 1996:260), or only to execute operational methods like a machine. It is, rather, a very creative activity of responsible text production. Others complain that "the translator's voice" is crying too loud in "domesticating the foreign" (Quale 1996). One will have to be critically aware of all these problems.

This hermeneutical approach is innovative in Translation Studies insofar as it focuses on presenting a "message" rather than a "source text". The practical task for translation pedagogics shifts now from analyzing equivalence on the language and grammar level to teaching text production in a social situation. Cultural education and scientific domain knowledge seem to be more important for translators than contrastive linguistics or comparative literature. And since the message understood is cognitively present in the translator's mind, nothing is being "transferred". Translators need writing models, but the idiomatic "choice points" are then handled intuitively, in view of the overall text and the translational categories we have described.

## 9.2 Discerning priorities in the texts

Any text is an individual entity, it represents very special features. The translator has to cope with all kinds of different texts, but the basic approach is always the same: try to understand it, identify with the message, and then write a translation in a way most intelligible for the audience intended. The strategy of social action is awareness, orientation, creation. There are problem priorities, and the translator will have to discern in every single case which aspect is dominant. Multifaceted texts include all these aspects on different levels of their holistic integrity, i.e. phonological peculiarities, semantic word fields, syntactic forms of style, pragmatic text construction.

The translator's approach to texts is more or less the same in literature and in specialist translation. The differences are to be seen in the knowledge base required, in the language proficiency, and in the function of the translation as a text. Whereas cultural and historical *knowledge* is necessary in literature, the knowledge relevant for specialized texts concerns the respective domain of science. Whereas literature uses the full potential of a language and thus requires *linguistic creativity* in the translator, technical translations will have to observe certain *functional styles* as a restricted sector within the overall language. Then the translations will be recognized as authoritative texts. The translation's *function* in literature is the task to open a new world of thinking to readers, to create interest in the foreign world, whereas in communication for specific purposes this function consists in continuing the original communication, now across the language border.

The individual coordination hierarchy of the various aspects of quality assurance in terms of translation priority has to be determined in every single case of translation anew, there is no general rule for that. "Every text poses different problems" (Eco 2006:13, n. 5). The translator will have to determine what appears to be the most important characteristic of the text at hand. The revision of translation drafts may then be based on linguistic aspects, as the translation task, in the final instance, is language production.

The cognitive environment relevant for understanding a text is different every time. Informative texts in communication for specific purposes require more factual knowledge and offer less linguistic freedom, as they show text type models to be followed, while literary texts against a cultural background call for receptivity in the human world, and for linguistic creativity. This has ever been accepted for the difference between literature and specialist texts, but there are even more variations within those text genres themselves.

In evaluating the text for understanding, the translator has to find out which approach may be adequate for the respective text at hand, in order to take the right priorities. It is the translator's cognitive processing which posits the relevant cognitive background for the text, it is not an inference generated from a text analysis. Hermeneutics suggests that "truth reveals itself to the reader". In this sense, every text says itself what is important, and this is the fundamental characteristic of translational competence in an hermeneutical approach. Any individual text presents a specific problem that will determine the translator's hierarchy of decision-making. The competent translator will have to discern this:

- In the case of *instructive texts*, for instance user manuals, the readability and its logical structure for a lay audience is the prominent feature dominating other aspects. Terminology must be coherent. Even if the translator must not be a technician, some basic technical understanding and the ability to think independently is necessary.

- In a *technical specification*, the exact terminology is most important, and checking for synonyms as well as data base retrieval skills are needed for adequate translation. But the rules of word formation and the principles of logical structuring shall not be forgotten over that.

- In a *hypertext translation* the problems of electronic data management might actually be more determining than questions of content and terminology. A holistic view on the various text parts is necessary for their inner coherence.

- In one *legal text*, the difference between the two law systems concerned, showing in key terms, might be dominant. As legal key terms often are linguistically vague, specialist knowledge making use of comparative law is needed for disambiguation.

- In another *legal translation*, e.g. a court sentence, it might be the functional style with its antiquated formulae what causes problems, and in a third one it will be the document character of the text.

- A *scholarly paper* appears to be different in style, e.g. more 'academic' in the German and more colloquial in the English speaking worlds (Stolze & Deppert 1998). This observation has consequences for the translation, as respective adaptation is needed.

- An *economic text* may show cultural specificity connected with a certain speakers' group, and also there is specific terminology to be correctly understood. In another case, corporate style and guidelines may be prominent.
- In one *advertising text*, the linking of contemporary word formation with culturally specific associations might be prevalent, whereas in another one the expressive linguistic forms and rhetorical phrases are prominent, and cultural specificity is found more in the visual area.
- An allegedly specialist text on a *product presentation* may turn out to be filled with management terms and only contain very few technical terms on a general level.
- In translating *business correspondence*, there might be required in one case some business knowledge, in another case client-oriented formulation, in a third case the sensibility for cultural differences, in a fourth case the precision regarding legal speech acts. In each translation, the relevant feature will be primary in the translational decision-making. However, secondary aspects like technical word formation, anonymous style, and layout shall not be eliminated by that.
- In a *political text* the underlying ideology of the author may be determining, what mirrors in the discourse field and its diction. Corrsponding metaphors should be discerned.
- Translating a *great speech* of a person already passed away long ago will not change the function and will try to render the emotional appeal in its rhetorical features.
- In a text presenting an *architectural draft* there may be no specialist terms found, but rather philosophical and cultural dissertations, and still the technical word formation is wanted as a functional style.
- For *popular psychology books* and self-help literature, an insight into the underlying ideology is indispensable, since the general language words used may easily lead to misconception.
- In a *newspaper article* to be read by laymen there might appear some technical terms to be rendered precisely in order not to change the information. Often there is relevant explanation in the text itself.
- *Children's books* need creative language, repetitive style, short sentences, and avoid morale (Oittinen 2003).
- In translating a *novel*, the particular style characterizing its author may be prominent, overruling any cultural aspects or genre type. Creative language may become a source of enthusiasm.
- At a *story from an exotic culture* it will be important to recreate the original scene mirroring in the metaphors and ideas on life. Language problems might be inferior.

- On the other hand, in translating *literature from a past century*, the historic epochal and cultural features might be prevalent in posing a translation difficulty.
- Translating a contemporary piece of *hybrid literature* is particularly challenging, because here the creolic influence of various migrant peoples, oral speech and social experiences has to be understood in order to find adequate linguistic frames.
- In a *poetic text* the rhythm might be the dominant feature to be respected, for instance, by means of reading aloud.
- In a *philosophical text* hermeneutical interpretation of the terms and argumentative style may be dominant.
- In a text on *church activities* the discourse field of the denomination will be relevant.
- In an *arts catalogue* where visible pictures are being described metaphorically by means of invisible ideas, much imagination will be required in the translator as well.
- *And so on, and so forth* (for more examples see Stolze 2003:299).

One might ask: How can I find out what is dominant in my text? Well, this is the work of intuition in grounded understanding. Translation competence includes the ability to discern a text's predominant specificity in every translation assignment. There is no general methodology yet for this task. Any specialist or literary or multimedia text presents an individual problematic to be solved by the translator. This will determine the individual hierarchy of translational decision-making.

The foregoing, of course, is an idealistic description of the basic problem. In practice, many translators will specialize on one certain aspect within the multiplicity of language. All this requires a sensitive holistic conscience as well as informed receptivity as part of the translational competence. In the final instance, responsibility for the result ever lies in the translating person herself.

## 9.3 The tool of lexicography

Dictionaries, glossaries, and data banks have ever been regarded as the main tools for translators. However, the use of dictionaries needs some knowledge about what they can offer and what not. There is also the question about the conception and recent developments in lexicography.

Since Medieval times, lexicons have been prepared to aid Bible translation. In order to reconstruct Greek *koiné* (a language spoken at the time of the New Testament but fairly different from classical Greek and from the modern language spoken in Greece today), researchers have, initiated by Frederick Danker, noted all occurrences of Greek lexemes found both in the Bible text and in other texts from that period of time. Based on traditional knowledge and the indications of context, a "general meaning" was extracted and indicated in the lexicon. And still today, lexicography works like that: you search for occurrences of a word in various contexts, try to find out the contextual meaning based on your world knowledge, and compare it with other meanings you had found earlier.

The underlying linguistic rule is that any word's meaning, separate from a context, is "far reaching, wide-spread, social and abstract", and only in an utterance it becomes "precisely defined, individual and concrete" (Weinrich 1970:16). "The meaning of a word is its use," said Wittgenstein (in *Philosophical Investigations* §43). Thus the meaning is a kind of a semiotic potential, rather vague, contrastively shown by means of glosses that constitute a word field. Meaning is grounded interpretability, to be disambiguated by the translator's grounded understanding. The Greek lexicon for the N.T. Greek (Bauer & Danker) simply makes the effort to list *all* occurrences found, in papyri and elsewhere, as a proof.

Several synonyms create a word field, a grouping of words that have something in common, semantic particles they share, we call them 'semes'. Example: *dialogue, conversation, contact, meeting, partnership, talks, verbal exchange, debate, negotiation, communication,* etc. are a word field about "talking together". In bilingual lexicography, several of those connected words will be listed, but they never constitute an exhaustive proposal for translation equivalents; you may ever find some other words from your own memory to be used in a translation.

Any novel context adds a new 'seme' to the meaning. So the only thing what lexicographers can do, is to agree on a "basic meaning potential", accepting the fact that there are no clear borders of meaning. That is the idea of the modern Prototype semantics (Kleiber 1993) where meaning is conceived of as an assembly of semes, more concentrated in the center, but with some offspring at the flexible borders.

No absolutely concise definition of meaning for general language words will ever be possible. "Open texture" is a term introduced by the philosopher Hart (cf. Endicott 2000:37) who has suggested that general words have an incontrovertible "core meaning" defined as standard instance in which no doubts are felt about its application, and around each vague word there is a margin of uncertainty called the "penumbra", others speak of fuzzziness.

Now there is the new lexicon in this tradition of Nida and Louw (1989), who present a new method of integrating "statements of meaning". Lee (2003) vehemently criticizes those statements as being not always convincing "definitions" of the meaning. He proposes another methodology of gathering, in order to obtain more reliable meaning indications that would overcome the lexicographer's inferring subjectivity. However, Lee seems to miss a clear idea of the process leading to the information in a dictionary.

In the sciences the process of knowledge goes from a definition describing the objects to a term. In the case of lexicography (not terminology) the process is just the other way round: the philologist tries to filter out a basic meaning of all the precise occurrences of the word found. This may well lead to a sort of prototypical "description of the meaning concept", but it remains a subjective endeavor, just as the meaning statements in BDAG (Danker 1993) and Nida & Louw (1989). It is not possible to find an ever valid "definition" for abstract concepts, such as *calling, revelation, understanding,* etc. and the large majority of the ambiguous words in New Testament Greek. Lee's "new method" proposes to collect all data possible in an electronic database, but this will still require the researchers to draw a conclusion, and when you put this through controlling teams, the discussion will never end, because meaning and use of words by people does not end. Also, why should all the old work done be not reliable, all of a sudden? Language is not entirely separable from peoples' thought.

## 9.4 The translator's growth

Sometimes there is complaint about the fact that the translator's status were not adequately perceived in public (Kußmaul 2000:32) and that we needed more self-confidence (Hönig 1993). In order to improve this, we propose here to see the profession in a systemic model. The goal of developing a translation competence consists in empowering the translator to cope with various textual jobs. The hermeneutical approach to translation puts much more responsibility in the translating person than traditional translation theories focusing only on text structures. This may enhance the translator's status.

Kußmaul (2007:100) mentions some holistic recommendations on a global approach to translation offered by practitioners, but this is not exact enough for him. He poses questions and elaborates on explanations on the word level, citing various contributions from cognitive science. But these questions are already answered by translational hermeneutics:

1. What is a global strategy and macro-analysis? (*my translation* from Kußmaul 2007:100). -- The global strategy follows the mentioned categories of orientation, proposing four aspects of macro-analysis (situative background, discourse field, meaning dimension, predicative mode).
2. Where should we direct our attention when we want to detect the meaning of a word from the previous or following context? -- We will find this meaning situated within a word field or isotopic web.
3. Which mental processes do we have to trigger in our mind? -- These processes begin intuitively in subconscious autopoiesis.
4. How do we activate our world knowledge for the text? Which kind of knowledge is relevant? -- Given knowledge is activated automatically by textual input. Subject knowledge regarding the topic treated is relevant.
5. How do we find an adequate paraphrasing for a word meaning, normally called free translation? -- We find it in imagining the respective scene talked about.
6. How can we detect the translation problems to be solved? -- Many problems will not even arise when we approach the text in grounded understanding. Most translation problems come from certain words where the external background is unknown and therefore has to be researched beforehand.

Within the field of Translation Studies there are numerous studies on the teaching of translation, on contrastive linguistics, software tools, terminography, text types, mental activity, comparative literature, etc. (Toury 1995:10). We might legitimately ask what the hidden link is among all these studies, and how all this could be brought together to constitute a visible discipline of TS.

One contribution to this effort might be a view of the translator in his or her personal growth by the professional activity performed. The translator will be able to act responsibly. E. Prunč (2007:341) requests rightly, that "the translator should engage self-confidently in the construction of senses and cultures, including the own translation culture. The precondition for this, however, is the ability to understand the power games being played in the social field of trans-cultural communication, to battle against the marginalization of the own profession, and to try to interfere as an equal partner based on his or her specialist competence" (*my translation*).

We had defined the act of understanding as a medial event. The philosopher Eberhard states:

> It is part of the ongoing effort of philosophy to find the right word. Finding the right word is the stammering characteristic of hermeneutics, and, as Grondin notes, 'hermeneutics is a humanism' (…). This does not mean that hermeneutics knows what man is. For Gadamer humanism is part of *Bildung*, culture, education, self-formation, (…). *Bildung* is a self-building, not a building that stands but a building in process, a building that understands, so to speak. It is 'building' in a verbal, not substantival, sense. Humanism, like metaphysics, is underway, always open to the other who might be right even in what it means to be human. (Eberhard 2004:62, note 1)

It is precisely in this way that a competent translator is growing, constantly being open to the new and unknown, thus becoming able to decide. Today this echoes in the common calling for "lifelong learning" for professional translators. Translation proves to be a directed process, a helical movement out of the translator's perspective. We can see this systemically.

## 9.5 A systemic model of translation

An old wisdom says that there are four areas most important in the life of humans: the *physical*, the *emotional*, the *cognitive* and the *spiritual* area. And each one of those worlds should be opened and entered at least once a day. That is how the ancient philosophical view of human life in its fullness sees it.

Now we may ask: Couldn't this be also relevant for a translator as a person in the system of her social activity? Transferred onto translation, we also perceive four aspects, though named a bit less philosophically:

⇨ the emotive motivation – i.e. the attitude towards clients including reasons for accepting or rejecting a commission;

⇨ the material outfit – i.e. office installations, experience and knowledge in the translator;

⇨ the cognitive process – i.e. the concrete application of one's translation competence in understanding the text and producing an adequate translation, considering the translational categories of orientation;

⇨ the intellectual enrichment – a life-long learning process as the outcome of the translation work and the basis for future motivation.

All these aspects are connected with each another and have to be integrated into the model of translation. A helical movement, then, becomes visible in the whole procedure. In the professional approach to texts, the translation process as such is decisively influenced by all the other areas of experience. Let us explain the model (see below):

(1) There is the *emotive motivation* affecting one's attitude towards clients. An "initiator" (Nord 1991:8) may address a translator asking for service. Now there are two reactions possible: either the commission is accepted and carried out, or not. In the first case the translator may have great service orientation, react openly, ask for which purpose the work is needed, show interest, etc. There are various reasons for this: S/he may be glad that there is adequate payment offered. S/he might have interest in that specific subject concerned in the assignment, which could even be a follow-up job to the previous one completed. Or there is only routine, perhaps the obligation to replace a colleague, or there is competitive pressure.

But a job may also be rejected. Reasons for this reaction may be: work overload, lack of time or lack of interest in the subject, negative experience with the client in earlier jobs, etc. There may also be uncertainty about the personal competence, or conscious limitation onto a few specific subject areas. The emotional state directly affects the way how translators are dealing with job offers. Such motivations for accepting or rejecting a job have occasionally been researched by means of questionnaires, however with a link to other, mostly financial aspects of translation.

(2) Then there is the issue of the ***material outfit*** needed for being able to do translation work at all. The translator will ask him or herself whether the physical, the social and the intellectual capacity for the job are given: is there a computer with TM-system, lexicons on CD-rom, special dictionaries, specialized literature, a court authorization, a third party liability insurance, membership in a professional association, a quality assurance system, etc.? A lack of necessary TM tools, as a principle, hinders participation in large technical translation projects (even if one were able to do it intellectually). Such equipment will be decisive for the success of the task, a lack of it might also lead to uncertainty and rejection of possibly interesting jobs. In practice, the lack of a liability insurance often prevents the acceptance of new challenging jobs in the field of technical and legal translation, even if those constitute the bulk of practical professional commissions.

> Alves & Gonçalves (2007:47) state that "subjective/emotional and physiological/motor aspects (are) involved in translation and constitute an important interface between body regulation and subjective consciousness which, in translating, can be related to typing skills, postural and ergonomic behavior, emotional balance and control under psychological stress, internal motivation etc. Despite being peripheral and less influential, the management of these aspects can either maximize or minimize cognitive resources that, in principle should mostly be concentrated on the processes taking place in the specific competence system."

The translator will also have to consider personal experience gathered so far: is there a formal special education, training courses attended, travels made, regular exchange with colleagues, previous work experience?

## A systemic model of translation

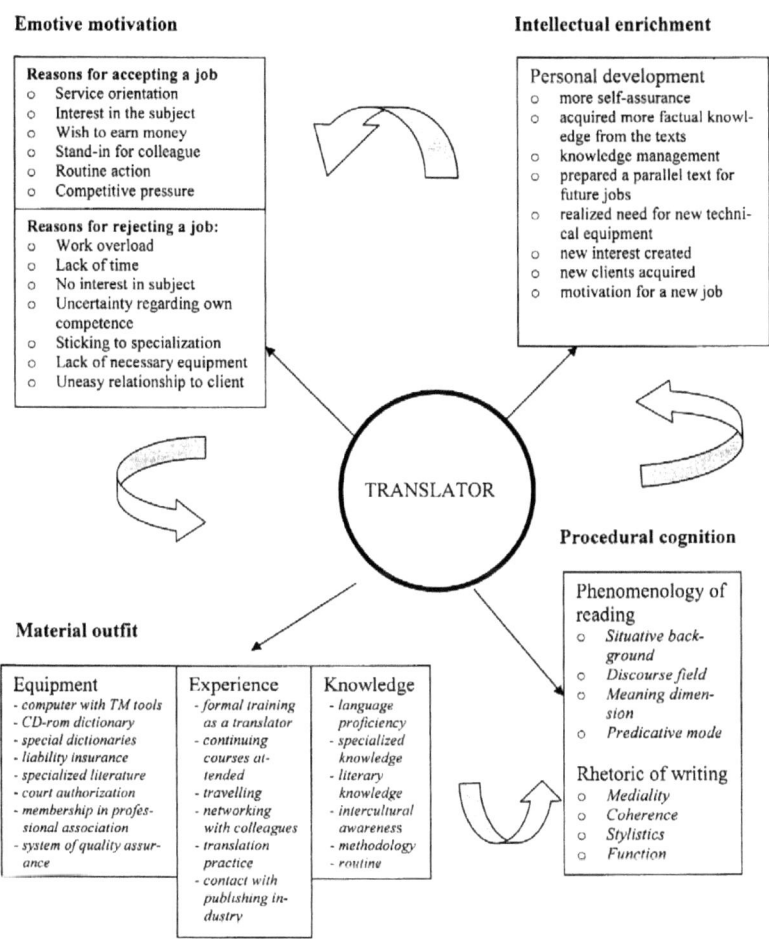

Networking is also a sign of professionals: E.W. Stein (1997), for instance, has proposed the method of network analysis, which identifies experts among professionals by analyzing the types and density of relationships among individuals within their professional context. The correspondent self-reflection on one's material outfit will not only influence the attitude towards clients, but also lead to more readiness to invest in office installation and further training.

No less important is the intellectual knowledge: language proficiency has to be constantly trained, knowledge of facts and developments, awareness of parallel literature and cultural specificities, the command of methodology and routine are needed. Both physical and intellectual equipment as a material outfit are necessary to do the job.

(3) The ***procedural cognition*** includes the concrete process of understanding a text and producing a translation in the other language. The relevant top-down- and bottom-up processes of dealing with the text have been described here earlier. Phenomenology of the situation and rhetorical aspects of writing are important for the translational strategy according to the translational categories of attention.

(4) After the translation job is finished, the area of ***intellectual growth***, a kind of spiritual enrichment, comes into our view. The entire procedure of doing translations provides for a learning process that will widen the translator's intellectual horizon. This aspect has not yet been researched in TS, but in an hermeneutical approach it is very important. By every single translation text encountered we learn something anew, our interest for other texts and working areas is being enhanced, memories from other texts are stirred up, the need for new tools is better understood.

Our knowledge gathered in one job will influence our achievement in the next one. Practitioners call this "utilizing knowledge". We have gained self-assurance, improved our routine, acquired new factual knowledge, prepared a parallel text for future translations, saw the need for novel office equipment, established links to other fields of encyclopedic knowledge, created new working interest, and found new clients, even made some bad experience. All this will in the end positively affect our emotional attitude towards future jobs. Modern techniques of individual knowledge management are being developed.

The various factors of the model might render new insights for translation criticism. Certain translational decisions can now be judged against a wider background and better understood in their reasons. There is never only one linguistic feature causing a translational reaction, as was long supposed in TS and is alluded by the idea of "translation rules". A glimpse of this has already been presented by studies concerning the "power relationships" in translation. Such studies themselves are influenced by those factors. Hence, an inadequate selection of subjects for a test may just reduce the relevance of the data collected.

We have finally come back – in a helical movement – to our starting point of the survey, at "motivation", but we arrived not at the same place. We are now on a hermeneutically higher level. It is a great shortcoming in Translation Studies that the act of translating has only been seen as a static transfer relationship, ignoring time and dynamics of social action. The translator's growth, however, is one of the most decisive factors in the whole procedure. Knowledge, social behavior, and even physical equipment are constantly evolving. They gradually lead to the level of "expertise" which, however, is difficult to define. Ericsson et al. (1993) promote the concept of "deliberate practice" – a goal-oriented activity, which integrates progressively increasing levels of difficulty, informative feedback and opportunities for repetition and correction of errors.

Alves and Gonçalves (2007:48) call for a "dynamic model of translator's competence". Instead of any growth of a text by multiple translations, we are looking here at a "growth of the translator".

> As cognitivist research has shown: "One observes changes of degree and kind in the levels of translator's competence as this competence develops and matures and procedural and declarative knowledge about translation become forms of specialized knowledge. ... We intend to show that translator's competence should be considered a particular cognitive configuration that allows translators to establish a balance between the periphery and the central layers of cognitive systems and, from a situated perspective, enables them to arrive at an inferentially driven interpretive resemblance between source and target texts. (Alves & Gonçalves 2007:53).

This is what hermeneutics has always affirmed. A dynamic view of a translator's competence should, therefore, move away from a static view of competence as a tangible, concrete ability and conceive of it as an ever changing system of cognitive interactions. The "consciousness of being affected by history"

(Gadamer 1990:301), what applies for texts as well as for persons, shall not be excluded from theoretical consideration. There are not only "texts-in-situation" (Nord 1991:14), there is even the translator-in-situation. All individual aspects of research and their results are only relevant in relation to the totality of the systemic process centered around the acting translator as a person.

We are pleading for an integrative view of the systemic translation process, also in translation teaching. Our four-phase model – motivation, outfit, cognition, enrichment – is relevant since all the phases are interlinked and influence one another. Translation competence is not only developed during classroom teaching, but rather in a lifelong learning process. This process concerns translational behavior, strategies of decision-making, and critical self-assessment. Only he who proceeds self-critically will be able to conduct socially adequate changes of behavior, or develop a kind of cognitive landscape that can help to secure and enlarge our knowledge. This is particularly true for translation which, in the final instance, is never absolutely complete: it remains a "work in progress".

The translator needs both good confidence in the own language proficiency and critical self-reflection, the ability to quickly familiarize with new fields of knowledge, and an interest in just everything. A broad view and versatility is more important than a depth of analysis. Then, translation as a service for communication will find its place in the society.

Translational hermeneutics becomes a research paradigm for TS when we look at its points of connection with cognitive linguistics. We ask *how* the many individual research projects may find their place in an overall world of science. Genshen Hu (2004) has developed the concept of "eco-translatology" where the field of translation research is seen in terms of the ecosystem with its living dynamics, macrocosm and balance, concurrence of the different, variation, growth and networking. These are also metaphors for the hermeneutical approach to translation. Others speak of "complexity theory": "In the ecological, post-structuralist spirit of complexity theory, syntactic competence is the ability to think historically and relationally, to produce complexity-based solutions in creative use of language, and to understand texts as non-linear evocations of meaning that are both universal and particular" (Kramsch 2008:54).

Hermeneutics is not so much a methodology, it is rather an epistemological attitude. It's not about "hermeneutical objects" such as a difficult texts to be understood and translated, but rather about the translator who wants to orientate himself in the world. Our theoretical conviction shall now be evidenced with the discussion of examples that were translated. The texts are taken from various fields of communication, each time doted with an extensive discussion of the translation. But first there is a consideration of perspectives on the quality of translations.

## 9.6 Perspectives on the quality of translations

In the foregoing we have presented a model of translational lines of orientation and fields of attention for the translator who strives to present a message authentically. This was done from an internal point of view as to translation competence. Academic research may of course also change the perspective to the outside, trying to objectivate observations. There are different visions of the "quality of translations". In talking about quality assessment or translation criticism or how to translate adequately, we should keep in mind that these questions are varying, depending on whether the translator himself or the translation client or the translation teacher is concerned.

### 9.6.1 The translator's dynamic interest for an adequate formulation

As a linguist and a cultural mediator, the translator has a *dynamic interest* of grounded understanding combined with language proficiency in trying to find adequate formulations for the message in the target language. Quality, in the eyes of the responsible translator, is the state where the translation actually comes up to the original goal of writing, when one feels to have really "found the right words" for the message fully understood. Of course this might appear as a rather idealistic concept, as in the professional reality there are many factors that work against this ideal, not least time pressure.

Playing with words in the creative "language play" (Wittgenstein) needs time. The best and satisfactory solution does rarely pop up immediately. Translation also includes the experience of uneasiness, when one is forced to stop the project and deliver the translation, even still feeling that some things could have been made better. That is why we have underlined the fact that the task of translating cannot be carried out in an absolutely perfect way, but only up to an optimal form.

On the other hand, the hermeneutical approach calling for subject-relevant pre-knowledge also helps to save time. When a text is initially grasped within its relevant background, the very time-consuming process of "translation-oriented text analysis" (Nord 1991) can be avoided, as the text is first understood holistically. The reference point for quality in the translator's eyes is the text's message bound to a culture or a scientific domain. Given this, any modification for the sake of genre or function requirements may be allowed for, and this allows creativity.

We have designed the task of translating as a presentation of the message in empathy with it. As we have seen, an ideological dealing with the text's message, also in terms of Skopos theory, may lead to more adaptation into the target culture, any strange features becoming invisible then. The translator's involvement in treating this text is greater, his/her voice is speaking loud. On the contrary, in a so-called "foreignizing" translation strategy, where we want to listen to the unknown author, the "translator's voice" *appears* loud in trying, with less personal involvement, to follow the strange text by means of creative language, sometimes even just translating literally. The strangeness of foreign ideas and language structures becomes more visible by less involvement of the translator.

### 9.6.2 The client's prospective interest for useful texts

Professional translation in practice is done for the purposes of special clients or in the service of editors. In the world of translation business there is the *prospective interest* of a client to receive translations useful for his own business goals. Quality, here, is what the client first has stated in his specification, quality is "fitness for purpose" (be it a precise translation, a conclusive survey, an informative rendering of the content, a new design for an advertising ad, a certified document translation, or a good-selling novel, etc.). The professional client in his prospective interest regarding business objectives will ask for the functional adequacy of the translation in his situation and simply presume that there is an equivalence relationship with the source text. The more precise this mandate is given, the better a translation can be adapted to it. Media adequacy and the coherent structure of the text, as well as the plausibility of argumentation are very important for the client. Regarding the specifics of the text genre, he will expect the typical macro-structure and fixed text blocks, independently of what was present in the original text.

The professional client will check the consistency of terminology from his point of view regarding the specialist domain and his own corporate preferences, but he will not check translation equivalence in the traditional sense. Any variation of terms might lead to a misunderstanding by the intended audience. The factor of time, again, is decisive here, because translations are only one step in a whole production process. If the translation comes too late, it will be useless, even if it is perfect.

A definition of quality requirements by the client, therefore, should always be requested, and this will help the translator in the decision-making process. The client's requirements can then be assessed adequately against the original message and its structure. Only after I know what to translate, I can also decide what to alter. Regarding style, the professional client will simply look at the idiomatic correctness of the translation concerning orthography, grammar and syntax. (Many translations in the practical field are already defective in that respect, and therefore the use of a spell checker is always recommended by commentators on quality assessment.) For the client, translation is a service paid for, and for lack of time he is not able to carry out any translation evaluation by comparing the version with the original. This gives back all the responsibility to the translator as the language expert who needs relevant encyclopedic, strategic and practical knowledge to be reliable.

In literary translation, the client's expectation may sometimes lead to transformations of the source text that are obviously contrary to the author's intention or induced by censorship. It is common ground by now that editors often ask for a suppression of lengthy or unwelcome passages (Eco 2006:124). The translator could, if necessary, become an advocate of his or her author and defend the faithful translation.

### 9.6.3 Translation criticism with a static analysis of shifts

The perspective on the quality of translation is somehow different in the case of classroom translation assessment. Here, a *static analysis* of source text structures and translation shifts is being used in order to check the student's view on the languages and grammar knowledge. Every semantic deviation or syntactic interference is marked as an error, in order to assess the degree of understanding the source text and the language proficiency of students. There is a need for linguistic criteria as a point of reference. It is not enough to ask that a translation should be "culturally adequate" or "adapted to the intended function", to criticize "sense missed" or "wrong word order", "false style" etc., since these well-known general remarks lack precision.

Therefore, translation criticism is an issue in pedagogics. Since "error analysis" (Spillner 1990) is a feature of language learning, it cannot be applied in the evaluation of professional translations. In comparative literary studies, however, comparisons and assessments of translations in regard to their original are a frequent topic of academic theses. Here, one will first have to define what is conceived of as an "error".

Within the interlingual paradigm of translation, one will note in one's translation criticism any deviation from the source text structure. Such formal non-equivalences or even "dynamic equivalence" (Nida) can be described as either "grammatical shifts" (tense, mode, number is changed) or as "lexical changes" in the sense of a semantically modified translation. Such formal changes in a translation are abundant. One will find the shift from past tense to present tense, from active to passive form, from the first to the third person in actions, and so on. This may be criticized as a "grammatical error" if it changes the meaning of the source text (which in fact is often the case). Besides that there will be wrong translations of words or terms as "lexical errors" based on misunderstanding. Though often some semantic aspects of partial equivalence (Koller 1992:229) are to be observed here too.

A critical evaluation of grammatical and lexical shifts and changes will also have to integrate stylistic considerations before any observed feature is called a grammatical or lexical "error" of translation. The so-called transfer procedures of Stylistique comparée (Vinay & Darbelnet 1995) cannot be applied here, as they merely describe differences in a language pair to be observed in preparing a translation. The general assessment of a translation should also take into account how far the understanding of the original message has been lessened by this version.

Here, the presented hermeneutical categories of attention for understanding and writing may also serve as a reference point. The exact meaning of words, the presence of equivalents, as well as the semantic and phraseological compatibility are a central question. There may be discussed several kinds of cultural incongruities and the solution of the resulting translation problems. A great source of translation errors is caused by the particular differences between language pairs, like false friends and linguistic polysemy on the word level, syntactic differences in idiomatic focusing structures, in sentence connection, and others, as interference by foreign standards is a constant source of translation errors. The application of our translational categories, though, is only possible when viewing both text and translation as a whole.

# 10 Practice: Discussion of translation examples

The foregoing presentation of the hermeneutical theory of translation has argued all the time from the perspective of the individual translator. That is why below we will discuss examples of translations, between the English and the German language in both directions, that have been prepared by myself. Sometimes there is a comparison with other translations in a kind of translation criticism. By no means these translation examples are meant to become a model of translation. Any further translated version will be and shall be different. The purpose of this presentation is only to show how the hermeneutical orientation is working. Here, the student may try to apply the same method.

## 10.1 Translating in communication for specific purposes

### 10.1.1 A technical text

Translating in the communication for specific purposes means a continuation of the scientific communication across the language border.

| | |
|---|---|
| | **Translation assignment**<br>Non ferrous scrap treatment.<br>We attest that the O. scrap plant operates under the authorisation no. 750... of the province L. |
| 5 | After maximum recovery of metallic parts, due to state of the art technology, the remaining non-metallic steriles are dumped on Class I authorised site of NN. (...) |
| | **A) First attempt by a translation office**<br>Nicht-Alteisen Behandlung oder Die Behandlung von Nicht-Alteisen.<br>Wir bestätigen, daß die O. Altwarenfabrik unter der Referenznummer (Lizenznummer) 750... des Gebietes/der Gemeinde L. arbeitet. |
| 5 | Nach einem Maximum an Wiederherstellung/Recycling von Metallteilen, gemäß dem neuesten Stand der Technik, werden die restlichen Leichtmetall (steriles?), nach meiner Genehmigung, auf dem (Bau-)Platz von NN. abgeladen. |
| | **B) Retranslation by a professional**<br>Verarbeitung von Nichteisenschrott.<br>Hiermit wird bescheinigt, dass die Schrottverarbeitungsfirma O. gemäß Genehmigungsbescheid Nr. 750..1. der Provinz L. tätig ist.<br>Nach weitestgehender Rückgewinnung der Metallteile mit modernster Technologie werden die verbleibenden unergiebigen Nichtmetallteile auf der nach Klasse I zugelassenen Deponie von NN. abgelagert. |

**Commentary**

The approach to texts here requires relevant subject knowledge in the respective domain dealt with, and proficiency in the functional norms of the language for specific purposes (LSP). Looking at the respective domain of SITUATIVE BACKGROUND, this extract from an English-German technical translation commission is obviously completely failed in version (A), because the translator didn't understand, that the text is situated in the metal industry. He translated with a general language understanding. (The translation agency had this feeling too, therefore they presented that attempt for correction).

Regarding the DISCOURSE FIELD of our example, the initiator of the translation assignment had indicated that it was an official certificate for a company. This of course mirrors at the text level: We can see it from the sentences *"authorization N° 750 of the province L."*, and *"Class I authorized site of N.N."* (line 5). The level of communication is official, as it appears that we have a certificate about the licence given to a company. This FUNCTION will also have to be realized in the translation.

Every discourse field has its particular MEANING DIMENSION, recurring in the texts. In our example the technical terms like *non-ferrous scrap treatment, scrap plant, recovery of metallic parts, non-metallic steriles* are clearly situated within the domain of metal industry, but were misunderstood by the translator (A) in the sense of *Alteisen – scrap iron* (1) as was collected by migrant traders in the past. This solution maybe was found in a general language dictionary. However, the information gained from the DISCOURSE FIELD should have taught there here one has to consult a specialized dictionary or term bank.

With respect to the intrinsic relationship between the text as a whole and its constitutional elements, the holistic view is complemented by an analysis of the PREDICATIVE MODE which shows in the style. The text is marked by the anonymous voice apt for general statements: *"the remaining non-metallic steriles are dumped on Class I authorized site of N.N."*(5) The translator misunderstood here "I authorized" (personal voice) and translated *"nach meiner Genehmigung"* (6).

When we have acquired a global idea of the text message, translation work will begin. The translator's first decision concerns the GENRE of the text as an extralinguistic feature. A certificate – being a legally relevant text – has to be translated in formal equivalence, in order to be comparable to the source text. So there will be no changes as to any text type or space here.

The STYLISTICS is dominated by the fact that the translation will have the appearance of a certificate as well. Passive voice is adequate here: *Hiermit wird bescheinigt* (*we attest*) instead of "wir bestätigen". "Bescheinigen" is even the administrative word for certifying, whereas "bestätigen" (*to confirm*) has the same meaning, but is used in ordinary language.

Regarding COHERENCE in such a technical text, of course, terminology is indispensable. Terms from the domain of metal industry have to be understood and translated as such, including adequate word compounding in the target language. In the translation (A) the terminology is definitely not equivalent. This leads to a revision in translation (B) in terms of the following: *Verarbeitung von Nichteisenschrott* instead of *Behandlung von Nicht-Alteisen; weitestgehende Rückgewinnung* instead of *Maximum an Wiederherstellung; Schrottverarbeitungsfirma* instead of *Altwarenfabrik.*

The FUNCTION of this translation is the same as that of the original text – a certificate. The relevant translational decisions have already been described above. We might point out, though, that for the requirement of presenting a text with legal appeal in the target language, it must not be understandable for any lay reader. It is a certificate for use in an authority. This is realized in translation (B) by the passive voice and also in the nominal style focusing terminology.

## 10.1.2 A science text

The following example is a passage from a scientific journal.

**Reliability Analysis of Open Drainage Channels under Multiple Failure Modes**
by Said M. Easa, Member, ASCE

**Abstract**: Open drainage channel design involves variables that are uncertain. Because the performance of the channel system is also uncertain, reliability analysis is used to
5   measure the reliability of the system performance. In this paper, the reliability of open drainage channels under three possible failure modes is examined. The first failure mode occurs when the runoff exceeds channel capacity. The runoff and channel capacity are random variables that are estimated using the rational method and the Manning equation, respectively. The second failure mode occurs when the actual flow velocity
10  exceeds the maximum allowable velocity for erosion control. The third failure mode occurs when the actual flow velocity is less than the minimum allowable velocity for deposition control. The minimum and maximum allowable velocities are considered random variables. The failure probability of each mode is estimated using the advanced first-order second-moment (AFOSM) method. The overall failure probability of the
15  system that accounts for the correlations between the failure modes is presented. The method was applied to an example and was verified using Monte Carlo simulation. In practice, the method can be used to find the reliability of an existing channel under multiple failures, to evaluate the effects of alternative improvements, and to design a new channel for a specified reliability level.
20  **Introduction**
Open drainage channel design is made under conditions of uncertainty in both the demand (runoff) and supply (channel capacity) components of the system. The runoff involves random temporal and areal fluctuations inherent in natural processes that almost always introduce a large amount of uncertainty into the process of runoff genera-
25  tion (Melching et al. 1990; Plate 1986). There is also uncertainty in the design variables related to channel capacity, most notably the friction factor. For a given channel type, minimum, normal, and maximum values of the friction factor have been established (Chow 1959). In both design components, there is often uncertainty in the data caused by measurement inaccuracy and error.
30  In hydrologic design, research has mostly been related to the reliability analysis of floods (Kite 1977; Kottegoda 1980) and watershed runoff (Melching et al. 1990; Parker 1972; Wood 1976). The output reliability of rainfall-runoff models was analysed by Melching et al. (1991) using the HEC-1 flood hydrograph package (*HEC-1* 1985) and the Australian RORB runoff routing program (Laurenson and Mein 1985). The design
35  of open drainage channels has traditionally been deterministic (Chow 1959; Bedient and Huber 1988). Probabilistic methods involving the uncertainties in the runoff and supply capacity were developed for storm sewer systems by Yen et al. (1976), and for open drainage channels by Easa (1992). The method for drainage channels addresses only one mode of failure (when runoff exceeds the channel capacity), and is useful
40  when channel erosion and other design criteria are not of concern.
In this paper, a reliability method for analysing open draining channels under three possible failure modes is presented. The first failure mode occurs when the runoff exceeds the channel capacity; the second failure mode occurs when the actual velocity exceeds the maximum allowable velocity for erosion control; and the third failure mode
45  occurs when the actual velocity is less than the minimum allowable velocity for deposi-

| | |
|---|---|
| 50 | tion control. Each failure mode has a certain probability of occurrence. However, the system failure probability must account for the correlations between the failure modes. A numerical example using the advanced first-order second-moment (AFOSM) reliability method is employed for open drainage channel analysis. The AFOSM method is widely used in structural engineering and soil mechanics (Ditlevsen 1981; Harr 1987; Madsen et al. 1986; Smith 1986). This paper does not consider model structure uncertainty due to imperfect representation of reality. Examples of studies addressing model uncertainty are Melching et al. (1990), Melching et al. (1991), and Ronold and Bjerager (1992). (…)<br>**In:** *Journal of Irrigation and Drainage Engineering.* Vol. 120, No. 6, November/December 1994. © ASCE, ISSN 0733-9437/94/0006-1007/$2.00 + $.25 per page. Paper No. 4830. |

**Commentary**

The translator's reading will first concentrate on the SITUATIVE BACKGROUND of this example of science writing. The text is a part from a paper in the *Journal of Irrigation and Drainage Engineering*. This extra-textual information about the text's embedding tells us that we are dealing with scientific communication in the domain of "drainage engineering". Other fields of engineering, e.g. machines or pipelines etc., will be neglected here.

The DISCOURSE FIELD is an internal communication among experts as readers of such journals, in the field of open drainage channel design (line 3). When specialist language is usually characterized by conspicuous language (Kalverkämper 1990:121), we find this text marked by scientific English word compounding: *open drainage channel design* (3, 21), *reliability analysis* (1, 4), *system performance* (5), *hydrologic design* (30), *deposition control* (12, 45), *runoff* (7, 22, 24, 31, 36, 39, 42). *routing program* (34), *storm sewer systems* (37), etc.

The MEANING DIMENSION shows in that exact technical terminology. The text speaks of *variables* (3, 8, 13, 25), *reliability analysis of a system* (5), *failure modes* (1, 6, 9, 15, 42), *models* (32, 52), *methods* (8, 14, 16, 36, 38, 41, 49), *simulation* (26). The content is not a description of any object but the presentation of methods for analyzing the reliability of a channel design in computer simulation. Concrete terms are to be found a. o. in *demand* (22), *floods (31), watershed runoff* (31) und *supply capacity* (22, 37), *flow velocity* (9, 11), *friction factor* (26, 27). We may put them at their place in a terminological system which shows their interrelation, in order to better comprehend about what the text is talking to us:

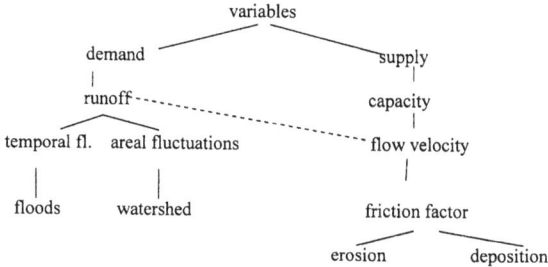

This helps for adequate understanding as a preparation for functional translation. This will also enable us to check the equivalent terminology in the target language, even before starting formulations.

Regarding the text's PREDICATIVE MODE we see anonymous voice or verbs in the third person and in present tense, as is required for scientific statements (Stolze 1999:135). Reference to past studies appears in the perfect tense: *research has mostly been related to* (30); *has traditionally been deterministic* (35).

After an initial global understanding of the text we may prepare a target language version. In view of its GENRE the text will also follow the text type of a scientific paper with an abstract. There will not be much formal difference to the source text, as long as target style guides would not require something else. STYLISTICS will observe the functional style of short sentences with a clear logical arrangement. There is no need for grammatical rephrasing, as in such texts the Anglo-Saxon model of writing tends to become universal (Stolze/Deppert 1998). However, the passive voice is more frequent in German texts of this type than in English ones.

The necessary COHERENCE requires equivalence of the terminology and unaltered terms throughout the text, as well as the use of technical word compounding, in this case in German. The terminology has already been checked, with the help of specialist dictionaries and term banks, in view of the concepts concerned here. A translation of "failure modes" with "Versagensarten", for instance, is also found in parallel reference texts in the Internet.

The final inclusion of the target text FUNCTION implies again an overall view of the text. Revision may eliminate all non logical statements, induce further research on semantic lacunae, revise individual sentence structures in relation to their context, and adapt the whole text to the relevant target text type model for such papers. Parallel texts may also be taken into consideration. Translation (A) shows the result of those considerations.

**Translation (A):**

**Zuverlässigkeitsanalyse für offene Entwässerungskanäle unter multiplen Versagensarten**
von M. Easa, ASCE-Mitglied

**Abstract:** Die Konstruktion offener Entwässerungskanäle impliziert Variablen, die unbestimmt sind. Da die Leistung des gesamten Kanalsystems gleichfalls unbestimmt ist, wird die Zuverlässigkeitsanalyse angewendet, um die Zuverlässigkeit der Systemleistung zu messen. In vorliegendem Beitrag wird die Zuverlässigkeit offener Entwässerungskanäle unter drei möglichen Versagensarten untersucht. Die erste Versagensart tritt auf, wenn die Abflussmenge die Kanalkapazität übersteigt. Die Abflussmenge und die Kanalkapazität sind Zufallsvariablen, die mit der Rationalen Methode bzw. der Manning-Gleichung geschätzt werden. Die zweite Versagensart tritt auf, wenn die tatsächliche Fließgeschwindigkeit die für die Erosionsbekämpfung zulässige Höchstgeschwindigkeit überschreitet. Die dritte Versagensart tritt auf, wenn die tatsächliche Fließgeschwindigkeit niedriger ist als die für die Bekämpfung von Ablagerungen zulässige Mindestgeschwindigkeit. Die zulässigen Mindest- und Höchstgeschwindigkeiten werden als Zufallsvariablen angesehen. Die Versagenswahrscheinlichkeit einer jeden Art wird eingeschätzt durch Anwendung der Advanced First-Order Second-Moment (AFOSM)-Methode. Die Gesamtversagenswahrscheinlichkeit des Systems, welche die Korrelationen zwischen den Versagensarten erklärt, wird dargestellt. Die Methode wurde auf ein Beispiel angewendet und mit der Monte Carlo-Simulation überprüft. In der Praxis kann die Methode dazu benutzt werden, die Zuverlässigkeit eines bestehenden Kanals unter verschiedenen Versagensarten zu erfassen, die Auswirkungen unterschiedlicher Verbesserungen zu berechnen, sowie einen neuen Kanal für ein bestimmtes Zuverlässigkeitsniveau zu entwerfen.

**Einleitung**

Die Konstruktion offener Entwässerungskanäle erfolgt unter Bedingungen der Unbestimmtheit, sowohl bei der Anforderungskomponente (Abfluss) als auch bei der Aufnahmekomponente (Kanalkapazität) des Systems. Der Abfluss beinhaltet zufällige zeitliche und räumliche Schwankungen, wie sie natürlichen Prozessen innewohnen, die fast immer sehr viel Unbestimmtheit in den Prozess der Abflussgenerierung einbringen (Melching et al. 1990; Plate 1986). Ferner gibt es Unbestimmtheit in den Konstruktionsvariablen hinsichtlich der Kanalkapazität, insbesondere beim Reibungsfaktor. Für einen gegebenen Kanaltyp sind Mindest-, Normal- und Höchstwerte des Reibungsfaktors festgelegt worden (Chow 1959). In beiden Konstruktionskomponenten findet sich oft eine Datenunsicherheit, die durch Ungenauigkeit und Fehler in der Messung verursacht ist.

In der hydrologischen Konstruktion haben sich Forschungsarbeiten bisher überwiegend auf die Zuverlässigkeitsanalyse des Abflusses bei Hochwasser (Kite 1977; Kottegoda 1980) und in Flussentwässerungsgebieten (Melching et al. 1990; Parker 1972; Wood 1976) konzentriert. Die Output-Zuverlässigkeit von Regenwasserabflussmodellen wurde von Melching et al. (1991) mit der HEC-1 Flutabflussmengenkurve (*HEC-1* 1985) und dem australischen Abflusslinienprogramm (Laurenson und Mein 1985) analysiert.

| | Die Konstruktion offener Entwässerungskanäle war traditionell deterministisch (Chow 1959; Bedient und Huber 1988). Probabilistische Methoden, welche die Unbe- |
|---|---|
| 45 | stimmtheiten in der Abfluss- und Aufnahmekapazität miteinbeziehen, wurden für Sturmsiel-Systeme von Yen et al. (1976), und für offene Entwässerungskanäle von Easa (1992) entwickelt. Die Methode für Entwässerungskanäle spricht nur eine Versagensart an (wenn der Abfluss die Kanalkapazität übersteigt) und ist brauchbar, wenn die Kanalerosion und andere Konstruktionskriterien ohne Belang sind. |
| 50 | In diesem Beitrag wird nun eine Zuverlässigkeitsmethode für die Analyse offener Entwässerungskanäle unter drei möglichen Versagensarten vorgelegt. Die erste Versagensart tritt auf, wenn die Abflussmenge die Kanalkapazität übersteigt; die zweite Versagensart tritt auf, wenn die tatsächliche Geschwindigkeit die zulässige Höchstgeschwindigkeit für die Erosionsbekämpfung überschreitet; und die dritte Versagensart |
| 55 | tritt auf, wenn die tatsächliche Geschwindigkeit geringer ist als die für die Ablagerungsbekämpfung erlaubte Mindestgeschwindigkeit. Jede Versagensart hat eine bestimmte Vorkommenswahrscheinlichkeit. Die Wahrscheinlichkeit des Systemversagens muss jedoch die Korrelationen zwischen den Versagensarten erklären. Dazu wird ein numerisches Beispiel mit der Advanced first-order second-moment (AFOSM)- |
| 60 | Zuverlässigkeitsmethode auf die Analyse offener Entwässerungskanäle angewendet. Die AFOSM-Methode findet im Bereich Tiefbau und Bodenmechanik weithin Verwendung (Ditlevsen 1981; Harr 1987; Madsen et al. 1986; Smith 1986). Im vorliegenden Beitrag wird die Unsicherheit in der Modellstruktur wegen unzureichender Darstellung der Wirklichkeit allerdings nicht berücksichtigt. Beispiele für Studien zur Modell- |
| 65 | unsicherheit sind Melching et al. (1990), Melching et al. (1991) und Ronold/Bjerager (1992). *(Translation R.Stolze)* |

The above translation (A) resulted from an application of the said translational categories of orientation by the translator, even though the domain of science was unknown before. In order to show the difference to the traditional translation approach, we may compare this version with a student translation (B) (see below), presented sentence by sentence in an English-German comparison. This way of presentation prevented any view of the text as a whole, and consequently the translation lacks COHERENCE, there is e.g. a constant alternation between *Versagen* and *Ausfall* (for "failure"). The translator also failed to position the text in the adequate DISCOURSE FIELD, and instead saw a text about "sewage installations", a domain of engineering, with lexemes like *Betriebssicherheitsanalyse, Entwässerungskanalanlage, Temperatur- und Flächenschwankungen, Anlagenkomponenten, Unsicherheit, Sicherheitsanalyse, Versorgung, Baustatik,* etc. "Ausfall" is, rather, a term of engineering. *Abriss* in lieu of "Abstract" gives evidence of lacking text type knowledge regarding German scientific articles.

Even if the text was conceived of as a "technical text" (and not as a general language text), the domain and DISCOURSE FIELD were missed. By an erroneous linguistic analysis of the English terminology, some false semantic relationships were established and translated, particularly in view of the verbs. No self-criticism leading to further research is visible.

**Examples**:

- *The minimum and maximum allowable velocities are considered random variables.*
- *Die minimal ... Geschwindigkeiten werden als unabhängige Variablen in Betracht gezogen (> angesehen).*
- *The method was applied to an example and was verified using the MC-Simulation.*
- *Die Methode wurde in einem Beispiel angewendet und mit der MC-Simulation verglichen (> überprüft).*
- *The runoff involves random temporal and aereal fluctuatons inherent in natural processes that almost always introduce ... uncertainty.*
- *Der Abfluss schließt naturgegebene Prozesse, wie zufällige Temperatur- und Flächenschwankungen ein, die zumeist einen großen Unsicherheitsbetrag ... ausmachen (> einbringen).*

|    | **Translation (B):** |
|----|---|
|    | **Betriebssicherheitsanalyse offener Entwässerungskanäle unter verschiedenen Ausfallarten.**<br>vorgestellt von M. Easa, Mitglied des ASCE |
| 5  | **Abriss**: Eine offene <u>Entwässerungskanalanlage</u> schließt unbestimmte Variablen ein. Weil die Leistung des Kanalsystems auch unbestimmt ist, wird zur Messung der <u>Betriebssicherheit</u> der Systemleistung die <u>Betriebssicherheitsanalyse</u> benutzt. In diesem Beitrag wird die Betriebssicherheit offener Entwässerungskanäle unter drei möglichen <u>Ausfallarten</u> untersucht. Die erste Ausfallart liegt vor, wenn der Abfluss die Kanalkapazität überschreitet. Der Abfluss und die Kanalkapazität sind <u>unabhängige</u> Variablen, |
| 10 | die nach der rationalen Methode und der Manning Gleichung <u>abgeschätzt</u> werden. Die zweite <u>Versagensart</u> liegt vor, wenn die tatsächliche Fließgeschwindigkeit das Maximum der zulässigen Geschwindigkeit für den Erosionsschutz überschreitet. Die dritte Versagensart liegt vor, wenn die tatsächliche Fließgeschwindigkeit niedriger als das Minimum der zulässigen Geschwindigkeit für den Ablagerungsschutz ist. Die minimal |
| 15 | und maximal zulässigen Geschwindigkeiten werden als unabhängige Variablen in Betracht gezogen. Die Ausfallwahrscheinlichkeit der jeweiligen Art wird nach der verwendeten AFOSM-Methode abgeschätzt. Die Gesamtausfallwahrscheinlichkeit des Systems erklärt die Wechselwirkungen der auftretenden Ausfallarten. Die Methode wurde in einem Beispiel angewendet und mit der Monte Carlo Simulation <u>verglichen</u>. |
| 20 | In der Praxis kann die Methode angewandt werden, um die <u>Sicherheit</u> eines bestehenden Kanals unter verschiedenen Ausfällen zu bestimmen, die Wirkung von alternativen Verbesserungen zu berechnen und einen neuen Kanal auf einem vorgeschriebenen <u>Sicherheitsniveau</u> zu entwerfen. |

### Einleitung

Eine offene Entwässerungskanalanlage wird in Abhängigkeit von zwei Systemkomponenten, dem Bedarf (Abfluss) und der Versorgung (Kanalkapazität) entworfen. Der Ablass schließt naturgegebene Prozesse, wie zufällige Temperatur- und Flächenschwankungen ein, die zumeist einen großen Unsicherheitsbetrag im Prozess der Abflussgestaltung ausmachen (Melching und andere 1990; Plate 1986). Die Anlagenvariablen bezüglich der Kanalkapazität weisen vor allem durch den Reibungsfaktor Unsicherheit auf. Die minimalen, normalen und maximalen Werte des Reibungsfaktors sind bei einem gegebenen Kanaltyp festgelegt (Chow 1959). Messungenauigkeit und Fehler liefern bei beiden Anlagenkomponenten unzuverlässige Zahlenwerte.

Bei hydrologischen Verfahren bezieht sich die Forschung zumeist auf Sicherheitsanalysen bei Überschwemmungen (Kite 1977; Kottegoda 1980) und beim Wasserscheidenabfluss (Melching und andere 1990; Parker 1972; Wood 1976). Die Leistungssicherheit der Regenwasserabflussmodelle wurde von Melching und andere (1991) unter Benutzung der HEC-1 Hochwasserganglinien (*HEC-1* 1985) und des Australischen RORB Abflusswegprogramms (Laurenson und Mein 1985) analysiert. Der Plan eines offenen Entwässerungskanals ist traditionell bestimmt. Mögliche Verfahren, die sich durch die Unsicherheiten der Bedarfs- und Versorgungskapazität verkomplizieren, wurden von Yen und andere (1976) für Regenwasserleitungsnetze und von Easa (1992) für offene Entwässerungskanäle entwickelt. Die Methode für Entwässerungskanäle behandelt nur eine Versagensart (wenn der Abfluss die Kanalkapazität überschreitet) und ist nur brauchbar, wenn die Kanalerosion und andere Konstruktionskriterien nicht maßgebend sind.

Dieser Beitrag stellt ein Analyseverfahren der Betriebssicherheit offener Entwässerungskanäle unter drei möglichen Ausfallarten vor. Die erste Ausfallart liegt vor, wenn der Abfluss die Kanalkapazität überschreitet; die zweite Ausfallart liegt vor, wenn die tatsächliche Fließgeschwindigkeit das Maximum der zulässigen Geschwindigkeit für den Erosionsschutz überschreitet; und die dritte Ausfallart liegt vor, wenn die tatsächliche Fließgeschwindigkeit niedriger als das Minimum der zulässigen Geschwindigkeit für den Ablagerungsschutz ist. Jede Ausfallart besitzt eine verschiedene Auftretenswahrscheinlichkeit. Die Systemversagenswahrscheinlichkeit muss eine Erklärung für die Wechselwirkungen zwischen den Ausfallarten geben. Ein Zahlenbeispiel unter Verwendung der AFOSM-Methode beschäftigt sich mit der Betriebssicherheitsanalyse für offene Entwässerungskanäle. Die AFOSM-Methode findet in der Baustatik und der Bodenmechanik breite Anwendung (Ditlevsen 1981; Harr 1987; Madsen und andere 1986; Smith 1986). Dieser Beitrag bezieht nicht das Modell struktureller Unsicherheit aufgrund unvollständiger Darstellung der Realität ein. Beispiele für Studien des Unsicherheitsmodells finden sich bei Melching und andere (1990); Melching und andere (1991); und Ronold und Bjerager (1992).

*(Student translation, presented sentence by sentence in an English German version.)*

## 10.1.3 A legal text

Practical translation in the field of legal texts is mainly needed in the field of international trade, when agreements between business firms have to be translated. The translation of law texts from jurisdiction for the purposes of comparative law or the explanation of legal rules is also needed, but with less frequency. For this reason we may observe here some specificities of the legal language encountered in the texts of a contract or an agreement or the like. For reasons of space we can only present short extracts.

**Example:**

6. INDEMNITY. G. agrees to defend, indemnify, and hold harmless K. from and against any and all claims, damages, losses, and expenses (including attorneys' fees) of any nature whatsoever resulting from, by, or on account of any acts or omissions of G., its subcontractors, agents, or employees, or arising out of the performance
5  or non-performance of its duties under this Agreement (including but not limited to any automobile collision or casualty which occurs or is alleged to have occurred while in the performance of G.'s duties under this Agreement; the failure of G., its subcontractors, agents, or employees, to comply with all rules and regulations pertaining to X bases and installations; any misrepresentation made or alleged to have been made by
10 G., its subcontractors, agents, or employees; and/or any failure to comply with applicable laws, regulations, or ordinances or the equivalent thereof (including but not limited to those applicable to G.'s employment of G.'s employees and all duties associated therewith) within the Territory). (...)

19. DISPUTE RESOLUTION AND CONSENT TO JURISDICTION. All
15 disputes among G. and K. arising from this Agreement shall be submitted to binding arbitration, to be administered by the American Arbitration Association under its International Dispute Resolution Procedures. Arbitration of any dispute shall be conducted within (some places in) F. County, in the State of G. The award of the Arbitrator(s) shall be binding upon each of the parties hereto, and each of the parties
20 hereto intends and agrees that the award of the Arbitrator(s) shall be enforceable under the New York Convention on the Recognition and Enforcement of Foreign Arbitral Awards in the courts of the United States and the courts of Germany to which the party against whom the award is rendered is subject to jurisdiction. Notwithstanding anything herein to the contrary, nothing herein shall prohibit K. from seeking an injunction or
25 other equitable relief allowed by paragraph 4 of this Agreement or to enforce its indemnity rights under paragraph 5 of this Agreement in a court of law. With regard to such injunctive or equitable relief and/or enforcement of arbitral awards as described above: (a) the parties agree that any judicial action under this Agreement shall be adjudicated in the Superior Court of H. County, State of G., or the United States
30 District Court for the Northern District of G., (b) each of the parties hereto consents and voluntarily subjects itself to the jurisdiction of the Superior Court of H. County, State of G., and the United States District Court for the Northern District of G., and to venue in said Courts, and (c) G. hereby consents to the domestication and enforcement in any Court of Germany with jurisdiction over G. of any judgment entered against it by either
35 the Superior Court of H. County, Georgia, or the United States District Court for the Northern District of Georgia, and waives any right to challenge the domestication of

> any such judgment against it in any Court of Germany with jurisdiction over G. *(from a "Ales Representative Agreement", 2006).*

And here comes the German translation.

**Translation:**

6. SCHADLOSHALTUNG. G. vereinbart, K. von und gegen alle Forderungen, Schadensersatzklagen, Verluste und Auslagen (einschließlich Anwaltskosten) jeglicher Art zu verteidigen und schadlos zu halten, die aus, durch oder wegen Handlungen oder Unterlassungen durch die Firma G., ihre Subunternehmer, Bevollmächtigten oder Angestellten entstehen, oder sich aus der Erfüllung oder Nichterfüllung ihrer Pflichten nach diesem Vertrag ergeben (einschließlich aber nicht nur eines Verkehrsunfalls oder Schadensfalls, der sich tatsächlich oder angeblich während der Ausführung von Pflichten der G. nach diesem Vertrag ereignet hat; des Versäumnisses der G., ihrer Subunternehmer, von Bevollmächtigten oder Angestellten, alle Gesetze und Vorschriften bezüglich der X Militärbasen und Anlagen zu beachten; jeder Falschangabe, die tatsächlich oder angeblich von der G., ihren Subunternehmern, Bevollmächtigten oder Angestellten gemacht wurde; und/oder jeden Versäumnisses einer Befolgung geltender Gesetze, Vorschriften oder Anordnungen oder dergleichen (einschließlich aber nicht nur derer bezüglich der Beschäftigung von Angestellten durch G. und alle damit verbundenen Pflichten) innerhalb des Territoriums). (...).

19. LÖSUNG VON STREITIGKEITEN UND ZUSTIMMUNG ZUM GERICHTSSTAND. Alle aus diesem Vertrag entstehenden Streitigkeiten zwischen G. und K. werden der verbindlichen Schlichtung unterworfen, die von der American Arbitration Association in ihren Verfahren zur internationalen Streitschlichtung vorgenommen wird. Die Schlichtung eines jeden Streits erfolgt in Orten des F. County im Staate G. Der Schiedsspruch ist dann für beide Parteien verbindlich, und jede Partei intendiert und vereinbart, dass der Schiedsspruch vollstreckbar ist nach der Konvention von New York über die Anerkennung und Vollstreckung ausländischer Schiedssprüche in den Gerichten der Vereinigten Staaten und in den Gerichten Deutschlands, welchen die Partei, gegen die der Schiedsspruch ergeht, jeweils untersteht. Ungeachtet anderslautender Aussagen hierin ist K. durch keine Bestimmung hierin daran gehindert, ein gerichtliches Verbot oder eine andere billige Abhilfe zu erstreben, wie in Absatz 4 dieses Vertrages erlaubt, oder ihre Rechte auf Schadloshaltung nach Absatz 5 dieses Vertrags vor Gericht geltend zu machen. Im Hinblick auf solch eine gerichtliche Verfügung oder billige Abhilfe und/oder Vollstreckung von Schiedssprüchen wie oben beschrieben, gilt: (a) die Parteien vereinbaren, dass jede gerichtliche Klage nach diesem Vertrag vor dem erstinstanzlichen Gericht 'Superior Court of H. County' im Staate G., oder dem Bezirksgericht 'United States District Court for the Northern District of G.' verhandelt wird; (b) jede Partei stimmt zu und unterwirft sich freiwillig der Rechtsprechung des Superior Court of H. County, State of G., und des United States District Court for the Northern District of Georgia, sowie dem Verhandlungsort in den genannten Gerichten, und (c) G. stimmt hiermit der Einbürgerung und Vollstreckung bei jedem Gericht in Deutschland mit Jurisdiktion über G. für jedes Urteil zu, das entweder vom Superior Court of H. County, G., oder dem United States District Court for the Northern District of G. gegen sie ergangen ist, und verzichtet auf jegliches Recht, die Einbürgerung eines solchen Urteils gegen sie vor einem deutschen Gericht anzufechten. *(German translation in practical translation business commission).*

**Commentary**

In such a translation text the first problem in the field of the SITUATIVE BACKGROUND is caused by the fundamental difference between the US-American law system and the one in Germany based on the Roman tradition. This shows a.o. in terminology, and here especially in the names of legal institutions.

In an American sentence one might find the denomination of a *Superior Court* or *Circuit Court* or *District Court.* Each of these is an inferior court of a U.S. federal state. It corresponds, to some extent, to the German Landgericht, but it is not a "Landgericht". A correct translation might therefore be, rather generally, *Gericht,* or *erstinstanzliches Gericht* or *ordentliches Gericht,* versions that try to include additional information. The American *County Court,* on the other hand, serves as an appeal court for the municipal courts, which correspond to the British *County Courts,* a kind of communal courts which are not the same as the German *Ortsgericht,* rather like *Amtsgericht.* In order to prevent mistakes, the latter is being translated by *Local Court,* the *Landgericht* as *Regional Court* (Stolze 2003a:359).

It is very important not to present a false equivalence in the translation, because the legal effect of the text always remains within the source country. As a German court *is not* an American court, the lay persons would actually infer the wrong meaning from their own cultural situation if the court is translated with a German denomination.

In the MEANING DIMENSION, legal concepts with their varying levels of abstraction are a translation difficulty (Stolze 2003a). In the translation between two different law systems, the problem of terminological equivalence is crucial. At non-equivalent legal terms, the translator will use the translational principle of the "smallest common denominator" in word meaning (Bleckmann 1977:99). This may be realized by fusing a more general term in the translation, as the hyperonym always includes the hyponym, e.g. *superior court* as *erstinstanzliches Gericht,* or *Gericht.*

Focusing on the PREDICATIVE MODE of the text to be translated, there is the famous problem of speech acts (Trosborg 1994) and a complex syntax to be observed. The syntax is fulfilling the text's function of stating – e.g. in an agency agreement or a sales contract – all possible aspects of the text, so that nothing may be neglected which later could become a basis of litigation. This is why contractual formulae are so complex and difficult to understand for lay persons. But such texts are only read and analyzed by trained lawyers. We see this particularly marked in our example, e.g. in the sentence *agrees to defend, indemnify, and hold harmless from and against any and all claims, damages, losses, and expenses* (line 1). It is also true, by the way, that the different terms in the triple propositions each one represent a specific semantic content, it's not only an automatic duplication.

For the purpose of translation, we have to consider the GENRE of the translation which will show in the STYLISTICS. It will be again a paper version of a contract having a documentary function – since an agreement is always valid in its original version. The translation constitutes an aid for better understanding, and therefore it is adequate to try to represent the functional stylistic appearance as literally as possible. A respective translation commission normally is the order to "translate as precisely as possible", because target readers/lawyers simply want to know "what the text is saying", just to be on the safe side. And even in original German texts we often find very long and complex sentences with a variety of attributes.

**Example for German legal style:**

Die Vertragspartner beabsichtigen, in Verhandlungen betreffend der Etablierung einer Existenzgründung zur Entwicklung neuartiger Krebsimpfstoffe, basierend auf der spezifischen Immuntherapie unter Anwendung des Patents mit dem Aktenzeichen Nr. ----- beim Deutschen Patentamt (nachfolgend Projekt genannt), einzutreten. Sie vereinbaren, was folgt:

1. die Vertragspartner verpflichten sich gegenseitig, sämtliche ihnen von der jeweils anderen Vertragspartei übermittelten Kenntnisse und Informationen bei ihren Verhandlungen betreffend das Projekt

- während der Verhandlungen und für den Fall, dass diese nicht zum Erfolg führen, auch nach dem Abschluss geheim zu halten und Dritten nicht zu offenbaren,

- im Fall des Nichtzustandekommens des Projekts nicht zu nutzen und Dritten nicht zur Nutzung zu überlassen. (...)

(*Geheimhaltungsvertrag*)

However, the mentioned typical form of triple explanations regularly found in English contracts – e.g. *to defend, indemnify and hold harmless*; or *We grant you a non-exclusive license to use, store and view on your intranet* – is not found in German texts which present more implication.

The reason for this may be the difference between the Anglo-Saxon case law (stating previous cases) and the constitutional law used in Germany, where the scope of meaning covered by an article in law is already given in the legislative texts and their official commentaries. In the English text on the contrary they must be presented in the text itself. One could argue that this extensive formulation is not necessary in a German translation because it does not correspond to the target style. However, looking at the FUNCTION of the translation, which, here, is a documentary aid for understanding, we have to stick to that structure. The official translation of an American agreement will not change it into a German agreement.

### 10.1.4  A publicity ad

|    | **Text** |
|----|----------|
|    | *bebe* Rein&Klar |
| 5  | Sichtbar wirksam, spürbar sanft<br>Es ist keine Love Story<br>Aber es geht unter die Haut |
| 10 | Denn das *bebe* Rein&Klar Aktiv-Gel wirkt tief in den oberen Schichten der Gesichtshaut. Sein spezieller Wirkstoff Elubiol reguliert aktiv die erhöhte Talgproduktion, eine der Hauptursachen für die Entstehung von Pickeln. So hilft das Aktiv-Gel sichtbar wirksam, der Neubildung von Pickeln vorzubeugen – dennoch ist es spürbar sanft und schützt die Haut gleichzeitig vor dem Austrocknen.<br>Bei täglicher Anwendung sorgt es für ein reines und klares Hautbild.   (*551 letters*) |

This text, as to the SITUATIVE BACKGROUND, is a publicity ad for a skin cream to treat acne (*source unknown*). The DISCOURSE FIELD is young people suffering from this problem. Regarding the MEANING DIMENSION it presents some technical terms (*Gel, Gesichtshaut, Wirkstoff, Talgproduktion, Pickel, Austrocknen, Anwendung, Hautbild*). This appears in the nominal style as a functional norm.

As a feature of the PREDICATIVE MODE we see a so-called eye-cather in the appealing formulation at the beginning: *sichtbar wirksam, spürbar sanft*. And this is repeated in the following text, thus creating text coherence.

|   | **Translation 1** |
|---|---|
|   | Bebe<br>Pure and clear<br>Visibly effective, sensuously soft<br>It's not a love story<br>But it's more than skin deep |
| 5 |   |
|   | The *bebe* Pure&Clear Active-Gel goes deep into the upper layers of your facial skin. Its special ingredient Elubiol actively regulates the heightened production of grease, a major cause for the growth of spots. The active gel visibly helps to prevent the return of the spot – yet it is sensuously soft and at the same time protects the skin from dehydration. |
| 10 | Use it daily, and it will keep your skin looking peachy clean. *(students' version)* (519) |

This translation follows the source text rather closely. As to the MEANING DIMENSION, there were problems with the correct terms (*heightened production, grease, spots, peachy clean, return of spots*). In this way the message is not very clear. Also, the gel "goes deep into", instead of working there. The semantic string in the repetition of "visibly effective and sensuously soft" was partially reproduced in the translation, probably by chance. Regarding STYLISTICS the word "sensuously" seems to come from another area. The statement "But it's more than skin deep" is not very understandable and not appealing. In view of the FUNCTION as an advertising text, the translational quality is poor.

|   | **Translation 2** |
|---|---|
|   | Bebe<br>Clean&clear<br>Spot the difference. Sense the softness.<br>Not a love story yet deeper than skin deep. |
| 5 | Bebe Clean&Clear Active-Gel goes deep under your skin to treat your complexion from within. Its special active ingredient elubiole regulates the excess oil that can cause spots and acne. You can spot the difference as Active-Gel helps keep your skin clear of acne – and you can sense the softness as it helps protect your skin from dryness and damage. Use Active-Gel daily to keep your skin looking clean and clear. *(other student version)* (514) |

This translation focused on the FUNCTION as an advertising text. As in that country some other product called "Clean&Clear" is already known, the translators felt free to refer to this. They knew that in publicity a direct address of the audience is favorable for promotion, so this is applied here. However, die COHERENCE of the text is not convincing. The specialist terms, again, are inadequate (*complexion, excess oil, spots and acne, dryness and damage*). The term *complexion* is an unconscious reference to the local preferences in the country, where white skin is desired, but the cream is not meant for that purpose. The extending transposition here as a linguistic means ("spots and acne") shows a trend to over-interpretation and explicitation in the translators. The repetition of the eye catcher in the text was adequately rendered. The STYLE is not very elegant: *can cause spots..., you can spot... and you can sense...* All in all there is much distance to the source text, compensated by more advertising appeal in the language. But the message is still unclear.

---

**Translation 3**

*Bebe*
Clear&Clean

Visibly effective, sensibly soft.
It's no love story but a skin deep touch.

5　The *bebe* Clear&Clean Active-Gel works deep in the upper layers of your facial skin. Its special ingredient Elubiol actively regulates the increased sebum production which is one of the main causes for the apparition of pimples.
The Active-Gel is visibly effective in preventing the recreation of pimples and it is sensibly soft in protecting the skin against dehydration.
Daily application will give you a clear and clean skin. *(retranslation)*　(515)

---

All translations have more or less the same length. This one presents the correct specialist terms (*facial skin, pimples, dehydration, sebum production*). In the DISCOURSE FIELD of advertisement it is important to have a scientific appearance in order to create confidence for the product in the consumer. The text follows the source text closely to present its message authentically. The designation of the ingredient Elubiol was seen as a name, the chemical composition could be something else. Regarding STYLISTICS the eye catcher was repeated as in the other versions, even creating a symmetrical sentence construction. Also, the text was more structured to enhance the publicity effect wanted for the FUNCTION. Functional style in the use of active nouns (*in preventing, apparition, recreation, protecting, application*) was also used. The product name was changed, in order not to interfere with other names and to preserve individuality, and also because "clear&clean" sounds more elegantly. This translation attempts to create a coherent scene of an efficient cosmetic product.

## 10.1.5 An economic text

The pragmatic translation problem inherent to economic texts regarding their SITUATIVE BACKGROUND is mainly to be seen in the inhomogeneous groups of persons participating in the communication process. There are rather diverse people appearing as authors or readers of texts in economy, and they are not always specialists but rather generalists. Besides the areas of politics and national economy, the economic communication is mainly realized within the companies and agencies themselves, and even the law is touched. Beyond commercial correspondence, the whole area of marketing is a complex field, comprising disciplines like foreign trade, business administration, cost accounting, storage, up until public relations and advertisement.

In addition to this specific information context, the varying language levels within the business communication, and the linguistic competence of the authors gain importance here. Rather often, economic texts practically contain less features of LSP, they even are part of everyday communication (business letters, tenders, reminders, advertisement, etc.). But the communicative world of business firms as the primary economic institution is the central background of economic texts.

Where terminology is given, the terms from the mentioned working fields are relevant. The inhomogeneous speakers' groups in economic communication as a DISCOURSE FIELD correspond to those various working fields which are interrelated in an enterprise. Bolten (1992) uses the model of a big company and combines it with the well-known threefold stratification model of the levels of language usage: a) language of theory, b) language of the profession, c) colloquial language at works and with clients (Stolze 1999:24).

Whereas the language of theory is mainly reserved to the level of planning and management in a firm, the professional language and works language is widely talked throughout the company.

Within an individual business firm, we may have departments for production, legal affairs, public relations, financing, personnel: more specifically research & product development, production management with construction, works preparation & fabrication, material management & disposition, buying & storage, marketing with market research, sales, distribution & logistics, administration with technical and commercial accounting & cashier.

Such a structuring helps to prevent in a text analysis both the limitation onto theoretical disciplines only, and to a classification according to an incalculable number of branches. Also, it is true that most practical translation assignments concern institutional communication among businesses.

Varying groups of authors also correspond to varying groups of addressees. With Beneke (1988:208) we might talk in view of advertising texts for special buyers of "texts with a double addressee", or of a "highly organized text type". Such a text is designed to fulfill several pragmatic functions. We have an example for this:

> *Text*: **Erstmals als Granulat: pflanzliche Haarfärbemittel**
>
> Naturprodukte stehen in der Gunst der Verbraucher weit oben. Dies gilt auch für Farben aus der Natur. Pflanzenfarben fürs Haar zum Beispiel sind ein bewährtes Kosmetikum: Schon im alten Ägypten haben vornehme Damen sich ihre Haare mit Henna gefärbt. Seit wenigen Wochen bietet N. bundesdeutschen Friseuren mit „Living Colors
> 5 Pflanzenhaarfarbe" nicht nur erstmals ein pflanzliches Haarfärbemittel als Markenartikel, sondern eine völlig neue Dienstleistung. „Wir sind weltweit das erste Unternehmen, das Pflanzenhaarfarbe als Granulat auf den Markt gebracht hat", sagt Karsten Wachowitz (Produktmanagement Kabinett Farbe). Die wesentlichen Vorteile des Granulats - es sieht aus wie löslicher Kaffee - gegenüber dem Pulver: geringste Staubent-
> 10 wicklung und damit kaum Inhalation, exakteres Dosieren, besseres Zubereiten und Anwenden sowie leichtes Ausspülen.
> Krappwurzel, Indigo, Henna, Kamille und Salbei sind nur einige von vielen Rohstoffen für die naturreinen, qualitativ hochwertigen Farben von „Living Colors". Unter anderem kommen sie aus Indien, Indonesien, Mexiko und dem Vorderen Orient. Alle Pflan-
> 15 zen werden aus kontrollierten Anbaugebieten bezogen.
> Die Bestandteile sind frei von synthetischen Farbstoffzusätzen und Konservierungsstoffen und untersucht nach dem Lebensmittelgesetz. Basierend auf Henna stehen in Kombination mit anderen Rohstoffen elf Nuancen zu Verfügung, die im Salon miteinander gemischt werden können. Durch ein patentiertes Verfahren ist es möglich, mit „Pre-
> 20 Color" und dem pflanzlichen Haarfärbemittel selbst den Weißanteil im Haar ohne Oxidation farblich dauerhaft zu verändern. (...)

> *Translation*: **Newly a granulated compound: Vegetable Hair-Dyes**
>
> Natural products <u>are high in the consumer's favour</u>. That is true for colours from the nature as well. <u>Vegetable hair-tints</u> for instance are a <u>reliable cosmetic</u>: even <u>in the Ancient Egypt</u> distinguished ladies had tinted their hair with henna. Since a few weeks, N. is <u>offering</u> with "Living Colors Hair Dyes" not only a novel <u>vegetable hair-tint</u> as a <u>brand</u>, but a completely <u>new service to the hairdressers</u> as well. "We are <u>the first business in the world</u> to <u>market</u> vegetable hair-tint as a granulated compound", <u>says Karsten Wachowitz</u> (Product Management Cabinet Color). The essential advantages of the <u>granulated compound – it looks like instant coffee</u> – compared with <u>powder</u> are: <u>lowest dust creation</u> and thus <u>little inhalation, exact dosage</u>, better preparation and application as well as <u>easy rinsing</u>.
>
> <u>Dyer's-weed, indigo, henna, camomile</u> and <u>sage</u> are only some of the many raw materials for the <u>natural high-quality colours</u> of "<u>Living Colours</u>". Among others they come from India, Indonesia, Mexico and the Middle East. All plants are bought <u>from controlled cultivations</u>. The ingredients are <u>free from synthetic pigment</u> admixtures and preservatives, and have been controlled according to the Food Act. Eleven shades <u>are available</u> on the basis of henna in combination with other raw materials. They may be mixed with one another in the salon.. A <u>patented procedure</u> enables to vary personally the permanent part of white in the hair without oxidation, using "Pre-Color" together with the <u>vegetable</u> hair-tint. (…)

Since all semantic aspects contribute to the overall meaning of the text, a translator should try, in view of its GENRE, to preserve as much as possible from the original message. Such poly-addressing appears as a kind of pragmatic "vagueness" in economic texts and constitutes a translation problem. Our example is a business report by a German producer of hair care products. It appeared in the firm's newsletter addressing the internal employees, hairdresser salons as the direct clients, and the local press for information of the public. And it had to be translated into English to be published in the Information Bulletin for international trade partners as well.

The text combines three functions: client information <u>and public relations to build-up confidence</u>, what is linguistically realized by the reference to natural products (*naturrein*), by a common simile (*löslicher Kaffee*), and by personal citations (*sagt Karsten Wachowitz*). These linguistic means of expert-lay communication have been analyzed by Beier (1983:96). Then there is also <u>specialized information for hairdressers</u> with terminology (*Granulat, Weißanteil*), as well as <u>marketing information for sales persons</u> about the product line and the firm's corporate identity with marketing terms (*Dienstleistung, Schulung, Einführung, Living Colors*). As we can see with our underlining, the three functions are lying on top of each other in the whole text. The translator will have to keep the different intentional features, and not for instance try to eliminate such "inadequate comparisons" as the 'instant coffee', thinking that this had nothing to do with a specialist text.

### 10.1.6 A pragmatic text

Economic texts show even more difficulties. A special problem in texts are terms that on the conceptual level are used both as hyperonymic terms, and as a more specific hyponymic term. Gerzymisch-Arbogast (1987:23) presents under the designation of „Passepartoutwörter" the vague usage of some terms in economics. General terms normally „have a high position on the scale of the conceptual *system*, but in *normal usage* they often take the position of a specific hyponym" (*my translation*). Such terms are rather wide in their meaning, comparable with general language prototypical lexemes. But passepartout words are specialist terms. The translation problem is to be seen in the lacking equivalence, that means their correspondent in the German language is not always an equally vague general term. Gerzymisch-Arbogast (1989:190) pleads for corrsponding entries in general dictionaries.

> Gerzymisch-Arbogast presents some examples from American economic English, such as *assets, property, money, income, profit, earnings, wealth, funds*, often used in one same text on various semantic levels of specification, this in contrast to de. *Aktiva, Vermögensgegenstände, Anlagevermögen, Anlagen, Geld*.
>
> Similar terms are also *agreement, contract, covenant, warranty* in contrastive comparison with German *Vertrag, Vereinbarung, Absprache, Abmachung, Übereinkunft, Abkommen, Zusicherung, Zusatzabrede, Gewährleistung*.

The translator should be aware of this problem and apply relevant factual knowledge in economics. The following example from a newspaper text, i.e. in expert-lay communication, presents this problem with the well-kown term of "management" that meanwhile even has entered the German language as a neologism. A semantic analysis regarding the text's MEANING DIMENSION will make clear that the concept at each position in the text is different, and this leads to various versions in the translation. According to contrastive linguistics, this would be called a "1-to-many equivalence relationship". However, this statement does not solve the translation problem of how to choose the right equivalent. The meaning of "management" has to be verified by a word field analysis.

| Text example | Translation |
|---|---|
| Manufacturing management₃ | Produktionslenkung |
| Time and motion studies, long dismissed as a primitive, divisive management₃ tool, have helped a GM-Toyota joint venture to succeed spectacularly.<br><br>FREDERICK WINSLOW TAYLOR is perhaps the most popular bogeyman of modern management₁ thinkers. One of the first people to study work systematically, Taylor argued that the productivity of physical labor could be increased greatly by measuring in minute detail the activities of workers, and then standardizing and accelerating their tasks. He called this "scientific management₁". Expounded in a book published in 1911, his methods were widely applied as mass production spread. (...) "Taylorism" is now vilified as the epitome of a hierarchical, authoritarian style of management₂ which caused decades of labor strife. No right-thinking manager₄ today would describe himself as a disciple of Taylor. (...)<br><br>[*The Economist*, January 23, 1993, p.73]<br><br>Management 1-4 | Zeit- und Bewegungsstudien, die lange als ein primitives, die Mitarbeiter spaltendes Organisationsinstrument verpönt waren, haben einem GM-Toyota Joint-venture zu spektakulärem Erfolg verholfen.<br><br>Der wohl bekannteste Buhmann bei den Vordenkern des modernen Managements ist wohl Frederick Winslow Taylor. Als einer der ersten, die Arbeitsverfahren systematisch untersuchten, argumentierte er, man könne die Produktivität körperlicher Arbeit dadurch stark erhöhen, dass die Tätigkeiten von Arbeitern bis ins kleinste Detail gemessen und ihre Aufgaben dann standardisiert und beschleunigt würden. Er nannte dies „wissenschaftliche Betriebsführung". Seine Methoden, die er in einem 1911 erschienenen Buch entwickelte, fanden breite Anwendung, als die Massenproduktion um sich griff. (...) Der „Taylorismus" wird heute als der Inbegriff eines hierarchischen und autoritären Führungsstils geschmäht, der jahrzehntelange Arbeitskämpfe ausgelöst hat. Kein vernünftig denkender Manager würde sich heute noch als Anhänger Taylors bezeichnen.<br><br>*(1) Unternehmensführung, Management als Theorie, (2) Führungsstil, (3) Organisationsstruktur, Lenkung, Steuerung, (4) Betriebsleitung, Direktion, Management, Leitungsmannschaft.* |

The example is from a newspaper, and we name it a „pragmatic text". The aim of such texts is to inform non-specialist readers in expert-lay communication about sciences and developments in economy and society. In order to make such texts intelligible for laymen readers, some linguistic tricks are applied, such as reference to persons, comparison with other things from life, explanation of terminological content. We see some of them also in our text example. The characteristics are found in German newspaper articles as well. Such rules are not only important for formulating such a pragmatic text, but also for its translation. The FUNCTION in the communicative situation of the DISCOURSE FIELD determines the text type to be used.

## 10.1.7 A multimedia text

**Birkart**
1   Ideen öffnen Wege –
Seit 1877 ist dies der Leitspruch des Familienunternehmens Johann Birkart, das nun schon in der vierten Generation Ideen durch Leistung in die Tat umzusetzen versteht. Weltweit mehr als 4000 Beschäftigte und 1100 eigene Fahrzeugeinheiten sind national und international für Sie im Einsatz.
2   Vergleichen wir die Leistungen einer Spedition mit dem Sport...
Optimale Vorbereitung, exakte Planung und Umsetzung führen zum Erfolg.
3   Immer in Bewegung –
Güter werden durch ein dichtes Verteilernetz termingerecht zu jedem Bestimmungsort transportiert. Zuverlässigkeit durch Spezialisierung. Wir haben für jede Güterart das passende System: Paketdienst, System-Glut, Deutsche Kleiderspedition, integrierte Transportleistung – von Haus zu Haus.
4   Wir fahren weltweit jeden Kilometer –
Die Verteilung von Gütern braucht viele Räder – ob national oder international, wir setzen sie in Bewegung.
4a   Freie Fahrt zu neuen Märkten -
Birkart kennt keine Grenzen. Mit uns haben Sie grünes Licht beim Zoll. Wir erledigen die Formalitäten und sparen Ihre Zeit.
5   Präzisionsinstrumente schaffen Lösungen nach Maß –
Die dks mit ihrem Angebot dies Transports und der Lagerung hängender Bekleidung ergänzt als Tochterunternehmen der Birkart-Gruppe die Serviceleistungen im Textilbereich.
6/7 Um Hürden zu meistern und Ziele zu erreichen, müssen Programm und Technik harmonieren. Modernste Technologie und Innovation bringen entscheidende Vorteile. – Ein kunden- und produktbezogenes, datengestütztes Verteilerprogramm steuert Lagerung, Kommissionierung und optimierten Versand.
8   Transportgut braucht Schubkräfte –
Nur wenige Flugstunden – und eilige Waren und Güter landen auf allen bedeutenden Flugplätzen der Erde. Die Birkart-Gruppe vermittelt jeden Lufttransport – unlimited. Unser Personal sorgt für individuelle Bearbeitung. wir prüfen Verlademöglichkeiten, erstellen Frachtkalkulation und bieten Ihnen spezielle Serviceleistungen.
9   Falcon-Service –
ein kombinierte Sea-/Air-Verkehr, ein weitere Bestandteil unsrer Luftfrachtpalette.
10   Eilt, Vorsicht.
Besondere Aufgaben verlangen besondere Lösungen - German Sky Express. Wir sorgen dafür, daß alles so ankommt, wie es ankommen soll – door to door.
11   Birkart international –
wir unterhalten global ein ausgedehntes Netz von eigenen Büros und Korrespondenten. Dies garantiert Ihnen Präsenz auf allen internationalen Märkten. Ob Europa, Afrika, Fernost, Australien, Nord- oder Südamerika – wohin sie auch Ihre Fracht verladen, wir sind überall zur Stelle – weltweit.
12   Die Meere der Welt sind Frachtrouten und Handelsstraßen. Ob kleinste Stückgüter, oder komplette Industrieanlagen – wir vermitteln die richtige Verschiffungsart und buchen den schnellsten Weg.
Die kostengünstiges und schnellste Verpackung für jedes passende Gut: der Container. Die Birkart-Gruppe organisiert Sammelladungen und für besondere Güter den Spezial-Container-Service – auch im Gateway-System.
Auch bei Seetransport arbeiten wir mit kompetenten und leistungsfähigen Partner. Die-

|  |  |
|---|---|
| 50 | se gewährleisten auch in der Verbindung Bahn, Binnenschiff und Lkw eine fachgerechte Behandlung und Beförderung.<br>Birkarts eigene Lkw's erledigen den Zubringer- und Abholdienst im Hafen oder im Binnenland.<br>13    Mit voller Kraft voraus. Ob zu Wasser, zu Lande oder in der Luft – wir schaffen logistische Möglichkeiten. |
| 55 | Bereitstellung, Organisation und Abwicklung sind die Kernbereiche der Logistik. Sie umfassen eine Fülle von Teilfunktionen, die, auf den Einzelfall abgestimmt, Effizienz garantieren.<br>Täglich werden wir nach Lösungen gefragt – einer Aufgabe, der wir uns gerne stellen.<br>*(Preparation: k+v design, Werbeagentur GmbH, Darmstadt 1991)* |

The text „Birkart" is the script of a publicity video, prepared by a German advertising agency. The text has to be spoken, as various pictures are linked, each one with a motto and a subsequent explanatory text heard while viewing the film scenes. This is a multimedia text, however with a specialist topic. It had to be translated into English for the company's international outreach. The SITUATIVE BACKGROUND is Germany with its many small and medium-sized enterprises, and you see their cars still running. This shows in the first paragraph when the firm's tradition is mentioned. Such a tradition is important for German family-owned businesses as it indicates reliability.

The DISCOURSE FIELD is the branch of forwarding agencies and logistics, and its MEANING DIMENSION reflects in specialist terms like *Fahrzeugeinheiten* (4), *Verteilernetz* (9), *Bestimmungsort* (9), *Paketdienst* (11), *System-Gut* (11), *Kleiderspedition* (11), *Lagerung* (20), *Kommissionierung* (26), *Verlademöglichkeiten* (30), *Frachtkalkulation* (31), *Luftfrachtpalette* (33), *Frachtrouten* (42), *Stückgüter* (42), *Container* (45), *Verschiffungsart* (43), *Sammelladungen* (46), *Zubringer- und Abholdienst* (51), *Seetransport* (48), *Logistik* (55), etc. These are exactly defined terms within the shipping business. At the same time – as it is also a publicity text – we also see repeated general language terms with a rather vague concept appealing to the client who is a logistics layman: *Leistung ((3), Einsatz* (5), *optimale Vorbereitung* (7), *Zuverlässigkeit* (10), *Spezialisierung* (10), *Bewegung* (15), *Lösungen nach Maß* (19), *Serviceleistungen* (21), *modernste Technologie* (24), *Aufgaben* (35), *Möglichkeiten* (30, 54), *Effizienz* (56). The author's intention, here, is confidence-building by individual interpretation. (This is a similar function like in our economic text.)

The PREDICATIVE MODE shows idioms referring to traffic: *freie Fahrt* (16), *grünes Licht* (17), *Räder in Bewegung* (15), *mit voller Kraft vorau* (13); and some metaphorical affirmations in the present tense, with a tendency to overstatement. Some text structures reiterate: *national oder international* (4, 14, 39), *von Haus zu Haus* (12), *weltweit* (4, 13, 41). A peculiar feature are several incomplete sentences indicating an idea, but this effect will not work in the English language. And finally: English names for German services is a characteristic of publicity texts here, see *German Sky Express*.

|  | **Translation (A)** |
|---|---|
|  | *Helicopter approaches* |
|  | 1 Ideas open up the world – |
|  | This has been the motto of the family-owned enterprise Johann Birkart ever since 1877. Ideas are put into action by efficiency, meanwhile in the forth generation. More than 4,000 employees and 1,100 vehicles worldwide are ready for duty in your service – at |
| 5 | home or abroad. |
|  | *Stadium* |
|  | 2 Let's compare the performance of a forwarding agent with sports… Optimal preparation, exact planning and implementation lead to success. |
|  | *Truck in Frankfurt* |
| 10 | 3 Always on the move – |
|  | Through a dense distribution network, goods are being transported to any destination on schedule. This is reliability by specialisation. We have the suitable system for any kind of goods: parcel delivery, system-freight, German clothes haulage (DKS), integrated transports – from door to door. |
| 15 | *German highway – crossing over to London* |
|  | 4 We cover every mile in the world – |
|  | The distribution of goods needs many wheels, and we set them all in motion – at home or abroad. |
|  | *Picture of Harrods/British policeman* |
| 20 | 4a Clear road towards new markets – |
|  | Birkart ignores borders. Together with us you will have green lights at customs. We attend to red tape and thus save your time. |
|  | *Picture of DKS/ phone picked up* |
|  | 5 Precision instruments create tailor-made solutions – |
| 25 | DKS with its offer of transportation and storage of hanging clothing is a subsidiary of the Birkart Group completing the services in the textile sector. |
|  | *Hurdler/sorting cycle/truck* |
|  | 6/7 Program and technology must go together if you want to master hurdles and reach goals. – Progressive technology and innovation bring decisive advantages. – |
| 30 | A customized and product-oriented, data-driven distribution program controls storage, commissioning and optimised shipment. |
|  | *Lufthansa* |
|  | 8 Cargo needs thrust – |
|  | Only a few hours of flight – and urgent products and goods land at all major airports in |
| 35 | the world. The Birkart Group arranges any air transport – without limits. |

|  |  |
|---|---|
| 40 | Our staff ensures individual handling. We study the loading possibilities, establish the estimate for freight, and offer you special services.<br>*Pole vaulter/lifting equipment*<br>9 Falcon-Service –<br>the combined sea-air link is another element of our airfreight range.<br>*Cockpit at takeoff/telephone picked up*<br>10 Urgent! Fragile!<br>Special tasks require special solutions – German Sky Express. We take care that everything arrives exactly as expected – from door to door. |
| 45 | *Display panel "Ideas open up..."*<br>11 Birkart international –<br>We are operating a wide-spread global network with our own offices and correspondents. This guarantees your presence in all international markets. Be it in Europe, Africa, the Far East, Australia, North or South America – wherever you will ship your freight, we are on the spot – worldwide. |
| 50 |  |
|  | *Freighter at the pier*<br>12 The oceans are freight routes and trade channels. Whether smallest pieces of mixed cargo or complete industrial plants – we obtain the right type of shipment and book the fastest route for you. |
| 55 | The most cost-effective and quickest packing for every suitable good is the container. The Birkart Group organizes collective consignments, and for special goods there is the Special Container Service, even in the gateway system.<br>In marine transport too we are cooperating with competent and efficient partners. They guarantee an expert handling and forwarding of your goods – even in the combination |
| 60 | of rail, inland waterway and motor transport.<br>*When Birkart truck appears*<br>Birkart's own trucks carry out the feeder and pickup service at the ports or in the inland. |
|  | *Pictures run/when swimmers appear* |
| 65 | 13 Full speed ahead! Whether by water, by land or in the air – we create logistic options.<br>Ready position, apt organisation and processing are the key areas of logistics. They comprise a variety of partial functions that ensure efficiency adjusted to the individual case. |
| 70 | Every day we are asked for answers – we love to face this challenge.<br><br>*(Translation R. Stolze 1992)* |

When the translator deals with this text, GENRE is of utmost importance. The result must become an appealing video-text easy to speak. Time is relevant in connection with the video and delimits speech rhythm, and the translation (A) tries to cope with this challenge.

Translation (B) (see below) does not come up to that. Direct verbal address of the audience according to the PREDICATIVE MODE might be adequate, as is also found in the text itself: *wir sind für Sie im Einsatz; wir bieten Ihnen spezielle Serviceleistungen; wir erledigen die Formalitäten und sparen Ihre Zeit*. Instead, in translation (B) the speaker's perspective was changed to a neutral statement: *Customs formalities are handled for you, saving your time.* On the other hand, the specialist terms must be translated correctly, so to signal precision as the basic value of a forwarding agent, what again was failed in translation (B) which obviously was not written from a technical perspective, but rather from a sportive one. The intended FUNCTION of the translation is not fully achieved.

The aspect of COHERENCE in translation will show both in the equivalence of technical terminology and in the compatibility of a word field in the text around "reliability" and "efficiency". Searching for corresponding lexemes, such as *achievement, performance, competence, reliability, service-orientation, answers, trust, confidence,* etc. instead of sequential phrase-related decisions would have helped the translator to create a more convincing text.

On the contrary, the authors of translation (B) obviously were animated to much talkativeness by the sports pictures of the film and the abstract scenes (*ideas, motion*) and took their frames rather freely. But the two central word fields as to the MEANING DIMENSION relevant here were neglected, i.e. (1) *ideas, preparation, success, task, solution* and (2) *movement, ways, distribution, transport, in motion*.

STYLISTICS will require an adequate idiomatic expressiveness. The rhythm of a spoken text has to be observed, and this might have been the main drawback in translation (B) which had been rejected by the client firm. Various cases of translationese by interference are also found there, e.g. *"To get over hurdles and achieve objectives, schedule and technology must be harmonized."* Or: *"And then came the achievement of a family business."* Such a sentence structure is not possible in English, and idiomatic translations often require non literal formulations. Besides that, in translation (B), the terminology is defective or missing: **service, *family business (= firm), *handle formalities, *data-supported, *dispatching, *fastest packaging, *consignment by sea,* etc. The technical part of the text was not realized.

**Translation (B):**

IDEAS OPEN UP THE WORLD

1    The idea took shape a long time ago in 1877! And then came the achievement of a family business, now in its forth generation! Together they have created, throughout these years, the Birkart Group, its ideas continuing to open up the world now and in the future.

2    Let us compare the idea with sport. Optimum performance requires precise preparation. Regular training, belief and willpower produce the success striven for.

3    A network with the most intricate links! A tailor-made system for every type of goods! Parcel service, systems, the DKS clothes forwarding service, integrated transport services – door to door!

4    We cover every mile of the world! So many wheels are needed to distribute goods. The Birkart Groups sets them all in motion at home and abroad.

5    A clear road to new markets! – No stopping at borders! Customs formalities are handled for you, saving your time!

5a    Precision instruments achieve tailor-made solutions! As a subsidiary of Birkart-Spedition, DKS with its transportation and storage service for hanging clothes provides an additional service in the textile sector. Let these pictures set you thinking. – Birkart does not stop there!

6    To get over hurdles and achieve objectives, schedule and technology must be harmonized. The latest communication systems allow good ideas to succeed – in seconds! Worldwide!

7    JB Logistics – developed by Birkart.
A customer and product-related, data-supported distribution program controls storage, ordering and optimised dispatching.

8    Endurance – quality – performance mean success. Success mobilizes new forces.

9    Transport needs thrust like this! Only a few hours' flight and urgent goods arrive at all the major airports in the world. The Birkart Group can arrange any air transport and is represented everywhere in the world!

10    Our partners with this thrust must be first-class and must match the Birkart performance standard.

11    Urgent. Fragile. Valuable. You need German Sky Express. Birkart makes sure that everything arrives as and when expected, anywhere in the world!

12    Falcon Service – combined sea/air transport – another component of the air freight range!

13    The Birkart Group has its own firms or branches in every continent.

14    The world's seas are freight and trade routes: The Birkart Group knows its way around. It arranges the right type of shipping and picks the quickest route, whether for very small general cargoes or complete industrial plants, and arranges the correct packaging.

The cheapest and fastest packaging for any goods that fit is the container. Birkart organizes collective consignments and has special containers for special goods. Gateway shipping – the expert system.

Reputable and efficient partners are selected for sea transport too.

Our partners ensure that handling and transport are of the highest standard, whether by inland waterway, rail or road.

Item after item goes overseas – even as conventional sea freight, from industrial plant to cotton reels – consignment by sea and arrangement of correct packaging run smoothly for every item.

15    Birkart's own lorries provide a transfer or pickup service at ports or inland.

| | |
|---|---|
| 50 | We create logistical options! Preparation, organization and performance – these are the key areas of logistics. They comprise a wealth of individual functions guaranteeing efficiency by adjusting to individual situations. This alone is the measure of the Birkart Group and will distinguish their solution from standard solution. |
| 55 | 16   At full throttle – whether on water, land or in the air – with the latest methods and equipment the family business has as many ideas now as it had in 1877, but with a positive difference: now and for the future ideas and achievements make Birkart at home throughout the world and allow Birkart and its many employees to open up, promote and maintain markets. |
| 60 | Listen to Birkart's ideas, or better still, let us convince you with results. *(English translation of the video script 1991, rejected by the advertiser as a client.)* |

## 10.2   Translating literature

### 10.2.1   Extract from a novel

| | |
|---|---|
| | PROLOGUE *Morgaine speaks...* |
| 5 | IN MY TIME I have been called many things: sister, lover, **priestess**, wise-woman, queen. Now, in truth I have come to be **wise-woman**, and a time may come when these things may need to be known. But in sober truth, I think it is the **Christians** who will tell the last **tale**. For ever the **world of Fairy** drifts further from the world in which the Christ holds sway. I have no quarrel with the **Christ**, only with his **priests**, who call the Great Goddess a demon and deny that she ever held power in this world. At best, they say that her power was of **Satan**. Or else they clothe her in the blue robe of the Lady of **Nazareth** |
| 10 | who indeed had power in her way, too - and say that she was ever **virgin**. But what can a virgin know of the sorrows and travail of mankind? |
| | AND NOW, when the world has changed, and **Arthur** - my brother, my lover, king who was and king who shall be - lies dead (the common folk say sleeping) in the **Holy Isle of Avalon**, the tale should be told as it was before the priests of the White **Christ** came to |
| 15 | cover it all with their **saints** and **legends**. |
| | FOR, as I say, the world itself has changed. There was a time when a traveller, if he had the **will** and knew only a few of the **secrets**, could send his barge out into the Summer Sea and arrive not at **Glastonbury** of the **monks**, but at the Holy Isle of Avalon; FOR at that time **the gates between the worlds** drifted within the **mists**, and were open, one to |
| 20 | another, as the traveller **thought and willed**. FOR this is the great secret, which was known to all educated men in our day: that by what men think, we create the world around us, daily new. |
| | AND NOW the **priests**, thinking that this infringes upon the power of their **God, who created the world** once and for all to be unchanging, have closed those doors (which |
| 25 | were never doors, except in the minds of men), and the pathway leads only to **the priests' Isle**, which they have safeguarded with the sound of their **church bells**, driving away all thoughts of **another world** lying in the darkness. Indeed, they say *that* world, if it indeed exists, is the property of **Satan**, and the **doorway to Hell**, if not Hell itself. |

I do not know what their God may or may not have created. In spite of the tales that are told, I never knew much about their **priests** and never wore the **black** of one of their slave-**nuns**. If those at Arthur's court at Camelot chose to think me so when I came there (since I always wore the **dark robes** of the **Great Mother** in her guise as **wise-woman**), I did not undeceive them. And indeed, toward the end of Arthur's reign it would have been dangerous to do so, and I bowed my head to expediency as my **great mistress** would never have done: Viviane, **Lady of the Lake**, once Arthur's greatest friend, save for myself, and then his darkest enemy - again, save for myself.

BUT the strife is over; I could greet Arthur at last, when he lay dying, not as my enemy and the enemy of my Goddess, but only as my brother, and as a dying man in need of the Mother's aid, where all men come at last. Even the priests know this, with their ever-virgin **Mary** in her blue robe; for she too becomes the **World Mother** in the hour of death.

AND SO Arthur lay at last with his head in my lap, seeing in me neither sister nor lover nor foe, but only wise-woman, priestess, **Lady of the Lake**; and so he rested upon the breast of the Great Mother from whom he came to birth and to whom at last, as all men, he must go. And perhaps, as I guided the barge which bore him away, not this time to the Isle of the Priests, but to the true **Holy Isle in the dark** world behind our own, that Island of Avalon where, now, few but I could go, he repented the enmity that had come between us.

AS I TELL this **tale** I will speak at times of things which befell when I was too young to understand them, or of things which befell when I was not by; and my hearer will draw away, perhaps, and say: *This is her magic*. BUT I have always held the gift of **the Sight**, and of looking within the minds of men and women; AND in all this time I have been close to all of them. AND SO, at times, all that they thought was known to me in one way or another. And so I will tell this **tale**.

FOR one day the **priests** too will tell it, as it was known to them. Perhaps between the two, some glimmering of the truth may be seen.

FOR this is the thing the **priests** do not know, with their **One God** and **One Truth**: that there is no such thing as a true **tale**. Truth has many faces and the truth is like the old road to Avalon: it depends on your own will, and your own thoughts, whither the road will take you, AND whether, at the end, you arrive in the Holy Isle of Eternity or among the **priests** with their **bells** and their **death** and their **Satan** and **Hell** and **damnation**... BUT perhaps I am unjust even to them. Even the **Lady of the Lake**, who hated a priest's robe as she would have hated a poisonous viper, and with good cause too, chid me once for speaking evil of their **God**.

'FOR all the gods are one God', she said to me then, as she had said many times before, and as I have said to my own **novices** many times, and as every **priestess** who comes after me will say again, 'and all the goddesses are one Goddess, and there is only one **Initiator**. And to every man his own truth, and the god within.'

AND SO, perhaps, the truth winds somewhere between the road to Glastonbury, Isle of the Priests, and the road to Avalon, lost forever in the **mists** of the Summer sea.

BUT this is **my truth**; I who am Morgaine tell you these things, Morgaine who was in later days called Morgan le Fay.

*In*: Marion Bradley, *The Mists of Avalon*. Sphere Books, London/Sydney 1983, p. IX-XI.

Here are two German translations.

**Translation (A):** PROLOG

*Morgaine erzählt...*
Zu meiner Zeit <u>hat man mir viele Namen gegeben</u>: Schwester, Geliebte, Priesterin, weise Frau und Königin. Jetzt bin ich wirklich eine weise Frau geworden. Und vielleicht kommt eine Zeit, in der es wichtig ist, daß all diese Dinge bekannt werden. Aber ich glaube, die nüchterne Wahrheit wird sein, daß die Christen das letzte Wort haben. Denn die Welt der Feen entschwindet immer weiter, treibt ab von der Welt, in der die Christen herrschen. <u>Christus ist nicht mein Feind, aber seine Priester</u>, die die Große Göttin einen bösen Geist nennen. Sie leugnen, daß die Macht über diese Welt einmal in ihren Händen lag. Wenn überhaupt, so sagen sie, kam ihre Macht vom Teufel. Oder sie kleiden sie in das blaue Gewand der <u>Maria aus Nazareth</u> – die auf ihre Weise tatsächlich auch Macht besaß – und behaupten, sie sei immer <u>eine Jungfrau</u> gewesen. Aber was kann eine Jungfrau von <u>Leid und Mühsal der Menschen</u> wissen?

Jetzt, nachdem die Welt sich verändert hat und Artus mein Bruder, mein Geliebter, der König, der war und der König, der sein wird – <u>tot ist</u> (das einfache Volk sagt, er schläft) <u>und auf der Heiligen Insel Avalon ruht</u>, soll die Geschichte erzählt werden. Die Welt soll erfahren, wie es war, ehe die Priester des Weißen Christus in das Land kamen und alles unter ihren Heiligen und Legenden <u>begruben</u>.

<u>Wie ich gesagt habe</u>, die Welt selbst hat sich verändert. Es gab eine Zeit, in der ein Reisender, wenn er den Willen besaß und auch nur einige der Geheimnisse kannte, mit seinem Boot auf dem Sommersee hinausfahren konnte und nicht im Glastonbury der Mönche ankam, sondern auf der Heiligen Insel Avalon. Damals trieben die Pforten zwischen den Welten in den Nebeln und <u>waren in beide Richtungen offen</u> – wie der Reisende es dachte und wollte. Es ist das große Geheimnis, das in unserer Zeit jeder Wissende kannte: <u>Die Menschen schaffen die Welt</u>, die uns umgibt, durch das, was sie denken, jeden Tag neu.

Die Priester glauben, dies verkleinere die Macht ihres Gottes, der die Welt ein für allemal unveränderlich geschaffen hat, und haben die Tore geschlossen (die nur in der Vorstellung der Menschen Tore waren). Heute führt der Weg nur noch zur <u>Insel der Mönche</u>, die sie mit dem Läuten ihrer Kirchenglocken schützen. So vertreiben sie alle Gedanken an eine <u>andere Welt, die in der Dunkelheit liegt</u>. Sie sagen sogar, daß jene Welt – wenn es sie überhaupt gibt – <u>dem Teufel gehört</u> und daß die Pforten zur Hölle führen – vielleicht sei diese Welt sogar <u>die Hölle selbst</u>, behaupten sie...

Ich weiß nicht, was ihr Gott <u>möglicherweise</u> geschaffen oder nicht geschaffen hat. Entgegen der Geschichten, die verbreitet werden, wußte ich nie viel über ihre Priester. Ich habe auch nie das schwarze Gewand ihrer Sklavinnen, der Nonnen, getragen. Wenn man an König Artus' Hof in Camelot es vorzog, mich für eine Nonne zu halten (denn ich trug immer die dunklen Gewänder der großen Mutter in ihrer Erscheinung als weise Frau), so habe ich <u>den Irrtum nie aufgeklärt</u>. Gegen Ende von Artus' Herrschaft wäre es sogar gefährlich gewesen, dies zu tun. <u>Klugerweise beugte ich das Haupt, wie meine Große Meisterin</u> Viviane, die Herrin vom See, es niemals getan hätte. Einst war sie – abgesehen von mir – König Artus' beste Freundin und wurde dann seine größte Feindin –auch das abgesehen von mir.

Aber der Kampf ist vorbei. Als Artus im Sterben lag, konnte ich ihm nicht mehr als meinem Feind und dem Gegner meiner Göttin <u>gegenübertreten</u>, sondern nur noch als dem Bruder und als einem Sterbenden, der die Hilfe der Mutter braucht – denn dahin gelangen am Ende alle Menschen. Das wissen selbst die Priester mit ihrer ewig jungfräulichen <u>Maria in dem blauen Gewand</u> – auch sie wird für die <u>Kirchenmänner in der</u>

Stunde des Todes zur Mutter der Welt.

Und so hielt ich schließlich Artus' Kopf in meinem Schoß. Er sah in mir weder die Schwester noch die Geliebte, auch nicht die Feindin, sondern nur die weise Frau, die Priesterin, die Herrin vom See. Er ruhte an der Brust der Großen Mutter, von der er bei seiner Geburt kam und zu der er am Ende wie alle Menschen zurückkehren mußte. Vielleicht bereute er unsere Feindschaft, als ich die Barke lenkte, die ihn davontrug – dieses Mal nicht zu der Insel der Mönche, sondern zu der wahrhaft Heiligen Insel in der dunklen Welt hinter unserer Welt – zur Insel Avalon, wohin außer mir nur noch wenige gelangen können.

Im Verlauf dieser Geschichte spreche ich manchmal von Dingen, die sich ereigneten, als ich zu jung war, um sie zu begreifen, oder von Dingen, die sich nicht in meiner Anwesenheit ereigneten. Der Hörer wird sich vielleicht entsetzt abwenden und sagen: *Das ist ihre Magie!* Aber ich habe schon immer die Gabe des Gesichts besessen und konnte sehen, was Männer und Frauen dachten. So war ich ihnen allen die ganze Zeit über nahe. Deshalb wurde mir manchmal auf die eine oder andere Weise alles bekannt, was sie dachten, und ich kann diese Geschichte von Anfang bis Ende erzählen.

Eines Tages werden auch die Priester sie erzählen. Vielleicht liegt die Wahrheit zwischen beiden Geschichten und wird durch sie hindurchschimmern.

Denn das wissen die Priester mit ihrem Einen Gott und der Einen Wahrheit nicht: Die eine wahre Geschichte gibt es nie und nimmer. Die Wahrheit hat viele Gesichter, und die Wahrheit ist wie der alte Weg nach Avalon: Es hängt von deinem Willen und deinen Gedanken ab, wohin der Weg dich führt. Es hängt von dir ab, ob du am Ende die Heilige Insel der Ewigkeit erreichst, oder ob du bei den Mönchen mit ihren Glocken, ihrem Tod, ihrem Teufel, ihrer Hölle und ihrer Verdammnis ankommst... aber vielleicht bin ich ihnen gegenüber auch ungerecht. Selbst die Herrin vom See, die das Gewand eines Christuspriesters haßte wie ein giftige Schlange – und das aus gutem Grund -, tadelte mich einmal, weil ich schlecht über ihren Gott gesprochen hatte.

„Denn alle Götter sind ein Gott", sagte sie damals zu mir, wie sie es bereits oft getan hatte, und wie ich viele Male zu meinen Priesterschülerinnen gesagt habe, und wie jede Priesterin, die nach mir kommt, sagen wird. „Und alle Göttinnen sind eine Göttin, und es gibt nur einen Gott, mit dem alles begann. Jeder Mensch hat das Recht auf seine eigene Wahrheit und auf den Gott, der durch sie spricht."

Und so windet sich die Wahrheit vielleicht irgendwo zwischen dem Weg nach Glastonbury, der Insel der Priester, und dem Weg nach Avalon, das für immer in den Nebeln des Sommersees verloren ist.

Aber dies ist meine Wahrheit. Ich bin Morgaine, und ich erzähle euch diese Dinge... ich, Morgaine, die in späteren Zeiten Morgan le Fay genannt wurde – die Fee Morgana.

*Fischer, Frankfurt am Main 1983, Taschenbuchausgabe 1987, S. 7-9.*

xxxxxxxxxxx

**Translation (B):** PROLOG
*Morgaine spricht...*

Damals zu meiner Zeit hatte ich viele Namen: Schwester, Geliebte, **Priesterin**, Weise Frau, Königin. Nun bin ich wirklich die **Weise Frau** geworden, und irgendwann einmal wird vielleicht all dies bekannt werden müssen. Doch ganz nüchtern betrachtet glaube ich, nach den Christen werden keine Märchen mehr erzählt. Unaufhaltsam treibt die **Welt der Feen** fort von der Welt, in der der **Christus** herrscht. Ich habe nichts gegen den Christus, nur gegen seine Priester, die die **Große Göttin** als Dämon bezeichnen und leugnen, daß sie jemals in dieser Welt Macht gehabt hat. Bestenfalls sagen sie, ihre Macht sei vom **Satan** gewesen. Oder sie kleiden sie in das blaue Gewand der Dame von Nazareth - die tatsächlich auf ihre Weise auch Macht besaß - und behaupten, sie sei immer jungfräulich gewesen. Doch was kann schon eine Jungfrau vom Kummer und den Qualen der Menschheit wissen?

Und nun, da die Welt sich verändert hat, und Artus – mein Bruder, mein Geliebter, der König, der war und der sein wird - begraben liegt (die einfachen Leute sagen, er schläft) auf der Heiligen Insel von Avalon, da sollte die Geschichte erzählt werden, wie es war, bevor die Priester des Weißen Christus kamen, und alles mit ihren **Heiligen** und **Legenden** zudeckten.

Denn, wie ich sage, die Welt selbst hat sich verändert. Es gab einmal eine Zeit, da konnte ein Reisender, wenn er den Willen hatte und nur ein paar von den Geheimnissen kannte, seine Barke in den Sommersee hinausfahren lassen und nicht im Glastonbury der Mönche anlangen, sondern auf der Heiligen Insel von Avalon; denn zu jener Zeit trieben die Pforten zwischen den Welten dort in den Nebeln, und der Durchgang war offen von der einen zur anderen, so wie es der Reisende durch Gedanken und Willenskraft bewirkte. Denn dies große Geheimnis war allen Berufenen in unseren Tagen bekannt: daß wir uns durch unser Denken die Welt um uns her täglich neu erschaffen.

Und nun haben die **Priester** in dem Glauben, dies greife in die Macht ihres Gottes ein, der die Welt ein für alle Mal unveränderlich geschaffen hat, jene Tore verschlossen (die immer nur in der menschlichen Vorstellung Tore waren), und der Pfad führt nur noch zur **Priesterinsel**, die sie mit dem **Geläute** ihrer **Kirchenglocken** beschützten, die jeden Gedanken an eine **Anderswelt im Dunkel** verscheuchten. Sie behaupten sogar, *jene* Welt, so sie wirklich existiert, sei das Eigentum **Satans** und der direkte **Weg zur Hölle**, wenn nicht gar die **Hölle** selbst.

Ich weiß nicht, was ihr Gott geschaffen hat oder nicht. Trotz der Geschichten, die erzählt werden, wußte ich nie viel über ihre Priester und ich trug nie den **schwarzen Habit** wie eine ihrer sklavischen **Nonnen**. Wenn die Leute an Artus' Hof in Camelot mich als eine solche sehen wollten, wann ich dorthin kam (denn ich trug immer die **dunklen Gewänder** der **Großen Mutter** in ihrer Erscheinung als Weise Frau), dann nahm ich ihnen diesen Glauben nicht. Und gegen Ende von Artus' Herrschaft wäre dies sogar gefährlich gewesen, und ich beugte mich dem Gebot der Stunde, wie es **meine große Herrin** niemals getan hätte: Viviane, die **Dame vom See**, einst außer mir Artus' größte Freundin und dann seine ärgste Feindin, wiederum außer mir selbst.

Doch der Streit war vorüber; ich konnte Artus schließlich, als er im Sterben lag, ansprechen - nicht als meinen Feind und den Feind meiner Göttin, sondern nur als meinen Bruder und als sterbenden Mann, der die Hilfe der Mutter braucht, in einer Lage also, in die alle Menschen am Ende kommen. Auch die Priester mit ihrer ewig jungfräulichen **Maria** in ihrem **blauen Kleid** wissen das; denn auch sie wird zur **Weltenmutter** in der Stunde des Todes.

Und so lag Artus am Ende da, den Kopf in meinem Schoß, und sah in mir nicht die Schwester, noch die Geliebte, noch die Widersacherin, sondern nur die Weise Frau, die Priesterin, die Dame vom See; und so ruhte er an der Brust der Großen Mutter, von der er ins Leben kam und zu der er endlich, wie alle Menschen, wieder heimkehren muß. Und als ich die Barke, die ihn davontrug, dieses Mal nicht zur Insel der Priester sondern zu der wahrhaft Heiligen Insel in der **Dunkelwelt** hinter der unsrigen, zu jener Insel von Avalon lenkte, wo nunmehr außer mir nur noch wenige hinfanden, da bereute er vielleicht die Feindseligkeit, die zwischen uns getreten war.

|    | Im Erzählen dieser Geschichte werde ich bisweilen von Dingen reden, die sich ereigneten, als ich noch zu jung war, um sie zu verstehen, oder von Ereignissen, die sich in meiner Abwesenheit zutrugen; und der Hörer mag sich vielleicht abwenden und sagen: *Das ist ihre Zauberei.* Doch ich hatte immer das **Zweite Gesicht** und die Gabe, in den Gedanken von Männern und Frauen zu lesen; und die ganze Zeit über war ich ihnen allen nahe. Und so kam es, daß zu Zeiten alles, was sie dachten, mir auf diese oder jene Weise bewußt war. So werde ich diese Sage also berichten. |
|----|---|
| 60 | |
| 65 | Denn eines Tages werden auch die **Priester** sie erzählen, so wie sie sie kannten. Und vielleicht scheint dann zwischen den beiden etwas von der Wahrheit auf. |
|    | Denn dieses eben wissen die Priester mit ihrem **Einen Gott** und der **Einen Wahrheit** nicht: daß es so etwas wie eine wahre Geschichte gar nicht gibt. Die Wahrheit hat viele Gesichter, und die Wahrheit gleicht dem alten Weg nach Avalon; es hängt von deinem Willen und von deinen Gedanken ab, wohin dich die Straße führt, und ob du am |
| 70 | Ende auf der Heiligen Insel der Ewigkeit ankommst oder bei den **Priestern** mit ihren **Glocken** und ihrem **Tod** und ihrem **Satan** und der **Hölle** und der **Verdammnis**... aber vielleicht bin ich auch ungerecht gegen sie. Sogar die Dame vom See, die ein **Priestergewand** wie eine giftige Natter verabscheute, und das zudem mit gutem Grund, schalt mich einmal, weil ich schlecht von deren Gott geredet hatte. |
| 75 | 'Denn alle Götter sind ein Gott', sagte sie damals zu mir, wie sie schon viele Male zuvor gesprochen hatte, und wie ich es meinen **Novizinnen** oft gesagt habe, und wie es jede **Priesterin** nach mir wiederholen wird: 'und alle **Göttinnen** sind eine **Göttin**, und es gibt nur einen **Allurheber**. Und jedem Menschen seine Wahrheit, und der Gott ist darin.' |
| 80 | Und so ist die Wahrheit wohl irgendwo auf den verschlungenen Pfaden zwischen dem Weg nach Glastonbury, der **Priesterinsel**, und jenem nach Avalon, das für immer in den **Nebeln** des Sommersees verschwunden ist. |
|    | Aber das ist nun meine Wahrheit: Ich, Morgaine, erzähle Euch diese Dinge - Morgaine, die in späteren Zeiten Morgan le Fay, die Fee Morgana genannt wurde. |
|    | *Übersetzung: R. Stolze, 1988* |

In order to understand that text we might take a look at its SITUATIVE BACKGROUND. The example is the first chapter from the novel „The Mists of Avalon" by Marion Zimmer Bradley. According to the blurb, the novel is about the old tale from the 5$^{th}$ century on King Arthur, the prophet Merlin and the search for the Holy Grail. Arthur had been a king of the Celtic Britons who could defend the country against attacks by the Saxons for a while. Written witness on his life appears in the 12$^{th}$ century. This is what we have as a basic knowledge when we read this blurb before translating.

The source culture also determines the relevant DISCOURSE FIELD where the author is at home. For this purpose we read the author's epilogue. The author Marion Bradley is already internationally renowned for other science fiction and fantasy novels. She was born in 1930 in the US state New York. She says, that she dealt a lot, in her material research, with American non-Christian groups and feminist circles. This for us creates the relevant discourse field for the text. As for the GENRE, it is an example of the fantasy novel, a modern form of the tale. The story speaks a lot about fairy queens, who's Celtic origin is best preserved today in Irish popular beliefs.

Every discourse field has its particular MEANING DIMENSION, and this recurs in the texts, reflecting in cultural associations, isotopy, specific metaphors and key words to be found in a text. As already said, the text is about King Arthur who, as we all know, searched for the Holy Grail, and the prophet Merlin with his fairy queens. So, more specifically, the novel is about the confrontation between the ancient Celtic religions and the new Christian religion brought by missionaries to the British island. This is reflected in our text in the word field of the fairy tale and of the Catholic church. You find them marked in semi-bold and with underlining in our text.

> This observation already gives us a hint for criticizing the given printed translation (a) where for (text line74): *I have no quarrel with the Christ only with his priests* we read the translation (line 7) *Christus ist nicht mein Feind aber seine Priester*. Obviously the translators didn't know anything about Christianity, since the Christ never is anybody's enemy.
>
> Or another example in this sense, even showing an inter-textual relationship is in the text, line 40: *for she too becomes the World mother in the hour of death*. This recalls a Christian prayer "Ave Maria", that ends in German: "bitte für uns Sünder in der Stunde unseres Todes" – exactly with this focus on the phrase end. Translation (a) says (47): *auch sie wird für die Kirchenmänner in der Stunde des Todes zur Mutter der Welt.* – a very strange formulation.

With respect to the intrinsic relationship between the text as a whole and its constitutional elements, the holistic view is complemented by an analysis of the PREDICATIVE MODE which shows in the particular mood of the textual message characterizing its author. There is example showing neglect of this aspect in translation (A). For reasons of language-pair differences, the semantic focus of personal oral speech was changed, a translational reaction which, however, is not inevitable:

> (line 3): Morgaine speaks... In my time I have been called many things: sister, lover, priestess, wise-woman, queen. Now, in truth I have come to be wise-woman, (...) I have no

quarrel with the Christ, only with his priests, who call the Great Goddess a demon and deny that she ever held power in this world.

It is she who speaks as a person. Translation (A) changes the voice (2): Zu meiner Zeit hat man mir viele Namen gegeben: Schwester, Geliebte, Priesterin, weise Frau und Königin. (...) Christus ist nicht mein Feind, aber seine Priester, die die Große Göttin einen bösen Geist nennen.

More precision, though, is possible, as is shown in translation (B) (line 3): Damals zu meiner Zeit hatte ich viele Namen: Schwester, Geliebte, Priesterin, Weise Frau, Königin. (...) Ich habe nichts gegen den Christus, nur gegen seine Priester, die die Große Göttin als Dämon bezeichnen.

Besides that, all the sentences begin with *now, and now, for* etc. as a signal of an oral talk. In translation (A) this was rendered incoherently.

The translator's first decision concerns the GENRE of the text as an extralinguistic feature. This is relevant, as it is the most determining factor in formatting the target text. In our case the translation will have to become a novel again.

The STYLISTICS of the whole text is as much an integrating element of sense as is the content, and cannot be detached from its form. Another example from our text (line 59f):

The truth is like the old road to Avalon: it depends on your own will, and your own thoughts, whither the road will take you, and whether, at the end, you arrive in the Holy Isle of Eternity or among the priests with their bells and their death and their Satan and Hell and damnation... Emotion shows in this by tendency to the end focus, accumulation of places.

This was translated (68f): "Die Wahrheit ist wie der alte Weg nach Avalon: Es hängt von deinem Willen und deinen Gedanken ab, wohin der Weg dich führt. Es hängt von dir ab, ob du am Ende die Heilige Insel der Ewigkeit erreichst, oder ob du bei den Mönchen mit ihren Glocken, ihrem Tod, ihrem Teufel, ihrer Hölle und ihrer Verdammnis ankommst." The emotional rhythm is totally missed by this blocking bracked phrase. And it would be so easy to keep this spoken rhythm, see translation (B) (68f):

Die Wahrheit gleicht dem alten Weg nach Avalon; es hängt von deinem Willen und von deinen Gedanken ab, wohin dich die Straße führt, und ob du am Ende auf der Heiligen Insel der Ewigkeit ankommst oder bei den Priestern mit ihren Glocken und ihrem Tod und ihrem Satan und der Hölle und der Verdammnis...

Also, there are indefinite formulations open to interpretation in texts; this is a well-known topic of literary and reception studies. Translators can try to keep this suspense in the text, rather than fix it into a very clear proposition, in order to enable interpretation for the readers as well.

> One **example**, where this is neglected, line (65f):
> 
> 'For all the gods are one God', she said to me then, as she had said many times before, (...) 'and all the goddesses are one Goddess, and there is only one Initiator. And to every man his own truth, and the god within.' --
> 
> **Translated** (75f): "Denn alle Götter sind ein Gott", sagte sie damals zu mir, wie sie es bereits oft getan hatte, und wie ich viele Male zu meinen Priesterschülerinnen gesagt habe, (...). "Und alle Göttinnen sind eine Göttin, und es gibt nur einen Gott, mit dem alles begann. Jeder Mensch hat das Recht auf seine eigene Wahrheit und auf den Gott, der durch sie spricht."

This is exactly what the author wants to say, but do we need to explain this? The reader can think this herself. I tried to keep the suspense (78):

> 'Denn alle Götter sind ein Gott', sagte sie damals zu mir, wie sie schon viele Male zuvor gesprochen hatte, und wie ich es meinen Novizinnen oft gesagt habe, (...): 'und alle Göttinnen sind eine Göttin, und es gibt nur einen Allurheber. Und jedem Menschen seine Wahrheit, und der Gott ist darin.'

Thematic COHERENCE in the target text may be realized by means of a semantic web. Having detected word fields of cultural concepts in holistic text understanding, one might search for corresponding lexemes within a word field in the other language.

> In our text, one should clearly distinguish between the word fields of fairy tale and of the Catholic church, as these are the two worlds struggling with one another. This was mixed up in translation (A). Terms like *Gewand eines Christuspriesters, Kirchenmänner, Maria aus Nazareth, eine Jungfrau, schwarzes Gewand der Nonnen, Maria in dem blauen Gewand, Priesterschülerinnen, Messgehilfen* are not part of Catholic discourse in German. More adequate words would be: *Priestergewand, Maria im blauen Kleid, jungfräulich, schwarzer Habit der Nonnen, Novizinnen, Messdiener.*
> 
> Our text very concretely speaks about the sexual relationship between Arthur and Morgaine, that is *brother & sister, man & beloved woman, Christian king & pagan priestess.* (This is even indicated in the first sentence, *I was called many things*). As this was not clearly denominated in the paragraph on Arthur's death in translation (A), the reader here does not develop a clear scenic idea of a dying man who laid his head in the lap of a woman. Due to grammatical transposition, a rather comical scene is even created here (49): *...hielt ich schließlich Artus' Kopf in meinem Schoß* (where was his body?).

Of course a text does not consist solely of words. In a quest for authenticity for the message, the translator focuses on the intended discourse field for the translation. The FUNCTION is important, as it affects the general set-up of the target text. Literary translation texts are placed within a certain genre, however representing the structure of the original, including tense, voice and style.

Translation (B) tried to use creative words in order to express the aspects of fairy: *Anderswelt, Weltenmutter, Dunkelwelt, Allurheber*, instead of the lengthy attributive constructions like in translation (A). Such expressions appeal to the relevant DISCOURSE FIELD of fantasy in the target language but they lack a direct formal equivalence to the source text structure.

### 10.2.2   A short story

| | Ernest Favenc (1845-1908) – „The Parson's Blackboy" |
|---|---|
| | The Rev. Joseph Simmondsen had been appointed by his Bishop to a cure of souls in the Far North, in the days when Queensland was an ungodly and unsanctified place. Naturally, the Rev. J., who was young, green, and zealous, saw a direct mission in front |
| 5 | of him. His predecessor had never gone twenty miles outside the little seaport that formed the commercial outlet of the district; but this did not suit Joseph's eager temperament. Once he felt his footing and gained a little experience, he determined on a lengthened tour that should embrace the uttermost limits of his fold. |
| 10 | Now, although beset with the conceit and priggishness inseparable from the early stages of parsonhood, Simmondsen was not a bad fellow, and glimpses of his manly nature would at times peep out in spite of himself. This, without his knowledge, ensured him a decent welcome; and he got a good distance inland under most favourable auspices, for, the weather being fine, everybody was willing to lend him a horse or drive him along to the next station upon his route. |
| 15 | The Rev. Joseph began to think that the roughness of the back country had been much exaggerated. In due course he arrived at a station which we will call Upton Downs; beyond it there were only a few newly-taken-up runs. On Upton Downs they were busy mustering, and when the parson enquired about his way for the next day the manager looked rather puzzled. "You see," he said, "we are rather shorthanded, and I |
| 20 | can't spare a man to send with you; at the same time the track from here to Gundewarra is not very plain, and I am afraid you might not be able to follow it. However, I will see what I can do." |
| 25 | Mr. Simmondsen was retiring to rest that night when a whispered conversation made itself audible in the next room. No words were distinguishable, but from the sounds of smothered laughter a good joke seemed to be in progress. "I think I can manage for you," said the manager at breakfast next morning. "When you leave here you will go to Gundewarra, twenty-five miles. From there it is thirty-five miles to Bilton's Camp, and then on to Blue Grass. From Blue Grass you can come straight back here across the bush, about forty miles. I will lend you a blackboy who knows the country well and will |
| 30 | see you round safely." |

The young clergyman thanked his host, and, after breakfast, prepared to leave. The blackboy, a good-looking little fellow arrayed in clean moles and twill shirt, was in attendance with a led pack-horse, and the two departed. For some miles the Reverend Joseph improved the occasion by a little pious talk to the boy, who spoke fairly good English, and showed a white set of teeth when he laughed, as he constantly did at everything the parson said. At midday they camped for an hour on the bank of a lagoon, in which Mr. Simmondsen had a refreshing swim. In the evening they arrived at their destination, and received the usual welcome.

"I see you adapt yourself to the customs of the country," said his host at mealtime, and a slight titter went round the table. The Rev. Joseph joined in, taking it for granted that his somewhat unclerical garb was alluded to. In reply to enquiries he was informed that Bilton's Camp was a rough place, and Blue Grass even worse; and he was pleased to hear it for until then his path had been too pleasant altogether; he hadn't had a chance to reprove anybody.

Bilton's Camp proved to be indeed a rough place. The men were civil, however, and as the parson had taken another exhilarating bath at the midday camp he appreciated the rude fare set before him; although here, as at the other place, there seemed to be a joke floating about that made everybody snigger.

The next day's journey, to Blue Grass, was but a short stage, and as the reverend gentleman had by this time become very friendly with Charley, the blackboy, the two rode along chatting pleasantly until they came somewhat unexpectedly on the new camp. A very greasy cook and two or three gins in dilapidated shirts were the only people at home, and they stood open-eyed to greet the stranger.

Although Mr. Simmondsen had suited his attire to his surroundings, he still retained enough of the clerical garb to signify his profession. The cook, therefore, at once took in the situation, and invited the parson under the tarpaulin which did temporary duty as a hut. He informed his visitor, at whom he looked rather curiously, that "everyone" was away, camped out, and that no one would return for a couple of days; that he was alone, excepting for two men who were at work in a yard a short distance off, and who would be in to dinner; in fact, they came up while he was speaking.

Mr. Simmondsen took a great interest in this, the first real "outside" camp he had seen; and as the two bushmen had gone down to the creek for a wash, and the cook was busy preparing a meal, he called Charley to ask him a few questions. "What are these black women doing about the place, Charley?"

"Oh, all about missus belongah white fellow," was the astonishing reply. It was some moments before Joseph could grasp the full sense of this communication; then he considered it his duty to read these sinners a severe lecture, and prepared one accordingly.

"Do you not understand," he said, when the three men were together, "the trespass you are committing against both social and Divine laws? If you do not respect one, perhaps you will the other." The cook stared at the bushmen in blank amazement, and the bushmen at the cook. "I allude to these unfortunate and misled beings," said the parson, waving his hand towards the half-clad gins. A roar of laughter was the reply. "Blest if that doesn't come well from you!" said the cook, when he could speak. The others chuckled in acquiescence.

"What do you mean?" said the indignant Joseph: "I speak by right of my office."
"Sit down and have some tucker," said the cook; "you're not a bad sort, I can see; but don't come the blooming innocent!" The indignant pastor refused. He saw that his words were treated lightly, that no one would listen to him, and he left in high dudgeon.

Charley had told him that there was a good lagoon about twelve miles on the road back to Upton Downs; he would go on there and camp - they had plenty of provisions on the packhorse - and taking his bridle and calling the boy he went to catch his horse.

As he came back he overheard the fag-end of a remark the cook was making to the others. "They came round the end of the scrub chatting as thick as thieves, and when I seed who it was – Lord! you could have wiped me out with one hand."

This was worse than Greek to the Rev. Joseph. Greek he might have understood.

In spite of a humble apology from the delinquent, he departed, and near sundown arrived at the lagoon Charley had spoken of. It was a lovely spot. One end was thick with broad-leaved water-lilies, but there was a clear patch at the other end promising the swim the good parson enjoyed so much.

When the tent was pitched he stood in Nature's garb about to enter the water, when Charley called to him. Pointing towards the lilies he told Mr. Simmondsen that he would get him some seed-pods which the blacks thought splendid eating.

The clergyman had only got up to his waist when he heard a plunge behind him and saw Charley's dark form half splashing, half swimming towards the lilies. Presently his head emerged from a dive, and he beckoned towards the clergyman to come over and taste the aboriginal luxury. The Rev. Joseph paddled lazily over and investigated. The seed-pods proved of very pleasant flavour, and as the sun was nearly down, Mr. Simmondsen wended his way to the bank and emerged in the shallow water, with Charley a few paces behind him.

For some reason he looked back. Shocking predicament!

There was no shirking the fact; all the quiet laughter about "the customs of the country", the unexplained allusions, the ribald manner of the cook, were intelligible in a flash.

Charley was a woman!

The wicked manager of Upton Downs had started him on his travels with ("after the custom of the country") a black gin dressed in boy's clothes as a valet, and that gin had been recognized by everyone on the road.

Mr. Simmondsen thought of the past and blushed. The night was spent in fervent prayer.

"My dear sir," said Davis, the super. of Upton Downs, "I did the best I could for you. Charlotte is as good as any blackboy, and knows all the country round here. Now, own up, didn't she look after you well?" "You forget the scandal that may arise," said the Rev. Joseph Simmondsen.

"Lord, man! who cares about what is done out here? Nobody will ever hear of it."

Davis was wrong.

Everybody did hear of it.

The Rev. Simmondsen received indignant letters from his Bishop, his churchwardens, several missionary societies, and, last and worst, a letter of eternal farewell from the young lady to whom he was engaged to be married.

Fortunately he inherited some money at the time, so he did the best thing possible - threw up the Church, went into squatting, and is now one of the most popular men in this district

**Translation** (A)

Ernest Favenc „Der Reisebegleiter des Pfarrers" – Übersetzung Elisabeth Schnack (1961)

Zu der Zeit, als Queensland noch ein gottloses und unbekehrtes Land war, wurde der Reverend Joseph Simmondsen von seinem Bischof auf ein Hilfspfarramt im hohen Norden berufen. Der Reverend Joseph, jung, ahnungslos und eifrig wie er war, sah darin natürlich eine Aufgabe. Sein Vorgänger hatte sich keine zwanzig Meilen nach außerhalb des kleinen Seehafens begeben, der für den ganzen Bezirk den Markt und Absatzplatz darstellte; so etwas hätte jedoch Josephs umtriebiger Wesensart nicht gelegen. Sobald er Fuß gefaßt und ein wenig Erfahrungen gesammelt hatte, beschloß er eine längere Rundreise, die auch die äußersten Grenzen seiner Gemeinde umfassen sollte.

Nun war Simmondsen, obwohl auch er bedroht war von Dünkel und Selbstgefälligkeit, die untrennbar zu den Anfängen jungen Pfarrherrntums gehören, doch kein unangenehmer Mann, und Anzeichen seiner männlichen Natur konnten sich zeitweise gegen seinen Willen bemerkbar machen. Das sicherte ihm, ohne daß er darum wußte, einen freundlichen Empfang. Da das Wetter schön war, gelangte er, unter günstigsten Umständen, eine gehörige Strecke ins Hinterland. Jedermann lieh ihm gern ein Pferd oder fuhr ihn bis zum nächsten Halt auf seiner Reise.

Der Reverend Joseph glaubte schon, daß ihm die rauhen Manieren des Hinterlandes reichlich übertrieben geschildert worden waren. So kam er schließlich auch an einen Ort, den wir Upton Downs nennen wollen; dahinter lagen nur noch ein paar erst kürzlich eingerichtete Routen. In Upton Downs war man gerade sehr mit der Viehzählung beschäftigt, und als der Pfarrer sich nach der nächsten Tagesstrecke erkundigte, wurde der Verwalter ziemlich verlegen. «Im Augenblick kann ich kaum jemand entbehren, den ich Ihnen mitgeben könnte», sagte er, «da wir Mangel an Hilfskräften haben; andrerseits ist die Wagenspur von hier nach Grundewarra nicht sehr deutlich, und ich fürchte, Sie könnten sie verfehlen. Doch will ich sehen, was sich machen läßt.»

Mr. Simmondsen zog sich in das Zimmer zurück, in dem er übernachten sollte, wurde aber auf eine getuschelte Unterhaltung aufmerksam, die im Nebenzimmer stattfand.

Worte konnte er nicht unterscheiden, doch, nach dem unterdrückten Lachen zu schließen, wurde ein guter Witz erzählt. «Ich glaube, ich kann ihnen behilflich sein», sagte der Verwalter am nächsten Morgen beim Frühstück. «Von hier haben Sie fünfundzwanzig Meilen bis Gundewarra. Von dort sind's hundertdreißig Meilen zu Biltons Camp und dann noch zehn Meilen nach Blue Grass. Von Blue Grass können Sie schnurgerade durch den Busch hierher zurückkommen, das sind etwa vierzig Meilen. Ich leihe Ihnen einen eingeborenen Diener, der die Gegend gut kennt und Sie wohlbehalten zurückführt.»

Der junge Geistliche dankte seinem Gastgeber und schickte sich nach dem Frühstück zum Aufbruch an. Der schwarze Diener, ein hübscher kleiner Bursche, der saubere Barchenthosen und ein Köperhemd anhatte, sorgte für ein Packpferd, und die beiden reisten ab. Während einiger Meilen benutzte Reverend Joseph die Gelegenheit, ein frommes kleines Gespräch mit dem Burschen anzuknüpfen, der recht nett Englisch sprach und blitzend weiße Zähne zeigte, wenn er lachte, und lachen tat er über alles, was der Pfarrer sagte. Um die Mittagszeit rasteten sie eine Stunde lang am Ufer einer Lagune, in welcher der Reverend ein erfrischendes Bad nahm. Am Abend kamen sie an ihrem Bestimmungsort an und wurden wie üblich willkommen geheißen.

«Wie ich sehe, passen Sie sich den Sitten des Landes an», sagte sein Gastgeber während des Essens, und ein unterdrücktes Lachen lief um den Tisch. Der Reverend stimmte ein, da er überzeugt war, die Bemerkung beziehe sich auf sein ungeistliches Gewand. Als Antwort auf seine Erkundigungen wurde ihm mitgeteilt, daß in Biltons Camp ein rauhes Lüftchen wehe, und in Blue Grass gehe es noch schlimmer zu; er freute sich jedoch, es zu hören, denn bisher war seine Reise viel zu angenehm verlaufen. Er hatte keinen Anlaß gehabt, jemanden zu rügen.

Biltons Camp erwies sich nun wirklich als primitiv; die Männer dort waren aber höflich, und da der Pfarrer bei der Mittagsrast wieder ein erfrischendes Bad genommen hatte, wußte er die rauhe Kost, die ihm nun vorgesetzt wurde, sehr zu schätzen, obwohl er wie am vorigen Abend, ein Spaß in der Luft zu hängen schien, über den jeder kicherte.

Der Treck nach Blue Grass am folgenden Tag war nur kurz, und da der Herr Pfarrer mittlerweile ein sehr freundliches Verhältnis zu Charley dem Eingeborenen, hatte, ritten sie fröhlich plaudernd ihres Weges und stießen ganz unerwartet auf das neue Camp. Ein sehr schmieriger Koch und zwei oder drei Eingeborenenweiber in zerlumpten Hemden waren die einzigen, die zu Hause geblieben waren, und die standen mit weit aufgerissenen Augen da, um den Fremden zu begrüßen.

Obwohl Mr. Simmondsen seine Kleidung den hiesigen Gepflogenheiten angepaßt hatte, behielt er doch so viel vom geistlichen Gewand bei, daß sein Beruf angedeutet war.

Der Koch erfaßte daher die Lage im Nu und lud den Pfarrer höflich ein, unter das Zeltdach zu treten, das einstweilen als Hütte dienen mußte. Er erzählte seinem Besucher, den er ziemlich neugierig betrachtete, daß «alle» weg seien und außerhalb übernachteten und erst nach einigen Tagen zurückkehren würden; er sei allein, abgesehen von zwei Männern, die in einiger Entfernung auf einer Koppel arbeiteten; sie würden zum Essen ins Camp kommen. Sie kamen sogar schon etwas vorher, während er noch sprach.

Mr. Simmondsen interessierte sich für alles, da es die erste echte Außenstation war, die er je gesehen hatte, und weil die beiden Männer zum Waschen an den Fluß gegangen waren und der Koch damit beschäftigt war, die Mahlzeit vorzubereiten, rief er Charley herbei, um ihm ein paar Fragen zu stellen. «Was haben die schwarzen Frauen hier zu tun, Charley?»

«Oh, Frauen gehören überall zu weiße Mann», war die überraschende Antwort. Es dauerte einige Augenblicke, bis Joseph den vollen Sinn dieser Mitteilung erfaßte; dann hielt er es für seine Pflicht, den Sündern eine kräftige Lektion zu erteilen, und hatte auch eine bei der Hand.

«Versteht ihr nicht», sagte er, als die drei Männer beisammen waren, «daß ihr sowohl gegen menschliches wie gegen göttliches Gesetz verstoßt? Wenn ihr das eine nicht respektieren wollt, dann doch wenigstens das andre!» Der Koch starrte die beiden Siedler in ratlosem Nichtbegreifen an, und die beiden Siedler starrten erstaunt auf den Koch. «Ich meine die beiden unglücklichen, irregeführten Geschöpfe dort drüben», sagte der Pfarrer und zeigte auf die halb bekleideten Eingeborenenweiber. Brüllendes Gelächter war die Antwort. «Verdammt lustig, daß so was ausgerechnet von Ihnen kommt!» sagte der Koch, als er die Sprache wiedergefunden hatte. Die andern kicherten beifällig.

«Was meinen Sie damit?» fragte der empörte Joseph. «Ich spreche kraft meines Amtes!» «Setzen Sie sich, und langen Sie zu!» rief der Koch. «Sie sind kein übler Bursche, scheint mir - aber spielen Sie nicht den Unschuldigen!» Der Pfarrer lehnte es unwillig ab, mit ihnen zu essen. Er sah, daß seine Worte leichtfertig aufgenommen wurden und daß keiner auf ihn hören wollte; so verließ er sie in großem Zorn. -

Charley hatte ihm erzählt, auf dem Rückweg nach Upton Downs kämen sie nach etwa zwölf Meilen zu einer sauberen Lagune; dort wollte er zelten - sie hatten reichlich Vorräte auf dem Packpferd -, und nun nahm er sein Zaumzeug und rief dem Jungen zu, er solle sein Pferd holen.

Als er zurückkehrte, schnappte er noch den Rest einer Bemerkung auf, die der Koch zu den anderen gemacht hatte. «Sie kamen aus dem Busch und schwatzten wie die dicksten Freunde miteinander, und als ich sah, wer's war, da hätt mich doch, weiß Gott, fast der Schlag getroffen!»

Für den Reverend Joseph klang es unverständlicher als Griechisch. Griechisch hätte er vielleicht sogar verstanden.

Trotz einer demütigen Entschuldigung von Seiten des Missetäters brach er also auf, und sie gelangten bei Sonnenuntergang zu der Lagune, von der Charley gesprochen hatte. Es war ein reizendes Fleckchen. Ein Teil des Wassers war dicht mit breitblättrigen Seerosen bedeckt, aber am andern Ende war eine freie Stelle, die zum Schwimmen geeignet schien, worauf sich der gute Pfarrer schon so gefreut hatte.

Bald war das Zelt aufgeschlagen, und er stand im Adamskostüm da und wollte ins Wasser gehen, als Charley ihn rief. Er deutete auf die Seerosen und erzählte Mr. Simmondsen, er wolle ihm ein paar Samenhülsen holen, denn die Schwarzen wüßten, daß sie köstlich schmeckten.

Der Geistliche war erst bis zu den Hüften im Wasser, als er hinter sich das Aufklatschen hörte und dann sah, wie Charley halb strampelnd und halb schwimmend auf die Seerosen lossteuerte. Bald tauchte ein Kopf aus dem Wasser auf; Charley winkte dem Geistlichen, zu ihm hinüberzukommen und die Eingeborenenleckerbissen zu kosten. Reverend Joseph schwamm gemächlich zu ihm hin. Die Seerosenkapseln hatten tatsächlich einen sehr angenehmen Geschmack. Da die Sonne nun fast untergegangen war, hielt Mr. Simmondsen aufs Ufer zu und kam dann im flachen Wasser auf die Füße zu stehen.

Aus irgendeinem Grund sah er sich um. Entsetzliche Bescherung!

Doch die Tatsache ließ sich nicht aus der Welt schaffen: all das verstohlene Lachen wegen der «Sitten des Landes», alle unerklärlichen Anspielungen und die dreiste Art des Kochs wurden ihm blitzschnell klar. Charley war eine Frau!

Der vermaledeite Verwalter von Upton Downs hatte ihm nach «Landessitte» eine schwarze Eingeborenenfrau in Jungenkleidung auf die Reise mitgegeben, und diese Frau war von allen Leuten entlang seiner Reiseroute erkannt worden.

Mr. Simmondsen dachte an die Reisetage und errötete. Die Nacht verbrachte er in inbrünstigem Gebet.

«Aber mein lieber Herr», sagte der Verwalter von Upton Downs, «ich habe mein möglichstes für Sie getan. Charlotte ist genau so tüchtig wie ein schwarzer Bursche, und sie kennt die ganze Gegend. Müssen Sie nicht selber zugeben, daß sie gut für Sie gesorgt hat?» «Sie denken wohl nicht an den Skandal, der daraus entstehen kann», sagte der Reverend Joseph Simmondsen.

«Lieber Himmel», rief der Verwalter, «wer kümmert sich drum, was hier draußen vor sich geht? Kein Mensch wird je etwas davon erfahren.»

Davis täuschte sich.

Alle Welt hörte davon.

Der Reverend Simmondsen erhielt empörte Briefe von seinem Bischof, vom Kirchenältesten, von mehreren Missionsgesellschaften und, was das Schlimmste war, einen Abschiedsbrief von der jungen Dame, mit der er verlobt war.

Glücklicherweise erbte er um die Zeit etwas Geld, daher tat er das Klügste, was er tun konnte: er ließ die Kirche Kirche sein, wurde Siedler und Herdenbesitzer und ist jetzt einer der beliebtesten Männer im ganzen Bezirk.

**Commentary**

This is a Short Story where it is important to reconstruct the text's cultural identity. We will have to ask whether this has been achieved in the printed translation (A). For that purpose we will first present the differences in a corresponding translation assessment based on error analysis from Contrastive linguistics, and then compare it with an approach in translational hermeneutics. This also will clearly show the divergent theoretical impacts of both analytical approaches.

There have been developed seven so-called translation procedures (Vinay & Darbelnet 1995) that are described syntactically. In a descriptive text cum translation analysis of our example "Favenc" all such possible shifts are evidenced.

An *emprunt*, a direct borrowing from the ST without a phonological or meaning change is to be found here in the name *"der Reverend J. S."* ("the Rev. Joseph Simmondsen", line 2) oder *"Mr. Simmondsen"* ("Mr. Simmondsen", 23), *"Lagune"* ("lagoon", 88). Regarding cultural elements we detect the marks of an anglophone environment, see also "Queensland" (3).

A *calque*, the linear translation of a ST form is found in "seaport" (5) – "Seehafen" (7); "parsonhood" (10) – "Pfarrherrentum" (13); "back country" (15) – "Hinterland" (19); "twill shirt", (32) – "Köperhemd" (41); "packhorse" (33) – "Packpferd" (41); "broad-leaved waterlilies" (89) – "breitblättrige Wasserlilien/Seerosen" (112); "seed-pods" (93) – "Samenhülsen/Seerosenkapseln" (116/122); "church wardens" (118) – "Kirchenältester" (144).

So-called *errors* as a lexical non-equivalence are found e.g. at "unsanctified" (3) – "unbekehrt" " (3); "inland" (12) – "Hinterland" (17); "route" (14) – "Reise" (18); "journey" (49) – "Treck" (60); "man" (20) - "jemand" (24), "Lord, man" (115) - "lieber Himmel" (140); *"was in attendance* with a lead pack-horse" (33) – *"sorgte für* ein Packpferd" (41); "read a lecture, and *prepared* one accordingly" (67) – „und *hatte* auch eine bei der Hand" (84) (no equivalence of semantic content).

A *literal translation* following directly the ST syntagm is given in: "twenty miles outside (5) – "zwanzig Meilen nach außerhalb" (6); "beyond it" (17) – "dahinter" (21); "he was alone, excepting for" (59) – "er sei allein, abgesehen von" (72); "in a yard" (59) – "auf einer Koppel" (73); "Do you not understand, he said" (69) – ",Versteht ihr nicht', sagte er" (85); "What do you mean?" (76) – „Was meinen Sie damit?" (94); "I speak by right of my office" (76) – "Ich spreche kraft meines Amtes" (94).

Such descriptions according to syntax show differences between the language systems, shifts in the translation, without any evaluation as to a good or a bad translation. But we don't get information about any cultural elements in the text. We can evidence idiomatic adequacy or interference, e.g. "a whispered conversation" (23) – "eine getuschelte Unterhaltung" (29) is unidiomatical in German, just like "for some miles" (33) – "während einiger Meilen" (42).

> A more frequently mentioned feature in text analysis, then, is ***transposition*** as a category change in the words. The content of a ST sign is being transferred onto signs of TT words in a different category, see: "a cure of souls" (2) – "Hilfspfarramt" (4) (*syntagm > composite*);
> "the next room" (24) – "das Nebenzimmer" (29) (*attributive form > composite*);
> "straight" (28) – "schnurgerade" (34) (*amplification*);
> "a white set of teeth" (35) – "blitzend weiße Zähne" (44) (*amplification/concentration*);
> "the reverend gentleman" (50) – "der Herr Pfarrer" (60) (*crisscross substitution*);
> "a roar of laughter" (73) – "brüllendes Gelächter" (90) (*phrase > adjektive/concentration*);
> "There was no **shirking** the fact" (102) – „die Tatsache ließ sich nicht aus der Welt schaffen" (127) (*nominalized verb > phrase/explicitation*);
> „Unexplain**ed**" (103) – „unerklär**lich**" (128) (*part.perf. > adjektive*);
> „you forget" (113) – „Sie denken wohl nicht an" (138) (*paraphrase*).

Such grammatical transformations in a translation generally aren't too frequent as they are not directly induced in a literal approach of translating. Such syntactical substitutions pop up only in case of grammar coercion, and various semantic paraphrasings can often be observed in translations. They constitute the central point in a translation critique. The problem of "faithful or free" translation becomes virulent here.

> So there is another procedure called ***modulation*** as a shift of perspective regarding the content of a phrase, e.g. "in **the Far North**" (3) – "im hohen Norden" (5) (instead of ‚im weiten'); "**commercial outlet**" (6) – "Markt- und Absatzplatz" (7) (*doubling*);
> „a **black**boy" (1/29/32/50/112) – „ein eingeborener Diener (a.o.)" (1,37,40,61,136) (*5x different*);
> "a conversation **made itself** audible" (24) – „**(er) wurde** auf eine Unterhaltung aufmerksam" (29) (*phrase subject changed*);
> "a little pious **talk** *to* the boy" (34) – "ein frommes kleines **Gespräch** *mit* dem Burschen" (43) (*reference changed*);
> „**as he** constantly did at everything" (35) – „und Lachen tat er über alles" (44) (*unidiomatic*);
> "took interest in **this, the first** real ‚outside' camp" (61) – „interessierte sich für **alles**, *da* es die erste Außenstation war" (76) (*other causal refereence*);
> „**these** black women" (64) – „**die** schwarzen Frauen" (79) (*wrong deixis*);

"The indignant pastor refused" (78) – „Der Pfarrer lehnte es unwillig ab, **mit ihnen zu essen**" (97) (*explicitation*).

An *équivalence* is given, when expressions are, for instance, exchanged by a proverb, see "that Bilton's Camp was a rough place" (42) – "dass in Biltons Camp **ein rauhes Lüftchen wehe**" (52);
"to read a severe lecture" (67) – „eine kräftige **Lektion zu erteilen**" (84);
"threw up the Church" (122) – „er **ließ** die Kirche Kirche **sein**" (148).

An *adaptation* is an explanation or even target language modification of cultural specifics or realia, here for instance "moles" (32) – "Barchenthosen" (41) (*instead of the forgotten 'Moleskin' or 'Englischleder'*); "bushmen" (62/71) – "Männer/Siedler" (77/87) (*instead of 'Arbeiter im Bush'*);
"went into squatting" (122) – "wurde Siedler und Herdenbesitzer" (148) (*what kind of herds?*).

These contrastive linguistic descriptions show similarities and deviations between the language structure in the text and its translation. But they cannot motivate their necessity or arbitrarity, because this is based on interpretation.

Hence the main subject of usual debate in translation criticism is the question how far such a shift can go before it becomes an illicit alteration, when the semantic information is changed too much. And such adaptations or changes are to be found in abundance in the present translation (A). This goes from the non-equivalent modification of words already mentioned, over ignored deixis, changes in temporal and numeral indications, from wrong clause referents up until the omission of whole phrases and sentences. Identical formulations in the text are sometimes translated differently, without making it clear why.

The following examples show an interpreting *modulation*:

"for, the weather being fine **everybody** was willing" (13) – "**da** das Wetter schön war, gelangte er…" (16) (*different sentence subject*);

"**he was retiring** to rest that night" (23) – „er zog sich **in das Zimmer** zurück, in dem er übernachten sollte" (182) (*perspective shifted:* er > das Zimmer);

"will **see you round** safely" (30) – „und Sie wohlbehalten **zurückführt**" (38) (*verb: change in semantics and tempus*);

"the blackboy **was in attendance with** a horse" (33) – „der schwarze Diener **sorgte für** ein Pferd" (41) (*semantics*);

"as at the **other place**" (47) – "genau wie am **vorigen Abend**" (58) (*place > time*);

"and calling the boy **he went to** catch his horse. As he came back" (82) – „und rief dem Jungen zu, **er solle** sein Pferd holen. Als er zurückkehrte" (who?), (103) (*change of referent*);

"This was worse than Greek" (86) – „klang dies **unverständlicher** als Griechisch" (107) (*superfluous explanation*);

"he saw Charleys's **dark form** swimming" (95) – "wie Charley --- schwimmend" (119) (*omission*);

"(he) emerged in the shallow water, with Charley a few paces behind him" (100) – (er) kam im flachen Wasser auf die Füße zu stehen. --/--" (124) (*sentence missing*);

"the wicked manager **had started him** on his travels with a black gin" (106) – "Der vermaledeite Verwalter hatte ihm eine... **auf die Reise mitgegeben**" (130) (*change of object*);

"the country **round here**" (112) – "die ganze Gegend" (137) (*incomplete deixis*);

"his churchwardens" (118) – „**vom** Kirchenältesten" (145) (*Pl./Sg.*);

"in **this** district" (123) – "im ganzen Bezirk" (149) (*wrong deixis*). –

There is a lot of other examples that could be listed. Over-interpretation, falsification and omissions are the problem of unreflected translation when we don't find a convincing motivation for that. But the question, whether the adaptations here are adequate or not, must still be discussed. Not everything is "wrong", is a grammatical or lexical error right away, maybe it will find its reason in more principal considerations going beyond sentence level.

The definition of "translation equivalence" along with syntactical and lexical causes in the sense of contrastive stylistics, therefore, is limited. A merely sentence-oriented discussion of equivalence is not useful in searching for a cultural identity in translated texts. Neither is the question whether we have here literal or non literal translation procedures leading us any further. They say nothing on our question about cultural elements in the text, but this is necessary for a reconstruction of cultural identity in translation with the goal of precision and authenticity.

The only hint that we could gain in our error analysis is perhaps the observation that the cultural background of this text maybe was not even recognized. The modulating translation with "im hohen Norden" (line 3) right at the beginning leads to an eurocentrical imagination, as has been rightly criticized by Venuti (1995:5).

A reader of translation (A) might actually think that this story is playing in the U.S.A. or in Canada.[120] Even the title "Der Reisebegleiter des Pfarrers" for "The Parson's Blackboy" does not contradict that. Later, we read about a "eingeborenen Diener" (l. 37), in Canada this would be an Indian. Afterwards we come across a "schwarzen Diener" (l. 40) and "schwarzen Burschen" (l. 136), and this is no more significant in simple reading. Of course one must know, where Queensland is located – it's a province in Australia. And then a translation with "im hohen Norden" is not adequate, because there it goes towards the equator. Something like "ganz weit im Norden", a literal translation for "in the Far North" would rather have been suitable.

The horizontal comparison of text parts has to be complemented by vertical observations, in order to detect cultural elements. The holistic hermeneutical criteria of orientation should also be integrated into the translation evaluation.

For dealing with the alien, that means with cultural elements in foreign texts, a holistic approach in an hermeneutical perspective is indispensable. Then even the text's background, the concrete situation implicitly talked about, will become visible. One needs a cognitive landscape to find one's way through the territory of the text. The categories of orientation offer a vertical vision of the text going from the outside to the inside, different from the horizontal perspective of the above equivalence discussion. Instead of analysing the syntactic structure of a text, the hermeneutical translator will pose questions to this text, in lateral thinking from various places of observation.

There is first a positioning of the text within its real situation, based on relevant encyclopaedical knowledge acquired by the translator. What is the SITUATIVE BACKGROUND, which country do we have here? Information about the author is as such already an indication of the content: the author Ernest Favenc (1845-1908) was an English pioneer who came to Australia in the 19<sup>th</sup> century. This can be researched. The name of "Queensland" in the text also refers us there. Once this situation as a background has been established, all other concepts will

---

[120] In various translation exercises and readers' enquiries the translation was always situated in that way. The designation "Queensland" is evoking, even today, in readers the idea of a queen, somewhere in England, Ireland or Northern America.

be excluded cognitively, and the imagination of the translator will now concentrate on Australia.

Of course this is easier if one has already collected some personal experiences, but even without that there are enough modern media, e.g. television, to get an idea of the country's nature. Since this continent is located in the south, the "North" there has the connotation of hot, sunny and dry, differently from Europe or Northern America.

This positioning of the text now will determine the interpretation and translation of the corresponding local designations in the text, the realia. The term "little seaport" (5) is an indication that the Englishmen, of course, colonized the country from the shore, and not from the "inland" (12) (*Landesinneres*). We detect some culture-specific indications:

> "Queensland" (3), "little seaport" (5), "inland" (12), "back country" (15), "Upton Downs" (17/111), "mustering" (18), "track" (20), "Bilton's Camp" (27/45), "Blue Grass" (28/49), "blackboy and gins" (50/52), "to camp out" (58), "bushmen" (62), "tucker" (77), "lagoon" (88), "waterlilies" (89), "aboriginal luxury" (97), "out here" (115), "squatting" (122).

The local names with "Camp" are an indication of the life in the Australian Outback, and a geographical name such as "Blue Grass" describes the abundant blueish plant growing there in the dry bushland, and the so-called "Eingeborene" are Aborigines with a black skin.

Then there is the DISCOURSE FIELD. In which social milieu is the text situated? Which genre are we confronted with? This text is a Short Story, printed in a bilingual booklet together with other stories.[121] We ask: has the author an ideology? We now read the whole text, cognitively oriented towards Australia.

That story is a literary report about life experiences of a young a bit naïve pastor, who for the first time gets beyond the circles of the British colonial power. Concretely it is the milieu of the puritan Protestant missionaries who had the idea that the whole world must be freed from paganism, be "sanctified", and should

---

[121] Printed in: Elisabeth Schnack: *Englische Kurzgeschichten. Australische Autoren / English Short Stories. Australian Authors.* Englisch-Deutsch, (Edition Langewiesche-Brandt) München DTV Deutscher Taschenbuchverlag, in wrappers 1992, p. 1-13.

be raised in morale and customs. European culture has been extended all over the world.

This statement has now to be proved with the help of textual features. We cannot only interpret this understanding into the text from the outside. Rather, we have to look for evidence to motivate our grounded understanding. For this purpose we will examine the MEANING DIMENSION on the text level. Culture-specific associations, key words, isotopic webs, metaphor and thematic strings have to be analysed.

> Besides the typical geographical indications, we also find a word field from **mission and church life**: "Bishop" (2), "cure of souls" (2), "ungodly" (3), "unsanctified" (3), "mission" (4), "parsonhood" (10), "sinners" (67), "lecture" (67), "trespass" (69), "clerical garb" (55), "parson" (56), "pastor" (78), "Greek" (86), "clergyman" (94), "churchwardens" (118), "missionary societies" (119), "Church" (122), – and a **moral** world field corresponding with that: "pious talk" (34), "chance to reprove" (44), "Divine laws" (70), "indignant" (76/78), "words treated lightly" (79), "innocent" (78), "dudgeon" (79), "Nature's garb" (91), "shocking" (101), "wicked" (106), "scandal" (113), etc.

The issue, here, is "decency", and the people in the camp are not reprimanded for exploiting the women as unpaid workers, but for taking them as a woman. And exactly that is the shocking point in the story: the young pastor travelled all the time himself in company of woman, and they even saw each other naked. This was absolutely impossible at that time around 1900.

One essential thematic string as a repetitive formulation in the text is "the blackboy" – *der schwarze Diener*, and a recurrent formulation is never meaningless in literary texts. Not stylistic variation is wanted for the translation here, but to get a glimpse of what this selection of terms is indicating connotatively. It indicates the central position of this character as the subject of the story, and "blackboy" was also the official designation for servants at colonial times.

In order to, finally, be able to fulfill the quest for precision in translating, we still have to take a closer look at the text level and check the PREDICATIVE MODE. The speaker's perspective, deixis, sentence subjects, focusing, idiolect, irony, intertextuality, quotations and the like are relevant for translation. The statement that something is a "transposition" or even a "modulation" is not very informative.

First of all there is the Rev. Simmondsen's world view as a speaker's perspective. He visits various stations on a route (not journey), and finally comes to "Upton Downs" what seems to be the end of the civilized world. The local reference "beyond it there were only a few newly taken up runs" (17) means "jenseits davon" from his view (more than only "dahinter"). At the end: "in this district" (123) designates the place of the speaker, not only "in dem ganzen Bezirk". Deixis is important as a cultural indicator.

Idiolect also includes the representation of spoken language, and we see this at several points in the text. There is, on the one hand, the effort for business talk in the manager of Upton Downs, then the rough comments of the cook at Blue Grass. Oral speech characterizes the persons, and this will have consequences in the translation. And the said moral, churchy way of expression of the pastor is part of it as well and it is enforced by a synsemantical context. Church language is not only how he speaks, but also the description of his moral world view: „ungodly", „to reprove", „a pious talk", „indignant", „shocking", „wicked", „high dudgeon".

And even irony as an aspect of the PREDICATIVE MODE is there in the text: "This was worse than Greek to the Rev. Joseph" (86), suportd by his title "Rev.". The question is whether one is able to transfer such observations into the translation.

When a text is finally understood, it can also be translated. In continuing the helical cognitive movement between translator and text, the translation will now be formulated, observing rhetorical fields of attention.

The GENRE of a Short Story could here be attained as well. A short story has an introduction, thematic climax and ends with a conclusion and a morale. The source text can be re-presented in its structure. The issue in that text is the clash of European-missionary concepts with the rough reality in the Australian bush, what led into a comical effect. A missionary is geared towards preaching the righteous behaviour, and in this story it is precisely himself who commits the sin. This understanding should also be verbalized in the translation, if the foreign shall be well understood and mediated accordingly for German readers.

One thing required for COHERENCE here is, of course, that the church special terms are used correctly, what is not the case in the translation.

See "parsonhood" (10) means ‚Pfarramt', ‚Pfarrersein', but not "junges Pfarrherrntum" (13). "Der Reverend" (19/49) for "The Rev. Joseph" (15/40) is unidiomatical in German because, here, it can only be used together with the name, otherwise "Pfarrer" or "Pfr. Joseph".

The minor change of numerus from "his church wardens" (118) to a singular "vom Kirchenältesten" (145) indicates that the translator was not quite aware of the directing body of a congregation (Kirchenvorstand, Ältestenrat, a council of church wardens). And "he threw up the Church" (122) means "he left the service as a clergyman", not the "church".

We had observed the **thematic string** of "the blackboy". This was varied in the translation what veiles the meaning („Reisebegleiter", „eingeborener Diener", „schwarzer Diener", „der Eingeborene", „ein schwarzer Bursche"). Maybe the translator did not have a clear idea of that person. A title like "Des Pfarrers schwarzer Diener" would perhaps have directed the reader earlier into the right cognitive scene.

For the text to create a meaningful cognitive scene in the reader, the translation must observe COHERENCE. The title could already indicate the theme. Semantic isotopies are created, where the church language and moral discourse field is also maintained in German. Then the pastor will appear authentically.

> **Deixis** is important for to get an idea of the localities: „his predecessor had never gone twenty miles outside" (5) (war nie weiter als zwanzig Meilen über ... hinaus gekommen) was translated unclearly: „keine zwanzig Meilen nach außerhalb" (7). With the particle „never" the isolation of the costal settlement is stressed. In the sentence "although here, as at the other place" (47), again, there is reference to the location in the Outback; the tranlslation arbitrarily interprets here: "wie am vorigen Abend" (58). And finally a concrete hint with an „aboriginal luxury" (97) is lost with the unspecific „Eingeborenenleckerbissen" (121) (better: Ureinwohnerdelikatesse).

Regarding STYLISTICS the observed style forms, such as verbal tense and mode, deixis, word plays, oral prosody, milieu characteristics etc. and they should find a corresponding frame. This task was not fulfilled in view of the word field of church language, as this obviously was not seen and often translated helplessly: !unbekehrtes Land" (rather ‚Heidenland'), „Hilfspfarramt" (‚kleine Pfarrei'), „Aufgabe" (‚Missionsauftrag'), „Pfarrherrentums" (‚Pfarramt'), „frommes Gespräch mit" (‚Vortrag an'), „Anlass zu rügen" (‚Chance zu tadeln'), „eine kräftige Lektion erteilen" (‚den Sündern die Leviten lesen'), „menschliches und göttliches Gesetz" (‚sittliches und göttliches Gesetz'), „empört" (‚entrüstet'), „entsetzliche Bescherung" (‚welch anstößige oder peinliche Lage'), „vermaledeit"

(‚niederträchtig'), etc. The translation (A) is not "wrong", but church language is missing, however this would be important to evoque the relevant scenery. This would have been a "reconstruction of cultural identity in translation".

The **locals' slang** is given in the only sentence of Charley: "Oh, all about missus belongah white fellow" (65), and this could be rendered in German for instance by linguistic grammar deviation: "Oh, überall Missus gehören weiße Kerl". In this respect the translation: "Oh, Frauen gehören überall zu weiße Mann" (81) is much too normal and elegant. When Charley talks like this, then the phrase "he spoke fairly good English" (35) cannot mean that he "recht nett Englisch sprach" (43), but rather something like "der weidlich/einigermaßen English konnte." Once and again we should also look beyond a sentence, on the whole entity, in order to grasp cultural elements. This is also true for the talk of the cook. The translation is much too literary: "...und als ich sah, wer's war, da hätt mich doch, weiß Gott, fast der Schlag getroffen!" (105). Does a worker in the bush really speak like that?

We mentioned the role of thematic strings for the "blackboy" already. But there is also the "gin", a negative designation for the aboriginal women. This, again, was translated diversely, once even as "Frau" (131), what blurs the message. Not only **repetitions** are interesting, but also their intentional breaking. We do not only read about "gins", the pastor asks about "black women" (64), he himself does not use this bad word. A translation could observe such difference.

And finally there is the implicit allusion to the **male sexual aspect**, what also has been neglegted or was coyly oppressed in the translation. We read about "his manly nature would peep out" (11), "we can't't spare a man" (20), "the men" (45), "the reverend gentleman" (50), up until a chaste keeping it secret: "in Nature's garb" (91), "Charley a few paces behind him. He looked back. Shocking predicament!" (100), or the euphemistic "Mr Simmondsen thought of the past and blushed" (109). What is not said here, is: "he saw her naked and she looked at him". The translation "Er dachte an die Reisetage und errötete" (133) does hardly capture this idea. But it would well be possbile to talk of ‚die Männer', ‚sein männlicher Charakter' and ‚der ehrwürdige Herr' instead of „der Herr Pfarrer" (60), in the translation.

Features of milieu, such as **irony**, were mentioned in view of idiolect and church speak. With the translation of "das klang unverständlicher als Griechisch. G. hätte er vielleicht sogar verstanden" (107), the ironical aspect is eliminated by the doubling. This is more than a mere "modulation". The idea that it was "incomprehensible" for him can be realized by the reader himself. So perhaps better: "Das war schlimmer als Griechisch..." (literal for "worse than Greek").

At the end, for revision, the translator will again lift his glance from the text level and take the FUNCTION of the target text into consideration. We return from the detail to the overall entity. The question is now whether the author's intention has been realized in this little ironical story, whether the text structuring is in overall correspondence with the source text, so that the target audience can be addressed with cultural information. Did the translator manage to visualize convincingly the cultural ideas in the period of the British Empire in Australia around 1900? In such a holistic view on the translation draft the omissions mentioned could perhaps still be detected and rectified, or the thematic strings as repetitive structures may become visible. This is not the case in the given translation. This one rather appears as the attempt to report about that text, instead of giving it a presence in empathy.

Coherence means that the allusions and local references become transparent. In this translation such expressions as "im hohen Norden" (5), "Reise" (18), "eingerichtete Routen" (22), "Barchenthosen" (41), "ein rauhes Lüftchen weht" (52), "rauhe Kost" (57), "Treck" (60), "außerhalb übernachten" (71), "Koppel" (73), "Siedler" (88) are actually referring to the concept of northern America (but there were no missionaries), it's the Wild West with trecks and horse yards. This lack of coherence is a sign of a lacking text comprehension.

The short story culminates in the encounter of the two in the water. And just this part is not rendered in the translation, insofar as the decisive sentence „Mr. Simmondsen wended his way to the bank and emerged in the shallow water, *with Charley a few paces behind him.* For some reason he looked back. Shocking predicament!" (99f) was dropped. Charley will not have swum dressed, if even the pastor didn't do that. (He only saw "his dark form" in the water, and this also is lacking in the translation.)

Visualising the scene of the story is the task of textual FUNCTION in literary translation, and this is missed in the translation (A). But a targeted scrutiny as to FUNCTION, e.g. regarding the location of Queensland, could still remedy it. The back country would then have the connotation of the Outback, where the Australian bush does not allow raising of animals according to the American model. The "bushmen" are workers in the bush, no settlers, because nothing grows there, the lagoons are Australian billabongs, and the black gins are aborigines.

The aboriginal luxury (97) points to this fact and their culture of eating fruits. And at the end: "he went into squatting" (122) means "er wurde Schafzüchter" (breeding sheep), and not settler like in North America. You find this solution even in a dictionary.

The geographical names like "camp" would be another indication that this could not be real "settlements", and the yard (59) is an area (Gelände) and no "Koppel" for horses in the European sense. There is no comment on what the people in Bilton's Camp were doing, it could also have been mining.

Our analysis is rather astonishing. The translator Elisabeth Schnack was a very famous and decorated translator in the 1960s of English, Irish, American and other Commonwealth literatures. But now it's not clear, whether these strange literatures have really been adopted in the German cultural environment, or whether Lawrence Venuti is right with his criticism at the manipulating, eurocentrical "rewriting" of texts.

We may conclude that contrastive linguistics is only an instrument for describing grammatical and syntactical differences between languages, and error analysis refers mainly to unidiomatic interference and to semantic violation of interlingual equivalence relationships. For an adequate translation of foreign cultural elements in texts, therefore, a holistic approach is needed, and the translational categories of orientation as shown are helpful in that. Below, I present a retranslation of this text, made according to the presented hermeneutical model.

|   | **Translation (B)** |
|---|---|
|   | Ernest Favenc „Des Pfarrers schwarzer Diener" |
| 5 | Einst, als Queensland noch ein gottloses Heidenland war, war der Reverend Joseph Simmondsen von seinem Bischof in eine kleine Pfarrei ganz weit im Norden entsandt worden. Und natürlich sah der junge Rev. J., ahnungslos und eifrig wie er war, darin einen unmittelbaren Missionsauftrag. Sein Vorgänger war nie weiter als zwanzig Meilen über den kleinen Seehafen hinaus gekommen, der den Handelsplatz des Distrikts bildete; doch solches entsprach nicht Josephs ungeduldigem Temperament. Nachdem |
| 10 | er ein wenig Fuß gefasst und etwas Erfahrung gesammelt hatte, entschloss er sich zu einer längeren Rundreise, die die äußersten Grenzen seiner Gemeinde einschließen sollte.<br>Nun war Simmondsen, wenngleich nicht frei vom Dünkel und der Pedanterie, wie sie für die Anfänge des Pfarramts typisch sind, durchaus kein schlechter Kerl, und flüchtige Eindrücke seines männlichen Charakters blitzten hin und wieder unwillkürlich auf. |

Dies sicherte ihm ohne sein Wissen einen schicklichen Empfang, und so drang er unter den günstigsten Vorzeichen ein gutes Stück weit ins Landesinnere vor. Bei dem schönen Wetter war jedermann bereit, ihm ein Pferd zu leihen oder ihn bis zur nächsten Station auf seiner Route zu kutschieren. Rev. Joseph glaubte schon fast, dass die Rauheit des Hinterlandes doch stark übertrieben worden wäre.

Zu gegebener Zeit erreichte er eine Station, die wir Upton Downs nennen wollen; jenseits davon gab es dann nur noch ein paar wenige neu eröffnete Pfade. In Upton Downs waren sie gerade mit dem Viehtrieb beschäftigt, und als der Pfarrer sich nach seinem Weg für den nächsten Tag erkundigte, sah der Verwalter etwas verdutzt drein.

„Sehen Sie", meinte er, „wir sind ziemlich knapp an Personal und ich kann keinen Mann entbehren, den wir Ihnen mitgeben könnten; aber die Strecke nach Gundewarra ist auch nicht gerade einfach und ich fürchte, Sie könnten sie verfehlen. Nun, ich will mal sehen, was ich machen kann."

Herr Simmondsen machte sich zur Nacht gerade zum Schlafen fertig, als im Nachbarzimmer eine geflüsterte Unterhaltung hörbar wurde. Worte konnte man nicht unterscheiden, aber nach den Geräuschen unterdrückten Lachens zu schließen wurde wohl ein guter Witz erzählt. „Ich glaube, ich kann da etwas für Sie tun", sagte der Verwalter am anderen Morgen beim Frühstück. „Von hier aus reisen Sie bis Gundewarra, das sind fünfundzwanzig Meilen. Von dort sind es dann fünfunddreißig Meilen bis Bilton's Camp, und noch zehn weiter bis Blue Grass. Von Blue Grass aus können Sie dann direkt durch den Bush wieder hierher zurück kommen, das sind ungefähr vierzig Meilen. Ich werde Ihnen einen schwarzen Diener leihen, der das Land gut kennt und Sie sicher überall hin führen wird."

Der junge Geistliche dankte seinem Gastgeber und machte sich nach dem Frühstück zum Aufbruch bereit. Der schwarze Diener, ein gutaussehender kleiner Bursche, ausstaffiert in sauberen Baumwollhosen und einem Köperhemd, wartete schon mit einem gesattelten Packpferd, und die beiden zogen los. Eine Zeit lang nutzte Pfarrer Joseph die Gelegenheit aus und hielt dem Jungen einen kleinen frommen Vortrag. Dieser sprach ganz weidlich Englisch und zeigte eine Reihe weißer Zähne, wenn er lachte, und das tat er beständig zu allem, was der Pfarrer sagte. Mittags rasteten sie eine Stunde am Ufer einer Lagune, in der Herr Simmondsen ein erfrischendes Bad nahm. Am Abend kamen sie an ihrem Ziel an und erhielten den üblichen Empfang.

„Ich sehe, Sie passen sich den Sitten des Landes an", sagte sein Gastgeber beim Essen, und ein leichtes Kichern ging um den Tisch. Pfr. Joseph stimmte ein, da er annahm, damit werde auf seine etwas unklerikale Kluft angespielt. Auf seine Nachfragen wurde ihm bedeutet, dass Bilton's Camp ein roher Ort wäre, und Blue Grass noch viel schlimmer; und er freute sich das zu hören, denn bislang war seine Reise eigentlich viel zu erfreulich verlaufen; er hatte nirgends eine Chance gehabt, jemanden zu tadeln.

Bilton's Camp erwies sich in der Tat als ein roher Ort. Immerhin waren die Männer höflich, und nachdem der Pfarrer bei der Mittagsrast wieder ein belebendes Bad genommen hatte, war er dankbar für die primitive Kost, die ihm vorgesetzt wurde; wiewohl auch hier, wie an dem andcren Platz, ein Spaß in der Luft zu hängen schien, der jedermann zum Kichern brachte.

Die Reise am nächsten Tag bis Blue Grass war nur ein kurzer Abschnitt, und da der ehrwürdige Herr sich inzwischen mit Charley, dem schwarzen Diener, recht gut angefreundet hatte, ritten die beiden fröhlich plaudernd dahin, bis sie etwas unverhofft auf das neue Lager stießen. Ein sehr schmuddeliger Koch und zwei oder drei Eingeborenenweiber in zerlumpten Hemden waren die einzigen Leute zuhause, und sie standen mit großen Augen da, um den Fremden zu begrüßen.

Obgleich Mr. Simmondsen seine Kleidung der Umgebung angepasst hatte, behielt er doch noch genügend von seiner geistlichen Tracht bei, um seinen Beruf anzuzeigen.

Der Koch erfasste daher die Lage sofort und lud den Pfarrer unter die Plane ein, die einstweilen als Hütte diente. Seinem Besucher, den er ziemlich neugierig musterte, teilte er mit, dass „alle" fort seien, draußen kampierten, und dass für ein paar Tage keiner zurückkommen würde; er sei allein da, bis auf zwei Männer, die auf einem Gelände in der Nähe arbeiteten und zum Abendessen da sein würden; tatsächlich tauchten sie auf, während er noch redete.

Mr. Simmondsen interessierte sich sehr für dieses erste echte „Außen-Camp", das er je gesehen hatte; und als die beiden Arbeiter zum Bach hinunter gegangen waren, um sich zu waschen, und der Koch das Essen vorbereitete, rief er Charley herbei, um ihm ein paar Fragen zu stellen. „Was machen diese schwarzen Frauen hier, Charley?"
„Oh, überall Missus gehören weiße Kerl", war die überraschende Antwort. Es dauerte eine Weile, bis Joseph den vollen Sinn dieser Mitteilung begreifen konnte; und dann sah er es als seine Pflicht an, diesen Sündern eine ernsthafte Strafpredigt zu halten und bereitete sich entsprechend vor.

„Seht ihr denn nicht ein", erklärte er, als die drei Männer beisammen waren, „welche Sünde ihr begeht, sowohl gegen die sittlichen als auch gegen die göttlichen Gesetze? Wenn ihr schon das eine nicht respektiert, so doch vielleicht das andere." Der Koch starrte in blanker Verblüffung zu den Arbeitern hinüber, und diese zum Koch. „Ich meine diese unglücklichen und irregeleiteten Wesen da", sprach der Pfarrer und machte eine Handbewegung zu den kaum bekleideten Eingeborenenweibern hin. Schallendes Gelächter war die Antwort. „Verdammt, und das kommt ausgerechnet von Ihnen!" rief der Koch, als er die Sprache wiedergefunden hatte. Die anderen glucksten beifällig.

„Was soll das heißen?" fragte Joseph entrüstet: „Ich spreche kraft meines Amtes."
„Setzt euch nur hin und langt zu", sagte der Koch; „Ihr seid keiner von der schlechten Sorte, das kann ich sehen; aber spielt nicht das brave Unschuldslamm!" Der erboste Pastor lehnte ab. Er merkte, dass seine Worte auf die leichte Schulter genommen wurden und niemand auf ihn hören wollte, und so verließ sie in höchstem Zorn. -

Charley hatte ihm erzählt, dass es etwa zwölf Meilen von hier an der Strecke zurück nach Upton Downs eine saubere Lagune gäbe; er würde also bis dorthin weiter ziehen und dort lagern - sie hatten reichlich Proviant auf dem Packpferd dabei -, und so nahm er sein Zaumzeug, rief nach dem Jungen und ging, um sein Pferd zu holen.

Als er zurück kam, schnappte er noch den Rest einer Bemerkung auf, die der Koch zu den anderen machte. „Die bogen ums Ende vom Bush und schwatzen wie die dicksten Freunde miteinander, und wie ich gesehen hab, wer das war – Himmel, da hätt' mich fast der Schlag getroffen." Das war schlimmer als Griechisch für den Reverend Joseph. Griechisch hätte er vielleicht noch verstanden.

Trotz einer ergebenen Entschuldigung seitens des Missetäters brach er auf und kam gegen Sonnenuntergang bei der Lagune an, von der Charley gesprochen hatte. Es war ein wunderschönes Plätzchen. Der eine Teil des Wassers war dicht mit breitblättrigen Wasserlilien bedeckt, aber am anderen Ende gab es eine klare Stelle, die zum Schwimmen einlud, was der gute Pfarrer so genoss.

Als das Zelt aufgeschlagen war, stand er im Adamskostüm da und wollte sich gerade ins Wasser begeben, als Charley nach ihm rief. Auf die Seerosen deutend, sagte er zu Mr. Simmondsen, er werde ihm ein paar Schoten holen, wie sie die Schwarzen sehr gerne essen.

Der Geistliche war erst bis zu den Hüften im Wasser, als er hinter sich ein Platschen hörte und dann Charleys dunkle Gestalt halb planschend, halb schwimmend auf die Seerosen zusteuern sah. Bald tauchte sein Kopf aus dem Wasser auf und er winkte dem Geistlichen zu, herüberzukommen und die Ureinwohnerdelikatesse zu kosten.

Reverend Joseph schwamm gemächlich hinüber und probierte. Die Fruchtkapseln er-

| | |
|---|---|
| | wiesen sich als äußerst wohlschmeckend, und als dann die Sonne schon fast untergegangen war, hielt Mr. Simmondsen aufs Ufer zu und richtete sich im seichten Wasser auf, Charley ein paar Schritte hinter ihm. |
| 120 | Aus irgendeinem Grund sah er sich um. Welch anstößige Lage! |
| | Die Sache war nicht von der Hand zu weisen; all das verstohlene Gelächter wegen der „Sitten des Landes", die ungeklärten Anspielungen, die derbe Art des Kochs wurden schlagartig klar: Charley war eine Frau! |
| | Der niederträchtige Verwalter von Upton Downs hatte ihn (nach der „Landessitte") mit |
| 125 | einer schwarzen Eingeborenen, in Knabenkleidung als Kammerdiener verkleidet, auf die Reise geschickt, und dieses Eingeborenenweib war von jedem entlang der Strecke erkannt worden. |
| | Mr. Simmondsen dachte an das Zurückliegende und wurde rot. Die Nacht verging in inbrünstigem Gebet. |
| 130 | „Aber mein lieber Herr", sagte der Aufseher von Upton Downs, „ich habe doch alles für Sie getan, was ich konnte. Charlotte ist so gut wie nur irgendein schwarzer Diener, und sie kennt die ganze Gegend hier herum. Sie müssen doch zugeben, hat sie Sie nicht bestens versorgt?" |
| | „Sie vergessen den Skandal, der daraus entstehen könnte", entgegnete der Reverend |
| 135 | Joseph Simmondsen. |
| | „Herr Gott, Mann", rief der Verwalter, „wer kümmert sich denn darum, was hier draußen geschieht? Niemand wird je davon erfahren." |
| | Doch Davis täuschte sich. |
| | Jedermann erfuhr davon. |
| 140 | Der Rev. Simmondsen erhielt empörte Briefe von seinem Bischof, seinen Kirchenältesten, mehreren Missionsgesellschaften und schließlich, was das Schlimmste war, einen Abschiedsbrief von dem jungen Fräulein, mit dem er verlobt war. Glücklicherweise erbte er zu der Zeit etwas Geld, und so tat er das Beste, was er machen konnte: er hängte den geistlichen Stand an den Nagel, wurde Schafzüchter, und |
| 145 | ist heute einer der populärsten Männer in diesem Distrikt. |
| | *Radegundis Stolze (2009)* |

### 10.2.3 Bible quotations in literature

Traces of religious language are often visible in literary texts. Ignorance of ecclesiological language usage and lacking knowledge about the presence of different bible translations for a specific audience or denomination, for instance in Germany and in the English speaking world, may have undesired effects in translations.[122] The translator should recognize those in the text, and reflect upon the denominational context in which they are placed.

---

[122] It is totally unclear why in the German edition of Jostein Gaarder's „Sofie's World" (J. Gaarder: *Sofies Welt. Roman über die Geschichte der Philosophie.* Aus dem Norwegischen von Gabriele Haefs. Carl Hanser Verlag, München/Wien 1993) the presentation of St. Paul's speech on the Areopagus (p. 193) has been quoted from an ancient bible, which is outdated linguistically and difficult to understand. The book is written for young

In English literary texts it is rather common to cite from the Bible, and this should be realized in a translation by adequate, valid quotations from official Bible editions, as the selection of the Bible version also determines the DISCOURSE FIELD in the sense of a denominational marking of the text. This concerns mainly the difference between the Roman-Catholic and the Protestant world of Christian confession with a whole variety of free churches.

In the example below this problematic was not seen. The translator cited from a German Catholic version, but should better have used a Protestant one for to be more precise, all the more as this Protestant world view is predominant in the Anglo-Saxon communities

| Example | Translation |
|---|---|
| (...) Mr. Fortune was a humble man of heart and he had the blessing which rests upon humility: an easy-going nature. (...) Even as a young man he had learnt that to jump in first doesn't make the bus start any sooner; and his favourite psalm was the one which begins: 'My soul truly waiteth still upon God.' | Aber Mr. Fortune war demütigen Herzens, und auf ihm ruhte der Segen, den solche Demut schenkt: Gelassenheit. (...) Schon als junger Mann hatte er begriffen, daß die Post nicht früher abgeht, bloß weil man als Erster aufsprang; und sein Lieblingspsalm begann so: „Bei Gott allein kommt meine Seele zur Ruhe..." |
| Mr. Fortune was not a scholar, he did not know that the psalms express bygone thoughts and a bygone way of life. In his literal way he believed that the sixty-second psalm applied to him. For many years he had been a clerk in the Hornsey branch of Lloyds Bank, but he had not liked it. Whenever he weighed out the golden sovereigns in the brass scales, which tacked and sidled like a yacht in a light breeze, he remembered uneasily that the children of men are deceitful upon the weights, that they are altogether lighter than vanity itself. In the bank, too, he had seen riches increase. But he had not set his heart upon | Mr. Fortune war kein Gelehrter, er wußte nicht, daß die Psalmen Ausdruck der Denkweise früherer Zeiten und einer längst überkommenen Lebensart sind. In seiner geradlinigen Art glaubte er wirklich, der zweiundsechzigste Psalm sei auf ihn gemünzt. Er war viele Jahre Angestellter bei der Lloyds Bank, Zweigstelle Hornsey gewesen, aber es hatte ihm dort nicht gefallen. Immer wenn er die goldenen Sovereigns auf der Messingwaage auswiegen mußte, die dann jedesmal in Schräglage ging wie eine Yacht am Wind, mußte er mit Unbehagen daran denken, wie die Kinder dieser Erde beim Wiegen betrügen, und schon ihre Eitelkeit die Waagschale in die |

people, and even all the other philosophers are presented in a clear, easy reading, sometimes even a bit colloquial manner. Thus, this text portion constitutes a totally inadequate, disturbing fracture in the overall entity, because the rest of the book is translated rather well. According to information from Denmark (Arnt L. Jacobsen), this deviation is not found in the Danish edition, for instance. There, St. Paul's speech has no register mark as to language level. So this seems not to be a stylistic feature in the original. Could it be, that the translator, in her need, asked grandpa for his old bible?

| | |
|---|---|
| them: and when his godmother, whose passbook he kept, died and left him one thousand pounds, he went to a training-college, was ordained deacon, and quitted England for St. Fabien, a port on an island of the Raratongan Archipelago in the Pacific. *[S.Townsend-Warner: Mr. Fortune's Maggot, p. 1-2.]* | Höhe schnellen läßt. In der Bank hatte er auch gesehen, wie sich Reichtümer anhäufen lassen. Aber er hängte sein Herz nicht an sie. Daher schrieb er sich, als seine Patentante starb, deren Sparbuch er verwaltet hatte, und ihm ein tausend Pfund hinterließ, in einer Katechetenschule ein, wurde Diakon und verließ England mit Kurs auf St. Fabien, Hafenstadt einer Insel des Raratonga-Archipels im Pazifik. *(S. Townsend-Warner: Mr. Fortunes Spleen. Deutsch von H. Weigelt. Zürich 1996)* |
| **Bible source**: Ps 62, 1;9 ¹<u>Truly my soul waiteth upon God</u>: from him cometh my salvation. ⁹Surely men of low degree are vanity, and men of high degree are a lie: to be <u>laid in the balance, they are altogether lighter than vanity</u>. [KING JAMES VERSION] ¹My soul finds rest in God alone; my salvation comes from him. ⁹Lowborn men are but a breath, the highborn are but a lie; if weighed on a balance, they are nothing; together they are only a breath. [NEW INTERNATIONAL VERSION] | **Bibelzitat**: Ps 62, 2;10 ²Meine Seele ist stille zu Gott, von dem mir Hilfe kommt. ¹⁰Aber Menschen sind ja nichts, große Leute täuschen auch; sie wiegen weniger als nichts, soviel ihrer sind. [LUTHER] ²<u>Bei Gott allein kommt meine Seele zur Ruhe</u>, von ihm kommt mir Hilfe. ¹⁰Nur ein Hauch sind die Menschen, die Leute nur <u>Lug und Trug. Auf der Waage schnellen sie empor</u>, leichter als ein Hauch sind sie alle. [Kath. EINHEITSÜBERSETZUNG] |

Similar mistakes get more frequent to the extent that translators are not aware of Christian specialist terminology. Such an uniformed dealing with texts results in the fact that the problem is overseen, and the term is not even researched. This we can note in a multitude of translations from the English language, as you find them everywhere in current translations (see also our discussion of the two previous text examples).

But there is the reverse problem as well: it happens that authors write about exotic beliefs in a foreign country which, however, they did not really understand. This could be the case, for instance, when a European author elaborates on Hindi beliefs in India. Here again, the translator will need relevant subject knowledge in order to see whether this is all correct. In translating one could then amend any error or misconception by the author, so that the target readers may not unnecessarily be offended, and also the author is not exposed to undue criticism for such a mistake. This is in line with functional theories of translation (Nord 1997) as oriented towards target readers' expectations. This, of course is only adequate if such errors are not intentional, and forms only a minor aspect in the overall source text.

It is clear that traces of religious language may appear in various texts in a different way. Neglect of those aspects may lead to a simplification up until inadequate transformation of content, or to missing functional adequacy of the translation.

### 10.2.4 Text from an arts catalogue

| | |
|---|---|
| | **Die Mathildenhöhe – Zeugnis eines legendären künstlerischen Reform-Projekts und Forum lebendiger Kulturarbeit** |
| 5 | Die Mathildenhöhe in Darmstadt, von 1899 bis 1914 der Schauplatz der legendären Künstlerkolonie ist heute als kulturelle Attraktion ersten Ranges und als lebendiger „Musenhügel" weltweit bekannt. Die nahe zum Stadtzentrum gelegene, eigentlich mäßige und trotzdem höchste Erhebung Darmstadts war in früheren Jahrhunderten erst ein Weinberg, dann ein höfischer Landschaftsgarten, bevor sie um 1900 zum aufsehenerregenden Experimentierfeld für künstlerische Innovationen ausgewählt wurde. |
| 10 | Damals versuchten ein aufgeschlossener Landesherr und eine Gruppe junger Künstler hier die Vision einer Verschmelzung von Kunst und Leben zu verwirklichen. Ziel des allumfassenden Reformprojekts war es, die Architektur sowie die gesamte häusliche Raumausstattung zu revolutionieren und damit eine Wohnkultur zu schaffen, die den Forderungen der Zeit entsprach. Ihre neue Ästhetik war ein Protest gegen die als falsch empfundene historisierende Stilmaskerade im wilhelminischen Zeitalter, sie war aber |
| 15 | auch ein utopisches Versprechen, das die Flucht aus den verkrusteten Verhältnissen des 19. Jahrhunderts ebenso ermöglichen sollte wie der Rückzug aus den sichtbar werdenden sozialen Problemen der entstehenden Industriegesellschaften. Es ging den Künstlern also um mehr als „nur" um neue Bau- und Wohnformen: Nach ihrem Willen sollte die ganze menschliche Lebensgestaltung reformiert werden, um an Schönheit |
| 20 | und Glück aber auch an Einfachheit und Zweckmäßigkeit zu gewinnen.<br>Diese ideologisch geprägte Maxime gilt insbesondere für den euphorischen Beginn, als die Künstlerkolonie noch unter dem Einfluß des Jugendstils und eines elitären Ästhetizismus stand. Schon nach 1901 wurde das Programm allmählich nüchterner und realitätsbezogener. Der ideelle Wandel ist u.a. in den zahlreichen Bauten faßbar, die von |
| 25 | 1900 bis 1914 auf der Mathildenhöhe entstanden und die dem breiten Publikum im Rahmen von vier großen Ausstellungen in den Jahren 1901, 1904, 1908 und 1914 vorgestellt wurden. (...) |
| | **Translation** |
| | **The Mathildenhöhe – Document of a legendary artistic reform project and forum of a lively cultural work** |
| 5 | Between 1899 and 1914, the Mathildenhöhe at Darmstadt was site of the legendary Artists' Colony. Today it is known world-wide as a first-class cultural attraction and a bustling "Muses' Hill". The moderate yet highest elevation of ground in Darmstadt, situated near the city centre, had once been a vineyard, then a formal landscape garden |

> in former centuries, before it was chosen around 1900 to become the sensational experimental field for artistic innovations. In those days, an open-minded sovereign and a group of young artists tried to realise here their vision of a fusion between art and life. The aim of the overall reform project was to revolutionise architecture as well as all aspects of interior design in order to create a living culture in correspondence with the demands of modern time. The novel aesthetics represent a protest against the historicising stylistic masquerade in the Wilhelminian age they regarded as wrong. However, they imply also an utopian promise of both the flight from the ossified conditions of the nineteenth century and a withdrawal from the obvious and growing social problems arising in an industrial society. The artists had more in mind than "merely" new forms of architecture and housing: according to their intention, the whole human life-style should be reformed to gain in beauty and happiness, as well as in simplicity and functionality. This ideological maxim is particularly true for the euphoric beginning, when the artists' colony still stood under the influence of Jugendstil and an elitist aestheticism. After 1901 the program became gradually more rational and realistic. The change of ideas is visible among other things in numerous buildings created on the Mathildenhöhe between 1900 and 1914. They were presented to the general public in four great exhibitions in 1901, 1904, 1908 and 1914. (...)
> (Künstlerkolonie Mathildenhöhe Darmstadt 1899-1914. *Das Buch zum Museum - The Museum Book*. Institute Mathildenhöhe Darmstadt 1999, 21-22.)

This text from a museum catalogue, situated as to its SITUATIVE BACKGROUND in the cultural sphere of modern Germany, and more specifically in the DISCOURSE FIELD of sophisticated museums, is a typical example of this text type. While the MEANING DIMENSION is mainly presented by reference to the topic of Jugendstil Reform, the peculiar feature of the text in its PREDICATIVE MODE is the large amount of adjectives. It seems to be a characteristic of arts texts to put the main centre of discussion into adjectives, and not so much into nouns, as in technical texts for example. Visible objects of art, such as sculptures, pictures, dance, textiles and other things, are being described by means of invisible ideas.

The translation has to observe, in view of the GENRE, an adaptation to the spatial requirements of a catalogue which intends to present the text in both languages side by side. The difference in length has to be kept limited. The need for idiomatic formulations appealing to museum visitors under STYLISTICS leads to some syntactic deviations from the source text structure, and the preferred end-focus in English language texts shows clearly. The aspect of numerous adjectives could be easily maintained.

> **Another example English-German**
>
> It is a challenge to define his complex and elusive style, for it is an ongoing dialectic process that involves an intuitive striving for expression, with many other expressive aspects. Neither Chinese, nor Western in his style, Hsiao expresses in varied mediums, though primarily in painting, his perceptions and search for wider meanings and understanding. The radiant colour fiedls of "The Eternal Garden" of 1993 appear to have been plowed with furrows and rows of light; it is a transcendent work, and yet at the same time rhythmic and unabashedly material and concrete in the best Western modernist tradition. Similarly, "The Great Chi" of 1994, with its immense scale and sweeping dry strokes of luminous pigment applied over unprimed, rippling cotton canvas conveys an unlikely, highly individual belief in the balance of nature. Fluid and bold, the painting's broad strokes are exactly what they literally suggest: the universal way, bringing order out of chaos. His works, however, can be quite nuanced, refined to a high degree and oblique. (...) (Sam Hunter: *Hsiao Chin's unique synthesis of East and West.* Catalogue, Milan).
>
> **Translation**
>
> Seinen komplexen und schwer fassbaren Stil zu definieren ist eine Herausforderung, denn er ist ein andauernder dialektischer Prozess, welcher einen intuitiven Ausdruckswillen mit noch vielen weiteren expressiven Aspekten einschließt. In seinem Stil, der weder chinesisch noch westlich ist, bringt Hsiao in unterschiedlichsten Medien, wenngleich vor allem in der Malerei, seine Auffassungen und Suche nach erweiterten Bedeutungen und einem vertieften Verstehen zum Ausdruck. Die leuchtenden Farbfelder im „Ewigen Garten" von 1993 erscheinen wie gepflügt mit Furchen und Reihen aus Licht, es ist ein transzendentes Werk, und doch zugleich rhythmisch und unverfroren materiell und konkret in bester modernistischer Tradition des Westens. Ähnlich vermittelt „Das Große Chi" von 1994, mit seinem riesigen Maßstab und den ausladenden trockenen Strichen leuchtenden Pigments auf ungrundiertem, kräuseligem Baumwolltuch, einen unwahrscheinlichen, höchst individuellen Glauben an die Balance der Natur. Flüssig und kühn sind die breiten Striche des Gemäldes genau das, was sie zu sein vorgeben: der universelle Weg, der Ordnung ins Chaos bringt. Seine Werke können jedoch auch sehr nuanciert, hochgradig verfeinert und vieldeutig sein.
> (*Translation R.Stolze*)

The example shows that the above described text type of arts catalogues is similar in various languages. The philosophical argumentation requires adequate representation in the translation. In the German language, the use of affixes is a special mark of philosophical writing as explained earlier, and it may be applied here. This signals the versatility of thought. Below there is the example of a German philosophical text probably showing typical signs of procedural style:

> Nietzsche aber, so verwandt seine Ausgangsmotive erscheinen, verläßt die menschenmögliche Perspektive. Das Subjekt seiner Kontemplation ist jener kalte Engel, der eine bereits vergangene Weltgeschichte überschaut. Der blaue Planet ist grau und leblos geworden. Für

den Intellekt ist die Bilanz aus der Geschichte der Gattung Mensch trostlos. Er hatte keinen Zweck, der über das menschliche Leben hinausreicht. Was die Geschichte des menschlichen Geistes, solange sie währte, ihm in Theologie und Philosophie und in den Wissenschaften überhaupt an Wahrheitsfähigkeit zutraute, war ein Mittel zur Steigerung der Lebensfähigkeit – mehr nicht. Denkprinzipien, Imperative und sprachliche Kommunikationsformen sind allesamt Ordnungsraster, in denen eine durchweg anthropomorphe Welt erbaut wird, die ihrem Wesen nach nicht kognitiv, sondern artistisch verfaßt ist. Das Zutrauen zur Allgemeingültigkeit und Verbindlichkeit intellektueller Anstrengung verdankt sich dem Vergessen der lebensförderlichen poetischen Antriebe, die aller menschlichen Tätigkeit zugrunde liegen. Der Philosoph erhält so die Aufgabe, zu demaskieren und zu dechiffrieren, das Heilsame der Illusionen im Wahrheitspathos zu enthüllen. (...)

[Hermann Braun: „Der kalte Engel. Friedrich Nietzsche – Verkünder des Unerhörten." In: *Evangelische Kommentare* 11/1994, S. 664+667.]

## 10.2.5   A poem

**W. H. Auden: If I Could Tell You**

Time will say nothing but I told you so,
Time only knows the price we have to pay;
If I Could Tell You I would let you know.

5   If we should weep when clowns put on their show,
If we should stumble when musicians play,
Time will say nothing but I told you so.

There are no furtunes to be told, although,
Because I love you more than I can say,
10   If I could tell you I would let you know.

The winds must come from somewhere when they blow,
There must be reasons why the leaves decay;
Time will say nothing but I told you so.

Perhaps the roses really want to grow,
15   The vision seriously intends to stay;
If I could tell you I would let you know.

Suppose the lions all get up and go,
And all the brooks and soldiers run away,
Will time say nothing but I told you so?
If I could tell you I would let you know.

October 1940   (In: Auden, Wystan Hugh; *Gedichte. Poems*. München: dtv, 1976, p. 32)

This poem – among of the author's most famous ones – knows already many translations, and it invites for even more attempts. It is a sophisticated example of a villanella, as was created by Passerat and Richelet in the 16th century. There are a special rythm and verse ends.[123] This formal structure, of course, constitutes the main difficulty in translating poems, but various translators have tried to realize this even in the target languages. It is achieved for the prize of semantic deviation, as described extensively by Acartürk-Höß (2010:105ff) under the principle of "alterity". On the other hand, it is also legitimate to try to translate such a poem just in view of its content, as one might conceive a poem as a message told to the reader. The translation depends on how we understand this message. Such a conception would then focus more on the content, and sacrifice the poetic forms, as is done in the example below:

**Translation (A)**[124]

Wenn ich es wüsste

Die Zeit wird schweigen, doch ich hab's dir gesagt,
die Zeit kennt nur den Preis, den wir bezahlen;
Wenn ich es wüsste, würd' ich's dir sagen.

Sollten wir weinen, wenn Clowns auftreten,
sollten wir schimpfen, wenn die Musiker spielen,
die Zeit wird schweigen, doch ich hab's dir gesagt.

Es gibt keine Glücksfälle zu erzählen, und wenn auch,
ich lieb' dich mehr als ich sagen kann, und
Wenn ich es wüsste, würd' ich's dir sagen.

Die Winde müssen von wo kommen, wenn sie wehen,
es muss wohl Gründe geben, dass die Blätter welken;
die Zeit wird schweigen, doch ich hab's dir gesagt.

Vielleicht wollen die Rosen wirklich wachsen,
das Wunschbild ernsthaft will verweilen;
Wenn ich es wüsste, würd' ich's dir sagen.

---

[123] See embracing rhymes with a final pair according to the model AbA' abA abA' abA abA' abAA' (lowercase letters indicating mere rhyme, capital letters indicating a literal repetition of the verse) (cf. Gero v. Wilpert, *Sachwörterbuch der Literatur* (Stuttgart: Kröner, 1989, p. 1005.)

[124] R. Stolze, 2006 (reprinted in Acartürk-Höß 2010:265)

> Stell dir vor, alle Löwen stehn auf und gehen,
> und alle Bäche und Soldaten laufen fort;
> Wird die Zeit schweigen, und hab ich's dir gesagt?
> Wenn ich es wüsste, würd' ich's dir sagen.

The time of creation of this poem in October 1940 is a strong indicator for the SITUATIVE BACKGROUND. It's the time right after the beginning of the Second World War. This important aspect is strengthened by the fact that Auden also wrote a poem called "1$^{st}$ September 1939", the date of the beginning of the war. We know that "in 1940 Auden began to go regularly to church again, and by October he had rejoined the Anglican Communion" (Osborne).[125] So it might not be totally wrong to assume that this beginning war had a decisive impact for Auden. Concerning the DISCOURSE FIELD we may interpet the "lyrical I" also as a personal character confessing his love to somebody. That interpretation is intuitive in a reader who only takes this text, without any influence by literary criticism. This is then confirmed in an overall view by the MEANING DIMENSION of corresponding words: *you, love, roses, leaves decay, vision.* Life is endangered, there is also a sense of insecurity about what time will bring about, and a personal warning: *the price we pay, if we should weep, no fortunes are to be told, solders run away.* Will there still be hope for the future? The author doesn't know. With such an understanding, the translator may try to use words adequate in the mentioned semantic field. In the above tentative translation (A), we also tried to present a sort of lyrical rhythm, partly with some awkward formulation, however the special end-verses could not be realized. We might call this attempt a sort of "naïve interpretation", a moral interpersonal interpretation with reference to its time of origination.

According to the hermeneutical approach in translation, such a version is provisional, it calls for further clarifying information. An informative learning process will certainly lead to a revision of that first version above.

Literary Studies have analyzed Auden's writings with much scrutiny (Acartürk-Höß 2010:27ff). In the epoch of Auden's "re-conversion to Anglo-Catholicism" the author dealt much with issues of the human existence, its finiteness and "anxiety in time" (Osborne). Time is conceived of as absolutely omnipotent, as "a

---

[125] See Charles Osborne: *W.H. Auden. The Life of a Poet.* London: Eyre Methuen, 1980.

destroyer as undiscriminating and implacable as death".[126] You cannot conquer time, humans are weak. Again, here, the SITUATIVE BACKGROUND of the Second World War becomes visible. Furthermore, Auden is reflecting about language as the feeble means of understanding reality.

The MEANING DIMENSION concerning the underlying conflict between humanity and time is seen mainly in the ambiguous interplay of the key word fields around *know, tell* and *say*. Is time the only speaker? The lyrical speaker, who counts himself among the powerless humanity and addresses it (*we* and *you* in verse 1) can still say something about time, thus already undermining the omnipotence of time. Poetry as such is powerful.

Looking more precisely at the PREDICATIVE MODE, we see that the outward appearance of the dominant time is being undermined by syntactic and semantic features: *"Time will say nothing but I told you so"* – not only time is a speaker. The personal pronoun "I" can be the time, but also the author. This ambiguity is given in the semantic openness of the conjunction *but*: It can be understood both as "außer" (except) stating what time is exclusively saying and has said already, and as "aber" (yet) allowing the lyrical I to speak himself

The second verse too has such an ambiguity in "only": *"Time only knows the price we have to pay"* is ambiguous. If *only* refers to time alone, time is really omnipotent and all-knowing ("The time only knows the price"). But *only* may also refer to the verbal process thus limiting the knowledge of time ("The time knows only the price", not more than that).

It becomes clear that we are confronted, here, with a different, deeper reading of the text, triggered by literary analysis. Such a different understanding, based on a kind of "informed interpretation" from literary studies will then lead in grounded understanding to a different translation (B) (see below). Its appeal is very open, sensitive, quasi "post-modern". Maybe this corresponds more to the author's intention. But we can never be sure about it, there is no "one single correct interpretation", not even all interpretations are equally valid.[127] Poems are an open piece of art (Iser 1978).

---

[126] See Edward Mendelson, *Later Auden*. (London: Faber & Faber, 1999, p. 8).

[127] Acartürk-Höß (2010:161) with reference to Eco.

**Translation (B)**

If I Could Tell You

Die Zeit wird nichts sagen, außer: es ist schon gesagt,
Die Zeit allein kennt den Preis, der zu bezahlen ist;
Ja, könnt' ich es sagen, ich ließ' es euch wissen.

Ob wir weinen sollten, wenn Clowns Faxen machen,
Ob wir stolpern sollten, wenn die Musiker spielen,
Die Zeit wird nichts sagen, außer: es ist schon gesagt.

Wahrsagereien gibt es nicht zu erzählen, und dennoch,
Weil ich euch mehr liebe als ich zu sagen weiß,
Gilt: könnt' ich es sagen, ich ließ' es euch wissen.

Die Winde kennen eine Richtung, aus der sie wehen,
Es gibt Gründe, warum die Blätter vergehen,
Die Zeit wird nichts sagen, außer: es ist schon gesagt,

Rosen müssen wohl irgendwo sprießen,
Die Vision hält sich hartnäckig fest,
Ja, könnt' ich es sagen, ich ließ' es euch wissen.

Denkt doch, die Löwen verziehen sich alle,
und Bäche und Soldaten laufen hinweg,
Wird die Zeit nichts sagen, außer: es ist schon gesagt?
Ja, könnt' ich es sagen, ich ließ' es euch wissen.

*(Translation R. Stolze, 2007).*

Here, the translation has "grown" – not by another attempt from a different person, but by new input to the translator herself. This version is quoted as "showing a clear enhancement of quality" in the study on literary translation quality done by Acartürk-Höß (2010:292). Every learning process will have an effect on our way of dealing with texts and formulating a translation.

This observation might be confirmed in the future by relevant research on the influence of previous reading on the output of a translator. That is just one example of possible research within the new paradigm of translational hermeneutics in Translation Studies.

# 11 References

Acartürk-Höß, Miriam. 2010. *...making the mirror visible... Deutsche Übersetzungen englischer Lyrik (W.H. Auden) Versuch einer Verwissenschaftlichung der Übersetzungskritik.* Frankfurt/Main: Lang.

Aitchison, Jean. 2003. *Words in the Mind. An Introduction to the Mental Lexicon.* [3$^{rd}$ ed.] Oxford: Blackwell.

Albrecht, Jörn. 1998. *Literarische Übersetzung. Geschichte – Theorie – Kulturelle Wirkung.* Darmstadt. Wissenschaftliche Buchgesellschaft.

Alves, Fabio and Gonçalves, José Luiz. 2007. "Modelling Translator's Competence: Relevance and Expertise under Scrutiny." In *Translation Studies - Doubts and Directions,* Y. Gambier & M. Shlesinger & R. Stolze (eds.), 41-55. Amsterdam/Philadelphia: John Benjamins.

Anderson, John R. 1983. *The Architecture of Cognition.* Cambridge, MS: Harvard University Press.

Antos, Gerd. 1982. *Grundlagen einer Theorie des Formulierens. Texterstellung in geschriebener und gesprochener Sprache.* Tübingen: Niemeyer.

Antos, Gerd. 1989. „Textproduktion: Ein einführender Überblick." In *Textproduktion. Ein interdisziplinärer Forschungsüberblick,* G. Antos & H. P. Krings (eds.), 5-57. Tübingen: Niemeyer.

Apel, Friedmar. 1982. *Sprachbewegung. Eine historisch-poetologische Untersuchung zum Problem des Übersetzens.* Heidelberg: Carl Winter Universitätsverlag.

Arntz, Reiner and Picht, Heribert and Mayer, Felix. 2002. *Einführung in die Terminologiearbeit.* [4$^{th}$ ed.] Hildesheim: Georg Olms.

Arrojo, Rosemary. 1994. "Fidelity and the Gendered Translation." In *TTR* 7(2), 147-64.

Arrojo, Rosemary. 1997. „Eine neue Definition des 'Originaltexts'. Aufsätze." In *Übersetzungswissenschaft in Brasilien. Beiträge zum Status von ‚Original' und Übersetzung,* M. Wolf (ed.), 25-48. Tübingen: Stauffenburg.

Baker, Mona. 1993. "Corpus linguistics and Translation Studies: Implications and applications." In *Text and Technology: In Honor of John Sinclair,* M. Baker & G. Francis & E. Tognini-Bonelli (eds.), 233–250. Amsterdam/Philadelphia: John Benjamins.

Bălăcescu, Ioana and Stefanink, Bernd. 2003. "Modèles explicatifs de la créativité en traduction." *META,* XLVIII, 4, 2003: 509-525.

Bălăcescu, Ioana and Stefanink, Bernd. 2006. "Kognitivismus und übersetzerische Kreativität". *Lebende Sprachen* 2/2006: 50-61.

Baldauf, Christa. 2003. „On the mixing of conceptual metaphors." In *Text, Context, Concepts (TTC 4)*, C. Zelinsky-Wibbelt (ed.), 47-63. Berlin/New York: Mouton de Gruyter.

Barthes, Roland. 1970. *S / Z*. Paris: Editions du Seuil.

Bassnett, Susan and Lefevere, André (eds.) 1998. *Constructing Cultures. Essays on literary translation*. Clevedon/Philadelphia: Multilingual Matters.

Bassnett, Susan and Trivedi, Nirmal H. (eds.). 1998. *Postcolonial Translation Theory*. London/New York: Routledge.

Bassnett, Susan. 2000. „Authenticity, travel and translation." In *Translationswissenschaft*. Festschrift für Mary Snell-Hornby zum 60. Geburtstag, M. Kadric & K. Kaindl & F. Pöchhacker (eds.), 105-114. Tübingen: Stauffenburg.

Baumann, Klaus Dieter. 1992. „Die Fachlichkeit von Texten als eine komplexe Vergleichsgröße". In *Kontrastive Fachsprachenforschung*, K.D. Baumann & H. Kalverkämper (eds.), 29-48. Tübingen: Narr.

Baumann, Klaus Dieter. 2008. "A cognitive-communicative analysis of the information transfer in LSP." In *AILA 15th World Congress of Applied Linguistics: Multilingualism, challenges and opportunities*. August 24-29, 2008 in Essen. Book of Abstracts, p. 92. Duisburg: Universitätsverlag Rhein-Ruhr OHG.

BDAG Bauer-Danker Lexikon. *A Greek-English Lexicon of the New Testament and other Early Christian Literature* (3rd ed. 2001). Chicago: University Press.

Beeby, Allison. 1996. *Teaching Translation from Spanish into English*. Ottawa: University Press.

Beier, Rudolf. 1983. "Fachexterne Kommunikation im Englischen. Umrisse eines forschungsbedürftigen Verwendungsbereichs der Sprache." In *Fachsprache und Fachliteratur*, B. Schlieben-Lange & H. Kreuzer (eds.), 91-109. Göttingen: Vandenhoeck-Ruprecht.

Beiner, Marcus. 2009. *Humanities. Was Geisteswissenschaft macht. Und was sie ausmacht.* (Berlin: University Press.) Darmstadt: Wissenschaftliche Buchgesellschaft.

Beneke, J. 1988. "Metaphorik in Fachtexten." In *Textlinguistik und Fachsprache. Akten des Internationalen übersetzungswissenschaftlichen AILA-Symposions Hildesheim*, 13.-16. April 1987, A. Arntz (ed.), 26-36. Hildesheim: Olms.

Benjamin, Walter. 1923. „Die Aufgabe des Übersetzers." Reprint in *Das Problem des Übersetzens* [2nd revised and modified ed.], H.J. Störig (ed.), 155-169. Darmstadt: Wissenschaftliche Buchgesellschaft.

Berger, Klaus and Nord, Christiane. 2000. „Verstandene Fremdheit: Ein neuer Skopos für alte Texte." In *Translationswissenschaft*. Festschrift für Mary Snell-Hornby, M. Kadric & K. Kaindl & F. Pöchhacker (eds.), 213-225. Tübingen: Stauffenburg.

Blank, Josef. 1977. „Im Anfang war das Wort. Die Interpretation des Johannes-Prologs bei Thomas von Aquin als Grundlegung einer theologischen Sprach-Theorie." In *IMAGO LINGUAE. Festschrift zum 60. Geburtstag von Fritz Paepcke*, K.H. Bender & K. Berger & M. Wandruszka (eds.), 81-94. München: Fink.

Bleckmann, Albert. 1977. "Ermessensmißbruch und détournement du pouvoir." In *IMAGO LINGUAE. Festschrift zum 60. Geburtstag von Fritz Paepcke*, K.H. Bender & K. Berger & M. Wandruszka (eds.), 95-101. München: Fink.

Boden, Margaret A. 2001. "Creativity and Knowledge." In *Creativity in Education*, A. Craft and B. Jeffrey and M. Leibling (eds.), 95-102. London/New York: Continuum.

Bolinger, D. 1976. "Meaning and Memory." *Forum Linguisticum*, 1 (1): 1-14.

Bolten, J. 1992. "<Fachsprache> oder <Sprachbereich>? Empirisch-pragmatische Grundlagen zur Beschreibung der deutschen Wirtschafts-, Medizin- und Rechtssprache." In *Beiträge zur Fachsprachenforschung: Sprache in Wissenschaft und Technik, Wirtschaft und Rechtswesen*, T. Bungarten (ed.), 57-72. Tostedt: Attikon.

Born, Anne. 1996. "The influence of place and climate as considerations for the translator with special reference to Scandinavia. In *XIV World Congress of the Fédération Internationale des Traducteurs (FIT)*, Vol. I, AUSIT (ed.), 14-17. Melbourne: AUSIT.

Bourdieu, Pierre. 1984. *Distinction: A Social Critique of the Judgment of Taste*. Cambridge, MS: Harvard University Press.

Brenner, Peter J. 1998. *Das Problem der Interpretation. Eine Einführung in die Grundlagen der Literaturwissenschaft*. Tübingen: Niemeyer.

Brodbeck, Karl-Heinz. 1995. *Entscheidung zur Kreativität. Wege aus dem Labyrinth der Gewohnheiten*. Darmstadt: Wissenschaftliche Buchgesellschaft.

Bubner, Rüdiger. 1976. *Handlung, Sprache und Vernunft*. Frankfurt/M: Suhrkamp.

Budin, Gerhard. 2002. „Wissensmanagement in der Translation.". In *Übersetzen und Dolmetschen*, J. Best & S. Kalina (eds.), 74-84. Tübingen: Francke.

Carbonell, Ovidi i Cortès. 2002. *Übersetzen ins Andere. Der Diskurs über das Andere und seine Übersetzung. Exotismus, Ideologie und neue Kanones in der englischsprachigen Literatur*. Tübingen: Stauffenburg.

Catford, J. C. 1965. *A Linguistic Theory of Translation. An Essay in Applied Linguistics*. London: Oxford University Press.

Cercel, Larisa (ed.). 2009. *Übersetzung und Hermeneutik, Traduction et herméneutique*. Bucharest: ZETA Books.

Cercel, Larisa 2010. „Subjektiv und intersubjektiv in der hermeneutischen Übersetzungstheorie". *Meta. Research in Hermeneutics, Phenomenology, and Practical Philosophy,* 3(2010): 84-104.

Chesterman, Andrew and Arrojo, Rosemary. 2000. "Shared ground in Translation Studies." *Target* 12: 151-160.

Chesterman, Andrew. 1993. "From 'is' to 'ought'. Laws, norms, and strategies in Translation Studies." *Target* 5:1: 1-20.

Chesterman, Andrew. 1997. *Memes of Translation.* Amsterdam/Philadelphia: John Benjamins.

Chesterman, Andrew. 1998. "Causes, Translations, Effects." *Target* 10: 201-230.

Chesterman, Andrew. 2001. "Proposal for a Hieronymic Oath." *The Translator* 7/2001, No.2: 139-154.

Chesterman, Andrew. 2004. „Hypotheses about translation universals". In *Claims, Changes and Challenges in Translation Studies,* G. Hansen & K. Malmkjaer & D. Gile (eds.), 1-13. Amsterdam/Philadelphia: John Benjamins.

Chi, M. and Feltovich, P. and Glaser, R. 1981. „Categorization and representation of physic problems by experts and novices." *Cognitive Science* 5: 121-152.

Christie, George C. 1964. "Vagueness and Legal Language." *48 Minn. Rev.* (1963-64): 885-911.

Clark, Andy. 1997. *Being There. Putting Brain, Body, and World Together Again.* Cambridge, MA: MIT Press.

Collini, S. 1992. „Introduction: Interpretation Terminable and Interminable." In *Interpretation and Overinterpretation. Umberto Eco with Richard Rorty, Jonathan Culler, Christine Brooke-Rose,* S. Collini (ed.), 1-21. Cambride, UK: Univ. Press.

Coseriu, Eugenio. 1980. *Textlinguistik. Eine Einführung* (ed. by J. Albrecht). Tübingen: Narr.

Cutts, Michael. 1996. "The author in literary translation: in search of idiom". In *XIV World Congress of the Fédération Internationale des Traducteurs (FIT),* Vol. I, AUSIT (ed.), 258-281. Melbourne: AUSIT.

Danker, Frederick W. 1993. *Multipurpose Tools for Bible Study.* Minneapolis: Fortress Press.

DeBono, Edward. 1970. *Lateral Thinking. A textbook of Creativity.* London: Ward Lock Educational.

Delisle, Jean and Woodsworth, Judith (eds.). 1995. *Translators through History.* Amsterdam/Philadelphia: John Benjamins.

Deppert, Alex. 2001. *Verstehen und Verständlichkeit. Wissenschaftstexte und die Rolle themaspezifischen Vorwissens.* Wiesbaden: Deutscher Universitäts-Verlag.

Dörner, Dietrich. 1976. *Problemlösen als Informationsverarbeitung.* Stuttgart/Berlin/Köln/Mainz: Kohlhammer.

Dostal, Robert J. 1994. "The Experience of Truth for Gadamer and Heidegger: Taking Time and Sudden Lighting" In *Hermeneutics and Truth*, B.R. Wachterhauser (ed.), n. 32. Evanston, IL: Northwestern University Press.

Eberhard, Philippe. 2004. *The Middle Voice in Gadamer's Hermeneutics. A Basic Interpretation with Some Theological Implications.* Tübingen: Mohr (Paul Siebeck).

Eco, Umberto. 2006. *Quasi dasselbe mit anderen Worten. Über das Übersetzen.* [German translation by B. Kroeber of "Dire quasi la stessa cosa. Esperienze di traduzione"]. München/Wien: Hanser.

Endicott, Timothy A. O. 2000. *Vagueness in Law.* Oxford: University Press.

Ericsson, K. Anders et al. 1993. "The role of deliberate practice in the acquisition of expert performance." Psychological Review, 100(3), 363-406.

Even-Zohar, Itamar. 1990. *Polysystem Studies.* Tel Aviv: The Porter Institute for Poetics and Semiotics.

Federman, Raymond. 1993. *Critification: Postmodern Essays.* New York: State University of New York Press.

Fillmore, Charles J. 1976. "Scenes-and-frames-semantics." In *Linguistic Structures Processing,* A. Zampolli (ed.), 55-81. Amsterdam: New Holland.

Fish, Stanley (1980): *Is There a Text in this Class? – The Authority of Interpretive Communities.* Massachusetts: Harvard University Press.

Fleischmann, Eberhard. 1997. „Überlegungen zur Gestaltung einer kulturwissenschaftlichen Komponente und zu ihrer Integration in das Übersetzer-/Dolmetscher-Studium." In *Translationsdidaktik. Grundfragen der Übersetzungswissenschaft,* F. Fleischmann et al. (eds.), 399-409. Tübingen: Narr.

Foltz, Peter W. 1996. "Comprehension, Coherence, and Strategies in Hypertext and Linear Text." In *Hypertext and Cognition,* J.-F. Rouet & J. Levonen & A. Dillon & R.J. Spiro (eds.), 109.136. Mahwah, NJ: Lawrence Erlbaum Associates.

Fontanet, Mathilde. 2005. « Temps de créativité en traduction. » *META* 50 (2): 432-447.

Forstner, Martin. 2005. „Bemerkungen zur Kreativität und Expertise." *Lebende Sprachen* 3/2005: 98-104.

Frank, Armin Paul. 1988 „'Längsachsen': Ein in der Textlinguistik vernachlässigtes Problem der literarischen Übersetzung." In *Textlinguistik und Fachsprache.* AILA-Symposion

Hildesheim 13.-15. April 1987. (Studien zu Sprache und Technik 1), R. Arntz (ed.), 485-497. Hildesheim/Zürich/New York: Olms.

Fuchs-Khakar, Christine. 1987. *Die Verwaltungssprache zwischen dem Anspruch auf Fachsprachlichkeit und Verständlichkeit.* Tübingen: Stauffenburg.

Gadamer, Hans-Georg. 1960. *Wahrheit und Methode. Grundzüge einer philosophischen Hermeneutik.* [5$^{th}$ ed. 1986]. Tübingen: J.C.B. Mohr (Paul Siebeck).

Gadamer, Hans-Georg. 1984. "Text und Interpretation." In *Text und Interpretation. Deutsch-französische Debatte mit Beiträgen von J. Derrida, Ph. Forget, M. Frank, H.-G. Gadamer, J. Greisch und F. Laruelle,* Ph. Forget (ed.), 24-55; 59-61. München: Fink.

Gadamer, Hans-Georg. 1990. *Truth and Method.* [Second revised edition. Translation by W. Glen-Doepel and revised by Joel Weinsheimer & Donald G. Marshall]. New York: Crossroad.

Gambier, Yves and Shlesinger, Miriam and Stolze, Radegundis (eds.). 2007. *Doubts and Directions in Translation Studies.* Amsterdam/Philadelphia: John Benjamins.

Gambier, Yves and van Doorslaer, Luc (eds.). 2007. *The Metalanguage of Translation.* (Special issue of Target, Vol. 19 No. 2). Amsterdam/Philadelphia: John Benjamins.

Gentzler, Edwin. 1993. *Contemporary Translation Theories.* London/New York: Routledge.

Gerzymisch-Arbogast, Heidrun. 1987. „Passepartoutwörter als fachsprachliches Übersetzungsproblem." *TEXTconTEXT*, vol. 2/1987: 23-31.

Gerzymisch-Arbogast, Heidrun. 1989. "The Role of Sense Relations in Translating Vague Business and Economic Texts." In *Translation and Lexicography. A special Monograph,* M. Snell-Hornby (ed.), 187-196. Paintbrush. A Journal of Poetry (Translations and Letters 16).

Gerzymisch-Arbogast, Heidrun et al. 2006. "Coherence, Theme/Rheme, Isotopy: Complementary Concepts in Text and Translation." In *Text and Translation. Theory and Methodology of Translation,* C. Heine & K. Schubert & H. Gerzymisch-Arbogast (eds.), 349-370. Tübingen: Gunter Narr Verlag.

Gile, Daniel and Hansen, Gyde. 2004. "The editorial process through the looking glass." In *Claims, Changes and Challenges in Translation Studies,* Hansen, G. & Malmkjær, K. & Gile, D. (eds.), 297-306. Amsterdam/Philadelphia: John Benjamins.

Gile, Daniel. 1991. „Methodological Aspects of Interpretation (and Translation) Research." *Target* 3: 153-174.

Gläser, Rosemarie. 1998. „Fachsprachen und Funktionalstile. Art. 16." In *HSK - Fachsprachen - Language for specific purposes I,* L. Hoffmann & H. Kalverkämper & H.E. Wiegand (eds.), 199-208. Berlin: Mouton de Gruyter.

Göpferich, Susanne. 1995. *Textsorten in Naturwissenschaft und Technik. Pragmatische Typologie – Kontrastierung – Translation.* Tübingen: Narr Verlag.

Göpferich, Susanne. 2002. *Textproduktion im Zeitalter der Globalisierung. Entwicklung einer Didaktik des Wissenstransfers.* Tübingen: Stauffenburg.

Göpferich, Susanne and Jakobsen, Arnt Lykke and Mees, Inger (eds). 2009. *Looking at Eyes: Eye Tracking Studies of Reading and Translation Processing.* (Copenhagen Studies in Language 36). Copenhagen: Samfundslitteratur.

Gouanvic, Jean-Marc. 2002. "The Stakes of translation in Literary Fields." *ACROSS Languages and Cultures* 3/2, 2002, 159-168.

Gouanvic, Jean-Marc. 2005. "A Bourdieusian Theory of Translation, or the Coincidence of Practical Instances: Field, 'Habitus', Capital and 'Illusio'". *The Translator* 11/2, 2005, 148-166.

Grice, H. P. 1975. „Logic and Conversation." In *Syntax and Semantics. Vol. 3: Speech Acts,* P. Cole and J. L. Morgan (eds.), 41-58. New York: Academic Press.

Grondin, Jean. 1993. "Die hermeneutische Dimension der Übersetzung". In *Übersetzen, Verstehen, Brücken bauen. Geisteswissenschaftliches und literarisches Übersetzen im internationalen Kulturaustausch,* A.P. Frank et al. (eds.), 151-157. Berlin: Erich Schmidt.

Grondin, Jean. 1994. Der Sinn für Hermeneutik. Darmstadt: Wissenschaftliche Buchgesellschaft.

Grzesik, Jürgen 1990. *Textverstehen – lernen und lehren. Geistige Operationen im Prozess des Textverstehens und typische Methoden für die Schulung zum kompetenten Leser.* Stuttgart: Klett.

Guilford, Joy Peter. 1968. *Intelligence, Creativity, and their Educational Implications.* San Diego: P. K. Knapp.

Guilford, Joy Peter. 1975. „Creativity: A Quarter Century of Progress." In *Perspectives in Creativity,* I.A. Taylor & J.W. Getzels (eds.), 37-59. Chicago: Aldine.

Gutt, Ernst-August. 2000. *Translation und Relevance. Cognition and Context.* (2nd edition). Manchester: St. Jerome.

Gutt, Ernst-August. 2004. "Challenges of Metarepresentation to Translation Competence." In *Translationskompetenz,* E. Fleischmann et al. (eds.), 77-89. Tübingen: Stauffenburg.

Haag, Ansgar (1984): „Übersetzen fürs Theater: Beispiel William Shakespeare." *Babel, International Journal of Translation,* Vol. XXX 4/1984, 228-235.

Hall, Edward T. 1976. *Beyond Culture.* Garden City, NY: Doubleday.

*Handbook of Translation Studies,* edited by Yves Gambier and Luc van Doorslaer (2010). Amsterdam/Philadelphia: John Benjamins

Hansen, Gyde. 2002. "Selbstaufmerksamkeit im Übersetzungsprozess." *Copenhagen Studies in Language* 27, 9-27. Copenhagen: Samfundslitteratur.

Hansen, Gyde. 2004. „Die Beschreibung von Übersetzungsprozessen." In *Translationskompetenz*, E. Fleischmann et al. (eds.), 91-101. Tübingen: Stauffenburg.

Hansen, Gyde. 2006. *Erfolgreich übersetzen. Entdecken und Beheben von Störquellen*. Tübingen: Narr.

Hayes, John Richard and Flower, Linda. 1980. "Identifying the organization of writing processes". In *Cognitive Processes in Writing*, L.W. Gregg & E.R. Steinberg (eds.), 3-30. Hillsdale, NJ: Erlbaum.

Heidegger, Martin. 1927. *Sein und Zeit*. (16$^{th}$ edition 1986). Tübingen: Max Niemeyer. Or: Special print from: „Jahrbuch für Philosophie und phänomenologische Forschung", vol. VIII, ed. by E. Husserl, Freiburg i. B. (Unaltered 5$^{th}$ edition 1941.)

Heidegger, Martin. 1962. *Being and Time*. (Translated by John Macquarrie and Edward Robinson). London: SCM Press Ltd.; New York/Evanston: Harper & Row.

Heine, Carmen. 2006. "Herausforderung Hypertextübersetzung". In *Text and Translation. Theory and Methodology of Translation*, C. Heine & K. Schubert & H. Gerzymisch-Arbogast (eds.), 17-39. Tübingen: Gunter Narr Verlag.

Heltai, Pál. 2004. "Ready-made language and translation." In *Claims, Changes and Challenges in Translation Studies*, G. Hansen & K. Malmkjaer & D. Gile (eds.), 51-71. Amsterdam/Philadelphia: John Benjamins.

Hendriks-Jansen, Horst. 1996. *Catching Ourselves in the Act. Situated Activity, Interactive Emergence, Evolution, and Human Thought*. Cambridge, MA: MIT Press.

Henschelmann, Käthe (1999): *Problem-bewusstes Übersetzen Französisch-Deutsch. Ein Arbeitsbuch*. Tübingen: Narr.

Hermans, Theo (ed.). 1985. *The Manipulation of Literature. Studies in Literary Translation*. London/Sidney: Croom Helm; New York: St. Martin's Press.

Hesseling, Ulla. 1982. *Praktische Übersetzungskritik, vorgeführt am Beispiel einer deutschen Übersetzung von Erich Fromm's "The Art of Loving"*. Tübingen: Stauffenburg.

Hintzman, D. L. 1986. „'Schema abstraction' in a multiple-trace memory model." *Psychological Review*, 93: 411-428.

Hönig, Hans G. 1986. „Übersetzen zwischen Reflex und Reflexion - ein Modell der übersetzungsrelevanten Textanalyse.". In *Übersetzungswissenschaft - Eine Neuorientierung*, M. Snell-Hornby (ed.), 230-251. Tübingen: Francke.

Hönig, Hans G. 1993. „Vom Selbst-Bewußtsein des Übersetzers." In *Traducere Navem. Festschrift für Katharina Reiß zum 70. Geburtstag*, J. Holz-Mänttäri & C. Nord (eds.), 77-90. Tampere: Tampereen Yliopisto.

Hönig, Hans G. 1995. *Konstruktives Übersetzen*. Tübingen: Stauffenburg.

Hönig, Hans G. and Kußmaul, Paul. 1992. *Strategie der Übersetzung. Ein Lehr- und Arbeitsbuch.* (4$^{th}$ ed. 1996). Tübingen: Narr.

Holmes, James S. 1988. *Translated! Papers on Literary Translation and Translation Studies,* (ed. by Raymond van den Broek). Amsterdam: Rodopi.

Hörmann, Hans. 1983. „Über einige Aspekte des Begriffs ‚Verstehen'." In *Kognition und Handeln,* L. Montada & K. Reusser & G. Steiner (eds.), 13-22. Stuttgart: Klett,

House, Juliane. 1997. *Translation Quality Assessment. A model revisited.* Tübingen: Narr.

Hu, Genshen. 2004. *An Approach to Translation as Adaptation and Selection.* Macao: Univ.

Humboldt, Wilhelm v. 1836/1971. *Linguistic Variability and Intellectual Development* (transl. by George C. Buck and Frithjof A. Raven, edition 1971). Coral Cables: University of Miami Press.

Husserl, Edmund. 1950. *Phänomenologie der Lebenswelt. Ausgewählte Texte I.* (Introduction and edition 1986 by K. Held). Stuttgart: Reclam.

Inghilleri, M. 2003. "Habitus, field and discourse. Interpreting as a socially situated activity." *Target* 15/2: 243-268.

Iser, Wolfgang. 1978. *The Act of Reading. A Theory of Aesthetic Response.* Baltimore/London: John Hopkins University Press. [Translation of "Der Akt des Lesens. Theorie ästhetischer Wirkung". Munich: Wilhelm Fink, 1976.]

Jääskeläinen, Riitta. 1996. "Hard work will bear beautiful fruit. A comparison of two think-aloud protocol studies". *META* XLI (1), 60-74.

Jakobson, Roman. 1959. "On Linguistic Aspects of Translation." In *On Translation*, R. A. Brower (ed.), 232-239. Cambridge, MA: Harvard University Press. [Reprint in: *The Translation Studies Reader,* L. Venuti (ed.), 113-118. London/New York: Routledge 2000].

Jakobson, Roman. 1981. "Linguistische Aspekte der Übersetzung." [Translation of "On Linguistic Aspects of Translation" (1959) by K.H. Freigang]. In *Übersetzungswissenschaft*, W. Wilss (ed.), 189-198. Darmstadt: Wissenschaftliche Buchgesellschaft.

Jamieson, John. 1993. "The 'Spoonful of Sugar' Principle in the translation into English of Sci-tech and Press Material". In *Current Trends and Developments in the field of translation: Towards the Global Sharing of Information and Technology. Proceedings of the In-*

*ternational Conference on Translation*, p. 135-142. Kuala Lumpur: Persekutan Penterjemah Malaysia dan Dewan Dahasa dan Pustaka.

Jeanrond, Werner G. 2009. „Textverstehen in der christlichen Tradition". In *Sprache und Religion,* Uwe Gerber & R. Hoberg (eds.), 83-101. Darmstadt: Wiss. Buchgesellschaft.

Johnson, Mark. 1987. *The Body in the Mind. The Bodily Basis of Meaning, Imagination and Reason.* Chicago: University Press.

Kade, Otto. 1968. "Kommunikationswissenschaftliche Probleme der Translation." In *Übersetzungswissenschaft,* W. Wilss (ed. 1981), 199-219. Darmstadt: Wissenschaftliche Buchgesellschaft.

Kaindl, Klaus. 1999. „Interdisziplinarität in der Translationswissenschaft. Theoretische und methodische Implikationen." In *Modelle der Translation. Grundlagen für Methodik, Bewertung, Computermodellierung,* Gil, A. & Haller, J. & Steiner, E., &. Gerzymisch-Arbogast, H. (eds.), 137-155. Frankfurt am Main etc.: Lang.

Kalverkämper, Hartwig. 1983. "Textuelle Fachsprachen-Linguistik als Aufgabe." In *Fachsprache und Literatur,* B. Schlieben-Lange & H. Kreuzer (eds.), 124-166. Göttingen: Vandenhoeck-Ruprecht.

Kalverkämper, Hartwig. 1988. „Fachexterne Kommunikation als Maßstab einer Fachsprachen-Hermeneutik: Verständlichkeit kernphysikalischer Fakten in spanischen Zeitungstexten." In *Fachsprachen in der Romania*, H. Kalverkämper (ed.), 151-193. Tübingen: Narr.

Kalverkämper, Hartwig. 1990. „Gemeinsprache und Fachsprachen – Plädoyer für eine integrierende Sichtweise." In *Deutsche Gegenwartssprache: Tendenzen und Perspektiven*, G. Stickel (ed.), 88-133. Berlin/New York: de Gruyter.

Kalverkämper, Hartwig. 1998. „Rahmenbedingungen für die Fachkommunikation." In *HSK - Languages for Special Purposes,* Vol. I, L. Hoffmann & H. Kalverkämper & H. E. Wiegand (eds.), 24-47. Berlin/New York: de Gruyter.

Kenny, Dorothy. 2009. "Corpora." In *Routledge Encyclopedia of Translation Studies,* Mona Baker & Gabriela Saldanha (eds.), 59–62. London & New York: Routledge.

Kintsch, Walter. 1998. *Comprehension: a paradigm for cognition.* Cambridge, MS: Univ. Press.

Kjaer, Anne Luise. 1999. "Überlegungen zum Verhältnis von Sprache und Recht bei der Übersetzung von Rechtstexten der europäischen Union." In *Übersetzen von Rechtstexten: Fachkommunikation im Spannungsfeld zwischen Rechtsordnung und Sprache*, P. Sandrini (ed.), 63-79. Tübingen: Narr.

Klaudy, Kinga. 2009. "Explicitation." In *Routledge Encyclopedia of Translation Studies,* M. Baker & G. Saldanha (eds.), 104–108. London & New York: Routledge.

Kleiber, Georges. 1993. *Prototypensemantik. Eine Einführung* (translated from the French by Michael Schreiber). Tübingen: Narr.

Koller, Werner. 1992. *Einführung in die Übersetzungswissenschaft.* (4$^{th}$ revised ed.). Heidelberg/Wiesbaden: Quelle & Meyer.

Kramsch, Claire. 2008. „Keynote: Language and culture." In *AILA 15$^{th}$ Wold Congress of Applied Linguistics: Multilingualism, challenges and opportunities.* August 24-29, 2008 in Essen. Book of Abstracts, p. 54. Duisburg: Universitätsverlag Rhein-Ruhr OHG.

Kupsch-Losereit, Sigrid. 2008. *Vom Ausgangstext zum Zieltext*, Berlin: Saxa.

Kußmaul, Paul. 1995. *Training the translator.* Amsterdam/Philadelphia: John Benjamins.

Kußmaul, Paul. 1997. "Comprehension processes and translation. A think-aloud protocol (TAP) study." In *Translation as Intercultural Communication. Selected papers from the EST Congress - Prague 1995*, M. Snell-Hornby & Z. Jettmarovà & K. Kaindl (eds.), 239-248. Amsterdam/Philadelphia: John Benjamins.

Kußmaul, Paul. 2000. *Kreatives Übersetzen.* Tübingen: Stauffenburg.

Kußmaul, Paul. 2000a. "Types of creative translating." In *Translation in Context. Selected Contributions from the EST Congress, Granada 1998,* A. Chesterman & N. Gallardo & Y. Gambier (eds.), 117-126. Amsterdam/Philadelphia: John Benjamins.

Kußmaul, Paul. 2007. *Verstehen und Übersetzen. Ein Lehr- und Arbeitsbuch.* Tübingen: Narr.

Ladmiral, Jean-René. 1993. « Sourciers et ciblistes ». In *Traducere Navem.* Festschrift für Katharina Reiß, J. Holz-Mänttäri & C. Nord (eds.), 287-300. Tampere: Tampereen Yliopisto.

Ladmiral, Jean-René. 1995. « Traduire, c'est à dire... Phénoménologies d'un concept pluriel ». *META*, XL. 3: 409-420.

Ladmiral, Jean-René. 2002. « La traduction - un concept aporétique ? » In: *identité, altérité, equivalence ? la traduction comme relation,* F. Israel (ed.), 117-140. Paris/Caen: lettres modernes minard.

Lakoff, George. 1987. *Women, Fire, and Dangerous Things: What Categories Reveal about the Mind.* Chicago, IL: University Press.

Lakoff, George 1990. "The Invariance Hypothesis: Is abstract reason based on image-schemas?" *Cognitive Linguistics* 1-1: 39-74.

Lakoff, George and Johnson, Mark. 1980. *Metaphors We Live By.* Chicago, IL: University Press.

Langacker, Ronald W. 1987. *Foundations of Cognitive Grammar.* Vol I. Stanford: Stanford University Press.

Laviosa, Sara. 2009. "Universals." In *Routledge Encyclopedia of Translation Studies*, M. Baker & G. Saldanha (eds.), 306–310. London & New York: Routledge.

Lee, John A. L. 2003. *A History of New Testament Lexicography*. New York etc.: Peter Lang.

Lefevere, André. 1977. *translating literature. The german tradition. From luther to rosenzweig*. Assen/Amsterdam: Van Gorcum.

Lefevere, André. 1992. *Translation, Rewriting and the Manipulation of Literary Fame*. London/New York: Routledge.

Levý, Jirí. 1969. *Die literarische Übersetzung. Theorie einer Kunstgattung*. Frankfurt am Main: Athenäum.

Lewandowska-Tomasczyk, Barbara. 2004. "Bilingual Competence and Translation in a Cognitive Framework". In: *Translationskompetenz*. E. Fleischmann et al. (eds.), 125-147. Tübingen, Stauffenburg.

Loffredo, Eugenia and Perteghella, Manuela (eds.). 2006. *Translation and Creativity. Perspectives on Creative Writing and Translation Studies*. London/New York: Continuum.

Luther, Martin. 1530. „Sendbrief vom Dolmetschen". Reprint in *Das Problem des Übersetzens* [2nd revised and modified ed.], H.J. Störig (ed. 1973), 14-32. Darmstadt: Wissenschaftliche Buchgesellschaft.

Malblanc, Alfred. 1968. *Stylistique comparée du français et de l'allemand. Essai de représentation linguistique comparée et étude de traduction*. Paris: Didier.

Malmkjær, Kirsten (ed.). 1998. *Translation and Language Teaching*. Manchester: St. Jerome.

Markman, Arthur. 1999. *Knowledge representation*. Hillsdale, NJ: Erlbaum.

McDowell, John. 1994. *Mind and World*. London/Cambridge, MA: Univ. Press.

Mossop, Brian. 1987. "Who is Addressing Us When We Read a Translation?" *TEXTconTEXT* 2/1: 1-22.

Mossop, Brian. 1998. "What Is a Translating Translator Doing?" *Target* 10 (2): 231-266.

Mounin, Georges. 1955. *Les belles infidèles*. Paris: Cahiers du Sud.

Mudersbach, Klaus and Gerzymisch-Arbogast, Heidrun. 1989. "Isotopy and Translation". In *Translator Training and Foreign Language pedagogy*, P.W. Krawutschke (ed.), 147-170. New York: SUNY.

Neubert, Albrecht. 1997. "Postulates for a Theory of Translation". In: *Cognitive Processes in Translating and Interpreting*, J. H. Danks et al. (eds.), 1-24. Thousand Oaks, C: Sage.

Neubert, Albrecht. 2000. "Competence in language, languages, and in translation". In *Developing Translation Competence,* C. Schaeffner & B. Adab (eds.), 3-18. Amsterdam/Philadelphia: John Benjamins.

Neumann, Stella and Hansen-Schirra, Silvia. 2008. "Learning from translators: A corpus-based examination of translation procedures." In *AILA 15th World Congress of Applied Linguistics: Multilingualism, challenges and opportunities.* August 24-29, 2008 in Essen. Book of Abstracts, p. 135. Duisburg: Universitätsverlag Rhein-Ruhr OHG.

Newmark, Peter. 1973. „Twenty-three Restricted Rules of Translation." *The Incorporated Linguist,* vol. 12, 1/1972: 12-19.

Newmark, Peter. 1979. „Sixty further Propositions on Translation (Part 2)." *The Incorporated Linguist,* vol. 18, 2/1979: 42-47.

Newmark, Peter. 1980. „Teaching specialized translation." In Angewandte Übersetzungswissenschaft, S.-O. Poulsen & W. Wilss (eds.), 127. Aarhus: Univ. Press.

Newmark, Peter. 1999. "Translating the allegorical dimension of literature." *Lebende Sprachen* 1/1999, 24-26

Nida, Eugene A. 1945. "Linguistics and ethnology in translation problems." In *Exploring semantic structures,* E.A. Nida (ed. 1974), 66-78. München: Fink.

Nida, Eugene A. 1964. *Toward a Science of Translating. With Special Reference to Principles and Procedures Involved in Bible Translating.* Leiden: E. J. Brill.

Nida, Eugene A. 1974. "Translation". In *Current Trends in Linguistics, Vol 12: Linguistics and Adjacent Arts and Sciences,* T.A. Sebeok (ed.), 1045-1068. The Hague/Paris: Mouton.

Nida, Eugene A. 1985. "Translation Means Translating Meaning – A Sociosemiotic Approach to Translation." In *X. Weltkongress der FIT.* H. Bühler (ed.), 119-125. Vienna: University Press.

Nida, Eugene A. and Louw, Johannes P. (eds.). 1989. *Greek-English Lexicon of the New Testament: based on Semantic domains.* New York: United Bible Societies.

Nida, Eugene A. and Taber, Charles R. 1974. *The Theory and Practice of Translation.* Published for the United Bible Societies. (2nd ed.). Leiden: E. J. Brill.

Nielsen, J. N. 1994. "Professions, Specific Purpose Languages, and Professional Texts. Elements of the Professional Translator's Knowledge." In *OFT Symposium Copenhagen Business School 11-12 April 1994, Translating LSP Texts. Conference Papers,* H. Bergenholtz et al. (eds.), 15-39. Copenhagen: CBS,

Nisbett, R. et al. (1977): "Telling More than we can Know: Verbal Reports on Mental Processes," in: *Psychological Review* 84.3: 231-259.

Nord, Christiane. 1991. *Text Analysis in Translation. Theory, Methodology, and Didactic Application of a Model for Translation-Oriented Text Analysis.* (translated by C. Nord and P. Sparrow). Amsterdam/Atlanta, GA: Rodopi.

Nord, Christiane. 1991a. "Scopos, Loyalty, and Translational Conventions." *Target* 3 /1991, No. 1: 91-109.

Nord, Christiane. 1997. *Translating as a Purposeful Activity. Functionalist Approaches Explained.* Manchester: St. Jerome.

Nord, Christiane. 2004. "Loyalität als ethisches Verhalten im Translationsprozess". In *Und sie bewegt sich doch... Translationswissenschaft in Ost und West* (Festschrift für Heidemarie Salevsky zum 60. Geburtstag), Ina Müller (ed.), 235-245. Frankfurt am Main: Peter Lang.

Oittinen, Riitta (ed.). 2003. *Traduction pour les enfants - Translation for children.* [META, vol. 48, No. 1-2, mai 2003]. Montréal: Presses de l'Université.

Paepcke, Fritz. 1986. *Im Übersetzen leben. Übersetzen und Textvergleich.* (Ed. by Klaus Berger and Hans-Michael Speier.) Tübingen: Narr.

Piaget, Jean. 1947. *La psychologie de l'intelligence.* Paris: Colin.

Pokorn, Nike K. 2007. "In Defense of Fuzziness". *Target* 19:2/2007, 327-336.

Pommer, Sieglinde. 2006. *Rechtsübersetzung und Rechtsvergleichung - Translatologische Fragen zur Interdisziplinarität.* Frankfurt/Main: Lang.

Preiser, Siegfried. 1976. *Kreativitätsforschung.* Darmstadt: Wissenschaftliche Buchgesellschaft.

Presas, Marisa. 2004. "Translatorische Kompetenz als Expertenwissen: eine Annäherung aus kognitiv-psychologischer Sicht." In *Translationskompetenz*, E. Fleischmann et al. (eds.), 199-207. Tübingen: Stauffenburg.

Prunč, Erich. 2007. *Entwicklungslinien der Translationswissenschaft. Von den Asymmetrien der Sprachen zu den Asymmetrien der Macht.* Berlin: Frank &Timme.

Putnam, Hilary. 1975. "The Meaning of 'Meaning'." In *Language, Mind and Knowledge.* Minnesota Studies in the Philosophy of Science, vol. 7, K. Gunderson (ed.), 131-193. Minneapolis: University of Minnesota Press. [Reprint in *Mind, Language and Reality* (1975), 215-271.]

Quale, Per. 1996. „Bless thee – thou art translated. The originator and the author of the translation." In *XIV World Congress of the Fédération Internationale des Traducteurs (FIT),* Vol. I, AUSIT (ed.), 642-647. Melbourne: AUSIT.

Reiß, Katharina and Vermeer, Hans J. 1984. *Grundlegung einer allgemeinen Translationstheorie.* Tübingen: Niemeyer.

Remael, Aline. 2010. "Audiovisual translation." In *Handbook of Translation Studies*, Y. Gambier & L. van Doorslaer (eds.), 8-18. Amsterdam/Philadelphia: John Benjamins.

Richter, Duncan. 2004. *Historical Dictionary of Wittgenstein's Philosophy.* Lanham, ML/Toronto/Oxford: The Scarecrow Press.

Rickheit, Gert and Strohner, Hans. 1993. *Grundlagen der kognitiven Sprachverarbeitung. Modelle, Methoden, Ergebnisse.* Tübingen/Basel: Francke.

Rickheit, Gert. 1995. "Verstehen und Verständlichkeit von Sprache." In: *Sprache: Verstehen und Verständlichkeit,* B. Spillner (ed.), 15-29. Frankfurt a. M: Lang.

Ricœur, Paul 1969. *Le conflit des interprétations.* Essais d'herméneutique. Paris: Seuil.

Ricœur, Paul. 2004. *Sur la traduction.* Paris: Bayard.

Risku, Hanna. 1998. *Translatorische Kompetenz. Kognitive Grundlagen des Übersetzens als Expertentätigkeit.* Tübingen: Stauffenburg.

Risku, Hanna. 1998a. "32. Kognitionswissenschaft". In *Handbuch Translation,* M. Snell-Hornby et al. (eds.), 119-122. Tübingen: Stauffenburg.

Risku, Hanna. 2000. "Situated Translation and Situated Cognition: ungleiche Schwestern." In *Translationswissenschaft.* Festschrift für Mary Snell-Hornby zum 60. Geburtstag, M. Kadric & K. Kaindl & F. Pöchhacker (eds.), 81-91. Tübingen: Stauffenburg.

Robinson, Douglas. 1991. *The Translator's Turn.* Baltimore/London: John Hopkins.

Robinson, Douglas. 1991a. *Who Translates?: Translator Subjectivities beyond Reason.* New York: State University Press.

Robinson, Douglas. 1998. "Hermeneutic Motion". In *Routledge Encyclopedia of Translation Studies,* M. Baker (ed.), 97-99. London and New York: Routledge.

*Routledge Encyclopedia of Translation Studies,* M. Baker (ed. 1998). London/New York: Routledge.

Rübberdt, Irene and Salevsky, Heidemarie. 1997. „New ideas from historical concepts: Schleiermacher and modern translation theory." In *Translation as Intercultural Communication.* Selected papers from the EST Congress – Prague 1995, M. Snell-Hornby & Z. Jettmarová & K. Kaindl (eds.), 301-312. Amsterdam/Philadelphia: John Benjamins.

Salevsky, Heidemarie. 2000. "Alles fließt... Vasilij Grossman in amerikanischer, west- und ostdeutscher Übersetzung." In: *Paradigmenwechsel in der Translation,* P.A. Schmitt (ed.), 177-203. Tübingen: Stauffenburg.

Santoyo, Julio César. 2004. "Self-Translation: Translational Competence Revisited (and Performance as well)". In *Translationskompetenz.* E. Fleischmann et al. (eds.), 223-235. Tübingen, Stauffenburg.

Šarčević, Susan. 1988. "The challenge of legal lexicography: Implications for bilingual and multilingual dictionaries." In *ZüriLEX '86 Proceedings.* Papers at the Euralex International Congress, M. Snell-Hornby (ed.), 307-314. Tübingen: Narr.

Schank, Roger. 1982. *Dynamic Memory. A theory of reminding and learning in computers and people.* London/New York: Cambridge University Press.

Schleiermacher, Friedrich. 1942. *Dialektik*. (Ed. by Rudolf Odebrecht. 1st ed. 1838) Leipzig: Suhrkamp.

Schleiermacher, Friedrich. 1977. "On the different methods of translating", in *translating literature: the german tradition. from luther to rosenzweig*, A. Lefevere (ed.), 66-89. Assen/Amsterdam: Van gorcum.

Schleiermacher, Friedrich. 1998. *Hermeneutics and Criticism and other Writings*. (German original 1838. Translated and edited by Andrew Bowie.) Cambridge: Univ. Press.

Schmitt, Peter A. 2004. „Ingenieur vs. Übersetzer: Wird Hochtechnologie zu hoch für Übersetzer?" In *Translationskompetenz*, E. Fleischmann et al. (eds.), 539-550. Tübingen: Stauffenburg.

Schopp, Jürgen F. 2005. *„Gut zum Druck"? Typographie und Layout im Übersetzungsprozess*. Tampere: University Press.

Schütz, A. 1970. *On Phenomenology and Social Relations*. (Ed. and with an introduction by H.R. Wagner.) Chicago: University of Chicago Press.

Shing-yue, Sheung. 2002. "Professional, Activist, or 'Example'?" In *Translation: New Ideas for a new Century*. Proceedings of the XVI F.I.T.-Congress, Vancouver, BC, Canada, August 7-10, 2002, 60-63.

Shuttleworth, M. and Cowie, M. 1997. Dictionary of Translation Studies, Manchester: St. Jerome.

Simon, Sherry. 1996. Gender in Translation. Cultural Identity and the Politics of Transmission. London: Routledge.

Sinclair, John. 1991. Corpus, Concordance, Collocation. Oxford: University Press.

Snell-Hornby, Mary. 1988. *Translation Studies - An Integrated Approach*. Amsterdam: John Benjamins

Snell-Hornby, Mary. 2004. "Venutis ‚foreignization': Das Erbe von Friedrich Schleiermacher in der Translationswissenschaft?" In: *Und sie bewegt sich doch... Translationswissenschaft in Ost und West*. Festschrift für Heidemarie Salevsky zum 60. Geburtstag, I. Müller (ed.), 333-344. Frankfurt am Main: Peter Lang.

Sperber, Dan and Wilson, Deirdre. 1986. *Relevance. Communication and Cognition*. Oxford: Blackwell.

Spillner, Bernd. 1990. *Error Analysis. A Comprehensive Bibliography*. Amsterdam/ Philadelphia: John Benjamins.

Stanley, John W. 2005. *Die gebrochene Tradition. Zur Genese der philosophischen Hermeneutik Hans-Georg Gadamers*. Würzburg: Königshausen & Neumann.

Stanley, John W. 2011. "Translational Hermeneutics and the Notion of Language Games – A New Paradigm for Synthesizing the Pragmatic and Cultural Turns in Translation Studies?" In *Translationsforschung. Leipziger Studien zur angewandten Linguistik und Translatologie* (2nd Vol.), Schmitt, P. & Herold, S. & Weilandt, A. (eds.). Frankfurt: Peter Lang.

Stecconi, Ubaldo. 2007. „Five reasons why semiotics is good for Translation Studies". In *Doubts and Directions in Translation Studies,* Y. Gambier, M. Shlesinger & R. Stolze (eds.), 15-26. Amsterdam: John Benjamins.

Stefanink, Bernd. 1997. "'Esprit de finesse' – 'Esprit de géometrie': Das Verhältnis von 'Intuition' und 'übersetzerrelevanter Textanalyse' beim Übersetzen". In *Linguistik und Literaturübersetzen,* R. Keller (ed.), 161-184. Tübingen: Narr.

Stein, Erik W. 1997. "A look at expertise from a social perspective." In *Expertise in Context: Human and Machine,* P.J. Feltovich & K.M. Ford & R.R. Hoffman (eds.), 181-194. Manlo Park, CA: AAAI.

Steiner, Erich. 2004. "Macro- and Micro-level Approaches to Translated Texts – Methodological Contradictions or Mutually Enriching Perspectives? In *Übersetzen, Interkulturelle Kommunikation, Spracherwerb und Sprachvermittlung – das Leben mit mehreren Sprachen.* Festschrift für Juliane House zum 60. Geburtstag. N. Baumgarten et al. (eds.), 15-19. Bochum: AKS-Verlag.

Steiner, George. 1975. *After Babel. Aspects of Language and Translation.* (2nd ed. 1992). Oxford/London: Oxford University Press.

Sternberg, Robert J. (ed.). 1999. *Handbook of Creativity.* Cambridge, MA: University Press.

Stolze, Radegundis and Deppert, Alex. 1998. "Übersetzung und Verständlichkeit deutscher und englischer Wissenschaftstexte." *FACHSPRACHE International Journal of LSP,* 20. Jg., 3-4/1998: 116-130.

Stolze, Radegundis. 1992. *Hermeneutisches Übersetzen. Linguistische Kategorien des Verstehens und Formulierens beim Übersetzen.* Tübingen: Narr.

Stolze, Radegundis. 1993. "Linguistic categories in support of the translator's choice." In XIII FIT World Congress, Translation - the vital link" 6-13 August 1993, Brighton. Proceedings. Volume 1, 649-658. London: Institute of Translation and Interpreting.

Stolze, Radegundis. 1999. *Die Fachübersetzung. Eine Einführung.* Tübingen: Narr.

Stolze, Radegundis. 2002. "Empathy with the message in translation." In *Current Writing. Text and Reception in Southern Africa.* [Volume 14(2) October 2002 "Translation, Diversity and Power"], I. Dimitriu (ed.), 19-31. Durban: Current Writing.

Stolze, Radegundis. 2003. *Hermeneutik und Translation.* Tübingen: Narr.

Stolze, Radegundis. 2003a. "Levels of abstraction in specialist concepts as a translation problem." In *Text, Context, Concepts*, C. Zelinsky-Wibbelt (ed.), 351-365. Berlin: Mouton de Gruyter.

Stolze, Radegundis. 2004. "Creating 'presence' in translation." In *Claims, Changes and Challenges in Translation Studies,* G. Hansen & K. Malmkjaer & D. Gile (eds.), 39-50. Amsterdam/Philadelphia: John Benjamins.

Stolze, Radegundis. 2005. "Transparentes Übersetzen im Bereich des Rechts". In *Kultur, Interpretation, Translation. Ausgewählte Beiträge aus 15 Jahren Forschungsseminar,* H. Salevsky (ed.), 275-290. Frankfurt am Main: Lang.

Stolze, Radegundis. 2008. *Übersetzungstheorien – Eine Einführung.* ($5^{th}$ edition). Tübingen: Narr.

Stolze, Radegundis. 2009. "Worlds of Discourse in Translation Studies." *ACROSS Languages and cultures.* Vol. 10/issue 1, 200: 1-19.

Störig, Hans Joachim (ed.). 1973. Das Problem des Übersetzens. ($2^{nd}$ revised and modified edition.) Darmstadt: Wissenschaftliche Buchgesellschaft.

Strauss, A. L. and Corbin, J. 1998. *Basics of Qualitative Research: Techniques and Procedures for Developing Grounded Theory.* London: Sage.

Strowe, Anna. 2011. "Is Simpatico Possible in Translation? The 1620 Translation of the Decameron and the Case for Similarity." *The Translator*, Vol. 17, No. 1/2011, 51-75.

Talmy, Leonard. 2000. *Toward a Cognitive Semantics*, Volume 1. Cambridge: MIT Press.

Teich, Elke. 2003. *Cross-Linguistic Variation in System and Text. A Methodology for the Investigation of Translations and Comparable Texts.* Berlin: Mouton de Gruyter.

Tirkkonen-Condit, Sonja (1997): "Who Verbalises What: A Linguistic Analysis of TAP Texts." *Target* 9:1, 69-84.

Toury, Gideon. 1995. *Descriptive Translation Studies and Beyond.* Amsterdam/Philadelphia: John Benjamins.

Toury, Gideon. 2004. "Probabilistic explanations in Translation Studies: Universals – or a challenge to the very concept?" In *Claims, Changes and Challenges in Translation Studies,* G. Hansen & K. Malmkjaer & D. Gile (eds.), 15-25. Amsterdam/Philadelphia: John Benjamins.

Trosborg, Anna. 1994. „'Acts' in contracts: Some guidelines for translation." In *Translation Studies an Interdiscipline,* M. Snell-Hornby & F. Pöchhacker & K. Kaindl (eds.), 309-318. Amsterdam/Philadelphia: John Benjamins.

Tymoczko, Maria. 2006. *Enlarging Translation, Empowering Translators.* Manchester: St. Jerome.

Tytler A. F. 1797. *Essay on the principles of translation*. (Reprint ed. J. F. Huntsman 1978.) Amsterdam: John Benjamins.

Ulmann, Gisela. 1968. *Kreativität. Neue amerikanische Ansätze zur Erweiterung des Intelligenzkonzepts*. Weinheim: Beltz.

Ventola, Eija and Mauranen, Anna. 1996. *Academic Writing: Intercultural and Textual Issues* Philadelphia: John Benjamins.

Venuti, Lawrence. 1995. *The Translator's Invisibility. A History of Translation*. London/New York: Routledge.

Venuti, Lawrence. 1998. *The Scandals of Translation – Towards an Ethics of Difference*. London/New York: Routledge.

Vermeer, Hans J. 1978. „Ein Rahmen für eine allgemeine Translationswissenschaft." *Lebende Sprachen* 3/1978, 99-102.

Vermeer, Hans J. 1982. "Translation als ‚Informationsangebot'." *Lebende Sprachen*, 3/1982: 97-101.

Vermeer, Hans J. 1986. „Übersetzen als kultureller Transfer." In *Übersetzungswissenschaft – Eine Neuorientierung*, M. Snell-Hornby (ed.), 30-53. Tübingen: Francke.

Vermeer, Hans J. 1994. „Hermeneutik und Übersetzung(swissenschaft)." *TEXTconTEXT*, 9 (1994), No. 3: 163-182.

Vermeer, Hans J. 1996a. *A Skopos theory of translation. (Some arguments for and against)*. Heidelberg: Textcontext Verlag.

Vermeer, Hans J. 1996b. *Die Welt, in der wir übersetzen. Drei translatologische Überlegungen zu Realität, Vergleich und Prozeß*. Heidelberg: Textcontext Verlag.

Vermeer, Hans J. 2000. "Skopos and Commission in Translational Action." In *The Translation Studies Reader*, L. Venuti (ed.), 221-232. London/New York: Routledge.

Vermeer, Hans J. 2003. "Versuch einer translatologischen Theoriebasis." In *Traducta Navis. Festschrift zum 60. Geburtstag von Christiane Nord*, B. Nord & P.A. Schmitt (eds.), 241-258. Tübingen: Stauffenburg.

Verspoor, Marjolijn et al. 2008. „Symposium: Cognitive linguistics in the second language classroom." In *AILA 15th Wold Congress of Applied Linguistics: Multilingualism, challenges and opportunities. August 24-29, 2008 in Essen. Book of Abstracts*, p. 21. Duisburg: Universitätsverlag Rhein-Ruhr OHG.

Viaggio, Sergio. 2000. "The overall importance of the hermeneutic package in teaching mediated interlingual intercultural communication." *Interpreters' Newsletter* 10, 129-145.

Vinay, Jean-Paul and Darbelnet, Jean. 1958. *Stylistique comparée du français et de l'anglais. Methode de traduction*. (4th ed. 1968.) Paris: Bibliothèque de stylistique comparée.

Vinay, Jean-Paul and Darbelnet, Jean. 1995. *Comparative Stylistics of French and English: A Methodology for Translation.* (Transl. and ed. by J.C. Sager & M.-J. Hamel). Amsterdam/Philadelphia: John Benjamins.

Weinrich, Harald. 1970. *Linguistik der Lüge.* Heidelberg: Lambert Schneider.

Weinrich, Harald. 1976. *Sprache in Texten.* Stuttgart: Klett.

Wichter, Sigurd. 1994. *Experten- und Laienwortschätze: Umriß einer Lexikologie der Vertikalität.* Tübingen: Niemeyer.

Wierzbicka, Anna. 1996. *Semantics: Primes and Universals.* Oxford: OUP.

Wilhelm, Jane E. 2009. „Pour une herméneutique du traduire." In Übersetzung und Hermeneutik, Traduction et herméneutique, L. Cercel (ed.), 91-115. Bucharest: ZETA Books.

Wilss, Wolfram. 1980. *Semiotik und Übersetzen.* Tübingen: Narr (Kodikas/code suppl. 4).

Wilss, Wolfram. 1982. *The Science of Translation. Problems and Methods.* Tübingen: Narr.

Wilss, Wolfram. 1988. *Kognition und Übersetzen. Zu Theorie und Praxis der menschlichen und der maschinellen Übersetzung.* Tübingen: Niemeyer.

Wilss, Wolfram. 1992. *Übersetzungsfertigkeit. Annäherungen an einen komplexen übersetzungspraktischen Begriff.* Tübingen: Narr.

Wilss, Wolfram. 1996. *Knowledge and Skills in Translator Behaviour.* Amsterdam/Philadelphia: John Benjamins.

Wittgenstein, Ludwig. 1953. *Philosophische Untersuchungen: Kritisch-Genetische Edition.* Frankfurt: Suhrkamp 2001. (*Philosophical Investigations.* Transl. G.E.M. Anscombe, ed. Anscombe and Rush Rhees. Oxford: Blackwell, 1953).

Zelinsky-Wibbelt, Cornelia. 2003. "Integrating translation theory and translation practice." In *Text, Context, Concepts,* C. Zelinsky-Wibbelt (ed.), 199-220. Berlin: de Gruyter.

# 12 Index

## 12.1 Subject index

addressees 23, 71, 72, 87, 95, 96, 122, 150, 168, 173, 175, 179, 218
adequacy 87, 128, 148, 150, 174, 196, 243, 260
alterity 56, 99, 102, 130, 264
analysis 16, 19, 20, 21, 23, 28, 29, 33, 37-41, 46, 49, 53, 55, 56, 60, 61, 64, 66, 69, 76, 78, 79, 81-89, 95, 101, 105, 106, 111, 114, 115, 120, 125, 126, 129, 131, 137, 144, 146, 151, 157, 159, 174, 175, 182, 187, 192, 194, 196, 198, 201-204, 208, 218, 220, 234, 243, 244, 247, 254, 266, 270
appearance 18, 58, 59, 68, 81, 117, 160, 175, 202, 213, 216, 266
approach 10, 11, 16, 25, 30, 31, 32, 33, 34, 39, 47, 52, 55, 64, 65, 69, 75, 76, 77, 78, 80, 81, 82, 83, 85, 88, 89, 91, 95, 96, 99, 100, 102, 105, 110, 112, 116, 120, 126, 131, 141, 144, 150, 159, 174, 177, 180, 181, 182, 187, 189, 192, 194, 196, 200, 207, 243, 244, 247, 254, 265
argumentation 23, 26, 33, 39, 40, 41, 44, 126, 161, 173, 197, 262
aspects 13, 16, 23, 27, 33, 34, 40, 47, 66, 71, 74, 76, 77, 78, 81-83, 85, 88, 97, 100, 115, 116, 123, 125, 126, 135, 137, 138, 148, 149, 150, 154, 161, 162, 172, 174,- 176, 178-183, 187, 189, 190, 192, 194, 198, 213, 219, 237, 260, 262
assignment 9, 10, 18, 30, 58, 149, 153, 165, 176, 184, 189, 200, 201
assumption 15, 27, 42, 50, 64, 91, 131, 136
audience 23, 39, 44, 50, 51, 69, 71, 73, 87, 94, 97, 126, 136, 149, 168, 172, 181, 182, 197, 216, 225, 253, 257
authenticity 132, 159, 167, 171, 179, 237
author 9, 10, 15, 17, 18, 20, 24, 34, 41, 43, 47, 48, 51, 52, 55, 62, 63, 67, 74, 75, 76, 79, 94, 96, 98, 101, 103, 106, 107, 111, 113, 114, 117, 125, 127, 128, 129, 130, 131, 132, 136, 140, 142, 151, 158, 164, 168, 172, 173, 180, 183, 196, 197, 223, 233, 234, 236, 247, 248, 253, 259, 264, 265, 266, 272, 282
awareness 15, 38, 40, 48, 60, 63, 68, 77, 78, 81, 82, 112, 116, 147, 151, 155, 161, 170, 178, 181, 192
background 11, 20, 42, 43, 49, 67, 68, 69, 71, 76, 78, 81, 82, 86, 96, 105, 106-120, 125, 127, 146, 148-150, 162, 171, 172, 179, 182, 187, 193, 196, 201, 204, 212, 214, 217, 223, 233, 247, 261, 265, 266
behavior 11, 13, 21, 26, 28, 29, 32, 34, 42, 51, 57, 58, 65, 67, 78, 88, 97, 112, 128, 139, 144, 145
brain 59, 62, 64, 65, 67, 137, 148, 169
cognition 10, 33, 42, 67, 68, 77, 136, 146, 179, 180, 192, 194, 278
cognitive environment 43, 50, 51, 68, 69, 70, 71, 72, 86, 89, 111, 124, 173, 179, 181
cognitive landscape 105, 194, 247
cognitive representation 51, 59, 133, 152, 164, 171
cognitive science 10, 11, 64, 65, 67, 83, 92, 135, 144, 146, 169, 187
cognitively present 30, 32, 74, 180
coherence 11, 23, 89, 120, 143, 150, 156, 157, 158, 159, 160, 172, 174, 179, 182, 202, 205, 207, 215, 216, 226, 236, 252, 253
commission 76, 87, 114, 153, 189, 201, 213
common sense 57, 62
communication 9, 11, 14, 15, 19, 28, 36, 49, 50, 51, 53, 56, 58, 68, 69, 70-72, 75, 81-86, 101, 102, 105, 106, 110-114, 120, 122, 125, 127, 132, 134, 135, 136, 138, 160, 166, 168, 171-173, 181, 185, 188, 194, 195, 200, 201, 204, 217, 218, 219, 220, 221, 227, 237, 288
competence 10, 11, 14, 16, 18, 63, 74, 76, 77, 81, 84, 102, 104, 113, 123, 128, 131, 136, 138, 142, 146, 150, 155, 176, 177, 178, 179, 180, 182, 184, 187, 188, 189, 190, 193, 194, 195, 217, 226

comprehension 30, 45, 48, 50, 51, 52, 64, 69, 75, 83, 84, 85, 95, 99, 100, 115, 131, 136, 137, 153, 173, 175, 253
concept 14, 15, 20, 22, 24, 28, 29, 30, 34, 39, 46, 53, 56, 62, 65, 66, 74, 76, 80, 85, 89, 92, 93, 97, 99, 100, 104, 117, 122, 124, 128-133, 135, 139, 146, 147, 156, 160, 168, 173, 177-179, 186, 193, 194, 195, 220, 223, 253, 279, 287
conscience 28, 59, 64, 184
content 15, 32, 37, 42, 43, 55, 64, 66, 68, 72, 76, 79, 89, 90, 98, 102, 104, 105, 119, 120, 122, 130, 131, 135, 141, 142, 156, 161, 168, 170, 179, 182, 196, 204, 213, 221, 235, 243, 244, 248, 260, 264
context 16, 23, 30, 42, 44, 48, 51, 69, 70, 74, 86, 107, 115, 141, 157, 185, 187, 192, 206, 217, 250, 257
corpus studies 27, 144
creativity 11, 23, 42, 43, 55, 100, 135, 138, 139, 140, 141, 142, 144, 146, 148, 155, 162, 172, 181, 182, 196
critical reflection 9, 33, 164
culture 9, 14, 18, 33, 35, 43, 49, 50, 55, 57, 58, 62, 69, 71-74, 85, 86, 87, 100, 102, 107, 108, 109, 110, 113, 117, 121, 124, 125, 127, 144, 146, 147, 148, 153, 159, 162, 163, 164, 169, 178, 183, 188, 196, 233, 248, 249, 254, 260, 279
decision 9, 10, 29, 32, 33, 42, 72, 74, 88, 89, 145, 149, 150, 151, 152, 153, 154, 167, 169, 170, 171, 179, 180, 182, 183, 184, 194, 197, 202, 235
description 16, 17, 20, 27, 28, 32, 37, 39, 40, 57, 61, 66, 67, 69, 74, 87, 91, 100, 106, 122, 131, 157, 158, 160, 184, 186, 204, 250
descriptive 10, 15, 21, 23, 28, 29, 30, 32, 100, 101, 102, 110, 145, 243
dialogue 50, 54, 56, 57, 89, 105, 185
didactics 28, 65, 168, 174
discourse 9, 11, 35, 36, 39, 40, 49, 50, 58, 84, 86, 95, 113-117, 120, 122, 125, 128, 162, 167, 171, 172, 177, 178, 179, 183, 184, 187, 201, 204, 207, 214, 216, 217, 221, 223, 233, 234, 236, 237, 248, 252, 258, 261, 265, 277
discussion process 44, 50
domain 9, 14, 63, 69, 86, 89, 95, 107, 110, 111, 114, 115, 122, 140, 148, 172, 173, 180, 181, 196, 197, 200, 201, 202, 204, 207
dynamic task 30, 32, 74, 144
editing 74
embodiment 43, 57, 67, 78, 99, 105, 130, 135, 136, 162
encyclopedic knowledge 62, 66, 192
environment 34, 45, 55, 63, 65-67, 69, 73, 76, 111, 135, 169, 174, 178, 243, 254
equivalent 19, 22, 26, 30, 92, 107, 116, 202, 205, 210, 212, 221, 245
evaluation 21, 22, 24, 88, 112, 138, 197, 198, 243, 247
evidence 17, 33, 37, 42, 46, 56, 58, 59, 66, 68, 173, 207, 243, 249
evolution 39, 99, 142
existence 48, 52, 56, 60, 61, 83, 90, 119, 121, 134, 265
expectation 71, 76, 87, 175, 197
experience 10, 27, 28, 42, 45, 54, 55, 56, 60, 63, 65, 66, 67, 73, 75, 76, 86, 100, 104, 118, 120, 138, 140, 143, 147, 148, 163, 169, 189, 190, 192, 195, 237
expert knowledge 13, 77
expertise 11, 14, 75, 98, 146, 193, 285
explicitation 32, 86, 164, 216, 244, 245
expression 47, 54, 57, 71, 98, 109, 124, 131, 134, 137, 138, 145, 173, 175, 250, 262
faithful translation 15, 16, 17, 18, 58, 97, 132, 140, 197
faithfulness 34, 71, 128
feelings 60, 81, 135
fields of attention 10, 11, 179, 195, 250
focusing 10, 24, 83, 96, 120, 125, 127, 137, 145, 148, 150, 187, 199, 202, 249
form 16, 20, 23, 24, 28, 32, 38, 42, 49, 50, 53, 66, 72, 79, 86, 94, 96, 97, 99, 102, 103, 120, 122, 123, 125-127, 130, 131, 136, 154, 160, 161, 165, 169, 196, 198, 214, 234-237, 243, 244, 246, 253, 260
formulation 31, 38, 98, 104, 114, 129, 130, 132, 135, 136, 138, 141, 143, 144, 145, 151, 152, 153, 155, 164, 172, 173, 178, 183, 195, 214, 215, 234, 249, 265
function 11, 22, 49, 59, 87, 88, 93, 97, 98, 118, 121, 122, 127, 135, 148, 171, 172, 173, 174, 179, 181, 183, 196, 198, 201, 202, 205, 212, 213, 214, 215, 216, 217, 221, 223, 226, 237, 253

functional style  114, 166, 173, 175, 182, 183, 205
fusion of horizons  62, 70, 84, 86, 120
fuzziness  41, 42
genre  11, 47, 78, 83, 85, 87, 127, 153, 155, 161, 166, 174, 178, 179, 183, 196, 197, 202, 205, 213, 219, 225, 234, 235, 237, 248, 250, 261
grounded understanding  69, 70, 72, 73, 74, 78, 79, 82, 105, 120, 128, 148, 184, 185, 187, 195, 249, 266
growth  10, 11, 73, 94, 95, 96, 156, 187, 188, 192, 193, 194, 215
habitus  56, 57, 58, 60, 113, 143
helical movement  84, 144, 149, 151, 180, 188, 189, 193
hermeneutical approach  39, 182
hermeneutical circle  60, 61, 64, 66, 68, 69, 76, 81, 83, 90, 107, 110, 149, 178
hermeneutics  9, 32, 33, 40, 43, 45, 46, 47, 48, 49, 52, 53, 54, 56, 64, 65, 66, 67, 70, 83, 84, 134, 144, 156, 168, 177, 187, 188, 193, 194, 243, 267
historical consciousness  67, 136
history  48, 49, 54, 55, 56, 57, 58, 67, 74, 83, 98, 106, 110, 122, 140, 193
holistic  11, 44, 63, 64, 75, 82, 83, 85, 89, 116, 126, 144, 149, 157, 174, 181, 182, 184, 187, 201, 234, 236, 247, 253, 254
human activity  9, 31, 32, 33, 34, 62, 135
human translation  9, 29, 104, 142, 177
hypotheses  14, 15, 18, 27, 39, 47
ideology  19, 70, 90, 98, 113, 114, 117, 127, 183, 248
individual  9, 17, 18, 20, 26, 27-29, 31-35, 40, 43, 46-48, 56, 58-63, 66, 67, 72, 75, 76, 79, 81, 82, 86, 88, 90, 92, 96, 100, 102, 105, 115, 123, 138, 145, 149, 151, 159, 163, 164, 170-173, 175, 181-185, 192, 194, 200, 205, 218, 223, 227, 262
individuality  19, 27, 33, 48, 83, 88, 138, 217
inference  31, 33, 41, 43, 52, 63, 120, 182
information  19, 20, 23, 51, 52, 59, 62, 64, 65, 66, 71, 72, 74, 75, 87, 94, 97, 106, 107, 111, 114, 118, 125, 130, 132, 157, 160, 168, 170, 178, 179, 183, 186, 201, 204, 212, 217, 219, 243, 245, 253, 258, 265, 270
input  16, 27, 38, 51, 52, 54, 55, 59, 63, 65, 73, 120, 175, 187, 267

instruction  27, 105, 107, 126, 154, 168
intelligibility  122, 150, 173, 175
intention  17, 39, 48, 50, 52, 73, 74, 76, 96, 98, 128, 142, 172, 175, 197, 223, 253, 260, 266
intentionality  59
interdisciplinarity  36, 141
interest  11, 14, 16, 23, 32, 39, 49, 55, 64, 65, 66, 67, 68, 76, 80, 87, 96, 97, 103, 104, 106, 109, 124, 132, 141, 172, 181, 189, 192, 194, 195, 196, 237, 245
interlingual transfer  19, 21, 25, 26, 38, 88, 101, 163
interpretation  16, 19, 27, 34, 43, 44, 45, 46, 47, 48, 50, 61, 64, 68, 70, 71, 72, 73, 76, 83, 86, 89-94, 96, 97, 100-102, 110, 121, 122, 127, 138, 139, 142, 146, 160, 164, 184, 216, 223, 235, 245, 246, 248, 265, 266
interpretive understanding  52, 53, 61, 68, 69, 89, 90, 91, 92, 94, 105
interviews  15, 67, 89
intuition  33, 42, 44, 46, 63, 65, 78, 79, 135, 136, 139, 147, 184
isotopy  117, 119, 127, 157, 158, 175, 234
key words  65, 69, 116, 117, 120, 127, 159, 234, 249
knowledge  9-14, 17, 27, 29, 31, 35, 36, 40-49, 56, 57, 61-63, 65-84, 86, 87, 89, 102, 103, 106, 107, 110-114, 116, 120, 122, 123, 132, 136, 137, 139, 140, 145, 148-150, 158, 161, 163, 169, 171-174, 177-187, 189, 192, 193, 194, 196, 197, 198, 200, 207, 220, 233, 237, 247, 257, 259, 266
language philosophy  9, 40, 45, 46, 64, 84, 134
language proficiency  80, 162, 170, 171, 177, 178, 180, 181, 192, 194, 195, 198
language usage  47, 48, 92, 138, 140, 142, 147, 149, 217, 257
lateral thinking  146, 147, 247
learning process  50, 62, 130, 179, 189, 192, 194, 265, 267
life-long learning  11, 14, 189
literature  10, 11, 13, 29, 32, 37, 49, 58, 80, 81, 84, 93, 107, 115, 128, 131, 145, 161, 162, 164, 180-184, 188, 190, 192, 228, 257, 280, 281, 284
LSP  97, 114, 126, 160, 166, 167, 175, 200, 217, 270, 281, 285

meaning 11, 14, 20, 22-24, 35, 41-44, 48, 49, 53, 63-66, 70, 79, 81, 83, 86, 92-100, 106, 107, 110, 112, 115-125, 129, 131, 135, 136, 142, 145, 146, 148, 150, 153, 156-162, 165, 172, 178, 179, 185-187, 194, 198, 199, 201, 202, 204, 212, 214, 215, 219, 220, 223, 226, 234, 243, 249, 251, 261, 265, 266
medial event 54, 64, 88, 188
mediality 53, 54
memory 60, 62, 63, 65, 75, 76, 109, 110, 112, 134, 135, 136, 148, 160, 163, 164, 174, 176, 177, 178, 179, 180, 185, 276
mental activity 21, 74, 112, 188
message 9, 10, 15-17, 23, 30, 32, 34, 38, 47, 48, 50, 51, 65, 67, 70-76, 81, 82, 85, 88, 96, 98, 100, 102, 104, 113, 120, 12-127, 129-133, 136, 139, 140, 142, 145, 149, 150, 153-157, 159, 163, 165, 171, 173, 177, 179-181, 195-197, 199, 202, 215, 216, 219, 234, 237, 252, 264, 286
metacognition 82
metaphor 35, 78, 249
method 10, 33, 37, 49, 79, 85, 103, 121, 145, 186, 192, 200, 203, 208
methodology 9, 18, 23, 28, 32, 36, 38, 47, 58, 78, 79, 81, 85, 143, 152, 157, 174, 184, 186, 192, 195
mind 23, 30, 32, 44, 46, 50, 51, 59, 64, 65, 66, 70, 74, 75, 77, 81, 86, 108, 118, 130, 132, 133, 134, 135, 136, 158, 180, 187, 195, 260
misunderstanding 18, 36, 40, 97, 123, 197, 198
model 20, 22, 23, 26, 29, 34, 37, 44, 57, 63, 74, 83, 85, 87, 88, 105, 115, 120, 122, 141, 145, 155, 177, 179, 187, 188, 189, 193, 194, 195, 200, 203, 205, 206, 217, 253, 254, 264, 276, 277
motivation 15, 17, 28, 32, 33, 39, 47, 48, 56, 67, 102, 138, 153, 177, 189, 190, 193, 194, 246
multiperspectivity 75, 95
openness 54, 55, 64, 70, 84, 102, 132, 266
orientation 10, 11, 22, 30, 40, 45, 74, 77, 82, 84, 88, 96, 105, 137, 144, 179, 181, 187, 189, 195, 200, 207, 226, 247, 254
original 9, 15, 16-18, 22, 24, 25, 27, 34, 43, 46, 47, 49, 51, 55, 69, 71, 73, 74, 75, 76, 87, 95, 96, 99, 102-104, 127-132, 136-138, 140, 141, 144, 153-155, 160,
163, 172, 173, 179, 181, 183, 195, 197, 198, 199, 202, 213, 219, 237, 258, 284
outlook 9, 34, 45, 68, 74, 76, 78, 80, 82, 105, 106, 124, 126, 131, 176
paradigm 9, 13, 19, 21, 26, 27, 30, 32, 39, 40, 45, 85, 88, 101, 114, 121, 194, 198, 267, 278
pattern 26, 28, 31, 86, 116, 144, 178
person 9, 10, 30-33, 35, 39, 45, 51, 62, 65, 67, 68, 74, 75, 77, 91, 101, 106, 108, 109, 113, 115, 122, 124, 126, 134, 135, 177, 183, 184, 187, 189, 194, 198, 205, 235, 251, 267
perspective 19, 27, 31, 32, 33, 36, 37, 38, 47, 56, 58, 59, 64, 69, 74, 75, 79, 82, 89, 95, 96, 106, 111, 115, 116, 118, 125, 127, 146, 156, 160, 162, 165, 188, 193, 195, 198, 200, 225, 244, 247, 249, 250, 285
phenomenology 43, 135, 164
phenomenon 38, 39, 41, 49, 61, 68, 75, 76, 123, 128, 134, 139, 148, 161, 177
polysemy 83, 86, 122, 161, 199
practice 11, 13, 14, 17, 26, 28, 49, 54, 57, 61, 68, 77, 91, 104, 110, 112, 150, 174, 184, 190, 193, 196, 203, 273, 288
pragmatics 57, 87, 95, 105
precision 36, 74, 79, 81, 122, 123, 126, 130, 183, 198, 226, 235, 249
predicative mode 11, 124, 125, 126, 153, 162, 165, 179, 187, 201, 205, 212, 215, 223, 225, 234, 249, 250, 261, 266
prescriptive 10, 14, 18, 25, 26, 27, 28, 32, 40, 74, 88, 145
presence 9, 23, 50, 127, 199, 224, 253, 257, 286
problem-solving 78, 112, 144, 145, 146, 147, 148, 149, 151, 158, 159, 163, 169, 170, 173, 179
procedure 16, 25, 47, 78, 79, 80, 95, 169, 189, 192, 193, 218, 244
process 9, 10, 11, 13, 16, 19, 27, 29, 30, 41, 42, 52, 53, 54, 60, 63, 64, 66, 67, 71, 73, 78, 83, 88, 89, 90, 93, 94, 95, 100, 102, 104, 120, 121, 128, 129, 131, 133, 134, 135, 137, 138, 140, 141, 149, 150, 151, 152, 159, 163, 167, 171, 179, 180, 186, 188, 189,탉192, 194, 196, 197, 203, 217, 262, 266, 274
production 11, 33, 38, 57, 72, 79, 88, 97, 106, 128, 131, 135, 137, 138, 147, 149,

150, 151, 153, 175, 180, 181, 197, 215, 216, 218, 221
profession 13, 187, 188, 217, 237
professionalism 13
proficiency 27, 142, 150, 155, 174, 200
purpose 10, 11, 14, 17, 21, 22, 23, 28, 53, 59, 64, 65, 82, 87, 95, 96, 97, 98, 101, 106, 171, 189, 196, 200, 213, 216, 233, 243, 249
qualities 60
quality assessment 11, 22, 195, 197
quality assurance 181, 190
rationale 33
reader 17, 20, 34, 44, 47, 48, 50, 51, 55, 59, 62, 63, 65, 68, 70, 72, 76, 77, 79, 82, 83, 89, 94, 95, 96, 103, 106, 109, 110, 112, 115, 116, 118, 131, 138, 147, 159, 168, 169, 180, 182, 202, 236, 247, 251, 252, 264, 265
reading 10, 11, 43, 44, 52, 53, 54, 55, 56, 62, 63, 64, 65, 75, 76, 77, 78, 80, 83, 94, 95, 96, 97, 101, 105, 106, 114, 116, 117, 120, 125, 127, 129, 130, 158, 173, 175, 179, 184, 204, 247, 258, 266, 267
reception 49, 55, 87, 88, 97, 115, 128, 137, 164, 235
receptivity 46, 54, 55, 65, 66, 67, 68, 72, 78, 80, 132, 151, 182, 184
recipient 55, 94, 95, 97, 132, 169
recurrence 27, 118
redundancy 115, 127, 157
reference 10, 20, 23, 24, 28, 37, 44, 47, 50, 57, 74, 76, 77, 82, 87, 88, 105, 109, 119, 125, 128, 130, 132, 134, 147, 160, 168, 169, 174, 178, 196-198, 199, 205, 216, 219, 221, 244, 250, 252, 261, 265, 267, 271
reflection 17, 18, 35, 43, 59, 61, 68, 75, 162, 178, 192, 194
relevance 11, 28, 30, 38, 42, 43, 45, 50, 51, 71, 121, 123, 149, 193
research 11, 13, 14, 19, 26, 27, 32, 33, 36, 37, 38, 39, 42, 43, 50, 55, 56, 59, 60, 63, 64, 65, 66, 67, 68, 69, 77, 100, 101, 105, 107, 111, 113, 114, 122, 137, 139, 146, 147, 151, 163, 166, 171, 177, 180, 193, 194, 195, 203, 205, 208, 218, 234, 267
responsibility 9, 15, 31, 34, 42, 58, 74, 76, 131, 143, 144, 146, 173, 180, 184, 187, 197
retranslation 174, 216

scenery 136, 156, 159, 172, 251
science 14, 18, 26, 29, 36, 37, 38, 44, 56, 62, 63, 64, 66, 70, 81, 89, 90, 110, 111, 113, 128, 168, 181, 194, 203, 204, 207, 233
semantic equivalence 107
semantic web 117, 118, 119, 122, 157, 158, 236
semantics 66, 104, 110, 116, 117, 120, 123, 185, 246, 273
sign 23, 68, 86, 92, 118, 156, 192, 244, 253
situation 9, 27, 32, 37, 45, 49, 51, 52, 59, 65, 67, 69, 77, 82, 85, 86, 88, 95, 98, 106, 109, 145, 170, 175, 179, 180, 192, 194, 196, 212, 221, 237, 247
social activity 57, 66, 189
sociolect 169
solution 73, 94, 147, 148, 170, 195, 199, 201, 226, 227, 254
source text 10, 11, 23, 24, 25, 26, 30, 32, 34, 59, 65, 69, 72, 74, 87, 88, 95, 96, 97, 101, 114, 127, 129, 133, 136, 139, 140, 142, 145, 149, 150, 153, 156, 161, 172, 173, 175, 178, 180, 196, 197, 198, 202, 205, 215, 216, 237, 250, 253, 260, 261
specialist terms 14, 69, 124, 161, 183, 216, 220, 223, 226
specialist translation 11, 110, 166, 181
speech acts 50, 126, 173, 183, 212
strategy 10, 29, 30, 50, 64, 65, 78, 80, 95, 101, 106, 145, 148, 149, 151, 158, 159, 181, 187, 192, 196
stylistics 11, 14, 20, 33, 161, 162, 166, 167, 171, 172, 174, 179, 202, 213, 215, 216, 235, 246, 251, 261
subject 15, 17, 18, 29, 31, 38, 46, 47, 49, 52-, 53, 54, 55, 56, 58, 62, 68, 75, 78, 84, 101, 104, 109, 128, 141, 164, 166, 167, 174, 177, 178, 180, 189, 196, 200, 210, 244, 245, 249, 259
subjectivity 33, 34, 35, 39, 41, 42, 47, 52, 56, 59, 60, 72, 84, 85, 89, 101, 105, 112, 138, 139, 141, 142, 186
system 15, 18, 19, 23, 31, 32, 41, 47, 48, 62, 65, 67, 72, 77, 81, 86, 92, 99, 110, 112, 113, 115, 116, 121, 124, 132, 138, 140, 148, 154, 160, 161, 169, 178, 189, 190, 193, 203, 204, 212, 220, 224, 227
target text 10, 17, 19, 24, 30, 32, 87, 88, 96, 111, 132, 133, 136, 137, 141, 142,

150, 156, 157, 171, 205, 235, 236, 237, 253
term 17, 24, 41, 42, 44, 55, 65, 86, 90, 92, 108, 109, 111, 121, 131, 134, 156, 159, 163, 169, 186, 201, 205, 207, 212, 216, 220, 248, 259
terminology 11, 36, 41, 42, 44, 116, 121, 122, 123, 124, 160, 180, 182, 183, 186, 197, 202, 204, 205, 208, 212, 217, 219, 226, 259
theory 9, 11, 13, 14, 16, 17, 19, 25, 26, 31, 34, 35, 38, 39, 41, 43, 46, 49, 50, 66, 71, 72, 81, 83, 87, 95, 98, 99, 102, 104, 109, 115, 121, 123, 131, 132, 134, 136, 137, 138, 147, 159, 169, 171, 194, 196, 200, 217, 218, 283, 284, 287, 288
thinking 15, 18, 25, 29, 43, 44, 46, 48, 64, 66, 67, 96, 109, 112, 114, 120, 134, 135, 139, 140, 141, 146, 151, 160, 163, 172, 181, 220, 221, 227, 228
thought 26, 31, 32, 35, 40, 41, 42, 53, 61, 64, 74, 94, 105, 115, 128, 134, 137, 143, 147, 151, 186, 228, 237, 252, 262
tradition 24, 39, 46, 49, 54, 55, 56, 57, 60, 62, 66, 67, 100, 111, 143, 186, 212, 223, 262, 280, 284
transfer 11, 16, 18, 19, 20, 21, 27, 29, 30, 33, 51, 53, 80, 84, 85, 87, 98, 102, 112, 113, 116, 124, 132, 139, 145, 146, 149, 153, 156, 173, 177, 178, 193, 198, 227, 250, 270
translating 9, 10, 15, 16, 21, 22, 23, 27, 28, 29, 30, 40, 46, 47, 50, 53, 57, 58, 67, 71-76, 84, 85, 87, 88, 90, 99, 102, 103, 111, 113, 120, 123, 129, 134, 135, 139, 144, 152, 155, 163, 171, 176, 183, 184, 187, 190, 193, 196, 200, 233, 244, 249, 259, 264, 279, 280, 284
translation activity 9, 21, 29
translation equivalence 19, 197, 246
translation problem 44, 76, 143, 161, 170, 217, 219, 220, 221, 286
translation studies 36, 75, 85, 99
translation teaching 10, 23, 87, 115, 145, 194

translation universal 146, 164
translational activity 28, 151
translational strategies 67, 171
translational writing 11, 143, 144, 153
translator 9, 10, 11, 15-20, 23, 26, 28-30, 32-35, 40, 45, 47, 48, 51, 52, 55, 56-60, 68-82, 85, 86, 88, 90, 91, 92, 94-111, 114-116, 120, 121, 124-126, 128-137, 139-149, 151-155, 158-167, 169-171, 173, 175, 177-182, 184-187, 188, 258
truth 22, 35, 41, 46, 48, 50, 51, 55, 56, 61, 62, 64, 68, 70, 76, 81, 95, 96, 130, 134, 136, 142, 144, 151, 163, 182, 228, 234, 235, 236
TS 10, 15, 20, 21, 25, 29, 32, 36, 37, 38, 39, 42, 43, 47, 82, 85, 89, 105, 132, 145, 188, 192, 193, 194
understanding 11, 16-18, 30, 32, 34-37, 40, 42-53, 55, 56, 59, 60- 75, 77, 78, 79, 81-84, 86, 88-92, 94, 96, 98-101, 103, 107, 109-111, 114, 116, 119-127, 130, 132, 134, 137, 139, 140, 141-145, 146, 149, 151, 161, 164, 179, 181, 182, 186, 188, 189, 192, 198, 199, 201, 205, 213, 214, 236, 249, 250, 262, 265, 266
utterance 27, 50, 51, 81, 134, 135, 138, 185
version 24, 129, 130, 140, 141, 144, 150, 152, 153, 156, 166, 175, 197, 199, 200, 205, 207, 208, 213, 215, 258, 265, 267
word 14, 17, 22, 42, 49, 51, 54, 60, 81, 83, 92, 93, 99, 107, 108, 109, 117-121, 123, 134, 136, 143, 147, 156-158, 160, 161, 167, 170, 171, 175, 181-188, 198, 199, 202, 204, 205, 212, 215, 221, 226, 234, 236, 249, 251, 252, 266
world view 33, 35, 55, 58, 59, 125, 127, 172, 250, 258
writing 17, 18, 30, 31, 36, 37, 44, 51, 60, 86, 90, 105, 130, 131, 134, 135, 137, 138, 144, 149-155, 161, 163, 166, 167, 172, 175, 179, 180, 192, 195, 199, 204, 205, 262, 276
written texts 47, 50, 51, 53, 63, 75, 120

## 12.2 Author index

Aitchison 147, 151, 269
Albrecht 98, 269, 272, 281
Alves 72, 190, 193, 269
Anderson 137, 180, 269
Antos 137, 138, 140, 150, 172, 269
Apel 49, 269
Arntz 122, 269, 270, 274
Arrojo 32, 43, 99, 101, 269, 272
Bălăcescu 47, 68, 119, 120, 139, 141, 147, 148, 149, 159, 162, 163, 269, 270
Bassnett 30, 74, 101, 102, 270
Baumann 114, 160, 167, 270
Begriff 104, 220
Beiner 38, 39, 49, 50, 122, 270
Benjamin 24, 133, 270
Berger 95, 121, 271, 282
Boden 137, 271
Bourdieu 57, 271
Brenner 16, 45, 100, 271
Brodbeck 55, 151, 271
Bubner 31, 271
Catford 19, 271
Cercel 47, 272, 288
Chesterman 18, 26, 27, 32, 43, 76, 135, 150, 161, 272, 279
Collini 31, 272
Coseriu 82, 272
Darbelnet 20, 156, 198, 288
Eberhard 53, 54, 70, 134, 188, 273
Eco 11, 50, 72, 89, 92, 102, 109, 112, 163, 181, 197, 267, 272, 273
Ericsson 193, 273
Fillmore 51, 109, 134, 138, 159, 273
Fleischmann 110, 273, 275, 276, 280, 282, 284
Forstner 140, 141, 273
Frank 120, 129, 274, 275, 282
Gadamer 47, 49, 51, 53, 54, 55, 56, 60, 61, 62, 70, 76, 78, 86, 89, 90, 91, 94, 120, 129, 132, 134, 136, 137, 188, 194, 273, 274
Gerzymisch-Arbogast 157, 158, 220, 274, 276, 278, 280
Gile 27, 34, 36, 38, 272, 274, 276, 286, 287
Gonçalves 72, 190, 193, 269
Göpferich 67, 126, 166, 275
Gouanvic 58, 275
Grondin 45, 134, 188, 275

Guilford 139, 145, 146, 163, 275
Gutt 51, 69, 71, 72, 89, 148, 149, 275
Hansen 15, 36, 60, 66, 105, 156, 272, 274, 276, 281, 286, 287
Heidegger 47, 49, 52, 53, 55, 61, 64, 70, 89, 90, 91, 93, 94, 98, 129, 134, 273, 276
Heltai 167, 276
Hermans 101, 276
Holmes 33, 277
Hönig 29, 106, 111, 187, 277
House 22, 23, 33, 71, 85, 126, 169, 277, 285
Husserl 35, 58, 59, 68, 146, 276, 277
Jakobson 30, 74, 92, 93, 143, 277
Johnson 35, 55, 148, 278, 280
Kalverkämper 14, 36, 111, 115, 168, 204, 270, 275, 278
Kintsch 62, 278
Koller 20, 29, 132, 150, 156, 198, 279
Kußmaul 23, 47, 85, 88, 106, 115, 120, 136, 139, 141, 158, 159, 187, 277, 279
Ladmiral 24, 25, 29, 279
Lakoff 35, 59, 63, 120, 148, 157, 279, 280
Langacker 146, 280
Lefevere 17, 24, 101, 102, 103, 104, 133, 270, 280, 284
Levý 30, 76, 280
Neubert 18, 140, 177, 178, 179, 281
Newmark 25, 26, 28, 162, 281
Nida 21, 22, 23, 34, 102, 107, 108, 109, 110, 121, 140, 143, 186, 198, 281
Nord 23, 76, 82, 85, 87, 88, 94, 95, 97, 98, 105, 106, 121, 132, 137, 155, 173, 189, 194, 196, 222, 259, 271, 277, 279, 282, 288
Paepcke 33, 42, 47, 63, 76, 78, 82, 83, 99, 101, 133, 135, 137, 178, 271, 282
Prunč 57, 99, 155, 188, 282
Reiß 23, 26, 87, 94, 171, 283
Rickheit 65, 137, 283
Ricœur 49, 50, 55, 61, 62, 95, 133, 283
Risku 40, 44, 77, 92, 98, 151, 283
Robinson 45, 90, 99, 100, 135, 276, 283
Schank 65, 122, 147, 158, 284
Schleiermacher 45, 46, 47, 48, 54, 55, 59, 69, 75, 78, 79, 80, 81, 82, 83, 85, 94, 103, 104, 117, 125, 129, 283, 284

Snell-Hornby 19, 104, 118, 130, 161, 270, 271, 274, 277, 279, 283, 284, 287
Sperber 285
Sprache 101
Stanley 40, 46, 58, 96, 120, 134, 273, 285
Stecconi 29, 137, 285
Stefanink 47, 68, 88, 120, 136, 139, 141, 147, 148, 149, 159, 162, 163, 269, 270, 285
Steiner 27, 60, 73, 95, 99, 100, 131, 132, 133, 277, 278, 285
Stolze 1, 16, 30, 36, 38, 40, 45, 47, 74, 76, 97, 114, 121, 123, 124, 130, 131, 134, 135, 136, 155, 160, 163, 168, 173, 182, 184, 205, 206, 212, 217, 224, 231, 254, 262, 267, 269, 274, 285, 286
Toury 21, 26, 29, 37, 62, 188, 286, 287
Tymoczko 101, 102, 287
Venuti 19, 101, 102, 103, 104, 131, 247, 254, 277, 287
Vermeer 23, 26, 35, 78, 79, 87, 89, 94, 110, 113, 132, 171, 283, 287, 288
Vinay 20, 156, 198, 288
Weinrich 288
Wierzbicka 117, 288
Wilson 285
Wilss 15, 16, 19, 20, 25, 27, 29, 30, 33, 34, 42, 80, 85, 94, 100, 106, 126, 132, 139, 140, 145, 146, 147, 169, 170, 171, 172, 277, 278, 281, 288
Wittgenstein 28, 49, 120, 185, 195, 283, 288

# TRANSÜD. Arbeiten zur Theorie und Praxis des Übersetzens und Dolmetschens

Die Bände 1 bis 5 sind bei der Peter Lang GmbH erschienen und dort zu beziehen.

Bd. 6  Przemysław Chojnowski: Zur Strategie und Poetik des Übersetzens. Eine Untersuchung der Anthologien zur polnischen Lyrik von Karl Dedecius. 300 Seiten. ISBN 978-3-86596-013-9

Bd. 7  Belén Santana López: Wie wird *das Komische* übersetzt? *Das Komische* als Kulturspezifikum bei der Übersetzung spanischer Gegenwartsliteratur. 456 Seiten. ISBN 978-3-86596-006-1

Bd. 8  Larisa Schippel (Hg.): Übersetzungsqualität: Kritik – Kriterien – Bewertungshandeln. 194 Seiten. ISBN 978-3-86596-075-7

Bd. 9  Anne-Kathrin D. Ende: Dolmetschen im Kommunikationsmarkt. Gezeigt am Beispiel Sachsen. 228 Seiten. ISBN 978-3-86596-073-3

Bd. 10  Sigrun Döring: Kulturspezifika im Film: Probleme ihrer Translation. 156 Seiten. ISBN 978-3-86596-100-6

Bd. 11  Hartwig Kalverkämper: „Textqualität". Die Evaluation von Kommunikationsprozessen seit der antiken Rhetorik bis zur Translationswissenschaft. ISBN 978-3-86596-110-5

Bd. 12  Yvonne Griesel: Die Inszenierung als Translat. Möglichkeiten und Grenzen der Theaterübertitelung. 362 Seiten. ISBN 978-3-86596-119-8

Bd. 13  Hans J. Vermeer: Ausgewählte Vorträge zur Translation und anderen Themen. Selected Papers on Translation and other Subjects. 286 Seiten. ISBN 978-3-86596-145-7

Bd. 14  Erich Prunč: Entwicklungslinien der Translationswissenschaft. Von den Asymmetrien der Sprachen zu den Asymmetrien der Macht. 442 Seiten. ISBN 978-3-86596-146-4 (vergriffen, siehe Band 43 der Reihe)

Bd. 15  Valentyna Ostapenko: Vernetzung von Fachtextsorten. Textsorten der Normung in der technischen Harmonisierung. 128 Seiten. ISBN 978-3-86596-155-6

Bd. 16  Larisa Schippel (Hg.): TRANSLATIONSKULTUR – ein innovatives und produktives Konzept. 340 Seiten. ISBN 978-3-86596-158-7

Bd. 17  Hartwig Kalverkämper/Larisa Schippel (Hg.): Simultandolmetschen in Erstbewährung: Der Nürnberger Prozess 1945. Mit einer orientierenden Einführung von Klaus Kastner und einer kommentierten fotografischen Dokumentation von Theodoros Radisoglou sowie mit einer dolmetsch-wissenschaftlichen Analyse von Katrin Rumprecht. 344 Seiten. ISBN 978-3-86596-161-7

Frank & Timme

# TRANSÜD. Arbeiten zur Theorie und Praxis des Übersetzens und Dolmetschens

Bd. 18    Regina Bouchehri: Filmtitel im interkulturellen Transfer. 174 Seiten. ISBN 978-3-86596-180-8

Bd. 19    Michael Krenz/Markus Ramlow: Maschinelle Übersetzung und XML im Übersetzungsprozess. Prozesse der Translation und Lokalisierung im Wandel. Zwei Beiträge, hg. von Uta Seewald-Heeg. 368 Seiten. ISBN 978-3-86596-184-6

Bd. 20    Hartwig Kalverkämper/Larisa Schippel (Hg.): Translation zwischen Text und Welt – Translationswissenschaft als historische Disziplin zwischen Moderne und Zukunft. 700 Seiten. ISBN 978-3-86596-202-7

Bd. 21    Nadja Grbić/Sonja Pöllabauer: Kommunaldolmetschen/Community Interpreting. Probleme – Perspektiven – Potenziale. Forschungsbeiträge aus Österreich. 380 Seiten. ISBN 978-3-86596-194-5

Bd. 22    Agnès Welu: Neuübersetzungen ins Französische – eine kulturhistorische Übersetzungskritik. Eichendorffs *Aus dem Leben eines Taugenichts*. 506 Seiten. ISBN 978-3-86596-193-8

Bd. 23    Martin Slawek: Interkulturell kompetente Geschäftskorrespondenz als Garant für den Geschäftserfolg. Linguistische Analysen und fachkommunikative Ratschläge für die Geschäftsbeziehungen nach Lateinamerika (Kolumbien). 206 Seiten. ISBN 978-3-86596-206-5

Bd. 24    Julia Richter: Kohärenz und Übersetzungskritik. Lucian Boias Analyse des rumänischen Geschichtsdiskurses in deutscher Übersetzung. 142 Seiten. ISBN 978-3-86596-221-8

Bd. 25    Anna Kucharska: Simultandolmetschen in defizitären Situationen. Strategien der translatorischen Optimierung. 170 Seiten. ISBN 978-3-86596-244-7

Bd. 26    Katarzyna Lukas: Das Weltbild und die literarische Konvention als Übersetzungsdeterminanten. Adam Mickiewicz in deutschsprachigen Übertragungen. 402 Seiten. ISBN 978-3-86596-238-6

Bd. 27    Markus Ramlow: Die maschinelle Simulierbarkeit des Humanübersetzens. Evaluation von Mensch-Maschine-Interaktion und der Translatqualität der Technik. 364 Seiten. ISBN 978-3-86596-260-7

Bd. 28    Ruth Levin: Der Beitrag des Prager Strukturalismus zur Translationswissenschaft. Linguistik und Semiotik der literarischen Übersetzung. 154 Seiten. ISBN 978-3-86596-262-1

Bd. 29    Iris Holl: Textología contrastiva, derecho comparado y traducción jurídica. Las sentencias de divorcio alemanas y españolas. 526 Seiten. ISBN 978-3-86596-324-6

Frank & Timme

# TRANSÜD. Arbeiten zur Theorie und Praxis des Übersetzens und Dolmetschens

Bd. 30   Christina Korak: Remote Interpreting via Skype. Anwendungsmöglichkeiten von VoIP-Software im Bereich Community Interpreting – Communicate everywhere? 202 Seiten. ISBN 978-3-86596-318-5

Bd. 31   Gemma Andújar/Jenny Brumme (eds.): Construir, deconstruir y reconstruir. Mímesis y traducción de la oralidad y la afectividad. 224 Seiten. ISBN 978-3-86596-234-8

Bd. 32   Christiane Nord: Funktionsgerechtigkeit und Loyalität. Theorie, Methode und Didaktik des funktionalen Übersetzens. 338 Seiten. ISBN 978-3-86596-330-7

Bd. 33   Christiane Nord: Funktionsgerechtigkeit und Loyalität. Die Übersetzung literarischer und religiöser Texte aus funktionaler Sicht. 304 Seiten. ISBN 978-3-86596-331-4

Bd. 34   Małgorzata Stanek: Dolmetschen bei der Polizei. Zur Problematik des Einsatzes unqualifizierter Dolmetscher. 262 Seiten. ISBN 978-3-86596-332-1

Bd. 35   Dorota Karolina Bereza: Die Neuübersetzung. Eine Hinführung zur Dynamik literarischer Translationskultur. 108 Seiten. ISBN 978-3-86596-255-3

Bd. 36   Montserrat Cunillera/Hildegard Resinger (eds.): Implicación emocional y oralidad en la traducción literaria. 230 Seiten. ISBN 978-3-86596-339-0

Bd. 37   Ewa Krauss: Roman Ingardens „Schematisierte Ansichten" und das Problem der Übersetzung. 226 Seiten. ISBN 978-3-86596-315-4

Bd. 38   Miriam Leibbrand: Grundlagen einer hermeneutischen Dolmetschforschung. 324 Seiten. ISBN 978-3-86596-343-7

Bd. 39   Pekka Kujamäki/Leena Kolehmainen/Esa Penttilä/Hannu Kemppanen (eds.): Beyond Borders – Translations Moving Languages, Literatures and Cultures. 272 Seiten. ISBN 978-3-86596-356-7

Bd. 40   Gisela Thome: Übersetzen als interlinguales und interkulturelles Sprachhandeln. Theorien – Methodologie – Ausbildung. 622 Seiten. ISBN 978-3-86596-352-9

Bd. 41   Radegundis Stolze: The Translator's Approach – Introduction to Translational Hermeneutics. Theory and Examples from Practice. 304 Seiten. ISBN 978-3-86596-373-4

Bd. 42   Silvia Roiss/Carlos Fortea Gil/María Ángeles Recio Ariza/Belén Santana López/ Petra Zimmermann González/Iris Holl (eds.): En las vertientes de la traducción e interpretación del/al alemán. 582 Seiten. ISBN 978-3-86596-326-0

F Frank & Timme

# TRANSÜD. Arbeiten zur Theorie und Praxis des Übersetzens und Dolmetschens

Bd. 43   Erich Prunč: Entwicklungslinien der Translationswissenschaft. 3., erweiterte und verbesserte Auflage (1. Aufl. 2007. ISBN 978-3-86596-146-4). 528 Seiten. ISBN 978-3-86596-422-9

Bd. 44   Mehmet Tahir Öncü: Die Rechtsübersetzung im Spannungsfeld von Rechtsvergleich und Rechtssprachvergleich. Zur deutschen und türkischen Strafgesetzgebung. 380 Seiten. ISBN 978-3-86596-424-3

Bd. 45   Hartwig Kalverkämper/Larisa Schippel (Hg.): „Vom Altern der Texte". Bausteine für eine Geschichte des interkulturellen Wissenstransfers. 456 Seiten. ISBN 978-3-86596-251-5

Bd. 46   Hannu Kemppanen/Marja Jänis/Alexandra Belikova (eds.): Domestication and Foreignization in Translation Studies. 240 Seiten. 978-3-86596-470-0

Bd. 47   Sergey Tyulenev: Translation and the Westernization of Eighteenth-Century Russia. A Social-Systemic Perspective. 272 Seiten. ISBN 978-3-86596-472-4

Bd. 48   Martin B. Fischer/Maria Wirf Naro (eds.): Translating Fictional Dialogue for Children and Young People. 422 Seiten. ISBN 978-3-86596-467-0

Bd. 49   Martina Behr: Evaluation und Stimmung. Ein neuer Blick auf Qualität im (Simultan-)Dolmetschen. 356 Seiten. ISBN 978-3-86596-485-4

Bd. 50   Anna Gopenko: Traduire le sublime. Les débats de l'Église orthodoxe russe sur la langue liturgique. 228 Seiten. ISBN 978-3-86596-486-1

Bd. 51   Lavinia Heller: Translationswissenschaftliche Begriffsbildung und das Problem der performativen Unauffälligkeit von Translation. 332 Seiten. ISBN 978-3-86596-470-0

Bd. 52   Claudia Dathe/Renata Makarska/Schamma Schahadat (Hg.): Zwischentexte. Literarisches Übersetzen in Theorie und Praxis. 300 Seiten. ISBN 978-3-86596-442-7

Bd. 53   Regina Bouchehri: Translation von Medien-Titeln. Der interkulturelle Transfer von Titeln in Literatur, Theater, Film und Bildender Kunst. 334 Seiten. ISBN 978-3-86596-400-7

Bd. 54   Nilgin Tanış Polat: Raum im (Hör-)Film. Zur Wahrnehmung und Repräsentation von räumlichen Informationen in deutschen und türkischen Audiodeskriptionstexten. 138 Seiten. ISBN 978-3-86596-508-0

Bd. 55   Eva Parra Membrives/Ángeles García Calderón (eds.): Traducción, mediación, adaptación. Reflexiones en torno al proceso de comunicación entre culturas. 336 Seiten. ISBN 978-3-86596-499-1

Frank & Timme

# TRANSÜD. Arbeiten zur Theorie und Praxis des Übersetzens und Dolmetschens

Bd. 56   Yvonne Sanz López: Videospiele übersetzen – Probleme und Optimierung. 126 Seiten. ISBN 978-3-86596-541-7

Bd. 57   Irina Bondas: Theaterdolmetschen – Phänomen, Funktionen, Perspektiven. 240 Seiten. ISBN 978-3-86596-540-0

Bd. 58   Dinah Krenzler-Behm: Authentische Aufträge in der Übersetzerausbildung. Ein Leitfaden für die Translationsdidaktik. 480 Seiten. ISBN 978-3-86596-498-4

Bd. 59   Anne-Kathrin Ende/Susann Herold/Annette Weilandt (Hg.): Alles hängt mit allem zusammen. Translatologische Interdependenzen. Festschrift für Peter A. Schmitt. 544 Seiten. ISBN 978-3-86596-504-2

Bd. 60   Saskia Weber: Kurz- und Kosenamen in russischen Romanen und ihre deutschen Übersetzungen. 256 Seiten. ISBN 978-3-7329-0002-2

Bd. 61   Silke Jansen/Martina Schrader-Kniffki (eds.): La traducción a través de los tiempos, espacios y disciplinas. 366 Seiten. ISBN 978-3-86596-524-0

Bd. 62   Annika Schmidt-Glenewinkel: Kinder als Dolmetscher in der Arzt-Patienten-Interaktion. 130 Seiten. ISBN 978-3-7329-0010-7

Bd. 63   Klaus-Dieter Baumann/Hartwig Kalverkämper (Hg.): Theorie und Praxis des Dolmetschens und Übersetzens in fachlichen Kontexten. 756 Seiten. ISBN 978-3-7329-0016-9

Bd. 64   Silvia Ruzzenenti: «Präzise, doch ungenau» – Tradurre il saggio. Un approccio olistico al *poetischer Essay* di Durs Grünbein. 406 Seiten. ISBN 978-3-7329-0026-8

Bd. 65   Margarita Zoe Giannoutsou: Kirchendolmetschen – Interpretieren oder Transformieren? 498 Seiten mit CD. ISBN 978-3-7329-0067-1

Bd. 66   Andreas F. Kelletat/Aleksey Tashinskiy (Hg.): Übersetzer als Entdecker. Ihr Leben und Werk als Gegenstand translationswissenschaftlicher und literaturgeschichtlicher Forschung. 376 Seiten. ISBN 978-3-7329-0060-2

Bd. 67   Ulrike Spieler: Übersetzer zwischen Identität, Professionalität und Kulturalität: Heinrich Enrique Beck. 340 Seiten. ISBN 978-3-7329-0107-4

Bd. 68   Carmen Klaus: Translationsqualität und Crowdsourced Translation. Untertitelung und ihre Bewertung – am Beispiel des audiovisuellen Mediums *TEDTalk*. 180 Seiten. ISBN 979-3-7329-0031-1

Bd. 69   Susanne J. Jekat/Heike Elisabeth Jüngst/Klaus Schubert/Claudia Villiger (Hg.): Sprache barrierefrei gestalten. Perspektiven aus der Angewandten Linguistik. 276 Seiten. ISBN 978-3-7329-0023-7

Frank & Timme

# TRANSÜD. Arbeiten zur Theorie und Praxis des Übersetzens und Dolmetschens

Bd. 70   Radegundis Stolze: Hermeneutische Übersetzungskompetenz. Grundlagen und Didaktik. 402 Seiten. ISBN 978-3-7329-0122-7

Bd. 71   María Teresa Sánchez Nieto (ed.): Corpus-based Translation and Interpreting Studies: From description to application / Estudios traductológicos basados en corpus: de la descripción a la aplicación. 268 Seiten. ISBN 978-3-7329-0084-8

Bd. 72   Karin Maksymski/Silke Gutermuth/Silvia Hansen-Schirra (eds.): Translation and Comprehensibility. 296 Seiten. ISBN 978-3-7329-0022-0

Bd. 73   Hildegard Spraul: Landeskunde Russland für Übersetzer. Sprache und Werte im Wandel. Ein Studienbuch. 360 Seiten. ISBN 978-3-7329-0109-8

Bd. 74   Ralph Krüger: The Interface between Scientific and Technical Translation Studies and Cognitive Linguistics. With Particular Emphasis on Explicitation and Implicitation as Indicators of Translational Text-Context Interaction. 482 Seiten. ISBN 978-3-7329-0136-4

Bd. 75   Erin Boggs: Interpreting U.S. Public Diplomacy Speeches. 154 Seiten. ISBN 978-3-7329-0150-0

Bd. 76   Nathalie Mälzer (Hg.): Comics – Übersetzungen und Adaptionen. 404 Seiten. ISBN 978-3-7329-0131-9

Bd. 77   Sophie Beese: Das (zweite) andere Geschlecht – der Diskurs „Frau" im Wandel. Simone de Beauvoirs *Le deuxième sexe* in deutscher Erst- und Neuübersetzung. 264 Seiten. ISBN 978-3-7329-0141-8

Bd. 78   Xenia Wenzel: Die Übersetzbarkeit philosophischer Diskurse. Eine Übersetzungskritik an den beiden englischen Übersetzungen von Heideggers *Sein und Zeit*. 162 Seiten. ISBN 978-3-7329-0199-9

Bd. 79   María-José Varela Salinas/Bernd Meyer (eds.): Translating and Interpreting Healthcare Discourses/Traducir e interpretar en el ámbito sanitario. 266 Seiten. ISBN 978-3-86596-367-3

Bd. 80   Susanne Hagemann: Einführung in das translationswissenschaftliche Arbeiten. Ein Lehr- und Übungsbuch. 360 Seiten. ISBN 978-3-7329-0125-8

Bd. 81   Anja Maibaum: Spielfilm-Synchronisation. Eine translationskritische Analyse am Beispiel amerikanischer Historienfilme über den Zweiten Weltkrieg. 144 Seiten mit CD. ISBN 978-3-7329-0220-0

Bd. 82   Sybille Schellheimer: La función evocadora de la fraseología en la oralidad ficcional y su traducción. 356 Seiten. ISBN 978-3-7329-0232-3

Frank & Timme

## TRANSÜD. Arbeiten zur Theorie und Praxis des Übersetzens und Dolmetschens

Bd. 83   Franziska Heidrich: Kommunikationsoptimierung im Fachübersetzungsprozess. 276 Seiten. ISBN 978-3-7329-0262-0

Bd. 84   Cristina Plaza Lara: Integración de la competencia instrumental-profesional en el aula de traducción. 222 Seiten mit CD. ISBN 978-3-7329-0309-2

Bd. 85   Andreas F. Kelletat/Aleksey Tashinskiy/Julija Boguna (Hg.): Übersetzerforschung. Neue Beiträge zur Literatur- und Kulturgeschichte des Übersetzens. 366 Seiten. ISBN 978-3-7329-0234-7

Bd. 86   Heidrun Witte: Blickwechsel. Interkulturelle Wahrnehmung im translatorischen Handeln. 274 Seiten. ISBN 978-3-7329-0333-7

Bd. 87   Susanne Hagemann/Julia Neu/Stephan Walter (Hg.): Translationslehre und Bologna-Prozess: Unterwegs zwischen Einheit und Vielfalt / Translation/Interpreting Teaching and the Bologna Process: Pathways between Unity and Diversity. 434 Seiten. ISBN 978-3-7329-0311-5

Bd. 88   Ursula Wienen/Laura Sergo/Tinka Reichmann/Ivonne Gutiérrez Aristizábal (Hg.): Translation und Ökonomie. 274 Seiten. ISBN 978-3-7329-0203-3

Bd. 89   Daniela Eichmeyer: Luftqualität in Dolmetschkabinen als Einflussfaktor auf die Dolmetschqualität. Interdisziplinäre Erkenntnisse und translationspraktische Konsequenzen. 144 Seiten. ISBN 978-3-7329-0362-7

Bd. 90   Alexander Künzli: Die Untertitelung – von der Produktion zur Rezeption. 264 Seiten. ISBN 978-3-7329-0393-1

Bd. 91   Christiane Nord: Traducir, una actividad con propósito. Introducción a los enfoques funcionalistas. 228 Seiten. ISBN 978-3-7329-0410-5

Bd. 92   Fabjan Hafner/Wolfgang Pöckl (Hg.): „... übersetzt von Peter Handke" – Philologische und translationswissenschaftliche Analysen. 294 Seiten. ISBN 978-3-7329-0443-3

Bd. 93   Elisabeth Gibbels: Lexikon der deutschen Übersetzerinnen 1200–1850. 216 Seiten. ISBN 978-3-7329-0422-8

Bd. 94   Encarnación Postigo Pinazo: Optimización de las competencias del traductor e intérprete. Nuevas tecnologías – procesos cognitivos – estrategias. 194 Seiten. ISBN 978-3-7329-0392-4

Bd. 95   Marta Estévez Grossi: Lingüística Migratoria e Interpretación en los Servicios Públicos. La comunidad gallega en Alemania. 574 Seiten. ISBN 978-3-7329-0411-2

Frank & Timme

# TRANSÜD. Arbeiten zur Theorie und Praxis des Übersetzens und Dolmetschens

Bd. 96   Ivana Havelka: Videodolmetschen im Gesundheitswesen. Dolmetschwissenschaftliche Untersuchung eines österreichischen Pilotprojektes. 346 Seiten. ISBN 978-3-7329-0490-7

Bd. 97   Maria Mushchinina (Hg.): Formate der Translation. 340 Seiten. ISBN 978-3-7329-0506-5

Bd. 98   Zehra Gülmüş: Übersetzungsverfahren beim literarischen Übersetzen. Ahmet Hamdi Tanpınars Roman „Das Uhrenstellinstitut". 196 Seiten. ISBN 978-3-7329-0498-3

Bd. 99   Peter Sandrini: Translationspolitik für Regional- oder Minderheitensprachen. Unter besonderer Berücksichtigung einer Strategie der Offenheit. 524 Seiten. ISBN 978-3-7329-0513-3

Bd. 100  Aleksey Tashinskiy/Julija Boguna (Hg.): Das WIE des Übersetzens. Beiträge zur historischen Übersetzerforschung. 248 Seiten. ISBN 978-3-7329-0536-2

Bd. 101  Heike Elisabeth Jüngst/Lisa Link/Klaus Schubert/Christiane Zehrer (eds.): Challenging Boundaries. New Approaches to Specialized Communication. 228 Seiten. ISBN 978-3-7329-0524-9

Bd. 102  Chuan Ding: „Peterchens Mondfahrt" in chinesischer Übersetzung. Eine Kritik. 124 Seiten. ISBN 978-3-7329-0528-7

Bd. 103  Changgun Kim: Übersetzen von Videospieltexten. Nekrotexte lesen und übersetzen. 164 Seiten. ISBN 978-3-7329-0379-5

Bd. 104  Guntars Dreijers/Agnese Dubova/Jānis Veckrācis (eds.): Bridging Languages and Cultures. Linguistics, Translation Studies and Intercultural Communication. 338 Seiten. ISBN 978-3-7329-0429-7

Bd. 105  Madeleine Schnierer: Qualitätssicherung. Die Praxis der Übersetzungsrevision im Zusammenhang mit EN 15038 und ISO 17100. 286 Seiten. ISBN 978-3-7329-0539-3

Bd. 106  Lavinia Heller/Tomasz Rozmysłowicz (Hg.): Translation und Interkulturelle Kommunikation / Translation and Intercultural Communication. Beiträge zur Theorie, Empirie und Praxis kultureller Austauschprozesse / Theoretical, Empirical and Practical Perspectives on Cultural Exchanges. 178 Seiten. ISBN 978-3-7329-0351-1

Bd. 107  Brita Dorer: Advance Translation as a Means of Improving Source Questionnaire Translatability? Findings from a Think-Aloud Study for French and German. 554 Seiten. ISBN 978-3-7329-0594-2

Bd. 108  Annegret Sturm: Theory of Mind in Translation. 334 Seiten. ISBN 978-3-7329-0492-1